Additional praise for *Salafism in Lebanon: From Apoliticism to Transnational Jihadism*

"Robert Rabil's new book, *Salafism in Lebanon: From Apoliticism to Transnational Jihadism*, is a major achievement. This important book underscores the dramatic implications Salafism has for regional and international security. It is an absolutely essential historical and contemporary analysis of Salafism in the Arab world in general and Lebanon in particular. Rabil's in-depth knowledge of the subject and his extensive research provide readers with a clear understanding of the development of Salafism as theology, religious-political ideology, political programing, and as a motivating factor potentially leading to violence."

—**Ralph Nurnberger**, adjunct professor of liberal studies,
Georgetown University

"Contrary to conventional wisdom, Rabil cogently demonstrates that the ideological lines among various Salafists become easily blurred in relation to Jihad as a means to claim the right to defend the Sunni community from internal and external foes. This is a must read book, which is by far the only, and most detailed and up-to-date study on Salafism in Lebanon, shedding the layers of confusion, and sometimes deliberate 'ignorance' wrapping this relatively new prominent religious movement."

—**Joseph Alagha** , professor of Islamic Studies,
Radboud University Nijmegen

"The Salafi movement amongst Lebanese Sunnis has never received much attention in English-language publications. With the Syrian civil war's aggravation of Sunni-Shi'a tensions in Lebanon, Professor Rabil's book could not be more well-timed to fill this gap in the literature. He explains the complex Salafi tendencies and movements in Lebanon in clear, lucid detail. Anyone wishing to understand more about Lebanon and the impact of the Syrian civil war on the region as a whole needs to read this book."

—**David Romano**, Thomas G. Strong Professor of Middle East Politics,
Missouri State University

Salafism in Lebanon

From Apoliticism to
Transnational Jihadism

Salafism in Lebanon

*From Apoliticism to
Transnational Jihadism*

Robert G. Rabil

Georgetown University Press
Washington, DC

Library of Congress Cataloging-in-Publication Data

Rabil, Robert G., author.
    Salafism in Lebanon : from apoliticism to transnational jihadism / Robert G. Rabil.
        pages cm
    Includes bibliographical references and index.
    ISBN 978-1-62616-116-0 (hardcover : alk. paper) — ISBN 978-1-62616-117-7 (pbk. : alk.
paper) — ISBN 978-1-62616-118-4 (ebook)
    1. Salafiyah—Lebanon.   2. Islam and politics—Lebanon.   3. Islamic fundamentalism—
Lebanon.   4. Identity politics—Lebanon. I. Title.
    BP195.S18R33   2014
    297.8'3—dc23

                                                                                    2014011322

Cover design by Faceout Studio, Emily Weigel. Cover image of al-Nour Square, Tripoli, is cour-
tesy of the author; border image is from Shutterstock.

15 14   9 8 7 6 5 4 3 2
First printing

Printed in the United States of America

For my brother,
Fadi Georges Rabil

Contents

Transliteration

The English transliteration from Arabic generally follows the rules of the *International Journal of Middle Eastern Studies*. Arabic names commonly used by the *New York Times* and whose spellings are thus becoming standard retain their original form as they appeared in that newspaper. Arabic terms and words are italicized with the exception of those that have become standard in their common use, such as jihad and intifada.

Acknowledgments

I am grateful to the Florida Atlantic University's community, especially the Florida Society for Middle East Studies, for its unwavering and encouraging support for my research and instruction, thanks to which I feel blessed as part of a robust, caring, and intellectually agile society. Special thanks go to Lou Sandler, Paul and Marilyn Cutler, and Bob Newmark. I thank the faculty and staff of the Department of Political Science at Florida Atlantic University, especially Professors Ed Schwerin, Tim Lenz, and Marshall Derosa for their moral, scholastic, and administrative support. I am grateful to the Lifelong Learning Society at Boca Raton and Jupiter campuses, especially René Friedman and Dr. Herb Shapiro, for their moral and financial support. My deep appreciation goes to my Lifelong Learning students, whose kindness and vast repertoire of experience and knowledge only sharpens my desire to be a better human being, researcher, and instructor. I thank my graduate students, who have never ceased to intellectually amaze and challenge me inasmuch as I have tried to challenge them.

I am grateful to my colleagues Professors Joseph Alagha, Franck Salameh, Asher Kaufman, and Walid Phares for their friendship and professional support. I am grateful to Tom Harb, secretary-general of the World Council for the Cedars Revolution, for his friendship and professional support in arranging interviews with Lebanese activists and officials. I am thankful to Fares Soueid, secretary-general of the March 14 Coalition, for arranging interviews with Lebanese officials, Salafists, and Islamists. I am grateful to Judge Joseph Rabil for spending significant time and exchanging ideas and debating Middle East issues with me. Special thanks go to Ahmad al-Ayubi, Regina Kantara, Ghada Saghieh, Karam Abou Rejeily, Cathy Tabbah, Adel Louis, retired brigadier general Khalil Helou, Tracy Chamoun, and the Ghaoui family for helping me in various ways conduct my research. I thank my colleagues at different branches of the US government whose invitation to participate in their sponsored seminars and forums on the Middle East proved instructive and invaluable to my work. I am indebted to my sister Pauline, who virtually scoured many libraries in Lebanon looking for primary sources essential for this book, let alone making contacts with Salafist sheikhs to get their books. Sheikhs Sa'd al-Din Kibbi and Salem al-Rafi'i provided important books and information essential to understand the heterogeneity and creed of Salafism. I am grateful to the municipal council of the city of Hazmieh, especially the president of the council Jean Asmar, for their generous welcome and support. My deep appreciation goes to all interviewees whose insightful and instructive information proved vital to this book. Special thanks go to several anonymous Lebanese officials and activists who helped broaden and sharpen my analysis on Lebanon and the region. I thank my mentors and colleagues Professors Avidor Levy and Sadek J. Al-Azm for their soothing sagacity, academic advice, and constructive criticism.

I thank my mother, Antoinette, and siblings, Fadi, Pauline, and William, for their unbounded love and firm belief in me, which carried me in times of doubt. I deeply thank my wife, Patricia, for putting up with me during times of vagaries, stress, and insane working hours. I am infinitely grateful to her for being tirelessly and selflessly ready to ballast our household with unconditional love. I am eternally grateful to her for giving me no less than miracles in my children, whose energy, compassion, tender love, amazing smiles and brightness, and noisy interruptions uplift my soul and nurture my thought. Georges, Grace, Nick, and Olivia have shown me the beauty, sanctity, and fragility of life and the importance of love and preserving a safe and peaceful environment for all children. Finally, I am ever grateful to my brother Fadi, to whom this book is dedicated, for showing time and again unique courage in facing the challenges of life. As the elder brother of three siblings, I have interacted with them in the capacity of a "protector" and a fatherlike figure who is ever ready to give advice. Little did I know how much I learned from them throughout the years. My journey with Fadi has been the most worrisome. I have tried to "protect" him as children in parochial schools, as young boys in an unforgiving civil war in Lebanon, and as young men and adults in our beloved country the United States, only to find out that his courage was appreciatively and admiringly beyond my means. This has been set in sharp relief as Fadi faces undauntedly the most difficult challenge of his life, a malignant disease. I thank you and love you, brother.

Boca Raton, Florida
March 2014

Introduction

Salafism had not attracted much attention before the September 11 terror attacks. Scholars focused more on political Islam since the assassination of Egyptian president Anwar Sadat in 1981. Yet, despite some significant studies by Western and Arab scholars, research on Salafism has, more or less, remained shrouded with misconception and confusion, given the various and different movements that operate in the orbit of Salafism in different parts of the Muslim world. More specifically, though the ideological background of Salafism in relation to both its historical evolutionary change and its crystallization as a multifaceted school of thought in Saudi Arabia has been fairly studied, little or random research has been undertaken on Salafism as a product and expression of its emergence and development in most countries.[1] The rebellions throughout the Arab world have renewed the interest in Salafism, as, to the surprise of many, Salafi movements have managed to stake a claim to power in some Arab states and to spearhead, in theory and practice, the battles against some Arab regimes, in particular the Syrian regime.

Considering this insufficient knowledge about and thus far prevailing lacuna of research on Salafism, this book traces and examines the emergence and development of Salafism in Lebanon in relation to the established transnational schools of Salafism and to its ideological and practical evolutionary change within the context of confessional politics in the country. Accordingly, the study examines the doctrines, religio-political ideologies, and visions of the Salafi schools in Lebanon in relation to questions about engaging politics and how they have been actually applied to politics. The underlining objective of the dynamic between ideology and praxis is (a) to emphasize the inherent tensions and ambiguities that have obscured a clear comprehension of Salafism, and (b) to better understand the constitutive elements of creed, ideology, and

1

manhaj (the methodology by which a Salafist implements his beliefs and *da'wa* [call to Islam] in relation to politics) of Salafism, in relation to the different schools of Salafism and to intra- and intercommunal relations and dynamics and their implications for Lebanon and regional security.

Doctrine

The term Salafist derives from the Arabic root word *salaf*, which means the past according to Qur'an verses (al-Baqara 275 and an-Nisa' 22). This term initially signified the pious forefathers (*al-salaf al-salih*) who represented the first three generations of Muslims. Not only did they witness the rise of Islam but also applied the Prophetic model as the correct way of life. The golden age of these generations made up the period of the four rightly guided caliphs (632–661). Subsequently those Muslims who were guided by and lived according to the Prophetic model as practiced by the *al-salaf al-salih* became part of the *salaf*.[2] Salafism took a theological meaning by *ahl al-Hadith* (partisans of the traditional accounts of the sayings and doings of Prophet Muhammad) during the Abbasid caliphate. They concentrated on the study of the Qur'an and *hadith* (traditional accounts of the sayings and doings of Prophet Muhammad) as a means to purge Islam of non-Muslim accretions, thereby returning the pristine purity of Islam. As such, they rejected *taqlid* (emulation) of the four Sunni canonical law schools (*madhabs*).[3] Therefore, they accepted *ijtihad* (individual interpretation of the Qur'an and *hadith*), albeit along strict and literalist reading of both sources.[4]

Nevertheless, despite its claim to purity, Salafism encountered tensions as it developed into a doctrine. Scholars such as Taqi al-Din ibn Taymiyah (d. 1328), Ahmad ibn Hanbal (d. 855), and Muhammad ibn Abd al-Wahhab (d. 1792) made conflicting contributions to the doctrine of Salafism, thereby making it conducive to ambiguities and contradictions. Al-Wahhab, the founder of the Wahhabi movement, asserted the belief in the oneness of God (*tawhid*) as the basis of the Islamic creed (*'aqida*). But al-Wahhab, in contrast to Ibn Hanbal and more in line with Ibn Taymiyah, called Muslims who did not adhere to the *tawhid* doctrine unbelievers (*kuffars*). As *kuffars* they could be excommunicated and have jihad waged against them. Moreover, while Wahhabis promoted *ijtihad*, in practice they continued to follow *taqlid* of the Hanbali school of Islamic jurisprudence (*fiqh*).

These inherent tensions in Salafism became more salient as new scholars and movements introduced new concepts to encounter modern challenges. Late-nineteenth-century reformist scholars such as Muhammad Abdu (d. 1905) rejected the antirationalist and literalist approach of al-Wahhab in favor of a rationalist *ijtihad*. Another scholar who shaped contemporary Salafism was

Nasir al-Din al-Albani (d. 1999). Al-Albani, in line with the medieval school of *ahl al-Hadith*, rejected the use of reason and *taqlid* and focused more on *'Ilm al-Hadith* (science of *Hadith*) as a means to address problems with no solution in the Qur'an. His interest in a renewal of *hadith* sanctioned a reassessment of certain *hadith* accepted by some *madhabs*. He advocated no involvement in politics so long as Muslims adhering to *tawhid* did not close their ranks, focusing on a comprehensive Islamic education of Muslim youths.

Parallel to these developments in Salafism, radical concepts by Muslim scholars helped deepen the schism over the concept of *manhaj* (the way or method by which Salafists live and implement their beliefs) in Salafism. More specifically, the concept of *manhaj* raised questions about politics. Muslim Brotherhood ideologue Sayyid Qutb (d. 1966) developed his political theory on the basis of three concepts: *hakimiyah*, *jahiliyah*, and jihad. He considered God's *hakimiyah* (sovereignty) as exclusive and maintained that faithful rulers should implement God's mandate on earth as set forth in the Qur'an. Rulers who failed to do so lapsed in Jahiliyah (the pre-Islamic pagan period in Arabia), and therefore jihad against them was a legitimate act. Qutb's political theory deepened the tensions and divisions among Salafists on questions of political engagement.

These inherent tensions in Salafism have become more relevant as Salafists could hardly follow the way of the pious ancestors without engaging in politics. In other words, how could a Salafist practice his or her beliefs and *da'wa* in relation to their political setting? This led to the emergence of three Salafi schools that demarcated and, in some instances, blurred the lines between the three categories. The first school is mainly identified with Nasir al-Din al-Albani's teachings but also with the Saudi scholars Muhammad Aman al-Jami and Rabi' al-Madkhali's teachings. Focusing on the correct Islamic upbringing and education of Muslim youth, this school opposes all forms of political organization and action and enjoins obedience to Muslim rulers. This school is referred to interchangeably as a quietest school, on account of its quietest posture, and as a scientific school (*al-Salafiyah al-Ilmiyah*), on account of its concern with education. The second school is identified with Salafists who advocate political activism. They are referred to as *harakis* (activists) and the school as the *haraki* school. Their provenance is traced to the ideological fusion of the Muslim Brotherhood's political culture and consciousness with Wahhabism's creed of *tawhid* in Saudi Arabia. They seek political reform and influence. The third school is identified as Salafi-jihadi, meaning it advocates violence as a means of change in Muslim society, in favor of reestablishing the Caliphate. Al-Qaeda represents the paradigmatic organization of this school.

No less significant, coterminous with Qutb's political theory and the ideological classification of Salafists, the creedal principle *al-wala' wal-bara'* (principle of confessing loyalty to Muslims and disavowal of non-Muslims) allowed Salafists to actively interfere in the public sphere. Accordingly, violence was sanctioned as a political instrument when this principle was radicalized. This principle became a contentious focal point among Salafists in relation to whether violence against non-Muslims can be sanctioned. Consequently these inherent tensions and ambiguities, together with Salafi fragmentation, have obscured a clear understanding of Salafists, especially those who accumulated political power in the form of harnessing a significant following and those who, regardless of being quietists or activists, decided to engage politics in the interest of defending the Sunni community. No case highlights more the confusion and misconception about Salafists than Salafism in Lebanon. No case underscores the serious implications of misunderstanding of Salafists for Lebanon and international security than Salafism in Lebanon. Due to the existing narrow and selective readings of Salafists in Lebanon, it is worthwhile to conduct an academic study on Lebanese Salafists in order to unveil the confusion, misconception, and misunderstanding about them.

This study investigates Salafism's theology, religio-political ideologies, political programs, visions, and outreach initiatives (*infitah*), examining in the process the interaction between Salafists and the Sunni community on one hand, and between Salafists and the state on the other, and assessing the impact of Salafi actions on Lebanon's communal coexistence and confessional system. It will undoubtedly contribute to a better understanding of Salafism in Lebanon and its serious and drastic implications for regional and international security.

Salafism in Lebanon

This study demonstrates that three schools of Salafism in Lebanon are, for the most part, broken down along the lines of the aforementioned classification: quietest Salafists, *haraki* (activist) Salafists, and Salafi jihadists. The late Sheikh Salem al-Shahal is credited with establishing the Salafi movement in Tripoli in 1946. As an autodidactic religious scholar and a Wahhabi-inspired Salafist, al-Shahal gained a reputation for propagating the Islamic faith (*da'wa*) and opposing all reprehensible innovations (*bida*) in Islam. Commenting on his movement, he stated that "we adhere to the [holy] book and the Sunna, and we believe in Islam as taught to us by the Prophet without any accretion."[5] Thanks to his close relationship with prominent Saudi sheikh Abd al-Aziz Abdallah ibn Baz, he managed to send dozens of Lebanese, including his sons Da'i al-Islam and Radi al-Islam, to Saudi Arabia to study at Saudi universities, in particular the Islamic University of Medina.[6] He established the initial link with the Saudi religious establishment that came to sponsor this school and therefore paved the way for Lebanese Salafists to become integral to the Salafi transnational networks that emerged from the contacts established by the graduates of Saudi universities.

In 1987, he established Jami'yat al-Hidaya wal-Ihsan al-Islamiyah (Islamic Association of Guidance and Charity), which focused on disseminating Wahhabi-Salafi jurisprudence.[7] Da'i al-Islam and Hassan al-Shahal, the son and son-in-law, respectively, of Salem al-Shahal, led this Salafi movement, until the latter decided to establish his own institute. The movement has grown into many organizations operating as religious schools and charitable associations. This scientific Salafism had, in principle, adopted a quietest, traditional posture, shunning politics. Nevertheless, al-Shahal Salafism has, in practice, engaged politics following the murder of former prime minister Rafiq Hariri in 2005.

Sheikh Sa'd al-Din ibn Muhammad al-Kibbi, the director of al-Imam Bukhari Institute in Akkar, inherited the mantle of the scientific Salafi school. Identified with al-Albani, al-Kibbi's school submits to political authority in order to obviate civil strife among Muslims and to focus on education. Sheikh Kibbi enjoins an apolitical approach to politics. He believes that adherence to the Prophetic model is now paramount for Muslim society. He acts on the example of Prophet Muhammad's initial *da'wa* through persuasion and insists on an Islamic comprehensive education of Muslims as the basis upon which to found the true Muslim community. He also rejects the philosophy of *takfir*, regarding it as a source of Muslim disunity and discord (*fitna*). In principle, many Salafi organizations adhere to this school. When Salafists were blamed for riots in Christian East Beirut in February 2006, a majority of Salafi organizations issued a statement under the name of the Salafi Associations in Lebanon, in which they deplored the riots but affirmed that "Salafiyah [Salafism] is neither a political party nor an organization; rather it is a firm scientific school that calls for upholding the [Holy] Book and Sunna according to the rightful understanding of the methodology of the righteous Salaf from the companions and followers [of the Prophet]."[8]

In practice, however, many of these organizations have been dabbling with politics. Hariri's assassination, the withdrawal of Syrian troops from Lebanon in the same year, and the endemic belief among Salafists that they have been neglected and oppressed by Lebanese (and Syrian) authorities have put societal pressure on this school of Salafism to take political stances. In fact, following the murder of Hariri, Hassan al-Shahal established the Islamic Political Office, which according to al-Shahal, "was created to follow daily events in Lebanon and to take legal political stances in light of what's happening, for the role of the partisans of the Sunna can no longer be marginalized."[9] Significantly, some leaders of this school, led by Sheikh Safwan al-Zu'bi and Dr. al-Shahal, have taken a decision to *infitah* (open up) to the political system and confessional communities, especially the Shi'a community as led by Hezbollah (the Party of God). They signed a memorandum of understanding with Hezbollah, which was immediately attacked and discredited by Salafists, including Da'i al-Islam. Salafists and the Sunni leadership considered the memorandum an instrument by which Hezbollah could penetrate and divide the Sunni community in general and the Salafists in particular. No sooner had the ink dried on the memorandum than it was "frozen" in response to the fury with which it was received among Salafists. Still, members of this school have been trying to maintain some sort of unity and solidarity among the Salafists and to prevent Sunni-Shi'a confrontations consequent upon the Syrian rebellion and the rise in sectarian Islamism.

The *haraki* school's political activism can be traced to the influence of Harakat al-Tawhid al-Islami (the Islamic Unity Movement) and al-Jama'a al-Islamiyah (the Islamic Association) in the early 1980s. However, its emergence and development cannot be separated from the internal and regional events and developments that reconfigured Lebanon's political system and shaped its politics.

Historical Background

Since the founding of Greater Lebanon in 1920 under the French mandate, the interplay between religion and politics has been a dominant feature of the country, defining its identity and political system. Pursuing a communitarian policy in line with entrenched traditions, the French weaved together small and large communities into a national quilt distinguished by its confessional/sectarian system, without giving any one sect (*taifa*) an absolute majority. The Lebanese constitution of 1926 consecrated the prevailing confessional system by recognizing the country's various sects. Besides scaffolding an imperfect communitarian equilibrium, the confessional system did not resolve the outstanding questions of identity and political orientation. Broadly speaking, Muslim elites identified with Arab nationalism and aspired for national sovereignty within the framework of unity with Syria, whereas Christians aspired for a sovereign Lebanon, asserting a Phoenician-Lebanese identity and a Western outlook. A national political platform was elaborated to bring about independence from the French and band the various sects together, whereby Christians would forsake Western tutelage and Muslims their penchant for unity with Syria. This was the famous National Pact (al-Mithaq al-Watani), which declared that "Lebanon is an independent state with an Arab face."

Ultimately the National Pact neither fostered nor forged a national identity. It was based on a compromise guided by the false assumptions that Muslims would "Arabize" the Christians, while Christians would "Lebanonize" Muslims. Admittedly, whereas the constitution consecrated the confessional system, the

National Pact consecrated political sectarianism (confessionalism) by organizing the structure of the system and how it worked. Yet the National Pact provided under certain domestic and regional circumstances a sense of national unity and the opportunity of dissent given its liberal substance.

This unity collapsed on more than one occasion under the double weight of what Malcolm H. Kerr famously termed "the Arab Cold War" and Arab nationalism. In the name of Arab nationalism, leftists, pan-Syrians, and pan-Arabs were more interested in removing a regime dominated by Maronite Christians—what they termed political Maronitism—than in reforming the system. The National Pact had become a mere illusionary term as the country split along sectarian lines, and Beirut emerged as the new battleground for the Arab-Israeli conflict and Palestinian militancy. As the civil war tore Lebanon apart and foreign armies encamped behind tenuous political and confessional alliances, attempts at national reconciliation were doomed in their infancy until 1989. The same year, Lebanese deputies, at the urging and pressure of Saudi Arabia and Syria, ironed out a constitutional compromise, the Document of National Understanding (Taif Accord), which helped end the civil war in 1990. The Taif Accord amended the constitution and by extension the National Pact. Lebanon was identified as an Arab state and the definitive homeland of all its members ("sons"). In reality, however, Lebanon fell under the thumb of Syrian hegemony. Syrian intelligence chiefs became the czars of the Second Republic, which they tried to shape in step with their oppressive rule and Ba'thist nationalist outlook.

Meanwhile, although Damascus maintained using secular radical organizations as proxy tools of state policy, the entry of various radical Islamist organizations into Lebanon's civil war underlined a new dimension of politics and militancy. Islamist organizations, supported directly or indirectly by Iran and Syria, became the purveyors of terrorism against Western interests and individuals in Lebanon in the 1980s. Hezbollah encapsulated the fervor of militant Islam. The ethnic and ideological cohesion of Hezbollah's leaders and the determination with which they tried to overcome their community's sociopolitical marginalization in Lebanon coincided with the party's ideological objective to promote Ayatollah Khomeini's version of fundamentalist Islam, which found its expression in armed struggle against Israel's occupation of Lebanon. In the 1980s, though their national security policies did not neatly overlap, Tehran and Damascus found in Hezbollah a terror instrument by which to strike at their own enemies, especially the United States. Damascus also used Hezbollah as a proxy terror tool to force Israel from Lebanon without incurring a head-on military confrontation with Israel's defense forces.

In the aftermath of the civil war in the 1990s, Tehran supported Hezbollah's transformation from a jihadi organization to a political party, without relinquishing its "resistance" image and jihadi organization. Nevertheless, Damascus remained the patron of Lebanon. In fact, following the defeat of Iraq in Kuwait, Damascus, with the blessing of Washington, institutionalized its occupation of Lebanon, and once Syria occupied Lebanon, it helped Hezbollah monopolize Islamic resistance against Israel. Before long, Hezbollah morphed into a sophisticated, hydra-like political and jihadi organization.

Parallel to these developments, the ascension to power of the secular and Alawi-dominated Ba'th Party in Syria in 1963 posed a significant threat to the ideology and praxis of the Syrian Muslim Brotherhood (al-Ikhwan), which had already been affected by the political trend set by secular, socialist, and national-ist parties. In 1964, a Muslim Brotherhood insurgency erupted in Hama, which the regime swiftly subdued. Nevertheless, the regime failed to pay attention to the organization's growing underground activity. The insurgency reerupted in 1976 on account of domestic and regional policies. The decisive and final show-down took place in Hama in 1982, whereupon the regime used indiscriminate and brute force to quell the rebellion. Since then, the regime had pursued a con-sistent policy toward all Islamist organizations, aimed at fragmenting them by neutralizing their radical elements and co-opting their moderate members. The regime paid special attention to Islamic activism in Tripoli, a city in northern Lebanon that had been historically connected to the Syrian heartland.

Tripoli as a Puritan Sunni City: The Rise of Salafism

In fact, immediately after the independence of Lebanon in 1943, Islamic activ-ism found a permissive political setting in the country in general and northern Lebanon and its major city Tripoli in particular. The city had been historically a religious focal point for the Mamluks (1250–1517) and the Ottomans (1299–1918). Desirous no less of projecting their piousness than of reducing Western and Christian culture consequent upon decades of interaction between indig-enous Christians and crusaders, they established enough Muslim mosques and institutions to religiously color the city. No less significant, the late-nineteenth-century Muslim reform movement found its way into the city and its hinter-land through the movement's literary organ *Al-Manar*, whose founder Rashid Rida hailed from al-Qalamoun, near Tripoli. Though Rida's initial openness to Western political thought transformed into a defensive ideology against Western policies, his reformist ideas touched many in northern Lebanon, including the founder of scientific Salafism in Lebanon, Salem al-Shahal. Nevertheless, pan-Arab, pan-Syrian, leftist, and communist parties dominated the politics of the Muslim community in Lebanon until the invasion of the country by Israel in 1982. The invasion, following two humiliating Arab defeats in 1967 and 1973, dealt a severe blow to Arab nationalism, which had suffered its initial setback in 1961 when the union between Egypt and Syria collapsed.

All of this had a consequential impact on Lebanon's Sunni Islamism, reflected by the emergence of radical Islamist organizations, including in the Palestinian refugee camps, which espoused jihad against Israel and a strong desire to impose their radical views and practices on Lebanon's society. Significantly, coinciding with Israel's invasion of Lebanon in 1982, a radical Islamist organization, the aforementioned Harakat al-Tawhid al-Islami, had gained ground in Tripoli, and from 1983 to 1985, it imposed its control over the city, including introducing Islamic law (*shari'a*). Interestingly enough, the strongmen of the movement who pledged their allegiance to its leader sheikh Sa'id Sha'ban had secular backgrounds in pan-Arab, leftist, and Palestinian parties. Their disillusion with Arab politics exacerbated their identity crisis, whose salvation was found in Islam and Islamism. The Iranian Revolution in 1979 only reinforced their newfound belief that Islamism was the answer to Arab and Muslim impotence and incompetence. The Islamic Unity Movement was a hybrid Islamist movement that included Salafi components and impulses. Muhammad Abi Samra identified it as a Salafi movement, led by a Salafi sheikh who sought to walk in the footsteps of the pious ancestors. Sheikh Sha'ban was among the first charismatic preachers to lambast Arab rulers for establishing *jahili* regimes far from Islamic law and Islam.[10] The Syrian regime and its allies in Lebanon were no exception to his harsh criticism. Most important, his harsh words were matched by harsh actions against Syria's allies in Tripoli. Sha'ban's takeover of the city was bloody. For example, Hisham Minqara, one of the main strongmen of the Islamic Unity Movement, is reputed to have killed dozens of communists in their headquarters in Tripoli.

However, the movement's meteoric rise in Tripoli was matched by a swift fall at the hands of the Syrian regime. The Syrian regime and its allies waged one of the most vicious campaigns against Tripoli in the history of Lebanon's civil war. Hundreds were killed and arrested throughout the city. But the neighborhood that bore the brunt of Syria's deadly campaign was Bab al-Tabbaneh. No wonder this most populous and impoverished neighborhood in Tripoli has emerged as a hub for Salafists, whose opposition to Syria and their allies in Lebanon has been unparalleled. For the citizens of northern Lebanon, the silence with which the regional and international community responded to the indiscriminate massacre of civilians was shocking. Tripolitans have resentfully told me that even the scholars of the Middle East rarely mention this Syrian atrocity, in contrast to that in Hama in 1982. Moreover, the city had to succumb to years of Syrian harassment, oppression, and marginalization by both Syrian intelligence and their loyalists in Lebanon's security apparatus. To be sure, Damascus pursued a two-pronged (though contradictory) policy toward Islamist movements. Gathering momentum in the 1990s during the regime's peace negotiations with Israel, the regime's policy had been to support Islamist movements that served Syria's regional interests and to either restrict or clamp down on Islamist movements deemed inimical to Syrian interest and politics.

Activist (*Haraki*) Salafists

Consequently many Islamists from Tripoli and northern Lebanon fled the country only to come back after Syria's humiliating withdrawal from Lebanon in 2005, rigorously invigorated to avenge their dead and oppression at the hands of the Syrian regime. Among those who returned was Sheikh Salem bin ʿAbd al-Ghani al-Rafiʾi, who has emerged as the leading anti-Hezbollah and anti-Syrian activist (*haraki*) Salafist in Tripoli. Little wonder that some residents of this region of Lebanon have been linked to al-Qaeda and other radical organizations. They are the product of dispossession, oppression, and marginalization that left them at the mercy of charismatic Salafi preachers who helped to reinforce their Islamic authentic identity but at the same time to transform many of them into Salafi jihadists. The constant educational, missionary, and emotional mobilization of Sunni youth by Salafi preachers, as Radwan al-Sayyid observed, have led them to rally around charismatic emirs under whose authority they can wage jihad.[11]

No less significant, *haraki* Salafists have been no less influenced by Sunni Islamists who insisted on political activism as a means to defend the Sunni community. In this respect, Fathi Yakan, a former pupil of Salem al-Shahal and cofounder and main ideologue of the Islamic Association, championed Islamic activism and therefore helped to pave the path for Salafists to engage in politics. Sheikh al-Rafiʾi, among others, admitted to me that most *haraki* Salafists "emerged from the womb of Yakan's Islamic Association." Amid the throes of civil war, Fathi Yakan contended that Islamists need not only to engage in politics but also to focus their energy on situating themselves at the center of the state. He explained the transitional objective of Islamism:

> It is stupid, in light of our confrontation with the challenge and the battle ground [of the struggle for Lebanon], to allow others to have the lion share in every matter and to acquiesce to that. . . . On the contrary, doing so is a betrayal of Islam, for that would help liquidate the Islamic presence and prevent the implementation of the creed [law] of Islam in society and state. . . . Islam today is in an asymmetrical war with *Jahiliyah* everywhere, and war is a ruse. . . . What cannot be taken in war cannot be forsaken,

and for the Muslims to win some positions in the way of a comprehensive Islamic change is better than losing all positions without reaching the aspired goal.[12]

He also supported Islamic political activism as a means to defend Islam and Muslims from secularization and Westernization.[13] Led by charismatic sheikhs, the *haraki* movement is still in its formative stage and does not yet have a political organization or a consensual political platform. In theory, it does not advocate violent political activism and, in line with Yakan and the Muslim Brotherhood's political theory, seeks political reform and power. Sheikh Zakariya 'Abd al-Razaq al-Masri has been at the forefront of Salafists championing political engagement. He adheres to the Salafi doctrine of *al-wala' wal-bara'*, whereby he believes that Muslims should be faithful and supportive of believers and unhelpful to *kuffars*. He conditions and limits leveling the charge of *takfir* to major prohibitions/sins. He denounces deviant (sinful) Muslims as hypocrites. He typifies jihad as offensive and defensive. He believes that only the caliph of the *ummah* (Muslim community) has the right to wage an offensive jihad to remove unbelieving leaders; but he asserts that defensive jihad to defend the Ummah is a legal duty. Significantly, he is close to Salafi jihadists in believing that the clash with the United States is "ideological, moral, social, economic and civilizational" and is a kind of self-defense that, including martyrdom operations, is affirmed by all heavenly messages.[14] No less significant, he has formulated a vision, based on bifurcating the world into believers and unbelievers, according to which he premised his political program. His program underscores the importance of waging jihad against *kuffars* but also provides a plan by which Lebanese Muslims could only pledge allegiance to Muslim rulers.

This broad *haraki* movement has taken a far-reaching political dimension following the uprising in Syria. Not only has the movement vocally supported the opposition but it also has made significant efforts to arm them and create makeshift hospitals and security areas in Tripoli and the Akkar region, both inaccessible to Lebanese authorities. At the same time, acting as the guardian of the Sunni community, it has denounced Hezbollah, Iran, and the regime of Bashar al-Asad in Damascus. The emerging leader of this movement is Sheikh Salem bin 'Abd al-Ghani al-Rafi'i. In a lengthy interview with al-Rafi'i, I inquired about the commitment of the Salafists to topple the regime. Al-Rafi'i's soft tone belied his steely poise when he asserted that "we are ready to sacrifice two million martyrs before we reconsider our policy towards the brutal Asad regime." The ease with which al-Rafi'i committed himself to deposing the regime at this staggering human cost underscores the *harakis'* rigidity and aspiration to power. In fact, al-Rafi'i, expressing his disappointment with the mainstream

Sunni al-Mustaqbal Party, affirmed that "they will establish a political party to better handle Sunni affairs."[15]

Takfiri Salafists

The last and most notorious group is the Salafi jihadists. This group advocates jihad against existing political orders and adheres to the theology of *takfir*. Tripoli, Dinniyah, and Beka', among other areas, have witnessed a growth of Salafi-jihadi cells affiliated with al-Qaeda. Lebanese authorities have clamped down on them. Nevertheless, nowhere was the impact of the region and Lebanon's cataclysmic events more transformative than on Salafi jihadists. Their local militancy transmuted into a global cause of jihadism against the United States and Syria. The Palestinian Salafi-jihadi Usbat al-Ansar reflected the new face of terrorism, which expanded the theoretical and practical focus of their militancy to global jihadism. Theirs was a global jihadi war waged in defense of the imaginary borders of their identity and authentic Sunni Islam.[16] Similarly, motivated no less by feelings of revenge than by an ideological obligation to wage jihad against the *kafir* Asad regime, Lebanese Salafi jihadists have made their battle against the Syrian regime a jihad in the path of Allah. In fact, it was *haraki* sheikhs al-Rafi'i and Ahmad al-Assir who made jihad in Syria an Islamic legal obligation. For Salafi jihadists and *haraki* Salafists, the rebellion in Syria is inseparable from their homeland. Not only do they believe that Tripoli is part of Bilad al-Sham (Greater Syria)[17] but also the stronghold of what Prophet Muhammad described as *al-firqa al-najiyah* (saved sect).[18] The rebellion, as seen by sheikh al-Rafi'i and other *haraki* Salafists, goes beyond removing the Asad regime. It is also as much about protecting the Sunni community from the Iranian regime and its Hezbollah proxy in Lebanon as getting rid of Sunni traitors (*khawarij*) and the anemic Sunni leadership. Though quietest Salafists have frowned upon the confrontational discourse and *takfiri* rhetoric of *haraki* Salafists, their efforts to unite Salafists and oppose *takfir* ideology have thus far not succeeded, given the fragmentation of Salafists and the strong belief championed by *harakis* that Sunnis have been turned into lambs for slaughter.

Synopsis of the Book

It is within this contextual interaction between Salafism, in all its variants, and confessional politics under the influence of Syria in Lebanon until 2005 and thereafter under Hezbollah's political and military ascendancy in the state that this book traces the development of Salafism as an expression of theology, religio-political ideology, political program, and vision, from *da'wa* to transnational jihad and from social marginalization to political empowerment. The book examines the ideological and sociopolitical foundation out of which Salafism emerged and developed in Lebanon and surveys the ways in which Salafists navigated the stormy waters of the country's civil war and its occupation by and then liberation from Syrian troops. It probes the ideological transformation of Salafists from opposing political engagement to supporting it, without legitimizing thus far the system. For example, Sheikh Zakariya al-Masri supports Muslim participation in Lebanon's confessional politics on the condition that Muslims should not express their fealty to the Christian president (see chapter 4). In fact, in seeking to dislodge the urban Sunni leadership, Salafists aspire to shape the country's political system and society in line with their beliefs and *da'wa*. Similarly, they have adopted political attitudes hermeneutically clear but ideologically open to interpretation, blurring the lines between and among the Salafi schools. For example, some quietest Salafists have called for arms against Hezbollah but have not leveled the charge of unbelief against the party to sanction jihad against it. And *haraki* Salafists have called for jihad, although they have ideologically opposed violence. Meanwhile, Salafism, despite its ideological fractionalization and factionalism, has followed the path of Islamism in opening up to other communities in Lebanon, but this *infitah* has collapsed under the weight of Sunni-Shi'a tension. A significant number of Salafists, supported implicitly by the Sunni leadership of the Sunni community, have scuttled the *infitah* to the Shi'a community because of their ideological and political opposition to Hezbollah.

In contrast to the conventional wisdom prevailing in the Sunni political community and among scholars that Salafism can be controlled and that its influence is overblown, this study demonstrates that activist and jihadi Salafists have got the better of the Sunni leadership. They have ideologically and/ or practically endorsed violence and jihad in response to the weakness of the Sunni political leadership and Shi'a ascendancy in the state and the region. At the same time, the study shows that the rebellion in Syria against the Alawi-led Syrian regime and the participation of the Shi'a Islamist party Hezbollah in the Syrian conflict on the side of the Syrian regime have only sharpened the determination of Salafists not only to support jihad in Syria but also to "rebel" against Lebanese authorities in general and the Sunni leadership in Lebanon in particular. The study reveals that this political and military rebellion has been linked to and fed by Salafi transnational networks that have purposefully supported their like-minded Salafi movements. This has made some of them purveyors of political power and militancy, regardless of their ideological standing. Nevertheless, notwithstanding Salafism's lack of political experience, Lebanon's confessional system, coupled with Salafism's factionalism and ideological and practical fractionalization, militates against Salafism's preeminence as a political bloc in Lebanon. This, however, does not reduce the disproportionate threat Salafists pose to the communal harmony and security of Lebanon and the region, thereby adding new layers of complexity to the roots and practices of *takfir* and jihad and their attendant violence.

My hypothesis is that Hezbollah's ascendency in Lebanon, coupled with the Syrian rebellion, has generated new sociopolitical dynamics in both Lebanon and Syria, creating immediate and long-term political uncertainties and challenges to Salafists. In response, Salafists, gripped by feelings of discontent and revanchist impulses, have been compelled to address political matters that go beyond their theology and religio-political ideologies, forcing them to consider rationales for political strategies. These rationales, taken up by some quietest and activist Salafists, underlie the objectives of a new phase of political activism that essentially seeks political influence and in the case of *harakis* to sanction transnational Jihad. As such, the study departs from the theoretical point that the rationale for Salafism's transformation is no less a product of the lethal interplay between the politics of discontent and communal-national-regional politics than an appeal to authentic Islam. Correspondingly, the focus of this book is to identify the factors underlying these rationales in relation to (1) the different schools of Salafism and the emergence of charismatic preachers, (2) the Sunni community and transnational networks of Salafists, (3) the intracommunal and intercommunal relations in Lebanon, and (4) the Syrian conflict.

Theoretical Analysis and Term Description

Since the term Islamism (political Islam) is sometimes interchangeably used with Islamic fundamentalism and is variably defined, the book employs a working definition of Islamism more specific to its Lebanese and regional milieu by reconciling Radwan al-Sayyid's definition of Islamism with that of Ayatollah Muhammad Hussein Fadlallah. Radwan al-Sayyid defined Islamism as follows:

> The Islamists in all their factions perceive that they are in disagreement with all intellectual and political currents in the Arab fatherland and the world. They possess a universal vision or a universal perspective, because they rely on Islam. This began in the Islamic reform era with the saying that Islam is a religion and world [*din wa dunia*], then came Hassan al-Bannah who said that Islam is a religion and state [*din wa dawlah*], and a [holy] book and sword. But in the contemporaneous era the efforts of the Islamic political movements have pivoted around the matter of the state.

In this respect, they see that Islam constitutes the fundamental legitimacy of every political system.[19]

This definition of Islamism relates to the political program of the Islamic Association, whose ideologue Fathi Yakan had paved the path to Islamic activism in Lebanon, including to *haraki* Salafism.

In response to a question about what is termed Islamic fundamentalism, the spiritual Lebanese Shi'a leader Ayatollah Fadlallah explained:

> There is no such thing here as "Islamic fundamentalism" as the West presents it—in other words, exclusive recourse to violence to bring about change and negation of the "Other." This description does not fit the Islamists. Concerning violence, *Jihad* in Islam is a defensive movement and deterrent. . . . We . . . consider the call to *Jihad* to be a call to protect the basic issues affecting human destiny from those who are committing aggression against us. . . . From an Islamic perspective, we compare violence to surgery: One only turns to it as a last resort. As for negating the Other, we read in the Book of God: "Say: 'O People of the Book! Come to common terms as between us and you: that we worship none but Allah; that we associate no partners with Him; that we erect not, from among ourselves, lords and patrons other than Allah'" (Al-'Imran:64). Christians and Jews differ with Muslims concerning the interpretation of the unity of God and the personality of God. Despite that, the Qur'an commands: Turn to the principle of unity—the unity of God and the unity of mankind. We interpret this to mean that we can meet Marxists on the common ground of standing up to the forces of international arrogance; we can meet nationalists, even secular nationalists, on the common ground of Arab causes, which are also Islamic causes. Islam recognizes the Other. . . . Therefore we Islamists are not fundamentalists the way Westerners see us. We refuse to be called fundamentalists. We are Islamic activists.[20]

Salafists share Fadlallah's concept of unity of God (*tawhid*), while *haraki* Salafists share his views that they are Islamic activists. Similarly, though the broad term Salafism (*Salafiyah*) remains hard to define on account of its ambiguity and fragmentation, its basic creedal tenets are well established. The study employs Sheikh Sa'd al-Din al-Kibbi's definition of Salafism:

> The Salafist school is the Islamic *Da'wa* that was transmitted to the messenger of God [Prophet Muhammad] and was recognized [understood] by the Prophet's companions, whose followers, may God have mercy on all of

them, embraced. The followers represent the victorious [saved] sect, Partisans of Sunna and the Group [*ahl-Sunna wal-jama'a*]. The Salafist school has been made known by the school of Partisans of Hadiths and Sunna [*ahl al-hadith wal-Sunna*], who aggrandized the *hadith* of the messenger of God and had a consensus on the Sunna during a period of time when groups, reported about by the messenger of God, rebelled [against Islam].[21]

Salafists of all stripes share this definition of Salafism, but disagree over the *manhaj* of Salafism.

Regarding the relational terminology of Salaf, Salafiyah, and Salafists, this study employs Muhammad Amarah's definitions. He defines Salaf as everyone who emulates and finds his or her tradition in the deeds and utterances of Prophet Muhammad and his Companions in Islam. Salafiyah (Salafism) implies the return to the Qur'an and Sunna as the original sources of Islam in the religion and the elimination of all accretions and all that contravenes the Qur'an and the Sunna. And Salafists are those who follow the path of the Salaf.[22]

This study pays attention to the theories of social movement, in particular to the definition that it is a "purposive collective actions whose outcome, in victory as in defeat, transforms the value and institutions of society."[23] It heeds Joseph Alagha's employment of the concept of resource mobilization in examining the Shi'a Islamist party Hezbollah.[24] Resource mobilization refers to the way a social movement mobilizes its resources, such as money, personnel, and political influence, to deal with difficult challenges facing it. Nevertheless, the methodological approach to the study will be qualitative, based on detecting and examining patterns and shifts in Salafi ideology and praxis. The application of the methodology draws on an understanding of the theological and religio-political ideologies of the Salafists but relies on examining two main variables, their political behavior and their discourse, which would allow us to understand the rationales they have considered for their political attitudes and strategies. Only in this way can we illustrate a detailed analysis of the emergence and development of Salafism and the political role Salafists have played in accordance with their theology and religio-political ideologies.

The theories of social movement have significant limitations, preventing a comprehensive understanding of the nuances and ideological overlaps within and among the Salafi schools. In fact, Salafists do not belong to an organization and do not consider themselves members of a movement, although the broad outlines of the Salafiyah movement are defined. Salafiyah is not a homogenous movement; it is more a heterogeneous movement sharing basic principles but divergent and even contradictory ideologies and tendencies. No less significant—although Salafists in Lebanon share a collective identity based on creed and a mission to cleanse Islam from foreign accretions and to create an ideal Islamic community—the creedal tenets of their *tawhid* and their *manhaj* are not uniform.

For example, *haraki* sheikh Zakariya al-Masri shares the basic creedal beliefs of the quietest school, mainly *tawhid* (oneness/unity) of God in His *rububiyah* (lordship), *uluhiyah* (godship), and *al-asma' wal-sifat* (names and attributes). However, Sheikh Masri, unlike quietest sheikh Sa'd al-Din al-Kibbi, does not refrain from leveling the charge of *kufr* (unbelief) on Muslims who commit major sins/prohibitions.[25] Nevertheless, Sheikh Masri, unlike Salafi jihadists, does not instruct jihad as an armed struggle against deviant or sinful Muslims, including rulers, unless they have consciously renounced Islam. Conversely, he, like Salafi jihadists, supports jihad against what he considers enemies of Islam, especially the Zionists and atheists. He advocates conditional engagement in politics in the interest of the Muslim community, though he harbors reservations about nationalism and patriotism.

Though Salafism has been the focus of a number of studies, hardly any work has been undertaken on the ideology and praxis of Salafism in Lebanon. To my knowledge, no contemporary study has addressed the development of Salafism in relation to the state and the country's confessional groups, in light of the dramatic developments of the Arab rebellions, especially in Syria. As such, our understanding of this highly determined and misconstrued movement is still quite rudimentary in relation to the fast-paced developments sweeping Lebanon and the region.

Notes

1. The main study on Salafism as a global movement remains that of Roel Meijer, ed., *Global Salafism: Islam's New Religious Movement* (London: Hurst, 2009).
2. See Muhammad Amarah, *Al-Salaf wa al-Salafiyah* (Cairo: Dar al-Hilal, 2010), 13–18. See also Muhammad Said Ramadan al-Bouti, *Al-Salafiyah Marhalah Zamaniyah Mubarakah La Madhab Islami* (Al-Salafiyah Is a Blessed Period Not an Islamic Canonical Law School) (Beirut: Dar al-Fikr al-Mu'asir, 2004), 9–13.
3. In Sunni Islam, there are four schools of jurisprudence: Hanbali, Shafi'i, Hanafi, and Maliki.
4. Amarah, *Al-Salaf wa al-Salafiyah*, 13–18, and al-Bouti, *Al-Salafiyah Marhalah Zamaniyah Mubarakah La Madhab Islami*, 9–13.
5. 'Abd al-Ghani 'Imad, *Al-Harakat al-Islamiyah fi Lubnan: Ishkaliat al-Din wa al-Siyasah Fi Mujtama' Mutanawe'* (Islamic Movements in Lebanon: The Ambiguity of Religion and Politics in a Diverse Society) (Beirut: Dar al-Tali'a, 2006), 314.
6. Ahmad Darwish, "Al-Salafiyun fi Lubnan," *Al-Shira'*, January 22, 1996.

7. 'Imad, *Al-Harakat al-Islamiyah fi Lubnan*, 310.

8. "Al-Mu'assassat al-Salfiyah Ijtama't wa Nadadat bi Ahdath al-Achrafieh" (Salafist Associations Met and Condemned Disturbances in Achrafieh), *An-Nahar*, February 9, 2006. The statement listed all associations that signed it.

9. See interview of al-Shahal in *Al-Mustaqbal*, May 12, 2005.

10. Muhammad Abi Samra, *Trablus: Sahat Allah wa Mina' Hadatha* (Tripoli, Lebanon: The Square of Allah and the Port of Modernity) (Beirut: Dar al-Saqi, 2011), 155.

11. "Khabiran fi al-Dirasat al-Islamiyah Yuhalilan 'Majmu'at al-Dinniyah'" (Two Experts in Islamic Studies Analyze the al-Dinniyeh Group), *An-Nahar*, January 12, 2000.

12. Fathi Yakan, *Abjadiyat al-Tasawor al-Haraki lil-'Amal al-Islami* (The Elementary Facts of the Conceptual Movement of Islamic Activism) (Beirut: Mu'assassat al-Risalah, 1981),166.

13. See Robert G. Rabil, "Al-Jama'a al-Islamiyah and Fathi Yakan: The Pioneer of Sunni Islamic Activism in Lebanon," in *Religion, National Identity, and Confessional Politics in Lebanon: The Challenge of Islamism* (New York: Palgrave Macmillan, 2011), 31–39.

14. Zakariya 'Abd al-Razaq al-Masri, *Al-Quwa al-Dawliyah fi Muwajahat al-Sahwah al-Islamiyah: Dawabet Shar'iyah fi al-'Amaliyat al-Jihadiyah* (International Forces Confronting the Islamic Awakening: Legal Safeguards for Jihadi Operations) (Tripoli, Lebanon: Maktabat al-Iman, 2004), 40–50, 93–97.

15. Author's interview with Sheikh Salem al-Rafi'i on July 19, 2012.

16. For Salafi-Jihadi details, see Fida' 'Itani, *Al-Jihadiyun fi Lubnan* (Jihadists in Lebanon) (Beirut: Dar al-Saqi, 2008). For Palestinian Salafi-Jihadi details, see Bernard Rougier, *Everyday Jihad: The Rise of Militant Islam among Palestinians in Lebanon* (Cambridge: Harvard University Press, 2007).

17. One day after the deadly bombings in Tripoli on August 25, 2013, the Council of Muslim Ulema, led by Sheikh al-Rafi'i, issued a statement in which it accused the Asad regime of being behind the strife that reached Tripoli, "al-Sham," in reference to (mythical) historical Greater Syria. For the full text of the statement, see the news website Mideast Observer, www.mideastobserver.com/v/19404 (accessed August 25, 2013).

18. The term "saved sect" derives from a *hadith* ascribed to Prophet Muhammad in which he said, "My *ummah* will split into seventy-three sects, all of whom will be in Hell except one."

19. Radwan al-Sayyid, *Siyasiyat al-Islam al-Mu'aser: Muraja'at wa Mutaba'at* (The Politics of Contemporaneous Islam: Revisions and Follow Ups) (Beirut: Dar al-Kitab al-'Arabi, 1997), 218.

20. Shaykh Muhammad Hussayn Fadlallah and Mahmoud Soueid, "Islamic Unity and Political Change: Interview with Shaykh Muhammad Hussayn Fadlallah," *Journal of Palestine Studies* 25, no. 1 (Autumn 1995), 63–64.

21. Sa'd al-Din ibn Muhammad al-Kibbi, *Ta'rif al-Bari'ah bi-Manhaj al-Madrasa al-Salafiyah: Ahl al-Hadith wal-Sunna)* (Introduction to What Is Created through the Methodology of the Salafist School: Partisans of Hadiths and Sunna) (Tripoli, Lebanon: Center of Islamic Science Research, 2009), 5–6.

22. Muhammad Amarah, *Al-Salaf wa al-Salafiyah*, 14–17.

23. Manuel Castells, *The Power of Identity: The Information Age; Economy, Society, and Culture, Volume II* (Oxford: Blackwell, 1998), 3.

24. Joseph Alagha, *The Shifts in Hizbullah's Ideology: Religious Ideology, Political Ideology, and Political Program* (Amsterdam: Amsterdam University Press, 2006).

25. Major sins are seven: *shirk* (polytheism), performing sorcery, committing murder, charging interest (usury), devouring the wealth of orphans, defaming innocent women, and fleeing from the battle.

Chapter One

The Creed, Ideology, and *Manhaj* (Methodology) of Salafism

A Historical and Contemporaneous Framework

This chapter traces and examines the emergence and development of Salafism as a Muslim school of thought. It emphasizes the historical, philosophical, and ideological debates that raged in the Arab classical period as a result of Arab conquests and defeats and their implications for society and religion. This helped engender and define Salafism as a doctrine and a movement, harking back to the pristine purity of Islam as reflected in the application of the prophetic model by the companions of the Prophet and their followers. It also investigates the emergence of the puritanical and revivalist Wahhabi religious movement, which transformed into a religio-political movement before becoming the religious authority and proponent of Wahhabi-Salafism in the Saudi state. At the same time, the chapter draws the background against which Salafism transformed into a multidimensional school of thought by surveying the ramifications of Arab and Muslim society's ideological and political attempt at meeting the composite cultural, military, and political challenge posed by the West to Arab and Muslim society in the modern period. The ramifications of meeting this challenge engendered ideological and political developments and dynamics whose interactions in Saudi society and universities fostered the creation of a hybrid Salafism. This entailed determining the methodology (*manhaj*) of Salafism, or the way by which Salafists can implement their beliefs and call to Islam (*da'wa*), which inadvertently raised questions about engaging politics. Consequently, three schools of thought—quietest, activist, and Salafi-jihadi—were identified with Salafism, which reflected their responses to and positions toward politics and political authority. Coterminous with this development, creedal principles dealing with how Muslims should practice their religion in relation to the pillars of Islam and the faith, to other Muslims, and to non-Muslims transformed into radical concepts expanding the theology of excommunication (*takfir*) and jihad.

This chapter, in addition to examining the development of Salafism as a heterogeneous movement, provides a historical and contemporaneous framework of reference essential for an adequate understanding of the emergence and development of Salafism in Lebanon.

Terminology and Creed

The term Salafism (or Salafiyah) derives from the Arabic root word *salaf*, which means the past according to Qur'anic verses (al-Baqara: Surat 275, al-Nisa': Surat 22, and Yunis: Surat 30). Since this term signified the past in Islam, it was religiously plausible to ascribe to the term a terminological foundation represented by the generation that established the religion of Islam and applied its *manhaj* (methodology). This was the generation of the companions of the Prophet, who lived in the era in which the revelation was transmitted to Prophet Muhammad. These pious forefathers (*al-salaf al-salih*) represented the golden age of Islam, which made up the period of the four rightly guided caliphs (632–61). Not only did they witness the rise of Islam, but they also applied the Prophetic model by walking in the footsteps of Prophet Muhammad as the correct way of life. Subsequently those Muslims who were guided by and lived according to the prophetic model as practiced by the *al-salaf al-salih* became part of the *salaf*.[1]

As Islamic conquests expanded the authority of the Muslim state, first under the Umayyad Dynasty (661–750) and then under the Abbasid Dynasty (750–1258), Salafism took a theological meaning by what came to be known as *ahl al-Hadith* (partisans of the tradition and sayings of Prophet Muhammad) during the Abbasid caliphate. The forming and expansion of the Muslim state brought under its rule various peoples and cultures, which inadvertently affected the way by which the new Muslim state interacted and governed its subjects. Broadly speaking, Persian and Greco-Roman cultures and traditions colored the governing style of the Umayyads, who faced the challenge of not only establishing a state but also of ruling a vast, multiethnic, and multireligious empire. This led them to political compromises that brought upon them the charge that they, unlike the righteous caliphs, pursued worldly self-interested policies instead of devoting themselves to the well-being of religion.[2] Meanwhile, during the formative stage of the Muslim state, many fundamental questions revolving around God's nature, relationship with mankind, and unity and justice that reflected upon the legitimacy of human authority confronted Muslim religious scholars, thinkers, and rulers alike. This led to a systematic approach involving how to discover and consider these questions, which are implicit in the Qur'an. The belief that knowledge could be attained by human reason, which more or less shaped the intellectual life of the regions that came under Muslim rule, provided the background against which "rationalist" schools of thought emerged to address those fundamental questions.

Chief among them was the Mu'tazili school, which was founded in the eighth century. The thinkers of this school believed that truth could be reached by using reason on what is given in the Qur'an.[3] The *ulema* (Muslim religious scholars) frowned upon this "rationalist" approach that conflicted with their theological views. Significantly, the expansion of the vocabulary and idiom of the Arabic language, the medium through which the divine revelation was transmitted, as a result of copious translation of Greek works, notably by Aristotle and Plato, into Arabic, only bolstered this approach. Promoted by some Arab rulers to meet the challenge of scientific progress and intellectual curiosity, partly to enhance their power and success, the expansion of the Arabic language underscored the relevance of philosophy, medicine, mathematics, and astronomy. Reflecting on the indebtedness of Islamic philosophers to the Greeks, Richard Walzer remarked, "All of them [Islamic philosophers] agree that truth as obtained by philosophy transcends the borders of nations and religions, and that it in no way matters who was first to discover it."[4] This intellectual climate was reflected upon by the Islamic philosopher Ya'qub Ibn Ishaq al-Kindi (801–66). He wrote: "It is fitting to acknowledge the utmost gratitude to those who have contributed even a little to the truth, not to speak of those who have contributed much. . . . We should not be ashamed to acknowledge truth and assimilate it from whatever source it comes to us, even if it is brought to us by former generations and foreign peoples. For him who seeks the truth there is nothing of higher value than truth itself."[5]

Though they disagreed with this logic, the *ulema* were more concerned about the implication of using reason as a method of interpreting the Qur'an for the unity of Islam. They advanced the worth of maintaining the unity of "God's people" over the yearning of reaching agreement on matters of doctrine. *Fitna* (strife) within the Muslim community had to be avoided. The Qur'an, for them, was the basis upon which faith and communal peace rested. And in response to the intellectual climate that advanced reason, including the use of *ra'y* (opinion), *qiyas* (analogical reasoning), and *ta'wil* (metaphorical or allegorical interpretation) to explain the Qur'an, the *ulema* asserted that a return to the pristine purity of Islam of the righteous ancestors, or *al-salaf al-salih*, was paramount to salvage the Muslim community from the heretical intellectual vise of foreign influences.[6] This school of thought ushered in what Muhammad Amarah referred to as *al-Salafiyah al-Nususiyah* (Textual Salafiyah).[7]

At the forefront of religious scholars who led this school was Ahmad Ibn Hanbal (780–855). Ibn Hanbal, the eponym of the Hanbali *madhab* (school of jurisprudence), is alleged to be the first to use the term "Salaf" in expounding his theological stand. He stated:

> It has been transmitted from more than one of our ancestors [*salafina*] that they said "the Qur'an is the speech of God and is uncreated," and this is what I endorse. I do not engage in speculative theology and I hold that there is nothing to be said other than what is in God's Book [Qur'an], the traditions of His messenger or those of his companions and their follow-ers—may God have mercy on them. It is not praiseworthy to engage in theological discussion in matters not contained therein.[8]

By focusing on the texts of the Qur'an, Sunna, and *hadiths* (sayings) of the Prophet's companions and their followers, this school consecrated the texts and made them the only canonical source, whose interpretation involved only a lit-eralist reading. These texts contained God's will that mankind should respond to by manifest action and inner faith. The proponents of this school, countering what they considered the heretical stand of Islamic philosophers (see below), held firmly that "intellect is an instinct [*ghariza*], wisdom is recognition [*fut-nah*], and knowledge is revelation."[9] Correspondingly, Ibn Hanbal, partly to fend off heretical Greek influence over reading the texts and partly to define the methodological approach to the texts, defined five principles according to which questions were to be answered. First, if the answer to the question is found in the texts, then a literal reading of the relevant text is fully adequate. Second, if the answer is found in a legal opinion expressed by a companion of the Prophet, then it becomes certain. Third, if the answer is found in multiple sayings by the companions, then the answer most close to the Qur'an and the Sunna is most relevant. Fourth, if the answer is found only in a weak saying whose authenticity is in question, then it is preferable to analogy. Finally, if the answer is not found in the texts, then strict analogy is used only as a necessity.[10]

The partisans of this "Salafi" school, among whom were Muhammad ibn Isma'il al-Bukhari (810–70) and Muslim ibn al-Hajjaj (817–75), came to be known interchangeably as *ahl al-Hadith* and *ahl al-Sunna* (partisans of the Sunna) for their immense concern with the texts, in contrast to the partisans of the rationalist school, who came to be known as *Ahl al-Ra'y* (partisans of opinion).[11] The epistemological, theological struggle between the two schools, according to Radwan al-Sayyid, was not settled until the fourth Islamic century (tenth century C.E.). Al-Sayyid perceptively observed that this epistemological struggle had essentially a sociopolitical dimension. It revolved around the vision of society, the means of regulating (and governing) society, and the source of authority within and over society. Though *ahl al-Hadith* and *Ahl al-Ra'y* accepted that the means of regulating and governing society is *'aql* (intellect), they differed over the "what-ness" (essence) of intellect (*ma'iyat or mahiyat al-'Aql*).[12] Islamic philosophers affirmed that

> the intellect is an essence, not part of the cognitive or emotional physiology of the human being. It is an element bestowed from above to regulate and direct the life of the individual, and when life leaves the body, intellect returns to its world. And just like the intellect with respect to the individual is both an essence and a function, its relationship to society has crystallized in the same way, in the sense that society is governed and regulated in its private and public life by the intellectual elite whom the active intellect has endowed with the right to govern in the matters of behavior, conduct, education and culture. On the political level, the upshot of this view is that authority [the ruler] is the *'aql* (intellect) of society. And the intellect of society does not derive from within it but is given to it from above by the verdict of nature. Human society is comprised of instincts, tendencies, and cravings that if left to themselves would clash with each other until they perish, thus leading to near or complete annihilation of society. Hence the necessity of the governing, regulating social intellect represented in the Sultan [ruler].[13]

On the other hand, Radwan al-Sayyid explained *Ahl al-Sunna*'s perspective of the essence of intellect in contrast to that of the Islamic philosophers. He wrote:

> In contrast, *ahl al-Sunna*, who consider the intellect an instinct, see the intellect in the human being as common as the rest of his instincts. This means that the intellect is an integral part of the individual and a part of his physiology, whose function is to regulate from within. This is reflected on the social level in the view that society inherently and internally organizes and regulates itself, without any outside force compelling it to defer to the intellect for the sake of continuity and stability. The Islamic society has inhered and fused with the Islamic *shari'a* . . . making Islamic society the source of both social authority (customs and consensus as related to Islamic law) and political authority.[14]

Taking all this into consideration, it becomes clear upon further examination that the theological and sociopolitical views of *ahl al-Hadith* provided the ideological foundation for the development and crystallization of Salafi thought and *da'wa* (call to Islam, propagation of the faith) following the fall of the Abbasid dynasty at the hands of the Mongols in 1258. Abd al-Ghani 'Imad referred to this new phase as *al-Salafiyah al-Tarikhiyah* (Historical Salafiyah).[15]

Historical Salafiyah

The scholar most credited with sharpening and crystallizing the theological and sociopolitical views of *ahl al-Hadith* was none other than classical Muslim *ulema* Taqi al-Din Ibn Taymiyah (1263–1328). His contribution to and influence over Salafism as a theological school made the reference Historical Salafiyah most plausible because it became a foundational referral source to the development and justification of Salafi thought. Ibn Taymiyah was born in a period of enormous tribulations in the Muslim world. In 1258, the Mongols, led by Hulagu, razed the illustrious capital of the Abbasid dynasty to the ground and brought to an end the Abbasid Caliphate. Meanwhile, Syria and Egypt fell to the rule of the Mamluks (1250–1517). Ibn Taymiyah, who was born in Syria, witnessed fundamental changes in Muslim society that questioned the very essence of the relationship between God and mankind on one hand, and that between the ruler and the *ulema* on the other. He blamed those who engaged in what he considered *bida'* (reprehensible innovations) in belief and practice, such as the Sufists, Jahmis, Asha'ris, philosophers, and Shi'ites, for the catastrophe that befell the Muslim *ummah* (community of believers).[16]

Ibn Taymiyah had strong reservations about the Muslim faith of the Mongols and Mamluks, whom he considered superficial converts to Islam, and took it upon himself to remind them of the meaning of their faith, including their obligation as rulers to participate in carrying out God's will. But how should one interpret God's will? Ibn Taymiyah set out to affirm the creed on the basis of which human life should be lived in the service of God. He, like Ibn Hanbal, believed that a literal reading of the Qur'an, the *sunna*, and the *hadiths* of the companions of the Prophet and their followers provided all the answers to guide human life. According to a biography of Ibn Taymiyah by his disciple Shams al-Din al-Dhahabi (d. 1347–48), he "supported the pure Sunna and *al-Tariqa al-Salafiyah* (Salafiyah way or methodology)."[17] Ibn Taymiyah expounded this Salafi methodology in a *fatwa* (religious edict). He wrote:

> As for the Salafiyah it is as [Hamd ibn Muhammad] al-Khattabi and Abu Bakr al-Khatib [al-Baghdadi] and others have stated: The way of the Salaf is to interpret literally the Koranic verses and *hadiths* that relate to the Divine attributes [*ijra' ayat al-sifat wa ahadith al-sifat 'ala zahiriha*], and without attributing to Him anthropomorphic qualities [*ma' nafy al-kayfiyya wal-tashbih*]. So that one is not to state that the meaning of "hand" is power or that of "hearing" is knowledge.[18]

Bernard Haykel keenly discerned that this definition is not simply about physical aspects of God: More crucially it is about how to approach the texts of revelation and who is to be considered a true believer in Islam.[19] It follows from this that the charge of *kufr* (unbelief) could be leveled against a person who denied an attribute of God or be interpreted metaphorically or associated with someone other than God. Beyond this, there was a need to transmit religious knowledge in order to protect the truth of belief. Thus, Ibn Taymiyah, though he was not in principle against the principle of *taqlid* (emulation) of the four established *madhabs* (Shafi'i, Hanbali, Maliki, and Hanafi schools of jurisprudence), he promoted and enjoined *ijtihad* (individual interpretation of the sources of Islamic law, the Qur'an and *hadith*, as opposed to *taqlid*) so long as this did not conflict with Islamic law. Ibn Taymiyah's biographer, al-Dhahabi, explained:

> He was well informed of the legal views of the [Prophet's] companions and their followers, and he rarely talked about a subject without quoting the four schools of the imams. Yet, he contradicted the four schools in well-known matters about which he wrote and for which provided arguments from the Koran and the Sunna. He has compiled a work entitled *Politics According to Divine Law for Establishing Order for Sovereign and Subjects* and a book [called] *Removing the Reproach from the Learned Imams.* . . . For some years now he has not issued *fatwas* (legal opinions) according to a specific school, rather he bases these on the proof he has ascertained himself. He supported the pure Sunna and the way of Salafiyah.[20]

Similarly, Ibn Taymiyah's interest in theology did not only concern purging Islamic belief of what he considers heresies but also protecting the unity of the *ummah*. Albert Hourani explained that for Ibn Taymiyah, the unity of the *ummah*—a unity of belief in God and acceptance of the Prophet's message—did not imply political unity. Authority in the *ummah* was essential to maintain justice and keep individuals within their limits. Authority could be exercised by more than one ruler. How he obtained power was less important than how he used it. The just exercise of power was a kind of religious service. He should exercise statecraft within the bounds of *shari'a* (Islamic law) and should rule in cooperation with the *ulema*.[21] Conversely, the ruler had to be obeyed even if he were unjust. Revolt against him was justified only if he went against a command of God or His prophet.[22]

The broad basis of this theological school was reflected by Ibn Taymiyah's axiom: We worship only God, we worship Him through *shari'a* and not through reprehensible innovations. Fundamentally, the creedal tenets of the *al-Salafiyah al-Tarikhiyah* included the following: (1) a return to the authentic beliefs and practices of the pious ancestors; (2) upholding *tawhid* (oneness of God) in affirming the *tawhid al-rububiyah* (oneness of Lordship), whereby God's creational powers cannot be attributed to other than Him, *tawhid al-Uluhiyah* (oneness of Godship), whereby all forms of worship should be directed exclusively to Him, and *tawhid al-asma' wal-sifat* (oneness of the names and attributes), whereby God's depiction should be presented according to the texts of revelation without inquiring about modality or metaphorical interpretation; (3) confirming the faith of those who believe in the pillars of Islam, whereby the charge of unbelief cannot be leveled against them unless they practiced *shirk* (polytheism) or opposed the truth;[23] (4) advancing the revelation over the intellect and submitting to the texts of the Book and the Sunna, whose literal reading must not involve metaphorical or heretical interpretation; (5) disavowing the partisans of heretic tendencies and similar *madhabs*; and (6) obeying the ruler as an aspect of obeying God unless he violated His command.[24]

The partisans of this Salafiyah came also to be known as *ahl al-Sunna wal-jama'a* (partisans of the Sunna and the "Group" [congregation of believers]). They believed that they were part of the *al-firqa al-najiyah* (saved group), in reference to a *hadith* by Prophet Muhammad in which he said: "The sons of Israel have been divided into seventy-two sects, and my *ummah* has been divided into seventy-three sects. All of them except one have gone to Hell. . . . They are those who are upon what I and my companions are upon."[25] As we shall see, this *hadith* has become pivotal to contemporary Islamic and Salafi movements that act in what they consider the interest of preserving the "sacred/saved group."

Subsequently, as Abd al-Ghani 'Imad observed, this historic Salafiyah transformed into a scholastic Salafiyah with the appearance of Sheikh Muhammad Ibn Abd al-Wahhab (1703–1791) in the Arabian Peninsula. It changed into a confessional orientation within Islamic thought, having its own philosophy and political authority. What characterized this scholastic Salafiyah was its emergence as a revivalist, puritanical movement, which subsequently found its revivalist expression in the reformist modern Salafiyah of Sheikh Muhammad Abdu (1849–1905). This bipolar transformation only reinforced a trend among Salafists to chart their own *manhaj* (methodology) by describing the way by which they can live and implement their beliefs and *da'wa*. This caused, as we shall see, the emergence of various Salafi groups.

Scholastic Salafiyah

Sheikh Muhammad Ibn Abd al-Wahhab was born in Najd, in what is today Saudi Arabia, an area that, besides being at the periphery of the holy land of Islam, had little, if any, cultural links to the prosperous urban centers of Islam. Najd by the eighteenth century was marked by anarchy, violence, and conflict, as a result of the absence of either a tribal or central authority order. There flourished in this harsh landscape religious traditions and customs at variance with those of Sunni orthodox Islam. Besides a belief in animistic and Sufi practices, the practices of venerating and worshipping *awlia* (saints) and *tawassul* (requesting the mediation of the dead) were widespread in the Arabian Peninsula.[26] Influenced by the Hanbali school and Ibn Taymiyah, al-Wahhab set out to unify the population and purge the holy land of all reprehensible innovations. He sought a renewal (*tajdid*) of the faith and rejection of all that he considered illegitimate beliefs. He focused on theological questions, central among them being the concept of *tawhid*, by which *al-'aqida* (Islamic creed) could be purified. He preached a return to the orthodox ways of pious ancestors (*al-salaf al-salih*) and a strict obedience to the Qur'an and *hadith*, as understood by the Hanbali school and its disciples. Only in this way can all the reprehensible innovations and practices be severed from the true faith as reflected in the *'aqida*. But his concept and understanding of *tawhid* differed from that of the established pattern that divided it actionably and doctrinally into *tawhid al-rububiyah, tawhid al-uluhiyah*, and *tawhid al-asma' wal-sifat*. Al-Wahhab established a difference between *tawhid al-rububiyah* (oneness of lordship or affirmation that "God Is One") and *tawhid al-asma' wal-sifat* (oneness of the names and attributes) on one side, and *tawhid al-uluhiyah* (oneness of Godship or oneness of the object of worship) on the other. He argued that polytheists practiced *tawhid al-rububiyah* and not *tawhid al-uluhiyah*, which explains the preponderance of reprehensible innovations and beliefs. Therefore, he asserted that the act of worship is based on the fundamental of *tawhid al-uluhiyah*. If one is to be a true Muslim, then he or she has to proclaim *tawhid*, including primarily adhering to it in religious practice. Therefore, Wahhabis would like to be designated *al-Muwahidun* or *Ahl al-Tawhid* (Partisans of Tawhid).[27]

This centrality on *tawhid al-uluhiya*, which rejected any act of devotion other than that directed toward worshipping God, drew a barrier between Islam and *tawhid*, as embraced by Wahhabis, and *kufr* and *shirk*. In other words, Wahhabism, by focusing on its theological understanding of *tawhid*, created a bipolar world: a true and faithful Muslim world represented by the partisans of *tawhid* and a *mushrik and kafir* world. Correspondingly, al-Wahhab waged a campaign against Shi'ism, Sufism, and all that he considered polytheists, while at the same time proscribing all kinds of reprehensible innovations. He destroyed the tombs of the Prophet's companions, Shi'a holy shrines, and clamped down on widespread practices and beliefs, charging their practitioners with polytheism and unbelief. However, his campaign was set in motion only after he partnered with the Saudi tribe of al-Dir'iya. Forging a compact with the chief of the tribe and ruler of the city, Muhammad ibn Saud, al-Wahhab assured himself and his movement a permanent alliance, giving rise to a political entity that formed the embryonic structure of the Saudi state. Initially, the Saudi tribe acted as the political and military arm of the Wahhabi movement. True, the campaign to unite the population and impose the Wahhabi creed was protracted and arduous; nevertheless, the campaign succeeded with the establishment of the Saudi state in 1932, at the heart of which was the Wahhabi religious establishment. Since then, the Wahhabi religious establishment has acted as the guardian of the Wahhabi creed and the source of religio-political legitimacy for the Saudi royal family.

Significantly, given the fact that al-Wahhab concerned himself with theological questions, *fiqh* (jurisprudence) was secondary to his doctrine. He adopted the position that religious rulings can only be based on the Qur'an, the Sunna, and the *ijma'* (consensus) of the pious ancestors. As Stéphane Lacroix keenly observed, "theoretically, that comes down to a rejection of *taqlid* (emulation) of the four canonical legal schools, and to the establishment of *ijtihad* (interpretation) as the pillar of the law. In practice, nevertheless, Ibn 'Abd al-Wahhab continued to adhere to the rules of exegesis of Hanbalism, which imply a very literal reading of the sacred texts."[28]

This, as we shall see, created tensions among Salafists who adopted the Wahhabi creed but advocated *ijtihad*. Significantly, as Abd al-Ghani 'Imad remarked, "by inducting the orientation of *ahl al-Hadith* into the understanding of the pious ancestors, al-Wahhab added a durational dimension to the comprehension of the pious ancestors, which included not only the [Prophet's] companions and their followers, but also the scholars and orientation of *ahl al-Hadith*. . . . Hence *ahl al-Hadith* became the title indicating Salafism as well."[29] No less significant, by bifurcating the world into the abode of true Islam and the abode of *kufr*, al-Wahhab's vision helped broaden the concept by which leveling the charge of unbelief could be justified.[30] Taking all this into consideration, one could safely argue that Wahhabism has developed into a sect by distinguishing itself from other Islamic groups despite the denial of its partisans.[31]

Whereas this revivalist, puritanical movement emerged in large measure as a response to the deviation of Muslims from the orthodoxy of pious ancestors, a revivalist movement, though in contradistinction to Wahhabism, emerged in the nineteenth century as a response to the cultural challenge of the West. This movement came to be known interchangeably as the modern or enlightened Salafiyah movement. This only further attested to the development of Salafism into various movements, making it all the more difficult to paint Salafism with the same brush.

The enlightened Salafiyah movement grew out from the power disequilibrium between the Muslim world and the West and as a response to the cultural, military, and political challenge of the West to the Arab and Muslim world.

Napoleon's invasion of Egypt in 1798, the French defeat, respectively, of the Algerian forces in 1836–37 and Moroccan forces in 1844, and British suppression of the Mahdist forces in Sudan in 1898 demonstrated the futility of military confrontation with the West and underscored the weakness of Muslim society. Ominously, these defeats followed and coincided with Western cultural penetration of Muslim society. Muslim society that withstood time and again foreign challenges and threats appeared so vulnerable to Western cultural and military prowess.

It is against this background that a reformist movement emerged in the Muslim world that, in line with some previous efforts, believed the answer to the composite challenge of the West lay in borrowing and learning from the West. Three individuals from different parts of the Muslim world illustrated what L. Carl Brown described as the early Muslim accommodationist and modernizing responses to the Western challenge.[32] They were Khayr al-Din al-Tunisi (1810[20?]–79), Sayyid Ahmad Khan (1817–98), and Sheikh Muhammad Abdu (1849–1905). Though they more or less shared the same reformist beliefs, Abdu stood out among them. He was an *ulema* who challenged deep-rooted traditions in the Muslim world and pioneered, in sharp contrast to both the Wahhabi-Salafi school and Historical Salafiyah, the Salafiyah school of Islamic modernism.

Abdu believed that Islam properly understood and implemented was compatible with modernity. He emphasized that Islam "imposed upon believers the obligation to use their God-given reasoning powers in adapting the basic principles set out in the *shari'a* to changing conditions of life in each generation."[33] He also deemed that human action, based on rational and scientific principles, would best serve humanity. In this respect, he consistently affirmed that "Islam and its prescriptions were fully rational and consonant with the conclusions of modern science and philosophy."[34] Correspondingly, he held out that political leadership had to be grounded in reason.[35] Sylvia Haim observed that Abdu's "diagnosis of the present state of Islam can be summed in one word, stagnation (*jumud*). This stagnation is not inherent in Islam as such but is the result of despotic rule and obscurantist theology. Once they are removed—and they can be removed—science and religion . . . would walk side by side in fraternity, as the Koran envisaged."[36]

Abdu, unlike the antirationalist, literalist Salafists, adopted *ijtihad* on the basis of reason and a return to the ways of the *salaf al-salih*. This Salafi paradigmatic society could be reproduced by means of following the ways of the pious ancestors on the basis of rational reading of the sources of revelation. Certainly Abdu was not a literalist, nor was he interested in arguing about the authoritativeness of the *hadith*. As the pioneer of enlightened Salafiyah, Abdu, though he was against all reprehensible innovations related to superstition, was not concerned with questions that condemned Muslims for their theological heresies. His modernist Salafiyah school was not about drawing the boundary that separated true from false Muslims. Rather, it was about revitalizing Muslim society with the objective of lifting it out from its state of *jumud*. This demanded learning from the West—namely, the sciences—to equip Muslim society with the means to make the big leap into modernity without losing its Islamic spirit and character. As Haykel noted, "their [enlightened Salafist] vision was more inclusive, even ecumenical, and was concerned with uplifting Islamic civilization and all its members."[37]

Ominously, Abdu's emphasis on the golden age of Islam as the paradigm for later ages undercut his case for massive borrowing from the West. For traditionalists and conservatives, the rightly guided caliphs and their followers, mostly credited with establishing the golden age of Islam, did not borrow from the West; rather, their accomplishment was the result of adhering to the tenets of Islam and applying the Prophetic model. This created a paradox in Salafi thought, which soon morphed into fundamental questions related to the nature of the Salafists' relationship with political authority in a world marked by a disequilibrium of power disfavoring and affecting Muslim society.

In fact, this development was not limited to Salafism. The relationship between Islam and political authority, which was concentric with the relationship between the West and the Muslim world in the early twentieth century, preoccupied Islamic contemporary thought. The causal factors of this preoccupation lay within fundamental changes in the reformists' view of the West and their relationship with political authority. The unfolding of the first two decades of the twentieth century revealed in the words of Radwan al-Sayyid an "immense, deep Western enmity to the Muslim world, reflected in dominating most areas of the Muslim world and disgracing their religion and society. This culminated in the defeat of the Ottoman empire in World War One and apportioning its regions by the Western victors."[38] Consequently, whereas Abdu and his generation of reformists believed in learning from the scientific methods of Western civilization, Abdu's disciples perceived that Western civilization evoked and crystallized a long history of Western enmity to Islam and Muslims.[39] This change in perspective by Muslim reformists coincided with another fundamental change in the relationship between reformists and the state. The Turkish leader Mustafa Kemal abolished the caliphate in 1924 and in its stead established a secular, nationalist order overtly hostile to Islam. Though this radical transformation did not take place in northern Africa and the Levant, its manifestation began to gradually appear in the countries of these two regions under Western colonization. Western colonialists established in these countries political orders that, even though not professing enmity to Islam and its institutions, left no role for Islam in society.

This caused a crisis among Muslim reformists, who felt betrayed not only by the West but also by those nationalists, many of whom were brought to power by the West or came to power in response to Western policies. Nothing reflects this crisis more than the ideological transformation of Rashid Rida (1865–1935). Born in al-Qalamoun, a village near Tripoli in today's northern Lebanon, Rida was a pupil and intellectual heir of Abdu. Initially he believed in Islamic modernism (liberalism), which underscored Islam's compatibility with modernity, and learning from the West as means to revitalize Muslim society. He advocated *ijtihad* in interpreting the textual sources of the revelation and frowned upon the fossilized Islam of traditional *ulema*. From 1898 to 1935, he published *Al-Manar* (The Lighthouse), a review, to circulate his ideas and those of his reformist colleagues. It served as a platform to stimulate a *tajdid* (reinvigoration/renewal) of Islam and the Muslim world. He also revived the works of Ibn Taymiyah by publishing his writings and promoting his ideas. Subsequently, taking note of the cataclysmic events brought about by Western policies in the Muslim world and shocked by the abolition of the caliphate, he transformed into a Muslim intellectual mostly concerned about protecting Muslim culture, identity, and politics from Western influence. He supported a theory that essentially emphasized the necessity of an Islamic state in which the scholars of Islam would have a leading role. Commenting on Rida's theory, Kosugi Yasushi wrote: "When Rida wrote his theory of *Khalifa of the Mujtahid*, or governance by the jurists, in the 1920s, it was seen as an obsolete nostalgia harkening to classical theory. When Ayatullah Khomeini's theory of 'guardianship by the jurist' became the backbone of the new Islamic republic in Iran, few remembered the significance of Rida's theory."[40]

What Yasushi alluded to was that Rida was a forerunner of Islamist thought. He apparently intended to provide a theoretical platform for a modern Islamic state. His ideas were later incorporated in the works of Islamic scholars. Significantly, his ideas influenced none other than Hassan al-Bannah, founder of the Muslim Brotherhood in Egypt. In fact, as Yasushi observed, "Hassan al-Bannah inherited the ideas of *Al-Manar* for Islamic reform and revival, in a much simplified and popularized version."[41] In other words, Rida paved the intellectual path for the emergence of the Muslim Brotherhood. Bassam Tibi forthrightly commented that "Rida's Islamic fundamentalism has been taken up by the Muslim Brethren, a right wing radical movement founded in 1928, which has ever since been in inexorable opposition to secular nationalism."[42]

Enlightened Salafiyah, as we have seen, had been deeply affected by the sociopolitical turbulence in the Muslim world. Though it stood on the opposite end of the Historical Salafiyah advocating *ijtihad* and *tajdid*, it subsequently forced to the center of Islamic thought fundamental questions relating to the relationship of Muslims with political authority. As the Arab-Muslim world continued to experience under its conservative and nationalist leaders constant sociopolitical crises and military defeats at the hands of Israel, questions related to political authority became more relevant by the day. For Salafists of all stripes, the fundamental question of *manhaj* (methodology), or the way by which Salafists can live and implement their beliefs and *da'wa*, moved to the center of their ideological debate over how to approach politics. It follows from this Salafists, in principle, largely agree on creedal tenets, but, in practice, basically disagree on how to apply the prophetic model to the reality of the present. More specifically, they invariably differ in contextualizing and understanding the present reality and therefore diverge over how to change this reality in accordance with applying the prophetic model.

Though this author has broadly followed Abd al-Ghani 'Imad in his classification of Salafists, he, in terms of how Salafists engaged politics in relation to their *manhaj*, has inched closer to Bernard Haykel and Quintan Wiktorowicz's classification.[43] Thus Salafists broadly fall into three distinct categories: quietests, *harakis* (activists), and Salafi jihadists.[44]

The Quietests: The Scientific Salafiyah (*al-Salafiyah al-'Ilmiyah*)

Al-Salafiyah al-'Ilmiyah, also known as the quietest Salafi school, is principally associated with its founder Sheikh Muhammad Nasir al-Din al-Albani. Born in Albania in 1914, al-Albani left with his father for Damascus in 1923 following the compulsory application of secular practices. Though he learned from his *ulema* father and some of his friends, such as Sheikh Sa'id al-Barhani, al-Albani was mostly autodidactic. He was influenced by the studies and ideas published by Rashid Rida's *Al-Manar* and spent significant time at the al-Zahiriyah library in Damascus studying the books of *hadith*. In line with Muslim reformists (enlightened Salafists), he emphasized *ijtihad* and rejected *taqlid* of the four *madhabs*. But unlike the Muslim reformists and in step with the classical *ahl al-Hadith*, he was totally opposed to the use of reason and adamant about purging from Islam what he considered the accumulated reprehensible innovations. He devoted his life to the study of *hadith* and profoundly versed himself with many *hadith* books, including the well-known books of *hadith* by al-Bukhari and Muslim. He focused on *'ilm al-hadith* (science of *hadith*) as a foundational religious discipline, with the objective of identifying spurious and weak *hadith*. The science of *hadith* did not involve reason to authenticate a *hadith*. Rather, it involved a strict linguistic or grammatical critique of the *matn* (content) of a *hadith* and a thorough investigation of the *sanad* (chain of transmission). Only by examining the *sanad* can a *hadith* be authenticated. This entailed appraisal of the morality and reliability of the transmitter.[45] In addition to classifying a number of *hadiths* as spurious, Al-Albani, according to Kamaruddin Amin, identified 990 *hadiths* considered authentic by most Muslim scholars but that he considered weak (*da'if*), including some of the celebrated works by Muslim.[46]

Before long, al-Albani's reputation as a scholar of *hadith* earned him an invitation from the recently established University of Medina in Saudi Arabia. Upon the recommendation of then vice president of the university and future mufti of the Saudi state Sheikh Abd al-Aziz ibn Abdallah ibn Baz, al-Albani was appointed professor of *hadith* in 1961. Al-Albani's focus on *ijtihad* beyond the four *madhabs* brought to the surface the tension in the Wahhabi religious establishment, whereby Wahhabi scholars, in principle, adhered to the concept of *ijtihad* but in practice followed the Hanbali school.[47] This led to his departure from the kingdom in 1963 when his contract was not renewed. Al-Albani resumed his work in Damascus before leaving for Amman in 1979. Pressured by his friend and protector Sheikh ibn Baz, Saudi authorities made al-Albani a member of the High Council of the Islamic University in Medina in 1975. In addition to teaching there for a relatively short time, al-Albani frequently visited the kingdom both as a participant in Islamic conferences and as a pilgrim. Al-Albani's focus on *ijtihad* and *hadiths* and their authenticity earned him powerful friends and enemies alike and provoked schisms in Salafi currents relating to their attitude toward political authority and societal behavior.

Significantly, al-Albani was key in reviving popular Islam as a force to change societal behavior and attitude toward political authority.[48] As Salafist, the principal tenets of his scientific school are *tawhid*, *itba'* (following/according to), and *tazkiyah* (purification). He, like classical Salafists, adhered to the broad principle of *tawhid* by emphasizing *tawhid al-rububiyah*, *tawhid al-uluhiyah*, and *tawhid al-asma' wal-sifat*. In respect to the tenet of *itba'*, al-Albani stressed following only the Prophet in affirmation of the Muslim pillar of *shahada* (testimony)*:* I testify/bear witness that Muhammad is the messenger of God. This testimony would not be complete without the belief that Muhammad was a human being who received a divine revelation: the Qur'an and Sunna. And this testimony would be completed by loving the Prophet and emulating the beneficent first three generations in Islam.[49] It follows from this that al-Albani categorically rejected what he considered reprehensible innovations introduced to Islam by *Ahl al-Ra'y* (partisans of opinion) and like-minded "rationalist" groups, innovations that tarnished the creed of and worship in Islam. Therefore, he asserted that the foundational fundamentals of Salafism began with *ahl al-Hadith* who represented the saved sect and served as the paradigm group for Muslim society.

In respect to the final tenet, *al-tazkiyah*, al-Albani considered it as a primary purpose for which the messenger of God was sent. Its objective was "to cleanse and heal the soul" and "purge it of its abominations" by abiding by the revelation and creed and ethics of Islam, which achieve justice and benevolence.[50]

For al-Albani, these aforementioned tenets of scientific Salafism could not be properly understood and applied without engaging in *da'wa*, the vehicle of societal change. *Da'wa* is a priority for al-Albani's scientific Salafi school, for without it neither the upright Muslim nor the Muslim state could be brought about. Correspondingly, al-Albani premised the methodology (*manhaj*) of change inherent in his *da'wa* on the concept *al-tasfiyah wal-tarbiyah* (purification and education). He believed that, in order to effect the exemplary Muslim, Islam should be purified of everything that is alien and fraudulent. To that end, the Sunna must be purged of all forged and weak *hadiths* so that the revelation can be understood in light of authenticated *hadiths*. As for *tarbiyah*, al-Albani believed that only by instilling into the youthful generation the authentic Islamic creed, as outlined in the Qur'an and the Sunna, could a pure Islamic society be formed as the basis of an Islamic state. Al-Albani explained:

> The partisans of religious science should take it upon themselves to educate the youthful generation in light of what has been confirmed in the Koran and the Sunna. It is not right to allow people to become heirs of concepts and errors, some of which are unanimously absolutely false and some of which are disagreed upon in light of speculation, *ijtihad* and opinion. Some of this *ijtihad* and opinion are contrary to the Sunna. These matters need to be purified [*tasfiyah*], and the point of departure and the path to be followed should be clarified. It is essential to educate [*tarbiyat*] the new generation the correct religious science, for this education [*tarbiyah*] will produce the pure Islamic society, and therefore establish for us the state of Islam. Without these two preambles—the correct religious science and the correct education on the basis of this correct science—it's impossible, in my belief, to establish the pillars of Islam, the rule of Islam, or the state of Islam.[51]

It follows from this that al-Albani put the Salafi *'aqida* (creed), as implemented in the proper *manhaj* premised on his *da'wa* concept of *tasfiyah* and *tarbiyah*, before politics. Put in simple terms, unless religion is purified and rightly practiced, political action will lead to corruption and injustice in Muslim society. This explains al-Albani's opposition to Islamism (political Islam) as adopted by the Muslim Brotherhood and other *harakis* (see below). His Islamist detractors refer to his controversial Palestinian *fatwa*, in which he called for the

Palestinians to leave the occupied territories of Gaza and the West Bank because they could no longer practice their religion correctly there, to underscore what they consider his improper approach.[52]

Apparently al-Albani's concern with the purity of Islam and *da'wa* has its analogical basis in the Meccan period, when Prophet Muhammad first began his mission. During this period, the Prophet and his companions, being a minority and facing serious obstacles, preferred *da'wa* on the basis of persuasion and advice rather than overt opposition to the dominant Quraysh elite. Jihad, as a struggle in the path of God, entailed then peaceful efforts to promote Islam, not rebellions or dissent. Al-Albani saw this period as an endorsement of his *da'wa* and a refutation of political Islam and violent jihad. He argued: "History repeats itself. Everybody claims that the prophet is their role model. Our Prophet spent the first half of his message making *da'wa*, and he did not start with jihad."[53] This did not mean that al-Albani condemned politics. He, in fact, saw politics as part of Islam. Nevertheless, he believed that under the present circumstances it was "good politics" to stay away from politics. His famous saying *"min al-siyasah tark al-siyasah"* (from politics is to leave politics) became a hallmark of his school.[54]

To be sure, al-Albani's Salafi school also perceived politics in its Western contemporary concept as a reprehensible innovation based on *takfiri* (unbelief) principles, reflected in deception, dishonesty, and cunning. Similarly, al-Albani opposed Muslim participation in both elections and parliaments. He argued: "Elections according to democracy are unlawful, and parliaments that do not govern in accordance with the Qur'an and the Sunna, but rather on the basis of the majority's arbitrariness, are tyrannical. Parliaments cannot be recognized, and Muslims can neither seek nor cooperate to found them, for they contend (combat) God's revelation. And they are a Western technique made by the Jews and the Christians, who cannot be legally emulated."[55]

Paradoxically, al-Albani's views planted the seeds of division among his disciples, who conferred upon themselves the designation *ahl al-Hadith*, in reference to the classical *ahl al-Hadith*. They studied at Dar al-Hadith, a religious institution attached to the Islamic University in Medina. This institution operated informally as a department of *hadith* until its official inauguration in 1976. Despite their official claim of shunning politics, two currents emerged among their ranks, one of which advocated an active rejection of the state and its institutions, while the other sponsored unconditional support for the ruler. This division mainly developed in the association al-Jama'a al-Salafiyah al-Muhtasiba (JSM), which means "the Salafi Group That Promotes Virtue and Prevents Vice." The JSM was founded in Medina in the mid-1960s by disciples of al-Albani as a response to the growing influence of the Muslim Brotherhood and other *haraki* organizations such as Sahwa (Awakening). It developed under the patronage of Sheikh ibn Baz, who had become the head of the Wahhabi religious establishment in 1969. Members of JSM, like their teacher, renounced any interest in politics. At the same time, however, they regarded Saudi rule as illegitimate on the basis of the classical Salafi principle, shared by al-Albani, that only members of the Prophet's tribe, Quraysh, can rule the *ummah*.[56] Consequently, they considered that the *bay'a* (pledge of allegiance) of the Saudi subjects to the Saudi regime to be null. This did not mean, however, that the Saudi rulers should be excommunicated (*takfir*).[57]

Nevertheless, though the JSM's opposition to the Saudi regime did not stem from political considerations, it came to harness significant grievances against the royal family, who were seen as too corrupt and too close to the West. This led to a division in the JSM, with a small radical core rallying around Juhayman al-'Utaybi. Al-'Utaybi considered that present rulers of the Muslim world, especially the Saudi royal family, did not live up to the character of the caliph, whereupon the ruler of the *ummah* has to rule justly and not to follow his desires. He also argued that they did not rule in accordance with the Qur'an and Sunna, thereby causing the Muslim community to fall into despair and discord. Though he did not excommunicate the Saudi royals, he severely criticized them and accused them of wiping out Islam and destroying the Muslim creed. In referencing present Muslim and Saudi rulers, al-'Utaybi concluded in his *Risalat al-Imara wal-Bay'a wal-Ta'a* (The Message of Governance, Pledge of Allegiance and Obedience) that "these [Muslim] rulers have no pledge of allegiance from Muslims and they should not be obeyed. Yet, they should not be excommunicated. . . . We believe that by staying in power, these rulers will destroy the religion of God glorious and exalted, even if they professed Islam; we ask God to relieve us from all of them."[58]

This anathematization of the Saudi rulers soon manifested itself in the violent seizure of the Grand Mosque in Mecca in 1979 by al-'Utaybi and his companions. Many of them were either killed or arrested by Saudi authorities. Al-'Utaybi was executed in January 1980.[59]

This episode had a deep impact on the Saudi *ahl al-Hadith*, many of whom frowned upon the seizure of one of the holiest mosques in the land of the Prophet. This gave rise to a new current among the members of *ahl al-Hadith*, who rallied around two illustrious scholars at the *hadith* department, Sheikh Muhammad Aman al-Jami, under whose name (Jami) the current came to be known, and Sheikh Rabi' al-Madkhali. The Jamis professed unquestionable loyalty to the Saudi regime. Doctrinally they endorsed the views of al-Albani's scientific Salafi school, with the exception of rejecting the classical principle that denied legitimacy of a non-Qurayshi ruler. They considered the Saudi state a pure Islamic state.[60] Before long, this current, strongly supported by the Saudi regime, came to represent the official religious orientation in the kingdom's schools and institutions. As we shall see, critical events in the 1980s and the 1990s deepened the politicization of the *harakis* in the kingdom, provoking a backlash against the Saudi regime. This further affected Salafism, namely its attitude toward and engagement in politics.

The *Haraki* Salafi School

In principle, the Muslim Brotherhood, founded by Hassan al-Bannah in Egypt in 1928, was the first Islamist organization. Interestingly enough, it blended Salafi views with its political activism. Al-Bannah based the ideology of the Brotherhood on three principles: (a) Islam is a comprehensive system; (b) Islam emanates from and is based on two fundamental sources, the Qur'an and the Sunna; and (c) Islam is applicable to all times and places.[61] He described his movement as a Salafiyah message, a Sunni way, a Sufi reality, a political organization, an athletic group, a scientific and cultural society, an economic enterprise, and a social idea. This protean exposition so as to appeal to "all men" underlined the universal program of the Brotherhood that sought to "internationalize" the movement by stressing the liberation of the whole Islamic world from foreign control and to institute an Islamic government.[62] As such, the Brotherhood typified a revivalist, political movement stamped by a Salafi ideological imprint. As mentioned earlier, al-Bannah was influenced by the enlightened Salafiyah, as expounded by Muhammad Abdu and especially Rashid Rida. He envisioned an Islamic utopia modeled after the utopia that existed during the time of the Prophet and the rightly guided caliphs. Being a basic tenet of Salafiyah, al-Bannah's vision grew out of Salafi origins. But he transformed it into a restrictive "fundamentalist" ideology by placing religious value on worldly affairs. Correspondingly, the state, acting as a steppingstone to the caliphate, became the object of al-Bannah's activism, whereby state institutions would serve as instruments to instill Muslim morality, to implement Muslim social justice, and to enforce *shari'a* as a comprehensive code of conduct valid for all times and places.[63]

This concern with creating an Islamic state dedicated to advancing God's will implicitly sanctified dividing the world into "true believers" and "unbelievers," into good and evil. However, this division became ideologically operational and actionable when Brotherhood ideologue Sayyid Qutb overlaid the justification of jihad on Abu al-A'la Mawdudi's concept of *jahiliyah*. *Jahiliyah* literally means ignorance and connotes the pre-Islamic pagan period in the Arabian Peninsula. Distressed by British influence over the Indian subcontinent and furious with what he considered political attempts at nationalizing rather than Islamizing the newly independent country of Pakistan, Mawdudi set out to establish an Islamist ideology. The principal themes of his ideology affirmed that sovereignty (*hakimiyah*) is to God, that Muslim rulers should confine themselves to determining God's mandate as set forth in the Qur'an and Sunna, that Islam is comprehensive, covering public and private life, and that absent this divine mandate, governments lapse into *jahiliyah*.[64] As L. Carl Brown wrote, "this 'age of ignorance' is not just a historic era coming to an end with the arrival of God's message to mankind through His Prophet Muhammad. *Jahiliyah* exists in any time or any place in which the divinely ordained ideal community has not been realized."[65]

Sayyid Qutb, following his return to Egypt from an official visit to the United States (1949–50) as an employee of the Egyptian Ministry of Education, joined the Muslim Brotherhood. Shortly thereafter, he set out to formulate an actionable ideology to implement what he believed to be God's plan for mankind. Brown commented that "Qutb's American experience probably sharpened his sense of a clash of civilizations."[66] Qutb expounded his theory in his seminal work *Milestones*.[67] He affirmed the exclusiveness of God's *hakimiyah* (sovereignty). God alone is to be worshiped and obeyed. Rulers are to implement God's mandate, as prescribed in *shari'a*. Rulers who set aside this comprehensive divine mandate lapse into *jahiliyah*. In this respect, Qutb built on Mawdudi's ingenious reinterpretation of *jahiliyah* from a historical period to a condition that can exist at any time God's mandate has not been implemented. This includes professed Muslims who don't live in conformity with God's mandate. Correspondingly, jihad against these rulers is legitimate, and the ruler's claim to being a Muslim is null and void. Commenting on jihad against *jahiliyah*, Qutb argued:

> Since this [Islamic] movement comes into conflict with the Jahiliyah which prevails over ideas and beliefs, and which has a practical system of life and a political and material authority behind it, the Islamic movement had to produce parallel resources to confront this Jahiliyah. This movement uses the methods of preaching and persuasion for reforming ideas and beliefs; and it uses physical power and jihad for abolishing the organizations and authorities of the jahili system which prevents people from reforming their ideas and beliefs but forces them to obey their erroneous ways and make them serve human lords instead of the Almighty Lord.[68]

Put simply, Qutb sharply divided the world into a *jahili* society and a true Muslim society where governance belongs to God. There exists no neutral space between the two worlds. The *jahili* society has to be wiped out in order to reclaim God's sovereignty and rule as laid down in *shari'a*.

The Muslim Brotherhood experienced an exponential growth since its founding in 1928. It became assertively politicized in the 1930s. Muslim Brotherhood fought in the 1948 war, engaged in violence against British and Egyptian Jews accused of collusion with Zionism, and allegedly assassinated Egypt's prime minister in 1948. In response, Egypt's secret police reportedly murdered al-Bannah in 1949. Meanwhile, the Brotherhood established contacts with a group of army officers committed to deposing the corrupt *ancien régime*. This Free Officers group led a coup against the palace in 1952, following which Gamal Abdel Nasser emerged as the leading man in Egypt. Before long, the relationship between Nasser's regime and the Brotherhood deteriorated as their views of the future of Egypt clashed. Following an assassination attempt on Nasser by the Brotherhood in 1954, he clamped down harshly on the Muslim Brotherhood. The organization was banned, thousands of its members were arrested and tortured, and a number of its leaders were executed. Qutb would spend much of his life in prison, where he wrote most of his works.

In the meantime, Nasser emerged as the champion of Arab nationalism and a significant force in Arab politics. In the 1960s, Saudi Arabia under King Faisal adopted a pan-Islamic foreign policy as a counterbalance to Nasser's pan-Arabism.[69] At the center of this policy was an attempt to create an Islamic bloc organized around the official principle of "Islamic solidarity."[70] Malcolm Kerr's famous description of Arab politics as an Arab cold war could not be more apt. As part of his policy, King Faisal welcomed many members of the Muslim Brotherhood to Saudi Arabia, who found employment in the kingdom's educational system.[71] The kingdom also relied on the Brotherhood as a propagandist instrument to denounce Nasser's unabashed secularism. Who could better censure Nasser than his Islamist victims? True, Nasser passed away in 1970, yet the influx of members of the Muslim Brotherhood to Saudi Arabia did not stop. Enduring economic malaise and political discrimination in their home countries, they still found a refuge in Saudi Arabia, whose conservative foreign policy remained more or less at odds with Arab nationalism.

In the meantime, the number of Muslim Brethren gradually but steadily increased in the faculty of sciences and education at Saudi universities, especially at King Abd al-Aziz University in Jeddah and its extension, Umm al-Qura University, in Mecca; Islamic University in Medina; and King Saud University in Riyadh. It is there at the kingdom's universities where education was to a great extent premised on imparting knowledge and (Islamic) morality that the creed of Wahhabism encountered the Islamic activism of the Muslim Brotherhood. Out of this encounter, a movement emerged called al-Sahwa al-Islamiyah (the Islamic Awakening), also known as Sahwa, that embodied an ideological symbiosis blending the Brotherhood's political and cultural outlook with Wahhabi religious concepts.[72] Sahwa members, as Stéphane Lacroix observed, were essentially politicized Salafists. Thanks in no small measure to the support of the Saudi state partly as a response to al-'Utaybi's indictment of Saudi "ungodly" rule, Sahwa, which thus far did not question Saudi legitimacy, was able to institutionally integrate itself into Saudi society.

Alternatively, it was natural for the disciples of al-Albani, *ahl al-Hadith*, to frown upon the politicized Salafists and even set themselves apart from Sahwa members in their attire and grooming. Interestingly enough, as Fouad Ibrahim observed, al-'Utaybi's rebellion inspired a whole new Sahwa generation that came to challenge the Saudi regime.[73] However, Sahwa more or less formed the educational backbone of the Saudi regime until the Gulf War in 1990. Not only did Iraq's invasion of Kuwait shatter whatever illusion remained about Arab nationalism, but it also divided Sunni religious scholars. Sahwa protested the regime's decision to allow thousands of "infidel" American troops in the kingdom to protect it from a possible attack by Iraq. In spite of the fact that the Saudi regime mustered the support of the Wahhabi religious establishment, as reflected by the Mufti of the State ibn Baz's *fatwa* sanctioning the deployment of American troops on Saudi soil, Sahwa members were shocked by the controversial Saudi decision. Its members, besides being apprehensive about Saudi partnership with the United States against a brethren Arab-Muslim state, perceived the United States to be an imperialist *jahili* society and a staunch supporter of Israel. No less significant, they were enraged by what they considered was the mufti's collusion with the Saudi regime.

In fact, as events unfolded, the Sahwa protest went beyond criticism of the regime. It included condemnations of the monarchy similar to those mounted by al-'Utaybi and assertive demands for social and political reform that questioned the very essence of Saudi rule.[74] The religious opposition, broadly speaking, revolved around two prominent Sahwa sheikhs, Salman al-'Awda and Safar al-Hawali.[75] These Salafi scholars waged a public campaign against the monarchy that contributed significantly to shattering its religious legitimacy. What helped give their campaign a strong thrust was that it coincided with the reaction of the liberal middle class that called for greater political openness. Following an unremitting harsh criticism of Western military presence in the kingdom, al-'Awda and al-Hawali, along with other religious scholars, signed a "Letter of Demands" (Khitab al-Matalib) and presented it to King Fahd in May 1991. The letter called for, among other things, the creation of an "independent consultative council [*majlis al-shura*] with the actual power to determine the domestic and foreign policies of the country," "supervision and strict accountability of all officials without exception," and "development of a foreign policy to protect the interests of the *ummah*, avoiding alliances that violate the sharia."[76]

Commenting on the letter, Gilles Kepel perceptively remarked: "In veiled terms, the signatories criticized both the Al Saud family's monopoly of power and the monarchy's loss of Islamic credibility after it was bailed out by impious foreign armies. . . . This letter demanded that the regime include in the decision-making process the educated middle class who did not belong to the royal family. With this demand, it called into question the dynasty's authority, while claiming the mantle of impeccable Wahhabite and Islamist rectitude."[77]

This rare, unabashed Islamic activism took King Fahd by surprise, and he pragmatically opted to take these demands into consideration apparently to consolidate his religious base. Though the king made good on his promise to create a consultative council (and codify the fundamental laws of the kingdom), he made the representation in the council heavily favorable to the Najd area around Riyadh, the stronghold of the al-Saud family and more advantageous to the liberals than to Sahwa. The Sahwa activists responded by publishing a "Memorandum of Advice" (Mudhakirat al-Nasiha), which essentially served as the basis for the demands of the religious opposition.

The memorandum expressed to a great extent a similar message to that of the Letter of Demands but was more detailed, more defiant, and more bold. Its principal demand was to elevate the role of Islamic clerics to that of an overseer of all government agencies, ministries, and embassies so as to assure their adherence to Islam. Next, it called for the Islamization of all Saudi laws and regulations, employing government officials without favoritism and nepotism, and establishing a strong army motivated by the spirit of jihad.[78] Clearly, its aim was to delegitimize the Saudi regime on religious and moral grounds and to underscore its political and military weakness. This memorandum brought an immediate denunciation by the Mufti Ibn Baz and the Council of Senior Ulema. Nevertheless, the disconcertment with which the Saudi regime reacted encouraged more dissent. In May 1993, signatories of the memorandum founded an organization called al-Lajna li-Difa' al-Huquq al-Shari'ya (the Committee for the Defense of Legitimate Rights, or CDLR), which strove for organized political activities along the lines of the Letter of Demands and the Memorandum of Advice. This organization focused on universities and mosques, which witnessed a brisk development of religious opposition.

Faced with growing dissent, the Saudi regime slowly but steadily moved against Sahwa members and other religious dissenters. The regime imprisoned Sahwa members, including al-'Awda and al-Hawali, and counterattacked the message of the religious opposition with official *fatwas*. CDLR spokesman Muhammad al-Mas'ari fled to London in 1994, where his organization eventually lost its influence. In the meantime, Saudi authorities gradually transplanted Sahwa scholars from the kingdom's universities with the Salafist Jamis (and

Madkhalis), who professed unconditional support for the Saudi rulers. By the late mid-1990s, all religious opposition to the regime had petered out. However, this critical episode in the relationship between the monarchy and Sahwa only reinforced the trend and determination of Islamic activists to organize and be politically and socially active, with the objective of affecting and/or attaining power. Although, broadly speaking, they don't excommunicate the rulers, they act in the capacity of the guardians of Islamic society. In other words, these activist Salafists, whose political consciousness stems from the political and cultural outlook of the Muslim Brotherhood, strive to found Muslim governance on God's will as outlined in *shari'a*. Conversely, governments that base their governance on idolatrous foundations become a target of delegitimization. Significantly, their discourse and actions have more or less blurred the lines between protecting the *ummah* and implicitly excommunicating the "ungodly" ruler who does not govern in accordance with the Book and the Sunna by delegitimizing him, therefore justifying or paving the way for waging jihad against him.

The Salafi Jihadists

The ideological foundation of the Salafi jihadists can be traced to that of Sahwa. In fact, one could argue that the ideology of the Salafi jihadists is an extension to the ideology of politicized Salafists, which developed and crystallized around new concepts that became central to the vision of Salafi jihadists. The ideology of the Salafi jihadists has its roots in the hybrid ideology that was born out of the fusion of the Muslim Brotherhood's political and cultural outlook and Wahhabism's creed in Saudi Arabia. The Qutbist political dimension of the ideology of the Muslim Brotherhood, which revolved around the concepts of *hakimiyah* and *jahiliyah*, formed the conceptual core of this Brotherhood-Wahhabism cross-fertilization. Thanks to disciples of Qutb, especially his brother Muhammad Qutb, an ideological parallel between Qutb's *jahiliyah* and *hakimiyah* on one side and Ibn Abd al-Wahhab's *jahiliyah* and *tawhid* on the other was made in the interest of merging these concepts into one ideological hybrid. The purpose of this hybrid was to promote a politicized version of Wahhabism in the kingdom. Muhammad Qutb's answer, as Stéphane Lacroix observed, was to establish an equivalence between the full application of *shari'a*, which was at the core of the Muslim Brotherhood's demands, and the purification of creed, the central concern of Wahhabis.[79] Muhammad Qutb explained:

> There is no difference between the question of creed and the question of *shari'a*: either there is government according to God's revelations [*al-hukm bima anzala Allah*], or *jahiliyya* and *shirk* [the association of God with other entities]. For the knowledge of the Truth of God and just belief in Him

imply granting sovereignty [*hakimiyya*] only to Him as they imply directing adoration [*uluhiyya*] only to Him. . . . *'Aqida* [creed] and *shari'a* are the
two sides of a single question, they emanate from a single source and lead
to a single end. This source and this end are belief in God and submission
[*islam*] to Him.[80]

By establishing the ideological correlation between application of the *shar'ia*
and purification of creed Qutb actually laid the foundation for adding another
tenet to the three creedal tenets of *tawhid*, that of *tawhid al-hakimiyah* (the unity
of sovereignty). *Tawhid al-hakimiyah* meant that God alone is sovereign, and
therefore the application of *shari'a* is imperative. This new concept is completely
in line with the Salafi creed of *tawhid*, because it derives from the creedal tenet
of *tawhid al-uluhiyah*, which means that all forms of worship must be directed
exclusively toward God alone. This concept eventually came to occupy a central
position in the ideology of Sahwa. At the same time, another concept, *al-wala'
wal-bara'* (loyalty and disavowal), seeped into the ideology of Sahwa. Broadly
speaking, this concept enjoined Muslims to demonstrate solidarity with faithful
Muslims and enmity toward false Muslims and non-Muslims. Significantly, the
concept took a political meaning with the emergence of al-'Utaybi's opposition
to the Saudi regime. One could argue that this concept was an extension to the
concept of *tawhid al-hakimiyah,* in that as it developed it explicitly sanctioned
"disavowal" of rulers who don't apply *shari'a*, and therefore jihad against them.

Al-wala' wal-bara' is a classical Islamic concept. Though ibn Taymiyah referred
to it in relation to fighting *bid'a*, it was none other than the grandson of the
founder of the Wahhabi movement, Sulayman ibn 'Abdallah ibn Muhammad
ibn Abd al-Wahhab (1786–1818), who added to it a theological value. Not only
did Sulayman use *al-wala' wal-bara'* as a means to fight reprehensible innovations, but he also used it as an instrument to separate the faithful from the *kafir*
(infidel). Sulayman argued:

> Can religion be performed, knowledge of jihad or *al-amr bil-ma'ruf wal-
> nahi 'an al-munkar* (commanding right and forbidding wrong) be applied
> [practiced] without love of God and hatred of God, loyalty to God and
> enmity to God? Had the people agreed on one path and a devotion [ado-
> ration/love] void of enmity and abomination, there would have been no
> division between right and wrong, believers and infidels, and devotees of
> the merciful and devotees of the devil.[81]

It is also noteworthy that by subsuming the concept of "commanding right
and forbidding wrong under the concept of *al-wala' wal-bara',*" Sulayman elevated the latter into a prominent position in Islam. Ibn Taymiyah, for example,
regarded the practice of *al-amr bil-ma'ruf wal-nahi 'an al-munkar* (commanding

right and forbidding wrong), also known as the practice of *hisbah*, as an ulti-
mate form of jihad. This concept was employed and institutionalized in the
Wahhabi religious establishment to enforce public morality, to prevent devia-
tions such as smoking and worshipping at shrines, and to impose punctual
observance of prayers.[82]

Notably, the concept of *al-wala' wal-bara'* was taken a step further by a Hanbali scholar, Hamd ibn 'Ali ibn 'Atiq (d. 1883), who, as Joas Wagemakers perceptively observed, connected *al-wala' wal-bara'* with the concept that can be seen
as the very basis of Islam, the unity of God (*tawhid*).[83] In other words, a Muslim
cannot profess his belief in *tawhid*, and by extension Islam, if he does not demonstrate his enmity toward non-Muslims. Moreover, ibn 'Atiq used Qur'anic
verses, in particular Surat 60:4, to uphold the necessity of expressing *bara'*.[84]
The trend that 'Atiq established by binding *al-wala' wal-bara'* to the foundation
of Islam continued into the twentieth century, where it was taken up in Saudi
Arabia by religious scholars who supported or opposed the Saudi rulers. Broadly
speaking, those who supported the kingdom were mainly employed by Saudi
institutions including the religious establishment. They practiced a form of the
concept that focused more on social matters and the relations between Muslims
and non-Muslims than on the rulers. Conversely, those who opposed the Saudi
regime, led by al-'Utaybi, transformed *al-wala' wal-bara'* by politicizing it and
applying it to the Saudi regime. Al-'Utaybi, who severely criticized and accused
the Saudi regime of destroying Islam in his *Risalat* (see above), systematically
transformed *al-wala' wal-bara'* into a radical comprehensive religio-political doctrine. Central to the foundation of Islam, this doctrine not only deepened the
division between the faithful and the infidel but also consecrated an obligatory
mission to combat all those disavowed from Islam, be they artificial Muslims,
dissenters, or non-Muslims.

Actually, al-'Utaybi was the first to use literally the term *al-wala' wal-bara'*.[85]
He argued that faith is premised on *al-wala' wal-bara'*. Those who loved for the
sake of God and those who hated for the sake of God have fulfilled their faith.
The firmest tie of faith is love and hate for God's sake.[86] He instructed that loving God, His messenger, and the believers obligates the hatred of infidels (*kuffars*) and the enemies of God and His messenger.[87] In much the same vein as
Ibn 'Atiq, he condemned misplaced *wala'* and insisted on demonstrating *bara'*.
He supported this by referring to the Qur'anic admonition in Surat 60:4, which
enjoins emulating Abraham and those with him. Abraham and those with him
severed their ties with their people for associating the worship of God with others. They rejected them and affirmed their hatred for them forever, until they
believed in God alone. Al-'Utaybi stressed on demonstrating enmity toward
God's enemies and not keeping it in the heart.[88]

Next he expanded the theological reach of *al-wala' wal-bara'* by underscoring the sacrosanct status and mission of *millat Ibrahim* (the religion of Ibrahim), which, according to him, God has made the paradigm community for Muslims. He based the religion of Ibrahim in two principles: (1) loyal worship of God alone and (2) disavowal of polytheism and its partisans and showing enmity toward them. Significantly, he asserted that the appearance of the religion of Islam took place only when these two principles had been fulfilled.[89] Then, making sure that *millat Ibrahim* is supported and followed through, he distinguished three phases Muslims had to go through. First, he enjoined Muslims to confess the truth in the propagation of *tawhid* God; to disavow both polytheism and its partisans and reprehensible innovations and their partisans, and show enmity toward them; and to follow only Prophet Muhammad. Second, he posited that when this happens, harm ensues, and Muslims are forced from their homes. Correspondingly, Muslims should migrate to a place where they can gather. Finally, he asserted that subsequently *qital* (fighting) takes place.[90] Then he instructed Muslims that it is necessary to combat those polytheists who wield power and not to be allured by their material promises and false scholars.

Though al-'Utaybi did not excommunicate Saudi rulers, his doctrine, in principle, reinforced the concept that in order for one to be a true believer, he should demonstrate his enmity to polytheists, be they Muslim rulers, dissenters, or non-Muslims. In practice, however, his doctrine conditioned Muslims to the fact that their sacred battle against polytheists is difficult and entails significant sacrifices, but they should persevere, for their victory is guaranteed in the end. Those who carry out this sacred mission comprise *millat Ibrahim* and are the saved sect.

To be sure, this revolutionary religio-political doctrine was not written in isolation of other creedal attempts to discredit artificial rulers and therefore wage jihad against them. Prominent among these attempts was the theory of Muhammad 'Abd al-Salam Faraj's *al-Faridah al-Gha'ibah* (The Neglected Duty), best known as the creed of Egyptian president Anwar Sadat's assassins.[91] Faraj used the fundamentals of Islamic law (Qur'an, *hadith*, consensus, and analogy) to try to construct a hermetic and hermeneutic theory sanctioning jihad against what he considered the blasphemous rule into which Islamic society has lapsed. Faraj relied heavily on certain Qur'anic verses and selective *fatwas* by Ibn Taymiyah to bolster his arguments. Among the foremost topics he addressed were (1) the establishment of an Islamic state, (2) rulers of the Muslims today are in apostasy from Islam, (3) revolt against the ruler, (4) the answer to those who say that in Islam jihad is defensive only, and (5) the verse of the sword.

Faraj believed that establishing an Islamic state is a duty that has been rejected by some Muslims and neglected by others. He refers to the Qur'anic verse "whosoever does not rule by what God sent down, they are the unbelievers" in Surat

5:44 as a proof of this duty.[92] It follows from this that rulers of the Muslims today are apostates.[93] He argued that the rulers today "were raised at the tables of imperialism, be it Crusaderism, or Communism, or Zionism."[94] As such, they are apostates who must be killed, as Ibn Taymiyah has enjoined.[95] Then, he furthers his argument by citing a verse in Surat 7:39 that states, "Fight them until there is no dissension (*fitnah*) and the religion is entirely God's."[96] Next he justifies rebelling against the rulers by citing Ibn Taymiyah's *fatwa*: "Any group that rebels against any single prescript of the clear and reliably transmitted prescripts of Islam has to be fought . . . even if the members of this group pronounce the Islamic Confession of Faith."[97] Moreover, Faraj refutes those *ulema* who say that jihad is defensive. He premises his conviction on a *hadith* that instructs, "To fight is, in Islam, to make supreme the Word of God in this world, whether it be by attacking or defending."[98] Significantly, Faraj underscores the controversial so-called verse of the sword by making it a topic of its own, in the interest of abrogating any passage in the revelation sanctioning coexistence with polytheists. The verse in Surat 9:5 states, "Then when the sacred months have slipped away, slay the polytheists wherever ye find them, seize them, beset them, lie in ambush for them everywhere."[99]

Faraj's *Neglected Duty* was well received by Islamists. Its radical impact of *takfir al-hakim* (declaring the ruler an infidel) was certainly manifested by the assassination of President Sadat in 1981. Evidently it was no histrionic act when the assassin of Sadat, Khalid al-Istanbuli, shouted "I shot the Pharaoh!" during his trial.

Radical as it was, Farraj's theory of tyrannicide was nowhere close to the comprehensive, missionary, and Islamic central nature of *al-wala' wal-bara'*. This revolutionary religio-political doctrine was taken to its extreme end by radical scholars, chief among them the Palestinian-Jordanian Salafi-jihadi ideologue 'Isam ibn Muhammad ibn Tahir al-Barqawi, known as Abu Muhammad al-Maqdisi. Born in 1959, al-Maqdisi established the theological connection between politics and *takfir* within *al-wala' wal-bara'*, which al-'Utaybi failed to do. Hence, he founded the theological theory sanctioning jihad against what he considered the corrupt, idolatrous, tyrannical, and infidel Muslim rulers.

Al-Maqdisi, like al-'Utaybi, believes that *al-wala' wal-bara'* as embodied in *millat Ibrahim* is central to Islam. But, in formulating his ideas, he goes explicitly further than his ideological predecessor. He redefines *millat Ibrahim* by basing it in the same two principles of worshipping God alone and disavowing polytheism and its partisans but expands the meaning of first principle by adding to it "all what that word worship contains from meanings" (*bi-kul ma tahwih kalimat al-'ibada min ma'an*).[100] Clearly, he opened *al-wala'* to interpretations beyond the realm of religion, whereby worship could be equated with obedience to political authority or adhering to a country's temporal laws. Then, in addition to attesting that the principle of *tawhid* means "There is no god but God," he asserts that disavowal (*al-bara'*) of every revelation/law other than the revelation/law of God is the most important meaning of "There is no god but God."[101] In other words, he turned *al-wala' wal-bara'* into an integral part of the first pillar of Islam, *shahada* ("I testify that there is no god but God and Muhammad is His messenger"), which confirms the Islamic profession of the faith and is incumbent upon every Muslim. Therefore, it becomes incumbent on every Muslim to disavow temporal laws and show enmity to the *kuffars*.

Next, al-Maqdisi details the principles upon which basis Muslims must sever their relations with infidel rulers and consequently wage their jihad against these infidels: (1) providing an alternative to the *shari'a*, (2) legislating with God, (3) arbitrating their rule in accordance with those idols in the East and West, (4) supporting the enemies of God, and (5) antagonizing God's religion and righteous believers.[102] It follows from this that al-Maqdisi calls on every believer to wage jihad against these rulers. He states: "The *da'wa*, labor, and exercising the effort (*al-jahd*) to remove them [infidel rulers] is a duty on all Muslims, each with his/her own capacity. Those who cannot carry weapons can support those who do, even in supplication."[103]

Al-Maqdisi accused present Muslim rulers of polytheism and idolatry and therefore of being infidels. Nevertheless, he reserved his severest condemnation of Muslim rule to the Saudi regime. He explains:

> We see clearly that the so-called "Saudi" state deceives people by promoting *tawhid* and books on *tawhid* and by allowing and egging on *ulema* to combat the tombs, sufism, and the polytheism of talismans and stones . . . and all that does not . . . harm or influence its foreign and domestic policies. . . . So as long as this split and diminished *tawhid* is far from the sultans and their crowns, they will support and encourage it. Otherwise where are the books of Juhayman [al-'Utaybi], and his likes, may God have mercy on him, which are full and abound of *tawhid*.[104]

In conclusion, al-Maqdisi instructs that "*millat Ibrahim* is therefore the correct path of *da'wa* . . . that entails detachment from friends and cutting of necks."[105] It is no coincidence that al-Maqdisi has called his website The Pulpit of Tawhid and Jihad, for, as shown above, he adamantly believes that jihad is the only way to bring about *tawhid*. Significantly, he redefined the theory not only sanctioning jihad but also making it incumbent on all Muslims.

True, al-Qaeda represents the quintessential Salafi-jihadi organization; yet it is Salafi-jihadi ideologues who went beyond the concept of *Hakimiyat al-Tawhid*, which al-Qaeda has adopted, and defined the revolutionary and missionary theory of *al-wala' wal-bara'* that widened the ideological and operational realm of Salafi jihadism.[106]

Notes

1. See Muhammad Amarah, *Al-Salaf wa al-Salafiyah* (Cairo: Dar al-Hilal, 2010), 13–18. See also Muhammad Said Ramadan al-Bouti, *Al-Salafiyah Marhalah Zamaniyah Mubarakah La Madhab Islami* (Al-Salafiyah Is a Blessed Period Not an Islamic Canonical Law School) (Beirut: Dar al-Fikr al-Mu'asir, 2004), 9–13.
2. For a perceptive account, see Ovamir Anjun, *Politics, Law and Community in Islamic Thought: Taymiyyan Moment* (Cambridge: Cambridge University Press, 2012), 64.
3. Albert Hourani, *A History of the Arab Peoples* (Cambridge: Harvard University Press, 1991), 62–63.
4. Richard Walzer, *Greek into Arabic: Essays on Islamic Philosophy* (Cambridge: Harvard University Press, 1962), 12.
5. Ibid, 62. It is interesting that this excerpt by al-Kindi prefaced a metaphysical work in Arabic, which was dedicated to the then reigning caliph, al-Mu'tasim.
6. Hourani, *A History of Arab Peoples*, 63–64, and Amarah, *Al-Salaf wa al-Salafiyah*, 20–21. For an excellent explanation as to why the *ulema* sought unity of Muslims over other doctrinal and communal considerations, see Radwan al-Sayyid, *Al-Jama'a wal-Mujtama' wal-Dawla: Sultat al-Ideologiyah fi al-Majal al-Siyasi al-Islami* (The Association [Congregation of Believers], the Society and the State: The Ideological Authority in the Islamic Arabic Political Field) (Beirut: Dar al-Kitab al-'Arabi, 1997), 242–43.
7. Amarah, *Al-Salaf wa al-Salafiyah*, 32.
8. Quote cited from Bernard Haykel, "On the Nature of Salafi Thought and Action," in *Global Salafism: Islam's New Religious Movement*, ed. Roel Meijer (London: C. Hurst, 2009), 38, and from Abd al-Ghani 'Imad, *Al-Harakat al-Islamiyah fi Lubnan: Ishkaliyat al-Din wal-Siyasah fi Mujtama' Mutanawe'* (Islamic Movements in Lebanon: The Ambiguity of Religion and Politics in a Diverse Society) (Beirut: Dar al-Tali'a lil-Tiba'a wal-Nashr, 2006), 265.
9. This position was initially expressed by Ibn Hanbal and reiterated by his followers, commonly known as the Hanbalites. See al-Sayyid, *Al-Jama'a wal-Mujtama' wal-Dawla*, 241.
10. Amarah, *Al-Salaf wa al-Salafiyah*, 28–30.
11. *Ahl al-Ra'y* included in classical Islam groups such as Asha'ri's, Jahmis, and Murji'is, which held positions close yet at variance with those of *ahl al-Hadith*. For example, the Asha'ris, not unlike the *ahl al-Hadith*, believed in the literal interpretation of the Qur'an but maintained that this could be justified by reason.

12. Al-Sayyid, *Al-Jama'a wal-Mujtama' wal-Dawla*, 242–43.

13. Ibid, 243.

14. Ibid.

15. Abd al-Ghani 'Imad, *Al-Harakat al-Islamiyah fi Lubnan*, 265–66.

16. Ibid, 265; Hourani, *History of the Arab Peoples*, 144, and 179–80.

17. Caterina Bori, "A New Source for the Biography of Ibn Taymiyya," *Bulletin of the School of Oriental and African Studies* 67, no. 3 (2004), 333.

18. Taqi al-Din Ibn Taymiyah, *Al-Fatawa al-Kubra* (Great Religious Edicts), vol. 5 (Cairo: Dar al-Kutub al-Haditha, 1966), 152. This quote was first cited in Bernard Haykel, "On the Nature of Salafi Thought and Action," 38. The translation of the text remained Haykel's.

19. Haykel, "On the Nature of Salafi Thought and Action," 38.

20. Bori, "A New Source for the Biography of Ibn Taymiyya," 333.

21. Hourani, *A History of the Arab Peoples*, 144. For a detailed analysis of Ibn Taymiyah's views see Ovamir Anjun, *Politics, Law and Community in Islamic Thought.*

22. Ibid, 144–45.

23. On Takfir, Ibn Taymiyah said, "As for he knew the Truth but fought against it and opposed it, he is a damned unbeliever, like *Iblis* (Satan)." Bori, "A New Source for the Biography of Ibn Taymiyya," 337.

24. 'Imad, *Al-Harakat al-Islamiyah fi Lubnan*, 266–67. See also Haykel, "On the Nature of Salafi Thought and Action," 39.

25. 'Imad, *Al-Harakat al-Islamiyah fi Lubnan*, 266. See also Abd al-Ghani 'Imad, *Hakimiyat Allah wa Sultan al-Faqih: Qira'a fi Khitab al-Harakat al-Islamiyah al-Mu'asara* (Sovereignty of God and Jurisprudent Sultan: Reading in the Discourse of Contemporary Islamic Movements) (Beirut: Dar al-Tali'a, 2005), 64.

26. Abdulaziz H. Al-Fahad, "From Exclusivism to Accommodation: Doctrinal and Legal Evolution of Wahhabism," *New York University Law Review* 79 (2004), 3. Hourani, *A History of the Arab Peoples*, 257–58.

27. 'Imad, *Al-Harakat al-Islamiyah fi Lubnan*, 270–71; Al-Fahad, "From Exclusivism to Accommodation: Doctrinal and Legal Evolution of Wahhabism," 2–4; and Stéphane Lacroix, "Between Revolution and Apoliticism: Nasir al-Din al-Albani and his Impact on the Shaping of Contemporary Salafism," in Meijer, *Global Salafism*, 59–60. For a critical view see Hamid Algar, *Wahhabism: A Critical Essay* (Oneonta, NY: Islamic Publications International, 2002), 31–37.

28. Lacroix, "Between Revolution and Apoliticism," 60.

29. 'Imad, *Al-Harakat al-Islamiyah fi Lubnan*, 268.

30. In accordance with the Salafi creedal concept of *al-wala' wal-bara'* (loyalty and disavowal) that enjoins loyalty to Muslims and disavowal of non-Muslims, rules were established to punish violators. The following is a concise summary of the ten rules that apply to leveling the charge of unbelief: (1) *shirk* in worshipping

God, (2) intercession with God through mediums, (3) refraining from leveling the charge of unbelief on or doubting polytheists, (4) believing that someone's guidance is better than that of the Prophet, (5) loathing something handed down by the Prophet, (6) ridiculing something from the religion of the Prophet, (7) performing sorcery with the objective of changing what a person likes or dislikes, (8) supporting and cooperating with non-Muslims against Muslims, (9) believing that someone could disown the revelation of prophet Muhammad, and (10) shunning God's religion. Ibid., 271–72. See also Sheikh Abd al-Aziz bin Abdallah bin Baz, *Al-'Aqida al-Sahiha wa Nawaqed al-Islam* (The Correct Creed and Islamic Contestations [Violations]) (Beirut: Mu'assassat al-Risala, 1413 H.), 24–25.

31. For more details on the Wahhabi doctrine, see David Commins, *The Wahhabi Mission and Saudi Arabia* (London: I. B. Tauris, 2006).

32. L. Carl Brown, *Religion and State: The Muslim Approach to Politics* (New York: Columbia University Press, 2000), 93.

33. Ibid., 96.

34. Sylvia Haim, *Arab Nationalism: An Anthology* (Berkeley and Los Angeles: University of California Press, 1962), 17.

35. Ibid., 18, and Brown, *Religion and State*, 96–97.

36. Haim, *Arab Nationalism*, 18.

37. Haykel, "On the Nature of Salafi Thought and Action," 46.

38. Radwan al-Sayyid, *Siyasiyat al-Islam al-Mu'aser: Muraja'at wa-Mutaba'at* (Politics of Contemporary Islam: Revisions and Follow-Ups) (Beirut: Dar al-Kitab al-Arabi, 1997), 174.

39. Ibid., 174.

40. Kosugi Yasushi, "*Al-Manar* Revisited," in *Intellectuals in the Modern Islamic World: Transmission, Transformation, Communication*, edited by Stephane A. Dudoignon, Komatsu Hisao, and Kosugi Yasushi (New York: Routledge, 2006), 27.

41. Ibid., 26.

42. Bassam Tibi, *Arab Nationalism: A Critical Enquiry*, 2nd ed. (New York: St. Martin's, 1990), 93.

43. Wiktorowicz, Quintan, "Anatomy of the Salafi Movement," *Studies in Conflict and Terrorism*, no. 29 (2006).

44. Bernard Haykel refers to the first category as "Scholastic Salafism," a reference that mistakes "scholastic" with "scientific" and could be confused with the above-mentioned broad designation of "Scholastic Salafism." He also includes Traditionists, Ulema specialized in *hadiths*, in the *Salafiyah al-'Ilmiyah* (Scientific Salafiyah). Haykel, "On the Nature of Salafi Thought and Action," 48–49. Wiktorowicz uses the designation "purists" for "quietests."

45. Lacroix, "Between Revolution and Apoliticism," 64–65. For a critical analysis of al-Albani's works and methods, see Kamaruddin Amin, "Nasiruddin al-Albani

on Muslim's Sahih: A Critical Study of His Method," *Islamic Law and Society* 11, no. 2 (2004), 149–72. For a biography of al-Albani, see Ali Ibrahim Muhammad, *Muhammad Nasir al-Din al-Albani* (Damascus: Dar al-Qalam, 2001). For a review of al-Albani's religious edicts, see Adel ibn Sa'd, *Fatawa al-'Alama Nasir al-Din al-Albani* (Religious Edicts of Distinguished Scholar Nasir al-Din al-Albani) (Beirut: Dar al-Kutub al-'ilmiyah, 2011).

46. Amin, "Nasiruddin al-Albani on Muslim's Sahih," 150.

47. Lacroix, "Between Revolution and Apoliticism," 65–66.

48. Popular Islam refers to the practice of Islam in society in distinction from official (state) Islam and political Islam.

49. Abou Usama Salim bin 'Eid al-Hilali, *Ta'rif 'Am bi-Manhaj al-Salaf al-Kiram* (A General Introduction of the Methodology [Way] of Honorable Salaf) (Amman: Al-Dar al-Athariyah, 2004), 14, and Abd al-Rahman Abd al-Khaliq, *Al-Usul al-'ilmiyah lil-Da'wa al-Salafiyah* (The Scientific Fundamentals of the Salafi Propagation) (Kuwait: Sharikat Bayt al-Muqadas lil-Nashr wal-Tawzi'), 13; first cited in Mirwan Shahadah, *Tahawulat al-Khutab al-Salafi: Al-Harakat al-Jihadiyah-Halat Dirasa (1990–2007)* [(The Transformations of the Salafi Discourse: Jihadist Movements; A Case Study (1990–2007)] (Ras Beirut: Al-Shabaka al-Arabiyah lil-Abhath wal-Nashr, 2010), 52–53.

50. Shahadah, *Tahawulat al-Khutab al-Salafi*, 54.

51. Ibid, 56. For more details on the concept of *Tasfiyah wa Tarbiyah*, see Shawqi Banasi, *Al-Tasfiyah wal-Tarbiyah 'Inda al-Sheikh al-'Alamah Muhammad Nasir al-Din al-Albani* (Purification and Education of Distinguished Sheikh Muhammad Nasir al-Din al-Albani) (Beirut: Dar Ibn Hazm li-Tiba'a wal-Nashr wal-Tawzi', 2007).

52. Lacroix, "Between Revolution and Apoliticism," 70. For the *fatwa*, see Quintan Wiktorowicz, *The Management of Islamic Activism: Salafis, the Muslim Brotherhood, and State Power in Jordan* (New York: State University of New York Press, 2001), 169n76.

53. Quintan Wiktorowicz, "Anatomy of the Salafi Movement," *Studies in Conflict and Terrorism*, no. 29 (2006), 217.

54. Shahada, *Tahawulat al-Khutab al-Salafi*, 57.

55. Ibid, 59.

56. According to al-Albani's disciple Juhayman al-'Utaybi, a ruler of the *ummah* must be: (1) a Muslim, and the proof to that his saying, "Oh you believers, obey God, obey the messenger, and those of you who are in authority"; (2) from the tribe of Quraysh; and (3) supportive of the religion. See Juhayman al-'Utaybi, "Risalat al-Imara wal-Bay'a wal-Ta'a wa-Hukm Talbis al-Hukam 'ala Talabat al-'Ilm wal-'Amma," (The Message of Governance, Pledge of Allegiance and Obedience, and the Reign of Rulers' Deception of Students of Knowledge and Commoners), in

Manbar al-Tawhid wal-Jihad (The Pulpit of Tawhid and Jihad), available at www
.tawhed.ws/r1?i=6513&x=fcchouzr (accessed June 18, 2013).

57. Lacroix, "Between Revolution and Apoliticism," 75, and al-'Utaybi, "Risalat al-Imara wal-Bay'a wal-Ta'a."

58. Al-'Utaybi, "Risalat al-Imara wal-Bay'a wal-Ta'a," available at http://www.tawhed
.ws/r1?i=6516&x=fcchouzr.

59. For details on al-'Utaybi's rise and takeover of the Grand Mosque, see Thomas Hegghammer and Stéphane Lacroix, "Rejectionist Islamism in Saudi Arabia: The Story of Juhayman al-'Utaybi Revisited," *The International Journal of Middle East Studies* 39, no. 1 (2007), 97–116.

60. Lacroix, "Between Revolution and Apoliticism," 76.

61. Zakariya Sulayman Bayyumi, *Al-Ikwan al-Muslimun wa al-Jama'at al-Islamiyah fi al-Hayat al-Siyasiyah al-Misriyah, 1928–1948* (The Muslim Brothers and the Islamic Association in the Egyptian Political Life, 1928–1948) (Cairo: Maktabat Wahbah, 1979), 90.

62. Ibid., 90–91.

63. Brown, *Religion and State*, 143–48; Hamid Enayat, *Modern Islamic Political Thought: The Response of the Shi'i and Sunni Muslims to the Twentieth Century* (London: I. B. Tauris, 2005), 83–93; and Ahmad Moussalli, "The Views of Islamic Movements on Democracy and Political Pluralism," in *Islamic Movements Impact on Political Stability in the Arab World*, The Emirates Center for Strategic Studies and Research (Abu Dhabi: The Emirates Center for Strategic Studies and Research, 2003), 129–34.

64. Brown, *Religion and Politics*, 152–53; for details on Mawdudi's Islamic order (state), see Enayat, *Modern Islamic Political Thought*.

65. Brown, *Religion and Politics*, 153.

66. Ibid., 155.

67. Sayyid Qutb, *Milestones* (Cedar Rapids, IA: The Mother Mosque Foundation, n.d.).

68. Ibid., 55.

69. Thomas Hegghammer, "Islamist Violence and Regime Stability in Saudi Arabia," *International Affairs* 84, no. 4 (2008), 704.

70. Stéphane Lacroix, *Awakening Islam: The Politics of Religious Dissent in Contemporary Saudi Arabia* (Cambridge, MA: Harvard University Press, 2011, translated by George Holoch), 41.

71. Members of the Muslim Brotherhood in Syria and Iraq also left their countries for Saudi Arabia following their persecution in both Syria and Iraq by the secular nationalists, who assumed power in Iraq in 1958 and in Syria in 1963.

72. For a detailed survey on the development of Sahwa, see Lacroix, *Awakening Islam*, 37–80. Among those who helped shape the ideology of the *Sahwa* was Muhamad

Qutb, brother of Sayyid Qutb, who taught at the Faculty of Shari'a in Mecca. This Faculty became part of Umm al-Qura University in 1981. Muhammad Qutb's contribution, as Lacroix explained, "was to establish an equivalence between the full application of *Shari'a*, which was at the core of the Muslim Brotherhood's demands, and the purification of creed, the central concern of the Wahhabis." See Lacroix, *Awakening Islam*, 54. Safar al-Hawali, a prominent *Sahwa* leader, who challenged the Saudi regime in the early 1990s, was Qutb's student as was Usama bin-Laden.

73. Fouad Ibrahim, *Al-Salafiyah al-Jihadiyah fi al-Sa'udiyah* (Beirut: Dar al-Saqi, 2009), 67–69.

74. Condemnations of the Saudi regime, similar to those leveled by al-'Utaybi, questioned the "[Saudi] governance that professes its adherence to the Book and the Sunna." Ibid., 68.

75. Salman al-'Awda and Safar al-Hawali had been ideologically influenced by Muhammad Surur Zayn al-'Abidin. Known as Surur, this sheikh was a member of the Syrian Muslim Brotherhood. He subscribed to Sayyid Qutb's actionable ideology. In 1965, he left Syria for Saudi Arabia, where he was among the first religious scholars to blend Qutb's ideology with the creed of Wahhabism. He promoted a politicized version of Wahhabism in Saudi Arabia. In 1973, he left the kingdom for Kuwait, where he stayed for ten years before leaving for London and then Amman. He questioned the loyalty of Wahhabi scholars to the Saudi state but condemned attempts to excommunicate rulers and rebel against them, for he believed this would lead to *fitna* (civil strife). Sheikh Surur's followers are known as Sururis. See Imad, *Al-Harakat al-Islamiyah fi Lubnan*, 274; Joas Wagemakers, *A Quietest Jihadi: The Ideology and Influence of Abu Muhammad al-Maqdisi* (New York: Cambridge University Press, 2012), 34; and Meijer, *Global Salafism*, 435–36.

76. See the letter's complete English translation in R. Hrair Dekmejian, "The Rise of Political Islamism in Saudi Arabia," *Middle East Journal* 48, no. 4 (Autumn 1994), 630–31.

77. Gilles Kepel, *Jihad: The Trail of Political Islam*, trans. Anthony F. Roberts (Cambridge, MA: Belknap Press of Harvard University Press, 2002), 214.

78. See Memorandum of Advice's demands in Dekmejian, "The Rise of Political Islamism in Saudi Arabia," 633–34.

79. Lacroix, *Awakening Islam*, 54.

80. Muhammad Qutb, *Jahiliyat al-Qarn al-'Ishrin* (The *Jahiliyah* of the Twentieth Century) (Cairo: Dar al-Shuruq, 1995), 45–46. This quote was first cited in and taken in its entirety from Lacroix, ibid., 54.

81. Abd al-Malak al-Qasem, *"Al-wala' wal-bara',"* available at www.said.net/arabic/ar45.htm (accessed June 22, 2013). See also 'Imad, *Al-Harakat al-Islamiyah fi Lubnan*, 281–82.

82. For the relationship between jihad and *hisbah*, see Richard Bonney, *Jihad: From Qur'an to bin Laden* (New York: Palgrave Macmillan, 2004), 111–26. For details on the concept of *hisbah*, see Michael Cook, *Commanding Right and Forbidding Wrong in Islamic Thought* (Cambridge: Cambridge University Press, 2000).

83. Joas Wagemakers, "The Transformation of a Radical Concept: *Al-wala' wal-bara'* in the Ideology of Abu Muhammad al-Maqdisi," in Meijer, *Global Salafism*, 87–88. See also 'Imad, *Al-Harakat al-Islamiyah fi Lubnan*, 281–82.

84. Surat 60:4 states: "There is for you an excellent example [to follow] in Abraham and those with him, when they said to their people: 'We are clear of you and of whatever ye worship besides Allah: we have rejected You, and there has arisen between us and you, enmity and hatred forever, unless ye believe in Allah and Him alone.'"

85. Juhayman ibn Sayf al-'Utaybi, "Bab; fi Fadl al-Hub fi Llah wal-Bughd fi Llah," *Awthaq 'Ura al-Iman; al-Hub fi Llah wal-Bughd fi Llah* ("Door; in the Graciousness of Love for the Sake of God and Hatred [Enmity] for the Sake of God," Faith the Firmest of Ties; Love for the Sake of God and Hatred for the Sake of God), available at www.tawhed.ws/pr?i=2351 (accessed June 26, 2013).

86. Ibid.

87. Ibid., "Fasl; al-Mar' Ma'a Man Ahab" (Section; the Individual with Whom He Loves), www.tawhed.ws/pr?i=2352 (accessed June 26, 2013).

88. Ibid., "Muqadimah" (Introduction), www.tawhed.ws/pr?i=2348 (accessed June 26, 2013).

89. Juhayman ibn Sayf al-'Utaybi, "Fasl; fi Bayan Millat Ibrahim," (Section; in the Statement of the Religion of Ibrahim), *Raf' al-Iltibas 'an Millat man Ja'alahu Allah Imaman lil-Nas* (Removing the Ambiguity from the Religious Community that God Made an Imam for the People), www.tawhed.ws/pr?i=1349 (accessed June 27, 2013).

90. Ibid., "Minhaj Nasr al-DinYa-Talakhas fi Thalathat Umur" (The Methodology of Supporting Religion Is Summarized in Three Matters), www.tawhed.ws/pr?i=1351 (accessed June 27, 2013).

91. For the English translation of the text of Neglected Duty, see Johannes J. G. Jansen, *The Neglected Duty: The Creed of Sadat's Assassins and Islamic Resurgence in the Middle East* (New York: Macmillan, 1986), 159–230.

92. Ibid., 165–66.

93. Ibid., 169.

94. Ibid., 169.

95. Ibid., 169–70.

96. Ibid., 171.

97. Ibid., 192.

98. Ibid., 193.

99. Ibid., 195.

100. Abu Muhammad al-Maqdisi, "Al-Fasl al-Awal; fi Bayan Millat Ibrahim" (First Section; In the Statement of the Religion of Ibrahim), *Millat Ibrahim wa-Da'wat al-Anbiya'wal-Mursalin* (The Religion of Ibrahim and the Propagation of the Prophets and Messengers), 1, available at www.tawhed.ws/pr?i=1394 (accessed June 27, 2013).

101. Abu Muhammad al-Maqdisi, "Al-Bara' min Kul Shar' Ghayr Shar' Llah min Aham Ma'ani 'La Ilah ila Llah" (Disavowal of Every Revelation [Law] Other than the Revelation [Law] of God Is the Most Important Meaning of 'There Is No God but God'), *Kashf al-Niqab 'An Shari'at al-Ghab* (Removing the Veil from the Law of the Jungle), available at www.tawhed.ws/pr?i=5367 (accessed June 27, 2013).

102. Abu Muhammad al-Maqdisi, "Al-Jihad wal-Khuruj" (Jihad and Egression/Rebellion), *Hadhihi 'Aqidatuna* (This Is Our Creed), available at www.tawhed.ws/pr?i=4784, 1–2 (accessed June 27, 2013).

103. Ibid., 2.

104. Al-Maqdisi, "Al-Fasl al-Awal; fi Bayan Millat Ibrahim," 3.

105. Ibid., 18.

106. The Jordanian terrorist Abu Mus'ab al-Zarqawi, who wreaked havoc in Iraq, mostly targeting the Shi'ites and the Americans there, was a disciple of al-Maqdisi.

Chapter Two

The Path to Salafism

This chapter illustrates the creation of Lebanon and its confessional system, which has brought together various sects and distributed power along religious lines. This system, however, has fostered neither a strong national identity nor a durable state. Yet, its quasi-democratic structure and liberal tendencies have made the country a lightning rod for political movements sweeping the Arab world. Quietest Salafism and Islamism (political Islam) found their way into Lebanon. The Islamic Association, led by its cofounder and ideologue Fathi Yakan, ideologically paved the way for Salafists to redefine their approach to the state. However, it was the rise and fall of the Islamic Unity Movement that practically underscored for Salafists the importance of adjusting their *da'wa* (call to Islam) to the political conditions of the country. The horrific suppression of the Islamic Unity Movement and the harassment of Islamists at the hands of the Syrians and their allies in Lebanon not only left deep scars in the collective consciousness of Islamists but also hardened revanchist impulses among Salafists, especially *haraki* (activist) ones. Yet it was in the shadow of Syrian occupation of Lebanon that Salafism grew. Concerned with anti-Syrian groups and parties, Syrian policy in Lebanon offered sociopolitical opportunities for Salafists to expand their *da'wa* and therefore to accrue political capital. Significantly, Salafi mobilization structures associated with informal interpersonal and transnational networks, linked to mosques, institutes, and schools, helped Salafism grow and Salafi institutions proliferate.

Lebanon's Confessional System and Weak National Identity

Lebanon, like other states in the heartland of the Middle East, emerged out of the ashes of the Ottoman Empire. Western colonial powers Great Britain and France, especially the latter, played a prominent role in creating Greater Lebanon in 1920. Though Lebanon's historical political community was Mount Lebanon, the abode of the Maronite and Druze communities, other areas were added to Mount Lebanon so as to make it a viable state. Tracing the beginning of its relationship with the Maronites to the Crusaders, France, by the beginning of the nineteenth century, had begun to systematically attempt to acculturate Christian society along French intellectual and cultural lines. Acting in the capacity of France's cultural arm, the French Jesuit order established a chain of schools, most important Saint Joseph University in 1875 in Beirut, which soon evolved into the nodal cultural center linking Beirut to Paris. It was there that Henri Lammens planted the ideological seeds of a separate Christian identity.[1]

Influenced by the intellectual atmosphere at Saint Joseph University, Maronite graduates drew the Phoenician ancestral link to a separate Christian identity, which found its expression in modern Greater Lebanon. Among them was Yusuf al-Sawda, who unequivocally spoke about the Phoenician origins of the Lebanese people while glorifying Phoenician culture and Lebanon's heritage. He asserted:

> Every nation has a strong desire to return to its roots by drawing from the well of its past to its present the glory of its pedigree. Italy is proud to be the heir of mighty Rome with its victories, its glory and its banner. The Greeks glorify their lineage to the important dynasty of personalities of the *Iliad* with its poets and philosophers. The civilized world thanks Italy and Greece and respects their descendants and the greatness of their forefathers. . . . As a nation is proud of its roots and draws its good virtues from its good progeny, so is Lebanon proud to remember and remind us that it is the cradle of civilization in the world. It was born at the slopes of its mountain and ripened on its shores, and from there, the Phoenicians carried it to the four corners of the earth. The same as Europe has to be committed to Italy and Greece it also has to be committed to a land that is the teacher of Rome and the mother of Greece.[2]

This perspective that the glory and contribution of Phoenicia to Western civilization—not least being the invention and dissemination of the alphabet by the mercantilistic Phoenicians—is embodied in Lebanon's cultural heritage and collective identity became the mantle of Phoenicianists in early twentieth century's Lebanon. Among others Michel Chiha and Charles Corm, the doyen of Phoenicianism, standardized and routinized Lebanon's Western orientation and national identity as an aspect of Phoenicianism. In 1919, Corm began publishing *La Revue Phenicienne*, which became the mouthpiece of the intellectual and political activity of the Phoenician idea, and subsequently, inspired by Maurice Barrès, wrote *La Montagne Inspirée*, which was regarded by many as the apotheosis of Phoenicianism.[3]

Parallel to this intellectual effort to reify Lebanon's Phoenician myth of origin and national character uniqueness, the assiduous work of the Maronite Church to create a separate non-Arab Christian identity culminated in providing the political foundation of the Phoenician idea in Greater Lebanon. This was illustrated by the decisive role played by Maronite patriarch Elyas Huwayek (also known as E. P. Hoyek) in creating Greater Lebanon. Patriarch Huwayek headed the Lebanese delegation to the Peace Conference in Versailles, where he called for the creation of Greater Lebanon as a separate Christian entity. He justified his claim on the grounds of the Phoenician idea.[4]

Initially the Muslims rejected out of hand the national concept of Greater Lebanon. The Sunni community, being socially and politically more advantaged than the Shi'a and Druze communities, led the opposition against the formation of Greater Lebanon. The Sunni leadership believed that Greater Lebanon was severed from Syria and thus advanced union with the latter. However, once the French had the mandate over Lebanon, they set about shaping its system. They fashioned a confessional system, whereby power is distributed along religious lines. The apportionment of representation in the parliament and the administration of the new state rested on a confessional basis, where every religious community (seventeen altogether) would be represented according to its demography.[5] Since the Maronites constituted a plurality, based on the first and thus far only census taken in 1932, they wielded most power.[6] The Sunni elite, most of whom were unionists (Arab nationalists advocating a union with Syria) from the three major coastal cities of Tripoli, Beirut and Sidon, continued to lead the opposition and tried to coordinate their efforts with Arab nationalists in Syria, namely the National Bloc leaders.[7]

Nevertheless, a combination of internal and external factors tempered the singleness of purpose and assiduity with which they pursued their political activism. The Maronite Church by the 1930s had become more or less critical of French policies, demanding Lebanon's full independence.[8] This position caused a thaw in the icy relationship between the church and the National Bloc leaders. Sunni elite frowned upon this budding political rapprochement, fearing a weakening of their "unionist" position.[9] Next, the Maronite leadership, represented by Beshara al-Khoury, began advocating a pro-Arab policy in the late 1930s, which was incompatible neither with the position of the Maronite Church nor with Christian elites calling for a Christian-Muslim national understanding. The growing base of this development within the Christian community helped ease Christian-Sunni tensions.[10] Finally, the Sunni leadership grew disenchanted and disillusioned with the policies of the National Bloc leaders. They felt betrayed by them negotiating a treaty with France that did not include the disputed territories added to Lebanon.[11] The cumulative effect of all of this tempered Sunni rejectionism and reinforced a trend advocated by the Sunni leader Riad al-Solh that an independent Lebanon could bring about internal unity as a precondition to Arab unity.[12]

Consequently, Khoury and Solh found in each other an ally to support their national vision. The corollary of this alliance was the birth of the National Pact (al-Mithaq al-Watani). While political power would be distributed along religious (confessional) lines according to the 1932 census,[13] Lebanon's identity would be characterized by an "Arab face" and manifested by the slogan "No East, No West."[14]

No doubt, Maronite-Sunni cooperation helped actualize independence. Nevertheless, other communities, especially the Shi'a community given its demographic significance, had little, if any, role in the process of concluding the National Pact. Evidently, the National Pact helped bring about under special circumstances communal conciliation and to some extent unity. But it neither fostered nor forged a national identity. It was based on a compromise guided by the false assumptions that Muslims would "Arabize" the Christians while Christians would "Lebanonize" the Muslims. This also is not to say that the National Pact was supported by a majority of Christians and Muslims. Émile Eddé, a rival of Khoury for the presidency, represented a deep current with variant impulses within the Maronite community, ranging from the belief of organic affiliation with the West to a Christian humanist character. Besides opposing Arabism and espousing the idea of Phoeninician origin, Éddé advocated a smaller Lebanon where Christians would constitute a majority.[15] Similarly, Muslim elites, such as Abdul Hamid Karame of Tripoli, had acquiesced to the National Pact and independent Lebanon not out of conviction but rather out of resignation, as they felt betrayed by the National Bloc leaders. No less significant, the National Pact was concluded by Muslim and Christian elites, leaving the masses either alienated from the process of national conciliation or torn by the hybridity and multiplicity of nationalist, Syrian, and pan-Arab ideologies.[16]

Commenting on the National Pact, Georges Naccashe, editor of the pro-Éddé *Le Jour*, published an article titled "Deux Negations Ne Font Pas Une Nation." He wrote:

> What kind of unity can one derive from such formula? It is easy to see what half the Lebanese do not want. And it is easy to see what the other half do not want. But what the two halves actually both want—that one cannot see. . . . The Lebanon that they stitched together was a homeland made up

of two fifth columns. . . . And in toiling to spurn both East and West, our leaders ended up losing their bearings. . . . The folly was in having elevated a compromise to the level of a state doctrine . . . in having believed that two "No's" can, in politics, produce a "Yes." . . . A state is not the same as a double negative.[17]

The Emergence of Quietest Salafism in Northern Lebanon: Al-Shahal, the Doyen of Salafism

Lebanon's weak national identity and quasi-democratic system made the country a lightning rod for almost all political currents sweeping the Arab world since the Arab defeat in the 1948 War and through what Malcolm Kerr famously described as an Arab cold war. Pan-Arab, pan-Syrian, and leftist parties dominated the political discourse in Lebanon, even though the country was home to Western-leaning Christian leaders. Nevertheless, the predominance of secular parties did not extinguish the assiduity and energy with which some *ulema* (Muslim religious scholars) carried out their religious activities in mosques and Muslim institutes. Tripoli and the Akkar region in northern Lebanon, especially the former, have been historically known as conservative Sunni strongholds, boasting a large number of mosques and institutes. Though Tripoli prides itself on being among the first cities to welcome Islam in the eastern Mediterranean, it was actually the Mamluks (1250–1516) who supported building mosques and religious activities in the city in the interest of eroding whatever religious, cultural, and sociopolitical vestiges the crusaders had during their rule there. This Mamluk policy was more or less followed by the Ottomans, keeping Tripoli and its vicinity a "fortress" of Islam, as many Muslims in Lebanon would like to say.

Subsequently the discourse of Enlightened Salafiyah found its way there thanks to efforts by Muslim reformers, chief among them Rashid Rida, who hailed from al-Qalamoun, near Tripoli. Rida's review *Al-Manar* circulated widely among Muslim reformers and scholars. Among those affected by the Islamic reformist discourse was Salem al-Shahal from Tripoli. Born in 1922, al-Shahal was, broadly speaking, autodidactic. He furthered his Islamic knowledge in Medina, where he became influenced by Nasir al-Din al-Albani's quietest and scientific Salafism. According to Hajj Ahmad Darwish, al-Shahal established in the late 1940s the first Salafi movement in Tripoli, Lebanon.[18] Basing his movement solely on *da'wa*, al-Shahal spent most of his life promoting the *manhaj* [methodology] of the pious ancestors as a way of life in poor Sunni neighborhoods in Tripoli and in impoverished villages scattered throughout the Akkar region. He subscribed to the Wahhabi creedal principle of "commanding good and forbidding wrong" to uphold Muslim morality and to the Salafi creed of propagating Islam in accordance with the Qur'an and the Sunna, without any accretion. He asserted that "Islam for Muslims cannot be true if it is not Salafist in its creed, which means that I don't accept novelties in the religion. It is like the sun that was seen by the companions, the sun that we see in the same way they did."[19]

Al-Shahal even refused to consider the birthday anniversary of the Prophet as a holiday, believing only in the two major Muslim holidays, Eid al-Adha and Eid al-Futr. As a Salafist, he believed that polytheism is a form of *takfir* (unbelief), but he rejected and deplored issuing a *fatwa* (religious edict) sanctioning the murder of a *kafir* (infidel/unbeliever). In this respect, he also rejected excommunicating the Shi'ites, believing that God will judge them. As a quietest, traditionalist Salafist, he maintained an arm's length from politics and did not question political authority even on highly sensitive matters. When pressed about the possibility of making peace with Israel, he stated that Jews "are strangers who appropriated the people's land and properties . . . [but] making peace under crucial circumstances is sanctioned [*yajuz*]. . . . If the rulers consider that making peace with Israel is an inevitable necessity, then their judgment is with God."[20]

In the late 1940s, al-Shahal established Shabab Muhammad (The Youth of Muhammad), a Salafi youth organization, to advance his *da'wa* among the youth, and in 1976, during the beginning of Lebanon's civil war, he established Nuwat al-Jaysh al-Islami (The Nucleus of the Islamic Army), apparently as a vehicle of Muslim mobilization against the Christians of the Zgharta region, near Tripoli. On closer examination, however, the creation of the organization was a disheartened attempt to compete with the proliferation of secular militant organizations that pervaded Tripoli. The organization remained a name without a content, participating neither in political nor military activities until its dissolution months later.[21] Meanwhile, al-Shahal focused his religious and educational *da'wa* especially on the neighborhoods of Abu Samra, Bab al-Tabbaneh, and al-Qibbi in Tripoli. In his efforts, he was joined by his sons Da'i al-Islam, Radi al-Islam, and Abu Bakr, all of whom were graduates of the Islamic University in Medina. According to Muhammad Abi Samra, the appellation of the first names of al-Shahal's sons pointed to his commitment to Salafism. His first son was called Da'i al-Islam in reference to the one who commits himself to *da'wa*, his second son was called Radi al-Islam in reference to the one who is convinced of *da'wa* and of its persistence, and his third son was called Abu Bakr in reference to the companion of the Prophet and first rightly guided caliph. Influenced by "quietest" Wahhabi Salafism and supported financially by Saudis, al-Shahals promoted their *da'wa* by establishing an association called Muslimun (Muslims) to take care of orphans.[22]

No doubt, al-Shahal's *da'wa* planted the seeds of Salafism in Lebanon. His *da'wa* found a welcoming populace in the impoverished areas of northern

Lebanon. His designation both as an emir and a sheikh points to the respect he elicited there.[23] In practice, however, his *da'wa* had little impact on the larger Muslim society, for it remained on the margins of religious and social activities in northern Lebanon until the late 1980s. Two developments helped Salafism grow and branch out ideologically. First, it was to large extent the emergence of al-Jama'a al-Islamiyah (the Islamic Association) as the first organized and activist Islamic movement that helped expand the ideology of Salafism and pave the way for activist Salafism. According to prominent Salafist sheikh Salem bin 'Abd al-Ghani al-Rafi'i, "the noble *al-jama'a al-islamiyah* was the womb out of which most Salafi sheikhs and activist Salafism emerged."[24] The other development was related to the rise and fall of the Islamic Unity Movement, which imposed Islamic rule on Tripoli from 1983 to 1985. Interestingly enough, the two persons mostly associated with al-Jama'a al-Islamiyah and the Islamic Unity Movement, Fathi Yakan and Sa'id Sha'ban respectively, were among the first members of al-Shahal's Youth of Muhammad.[25]

Fathi Yakan and al-Jama'a al-Islamiyah: The Pioneer of Islamic Activism

Notwithstanding the emergence of quietest Salafism in northern Lebanon, the first signs of Islamic activism transpired in Lebanon in the aftermath of the Palestinian debacle in 1948. A Muslim activist from Yafa (born in Beirut in 1933), Muhammad Umar al-Da'uq, distressed by the Arab defeat in Palestine, fled to Beirut, whereupon he established the Muslim organization Jama'at 'Ubad al-Rahman (the Association of the Worshippers of the Compassionate). His organization reflected his belief that the loss of Palestine was linked to the distance of Muslims from their religion and that it was imperative to prepare the future generation of Muslims to reclaim Palestine. He set about to bring Muslims back to "Islam as a faith, dogma, way of life, and moral values inspiring the spirit of Jihad and sacrifice."[26] He based his propagational (*da'wa*) activity on the educational, cultural, ethical, and spiritual tenets of Islam. By the early 1950s, his propagational activity reached many majority Sunni cities and towns, including the capital of northern Lebanon, Tripoli, where a center for Jama'at 'Ubad al-Rahman was opened.

Born in Tripoli in 1933 to a conservative Muslim family, Yakan, impressed by al-Da'uq's educational and cultural *da'wa*, left al-Shahal's organization and joined Da'uq's.[27] Around the same time, Mustafa al-Siba'i, the superintendent of al-Ikhwan (the Muslim Brotherhood) in Syria, moved to Beirut following the outlawing of al-Ikwan and the arrest of many of its cadres by the Syrian Shishakli regime in 1952.[28] Invited by Muslim associations to Tripoli, including Jam'iyyat Makarim al-Akhlaq al-Islamiyyah, al-Siba'i organized a series of lectures and forums that were well received. It was during these lectures and forums that Yakan came to know and forge a friendly relationship with al-Siba'i. Yakan was moved by al-Siba'i's Muslim Brotherhood's ideology and dedication to "liberating the Islamic nation from foreign rule" and "establishing a free Islamic state."[29] It is believed that this exposition of the ideology of the Muslim Brotherhood against the backdrop of tribulations that the Muslim world was going through motivated Yakan and his colleagues in Jama'at 'Ubad al-Rahman to move beyond Islamic cultural and educational activism.

At the same time, Da'uq wanted his organization to remain involved only in the Islamic cultural and educational fields so as to shield it from the lethal confrontation between the Egyptian Nasser regime and the Muslim Brotherhood. Yakan and his colleagues considered such a limited course of action as inadequate to withstand the challenges facing the Muslim *ummah* (community). Hence, they decided to found a movement similar to the Muslim Brotherhood. Reportedly, this movement began its activities in 1957 under the name of al-Jama'a al-Islamiyah (the Islamic Association), though it was officially licensed by Lebanon's Interior Ministry on June 18, 1964.[30]

Yakan, as a principal founder and first secretary-general of al-Jama'a al-Islamiyah, initially focused on building the hierarchy and structure of the organization and expanding its base of support. In doing so, he actively propagated the objectives and paramountcy of al-Jama'a in Tripoli and other Sunni-majority cities and villages as he relied on publicity, especially Islamic literature organs, to disseminate the organization's ideology and views to laymen and students.[31] It is noteworthy that al-Jama'a was then trying to compete with leftist and pan-Arabist organizations, especially Nasserist forces, which had a large repertoire of literature and wide public appeal. In fact, this period was marked by a sharp hostility to all Islamists from Egyptian president Gamal Abdel Nasser and his political forces throughout the Arab world. Commenting on this condition, Yakan sarcastically commented that "everything was permissible in Lebanon except Islamic activism or the Islamic Association."[32]

Still, during its incipient formative stage in 1958, the Islamic Association, despite its reservation about Nasser's harsh policies against the Muslim Brotherhood, decided to stand on the side of pan-Arab, Nasserist forces against the pro-Western Christian forces during Lebanon's 1958 civil strife. They aligned themselves with pan-Arabist leader Rashid Karame and opened offices for recruitment and training in Tripoli, as well as a radio station, The Voice of Free Lebanon, to influence Muslim mass public opinion.

However, this sharp thrust in domestic affairs did not entail a formulation of the Islamic Association's political program. In fact, throughout the 1960s, at the height of the Arab cold war, the organization preoccupied itself with educational, cultural, and philanthropic projects in order to expand its base of support and propagate its message to the Muslim community. This went hand in hand with the al-Jama'a's efforts to improve and strengthen its relationships with Islamic associations and groups, in particular the country's Dar al-Ifta' (Office of Legal Opinions), which handled personal status matters and *waqf* (religious endowments) under the supervision of the grand mufti of the Lebanese Republic.[33]

It is in this spirit of making the Islamic Association known to as many Muslims as possible, as well as to propagate its message, that it nominated Muhammad Ali Dinawi as a candidate for Tripoli for the 1972 parliamentary elections. Correspondingly it did not devise any political program or agenda, though this running for a seat in the parliament marked the first attempt by the Islamic Association to participate in Lebanon's politics.[34] The Islamic Association's detachment from Lebanon's political system was soon overshadowed by the country's civil war. It mobilized its members and created a militia, al-Mujahidun, and a radio station, Sawt al-Mujahidun (Voice of the Mujahidun). Throughout 1975 and most of 1976, al-Mujahidun fought on the side of leftist, pan-Arabist forces against the Christians. But unlike other parties, the association decided to dismantle its militia and move away from military activism. According to a leader and cofounder, "the Association voluntarily left this diabolical game . . . for it is not the work it believes in."[35] On a closer look, however, it appears that the entrance of Syrian troops in the summer of 1976 into Lebanon had changed the dynamics of the civil war, as they initially battled pan-Arabist and leftist forces led by Druze leader Kamal Jumblat. This direct Syrian involvement in Lebanon posed, then, a conundrum for the Islamic Association, for it neither had a political position vis-à-vis the state nor a political program defining its activities and vision for the state. Even more so, it was fighting on the side of pan-Arab and leftist forces with which it had serious ideological conflicts given its Islamist nature.

In hindsight, the Islamic Association's experience in Lebanon's civil war compelled it to define its outlook toward the state, as it was evidenced by the publication in 1979 of Yakan's *Al-Masa'la al-Lubnaniyah min Manthur Islami* (The Lebanese Question from an Islamic Perspective). Though falling short of outlining a political program for the Islamic Association's participation in Lebanon's politics, the book expressed in painstaking details the organization's perspective on Lebanon as a state and a confessional system.[36] Yakan believed that there was a "contradiction in the confessional belonging that made Lebanon throughout its history conducive to explosion."[37] He explained that the French mandate gave the Maronites an upper hand over the other communities by according them prerogatives that instituted Maronite ascendancy in all state matters. As such, the confessional system, which gave the Maronites political hegemony over the state, produced a confessional bureaucracy and administration that con-signed to the Maronites the top positions in the state, beginning with the presi-dency.[38] This contradiction, Yakan added, coincided with another one reflected in the various political currents in Lebanon, spanning the gamut from capitalist to Islamic to reactionary to progressive to communist. This made the allegiance of the Lebanese not to Lebanon, making the state incapable of imposing its authority on the Lebanese. This is so because the state itself is a bloc of con-tradictions.[39] Subsequently Yakan railed against this confessional system that did not give the Sunnis the rights that demonstrate their active participation in governing the state. He asserted that given the authority the Maronite president had over the Sunni prime minister, the post of the prime minister was function-ary and not authoritative.[40]

Yakan, significantly, short of calling outright for abrogating the confessional system, "linked the annulment of administrative confessionalism to annulling confessionalism on every level, calling for gradually subordinating all civil and non-civil positions to the logic of exchange and equity."[41] Years later in an inter-view with *Al-Diyar*, Yakan claimed that the Islamic Association was the first to pose the question of abrogating "political confessionalism (political sectarian-ism)" back in 1975, because the crises and civil wars tearing Lebanon apart were inherent in the prerogatives granted to one community at the expense of all other communities.[42]

In providing the background of the Lebanese crisis, Yakan maintained that behind every crisis in the region, including that of Lebanon, was the failure of temporal regimes to provide stability, justice, and freedom for human beings. He added that "peoples governed by Islam did not know extremism as all lived peacefully and securely in the shadow of the Islamic state."[43] He bolstered his statement by professing that *dhimmi* (Christians and Jews protected under Islamic rule) all had rights under Islamic law. Regarding the *jizya* (head tax) that the *dhimmi* were required to pay to the Islamic state for protection, Yakan averred that once Christians sought to fight alongside Muslims, the *jizya* would be lifted.[44]

Finally, taking into consideration the background of the causal factors of Lebanese crises, Yakan concluded that as a first step the solution, which could dissolve the deep-seated contradictions in the Lebanese entity, lay in the fusion of Lebanon into a bigger entity. In other words, Lebanon should go back to what it used to be before 1920: a part of Bilad al-Sham (Syria).[45]

The first impression of Yakan's solution to Lebanon's crisis leads one to observe that Yakan was as much a pan-Arab nationalist as Islamist. On closer examina-tion, however, his ideology and gradualist approach (*marhaliyah*) underline with no uncertainty his solution to the Lebanese crisis. Although his book did not outline a political program for the Islamic Association, it revealed the depth of the association's opposition to Lebanon's confessional system as headed by the Maronites. This opposition was more about Maronite prerogatives (*imtiyazat*) than about the confessional system. It follows from this that the Islamic Association did not call for the creation of an Islamic state on account of the presence of multiple confessions (communities) in the state, but it sought union with Syria as a means to strip the Maronites of their privileges. For Yakan, this was a first step in a long–term, gradual process to bring about the objectives of the Islamic Association. At the same time, the arguments and concerns proffered in the book about the secondary status of Sunni political and administrative power in Lebanon only helped to underscore the necessity for the Islamic Association to address this intolerable situation. No less significant, the success of the Islamic Revolution in Iran in 1979, besides inspiring Yakan and Islamists alike, such as future *haraki* Salafi sheikh Zakariya al-Masri, added a sense of urgency for the Islamic Association to ponder and address the nature of Islamic activism in Lebanon.

The Ideology of Fathi Yakan and the Nature of Islamic Activism in Lebanon

The ideology of the Muslim Brotherhood, as articulated by Hassan al-Bannah and Sayyid Qutb, formed the core of the ideological foundation out of which Fathi Yakan's Islamic activism and orientation had been expressed. Yakan, like Bannah and Qutb, believed that the *ummah* had lost its civilizational luster and become weak because Muslims had digressed from the principles and tenets of Islam as set forth by Prophet Muhammad and the pious ancestors (*al-salaf al-salih*). He, like them and Salafists, emphasized the early Muslim community as the political paradigm to be emulated. Nevertheless, Yakan's philosophy of Islamic activism did not neatly overlap with that of the Muslim Brotherhood, in particular that related to *jahiliyah* (the age of ignorance before God's message to Prophet Muhammad) as expounded by Qutb.

Yakan embraced and built on the definition of al-Bannah's Islamic movement. He regarded al-Bannah as "an eternal leader, the pre-eminent one in the history of Islam in the twentieth century . . . for he built a *da'wa* [Islamic propagation, call to Islam], created a [new] generation [of Muslims] and shook the modern history of Egypt."[46] Centering his definition of the Islamic movement on al-Bannah's ideology, he described the Islamic Association "as an Islamic movement, whose message is Islam and whose objective is to help people worship God as individuals and groups by establishing the Islamic community, which derives its rules and teachings from the book of Allah and His Prophet's

Sunna."[47] He added that the Islamic Association sought (a) to propagate clearly and wholesomely to the people the call for Islam, as related to the problems of the era and the requirements of the future, (b) to organize, educate, and nurture those who responded to the *da'wa* as the vanguard . . . to forge an Islamic public opinion, (c) to confront the challenge of Western civilization, and (d) to rally the different Muslim sects by going back to the fundamentals of Islam.[48] Clearly, his views revealed strong Salafi tendencies.

In much the same vein, like al-Bannah Yakan considered Islamic activism as essential, since Islam had been fighting a fateful battle. But he leaned more toward the actionable ideology of Qutb to face the battle's challenges. Yakan apparently believed in Qutb's jihadi ideology as he centered the methodology of Islamic activism on the *hakimiyah* (sovereignty) of Allah. He underscored the notion that the fundamental specificity of the methodology of Islamic activism is God's sovereignty, which can be accomplished by way of the Qur'an and the Sunna. From these two fundamental sources, *shari'a* (Islamic law) places people on an equal footing, where no one is better than another except for his or her *taqwa* (devoutness) to God. According to Yakan, this "Godly" methodological Islamic activism is superior to any temporal methodology because it is worldly and flexible and can grasp the multiple, diverse, and multifaceted problems of life.[49]

He also made uprooting *jahiliyah* a focal point of Islamic activism. Yakan believed that the existing political and economic system, complemented by a secular and materialistic ideology, threatened the very existence of Islam as a global paradigm of thought and way of life. He emphasized, as a priority of Islamic activism, the destruction of this *jahili* system and society and setting up in its stead an Islamic society.[50]

But, unlike Qutb who called for a break between Muslims and *jahiliyah*, Yakan believed in a gradualist strategy of activism and rejected Qutb's "isolation" as harmful to the comprehensive objective of Islam: the transformation of *jahili* society into an Islamic community. Qutb asserted that "there would be a break between the Muslim's present Islam and his past *jahiliyah* . . . as a result of which all his relationships with *jahiliyah* would be cut off and he would be joined completely to Islam."[51] Yakan, despite his assertion that Islamic transformation of all *jahiliyah* aspects is fundamental, defined Qutb's isolation as psychological. He believed that Islamic activism and *da'wa* are not possible if one is physically isolated. He explained that "psychological isolation and uplifting of faith in the course of the vastness of *jahiliyah* detects fakeness and confronts wickedness . . . but work, movement, interaction, and *da'wa* are not possible in isolation or seclusion."[52]

One could deduce from Yakan's postulations that, in spite of the fact that he believed in Qutb's jihadi ideology, he typified jihad more in terms of transformational than radical (revolutionary) activism. This does not mean that Yakan condemned jihad as a form of resistance; rather, he based his activism in the Islamic variegated situational context according to which his tactical efforts to uproot the *jahili* society are best served. Generally speaking, Yakan linked his Islamic activism to two operationalized concepts: *al-mabda'iyah* (principium) and *al-marhaliyah* (periodicization/gradualism). According to Yakan, *al-mabda'iyah* means "we should always be bonded to the principal objective of our existence as Muslims which is to make people worship God," whereas *marhaliyah* in Islamic activism means "to advance gradually from one step to another and to move from one stage to another . . . but within *al-Mabda'iyah*'s circle."[53]

This approach led some Muslim scholars to assume that Yakan's Islamic activism is either ambivalent or not in line with the Muslim Brotherhood's actionable ideology and activism.[54] In fact, Yakan's ideology and praxis manifested themselves in his attitude toward jihad as related to Palestine and Osama bin Laden and toward the Islamic Association's participation in Lebanon's realm of politics.

Yakan emphasized that the Palestine question is one of the highest priorities and duties for Muslims. He added that "the truth is military jihad is a duty prescribed by Islam to venerate this religion."[55] Significantly enough, speaking about bin Laden on the Arabic al-Jazeera television station, Yakan stated: "There is no doubt that sheikh Osama bin Laden has a high level of faithfulness, trustworthiness, and transparency. He is faithful to his religion and to jihad for the elevation of the word of Allah. . . . This man has a pure, honest and believing personality. He defends all that belongs to Islam and who renounces anything that is not Islamic, and therefore, he is a man after my own heart."[56]

In response to a question about bin Laden's terror attacks, Yakan commented: "If we examine the ideology of al-Qaeda and Bin Laden in depth, we see that he has become completely convinced that the only way to curb the disease that is afflicting the Islamic world . . . the only way to stop this octopus is to crush the serpent's head." Then, answering the question as to whether he shared bin Laden's opinion, Yakan stated: "It's fine with me. I might have crushed the serpent's head in a different way. I might have crushed it by means of the Islamic resistance in South Lebanon, by attacking Israel. But Bin Laden said: 'No, I will strike it in the World Trade Center, and shake its economic status.' This is his methodology, and he should bear responsibility for it, but I am not sad or depressed that this happened, and I do not condemn it. In all honesty, I have never condemned this. Just like it had negative ramifications, it had positive ones as well."[57]

Taking all this into consideration, one can safely argue that Yakan fashioned an Islamist ideology in Lebanon's Sunni milieu similar, though not identical, to that of politicized Salafists. It is a hybrid ideology fusing his transformation of the Muslim Brotherhood's ideology with the basic principles and activist outlook of activist (*haraki*) Salafists. This explains Sheikh al-Rafi'i's assertion that activist Salafism emerged from the womb of the Islamic Association.

But more than anything else, Yakan's ideology and praxis marked Sunni Islamic activism in Lebanon's confessional system and politics. Deliberating the rationale and nature of Islamic activism at a time of political upheaval in Lebanon, Yakan published *Abjadiyat al-Tasawor al-Haraki lil-'Amal al-Islami* (The Elementary Facts of the Conceptual Movement of Islamic Activism) in 1981, which complemented his previous book on Lebanon. Yakan, as secretary-general of the Islamic Association, justified Islamic activism in Lebanon within the contextual framework of how to reconcile the *mabda'iyah* of Islamic activism with the *marhaliyah* of Islamic activism. He recognized that (a) cultural pluralism and sectarian and party affiliations did not provide the appropriate grounds for establishing any ideological rule, be it Christian, Islamic, or leftist; (b) the public and economic structure of Lebanon was not adequate to create a state, let alone an ideological one; and (c) the Lebanese arena was not appropriate to achieve the principal objective of Islamic activism—the creation of an Islamic state. Correspondingly, Yakan emphasized that the gradualist work of Islamic activism should focus on (a) maintaining the unity of Lebanon and preventing its fragmentation into sectarian and ethnic ministates, (b) protecting Lebanese life from moral depredations and intellectual impairment so as to save the (future) generations from Westernization and secularism, and (c) taking advantage of profound social problems as proof of the failure of temporal regimes, thereby affirming that the fundamental solution was the return to Islam.[58]

In sum, Yakan justified Islamic activism in Lebanon on the grounds of saving Muslims. But in responding to the charge that this Islamic activism meant partnering with non-Muslims in governance, Yakan made the distinction between participation of Muslims and participation of Islam. He explained that participation did not mean participation of Islam in the rule of temporal regimes, nor was it the alternative to Islamic rule. Rather, the intention of participation (and its proposals) was to relieve Muslims from oppression and salvage their rights, while at the same time strengthening their social, economic, political, and military positions in order to better confront Westernization and degeneracy.[59]

Yakan, apparently, while calling for the abrogation of "political confessionalism," supported "equal participation" in Lebanon so as to check and prevent non-Muslims' monopoly of power, which in his opinion meant the extraction and dissolution of Islam.[60] However, Yakan's deliberations on Islamic activism blazed the ideological trail for Islamism's participation in Lebanon's realm of politics.[61] More specifically, Yakan's hybrid ideology paved the way for Salafism's engagement in Muslim society at large. Nevertheless, it took the rise and fall of the puritanical Islamic Unity Movement in Tripoli, which was designated by some scholars as a Salafi organization, that fueled the growth of Salafism in Lebanon.

Sa'id Sha'ban and the Islamic Unity Movement: The Rise and Fall of the Islamic Emirate in Tripoli

By the early 1980s, a combination of internal and regional factors intersected in Lebanon in general and in Tripoli in particular, leading to the creation of the first Muslim emirate in Lebanon (1983–85) under the rule of Sheikh Sa'id Sha'ban's Harakat al-Tahwid al-Islami (Islamic Unity Movement). Arab nationalism and other secular parties had experienced a gradual and steady decline of their political legitimacy beginning with the breakup of the union between Egypt and Syria in 1961 and peaking in the aftermath of the humiliating Arab defeat in the 1967 Arab-Israeli War. Meanwhile, the Islamists' call that "Islam is the solution" had only grown despite continued harassment by Arab rulers. Certainly, Ayatollah Khomeini's successful revolution in Iran in 1979 showcased for Islamists that their religiopolitical labor would eventually triumph. Nowhere was the impact of the Iranian Revolution more profound than in Lebanon. Not only did it invigorate Islamic activism there and pave the way for the creation of the Shi'a Islamist party Hezbollah, but it also helped further Iranian revolutionary reach into the country's diverse society. This simmering revolutionary fervor sharply intensified when Israel invaded Lebanon in the summer of 1982.

Among those somberly disillusioned with Arab politics and fervently supportive of the Iranian Revolution was Sheikh Sa'id Sha'ban (1930–98). Born in al-Batroun in northern Lebanon, Sha'ban is reportedly a convert from Shi'ism to Sunnism. Like Yakan, he was a member of al-Shahal's Youth of Muhammad before joining the Islamic Association. Also like Yakan, Sha'ban was influenced by Sayyid Qutb's radical ideology, but, unlike Yakan, he did not believe in a gradualist-pragmatic approach in the interest of strengthening Muslim society. He believed in Islamic rule under whatever circumstances. He subsequently left the Islamic Association and became one of the most charismatic preachers (*da'iya*) in Tripoli. His assertive personality and pungent oral delivery helped sharpen his *da'wa*, which was often expressed in fiery speeches. His call to Islam was couched no less in religious terms than in strident assaults on the Lebanese government, Christian groups, and all that is not Islamic. He was among the few Sunni Islamists who supported the Iranian Revolution and forged good relations with the Khomeini regime. Nevertheless, he did not champion the implementation of Khomeini's doctrine Wilayat al-Faqih (Rule by the Just Jurist/Governance by the Jurisprudent) or his Iranian-style order in Lebanon, for he knew this would alienate his Sunni followers. Responding to questions about his association with Shi'ism and the Iranian regime, including his visits to Iran, Sha'ban answered that since the first caliphate "there has not been an Islamic movement leading a state other than the Khomeini movement in Iran; it is a revolutionary Islamic movement." He added: "I am a Muslim, neither a Sunni nor a Shi'ite. I am a Muslim on the basis of the religion [*millat*] of our father Ibrahim. Sectarianism is mainly political sectarianism." He contended that "it was Hassan al-Bannah's idea to establish an Islamic project whose seeds were planted in Egypt that sprouted in Iran." And he added: "There are neither Sunni nor Shi'a Muslims. There are Muslims who need to follow the truth that should prevail over the earth."[62]

In its basic principles, Sha'ban's revolutionary ideology was similar to that of Salafi jihadists. Though ecumenical in his orientation, Sha'ban was abundantly clear that there was no alternative to Islamic rule, especially in Lebanon. He believed that Lebanon's religious and sectarian pluralism was at the heart of the country's problems. He affirmed that Islam "does not know pluralism, for it is the religion of oneness [*tawhid*]—oneness of God and oneness of humanity."[63] He perceived that nationalist and pan-Arab parties were not Islamic; rather, they were manifestations of Western intellectual thought. He contended that the only solution for Lebanon's religious pluralism was for non-Muslim communities to accept the Islamic *da'wa*, which had been delayed by Christian dismissal. In fact, he lamented the Syrian intervention in Lebanon in 1976 without which, according to him, the Maronites would have been chased out of the country to Cyprus and Latin America.[64] He stated that "there are as many idols in Lebanon as residents, and that ruin and corruption would remain in Lebanon until the era of atheism and religious pluralism is over and religion returns to God alone."[65] Sha'ban's political outlook stood in sharp contrast to that prevalent among Islamists, who considered "the regional climate is not suitable to creating an Islamic order in Lebanon." He elaborated: "Islam is a truth that needs to be presented far from social, political and regional circumstances, for it is politics, creation, association, and legislation. It is the alternative. . . . That's why I am not worried about the political surrounding, be it regional or international. I see that truth needs to be said even if the human being becomes a target of harassment and liquidation. A large number of the Prophet's companions were killed; but they triumphed in the end."[66]

Elaborating on his movement, Sha'ban considered his *tawhid* movement not as a new propagational (*da'wa*) movement but as an embodiment and continuation of the correct Islamic vision. He emphasized: "Our *da'wa* is the *da'wa* to hold onto the Book [Qur'an], the Sunna, and unity of the group that adhered to the Sunna." He added that "we called upon all parties to dismantle their organizations and enter anew the religion of God. Many parties and movements responded. . . . We believe in the return of our *ummah* to its Qur'anic essentiality [authenticity], we call upon our Islamic world in its various regimes to be united, and we call upon the Muslim peoples to return to one *ummah*."[67] One cannot fail but notice the Salafi component of Sha'ban ideology, reflected no less in the name of the movement than in a fundamental Salafi tenet: to carry out *da'wa* in accordance with the Qur'an and the Sunna. Clearly the Islamic Unity Movement was a hybrid Islamist movement that included Salafi components and impulses. Muhammad Abi Samra identified it as a Salafi movement, led by a Salafi sheikh who sought to walk in the footsteps of the pious ancestors. Moreover, Sheikh Sha'ban was among the first charismatic preachers to lambast Arab rulers for establishing *jahili* regimes far from Islamic law and Islam.[68]

Whereas Sha'ban's charisma and fiery Islamic populist discourse broadened his popular base of support, the repercussions of Israel's invasion of Lebanon, which forced a revision of the orientation of militant organizations in northern Lebanon, conditioned major militant emirs in Tripoli to pledge their allegiance (*bay'ah*) to Sha'ban. As a result, the Islamic Unity Movement was born in 1982.

Meanwhile, Syrian president Hafiz al-Asad had harbored reservations about the leader of the Palestine Liberation Organization (PLO), Yasser Arafat, based on the notion that Arafat's parochial and unilateral actions had been detrimental to Arab unity and stance vis-à-vis Israel. Conversely, Arafat had always been disquieted by Asad's attempt to control the PLO's decision-making process. During the course of Palestinian evacuation from Beirut in response to Israel's siege of the capital, Asad reversed his initial position and allowed a few thousand PLO fighters to move into Syrian-controlled areas in Lebanon, mainly in the Beka', whereupon their number had doubled. Arafat had also some two thousand fighters in Palestinian refugee camps near Tripoli and in the city itself. The dire situation Asad had found himself in at the time made it all the more necessary, from his standpoint, to have a compliant PLO leadership.[69] He tried to remove Arafat by force by provoking Palestinian dissidents against him, but as the PLO stood its ground, Asad mobilized a significant force to bring Arafat into submission. Taking wind of Syrian military preparation, Arafat escaped to Tripoli and set up his headquarters in the al-Baddawi Palestinian refugee camp, near the city. He also had supporters in the Nahr al-Bared refugee camp, ten miles north of the city. Shortly thereafter, PLO units from the Beka' managed to follow him, escaping the Syrian siege under the cover of night.

Asad immediately feared that Tripoli might become a lightning rod for the enemies of his regime, bringing together Islamists and the PLO. The Alawi-led Asad regime had barely survived a rebellion by the Muslim Brotherhood. In addition to being historically connected to the heartland of Syrian towns Homs and Hama, where the regime had faced a stiff rebellion by the Muslim Brotherhood in late 1970s and early 1980s, Tripoli had been a stronghold for Islamists. The Islamic Association, an offshoot of the Muslim Brotherhood, had been the most organized party in the city, though pan-Arab and leftist forces held the political upper hand. Ominously, coinciding with Israel's invasion of Lebanon, Sha'ban had gained ground and rallied around him both pan-Arabists and anti-Asad Islamists. In fact, a budding relationship had developed between the PLO and the Islamic Unity Movement to Asad's chagrin and concern.[70]

Under these complex circumstances, Asad had to clip the wings of the PLO before it constituted a grave threat to his national security. He assembled a motley force about eight thousand, which on November 3, 1983, moved on the Palestinian refugee camps, supported by heavy Syrian shelling. Surprisingly, Asad had an odd ally against Arafat. While Syrian forces shelled PLO units from land, Israeli gunboats shelled them from off Tripoli's coast. Apparently Israel was adamant about forcing Arafat from Lebanon. Hundreds of Palestinians were killed in about three weeks. Faced with an unrelenting and ruthless campaign against him, Arafat eventually agreed to leave the city with his men on December 20. But the battle of Tripoli was far from over.

Overstocked with arms left by the PLO, the Islamic Unity Movement continued to chase out all pro-Syrian parties and groups from Tripoli. From 1983 to 1985, it imposed its control over the city, including introducing *shari'a* law whereby, among other things, women had to wear the veil and liquor stores and nightclubs were forced to close.[71] At the same time, Sheikh Sha'ban lambasted Arab and secular rule. The Syrian regime and its allies in Lebanon were no exception to his harsh criticism. Most important, his harsh words were matched by harsh actions against Syria's allies in Tripoli. Sha'ban's takeover of the city was bloody. For example, Hisham Minqara, one of the main strongmen of the Islamic Unity Movement, is reputed to have killed dozens of communists in their headquarters in Tripoli. But its meteoric rise in Tripoli was matched by a swift fall. True, the movement was born in the house of a former Islamic Association leader, Sheikh Said Sha'ban, yet its militant leaders who pledged their allegiance to Sha'ban had come from various backgrounds, not all of which had an Islamic orientation. The three main groups that joined the movement were Harakat Lubnan al-Arabi (the Arabic Lebanese Movement), led by 'Usmat Murad; al-Muqawamah al-Sha'biyah (the Popular Resistance), led by Khalil 'Akkawi; and Jund Allah (the Army of God), led by Kan'an Naji and Fawaz Hussein Agha.[72] Hisham Minqara, a well-known and shrewd military strategist, served as Sha'ban's deputy.

The underlying reasons for the militant emirs to join the movement had been more or less associated with the bankruptcy of Arab nationalism, as starkly epitomized in the paralysis of Arab political and military activities in the face of

Israel's aggression. This forced a debate among the aforementioned movements, in particular in 'Akkawi's group, about their political orientations. 'Akkawi, a firm supporter of the Palestinian movement, had already been at odds with the Syrian regime since its intervention in Lebanon's civil war in 1976. He hid in the al-Baddawi refugee camp before moving to Bab al-Tabbaneh in Tripoli. There he grew more Islamic in his outer appearance and discourse, influenced no less by the Islamic conservative environment in Tripoli than by the success of the Islamic revolution in Iran. He came to the belief that Islamic resistance should supersede popular resistance and decided to pledge his allegiance to Sheikh Sha'ban, who by then had established himself as the most powerful religiopolitical leader in Tripoli.[73]

Despite Sha'ban's ability to rally around him various groups, his movement by 1984 began to face internal dissent, which led first to the secession in 1984 of 'Akkawi and then in 1985 of Naji. 'Akkawi and Naji had an ideological fallout with Sheikh Sha'ban, based on their strategic reorientation regarding the nature of rule in the country. They had come to believe that Sheikh Sha'ban's idea of imposing an Islamic order in Lebanon would not succeed.[74] At the same time, the movement opened a front along a "religious" line dividing Tripoli's Sunni majority Bab al-Tabbaneh from the Alawi majority Jabal (or Ba'l) Muhsin. The radical Sunni movement ruthlessly fought the Alawi-led Arab Democratic Party, which was supported by Syria. By this time, President Asad had dealt a severe blow to Amin Gemayel's government and was freed to deal with Sha'ban's movement. He rallied all pro-Syrian leftist, pan-Arab, and pan-Syrian parties and groups, including the Syrian Social Nationalist Party (SSNP), and supported their assault on the Islamic Unity Movement. Outgunned and outnumbered, the movement took a severe beating. However, it took the intercession of Iranian foreign minister Ali Akbar Velayati with President Asad to save Sha'ban and stop the assault. Velayati entered Tripoli and took Sha'ban with him to Damascus as Syrian troops entered the city. Hundreds were killed and arrested, and all signs of the movement's authority in the city were removed.[75]

As the Syrian army was forcing the movement to disarm, President Asad tried to co-opt Sha'ban by maintaining his leadership of the movement. Key commanders of the movement frowned upon Sha'ban's budding close contacts with the Syrians. On December 16, militants loyal to some of these commanders, including Hishim Minqara, launched a series of attacks on Syrian checkpoints throughout the city, killing fifteen Syrian soldiers. In response, Syrian forces sealed off parts of the city, including the al-Tabbaneh district, where the movement was headquartered, and at dawn the next day they launched an all-out attack on the movement's militants. Scores were arrested, including Minqara, and hundreds were killed, some of whom, according to Amnesty International, were deliberately murdered.[76] Through persuasion and/or brute force, President Asad managed to take control of the city and smother any potential threat to his regime and to his plans in Lebanon. Slowly but steadily, Syrian *mukhabarat* (secret police) continued their infamous policy of assassinating or arresting most Islamist activists deemed a threat to Syria's national interest in Lebanon. For example, the Islamic Unity Movement's leaders Sheikh Fouad al-Kurdi and Khalil 'Akkawi were murdered in February 1984 and February 1986, respectively.

Interestingly enough, throughout the whole ordeal, the Islamic Association, led by Fathi Yakan, did not come to the help of the Islamic Unity Movement, partly on account of Asad's co-optation of Yakan, and partly on account of Yakan's ideological distinction from that of Sha'ban. In addition, the Islamic Association took an active role in fighting the Israelis, as it established a significant political and military presence in the southern city of Sidon.[77]

As a result of Syrian heavy-handedness and repression, Tripoli and its environs were emptied of anti-Syrian Islamists and their sympathizers. Moreover, Syrian intelligence imposed a security cordon around the city that monitored and greatly restricted Islamic activism there. Undoubtedly, Syrian mutilation and subjugation of the city left deep wounds in the collective consciousness of Tripolitans, who not surprisingly, as we shall see, rebelled against the Syrian regime when the opportunity availed itself. Meanwhile, dozens of Islamists who were harassed into leaving Lebanon remained hopeful that someday they would return and "right the wrong that has been done to them at the hands of the Syrians and their allies in Lebanon."[78] Among those was none other than Sheikh Salem al-Rafi'i, who emerged after twenty years of forced exile as one of the most charismatic, anti-Syrian, anti-Hezbollah activist Salafists in northern Lebanon.

Paradoxically, Syrian subjugation of all but pro-Syrian parties and groups fostered a growth of Salafism, partly because Salafists became both more ideologically aware of Islamic activism and more attentive to Lebanon's confessional politics under Syrian tutelage and partly because they were left almost alone in the Islamist arena.

The Growth of Salafism in the Shadow of the State

In principle, apolitical Salafists, represented mainly by al-Shahal's quietest school, were the ones who indirectly benefited from the collapse of the Islamic Unity Movement. Their apolitical stance served to obviate any clash between them and Syrian intelligence in Lebanon. In practice, however, the growth of their movement cannot be disassociated from their political awareness, since part of their *da'wa* centered on their political grievances against the state, which neglected their areas and served as an arm of Syrian intelligence. Moreover, with the resumption of electoral politics following the end of civil war in 1990, apolitical Salafists could not afford to ignore being loosely involved in Lebanon's confessional system, which distributes political power and, by extension, political and economic spoils. Most insistently, quietest Salafists needed a political cover under which they could maintain and develop their missionary activities without institutional and/or security impediments. Consequently, they contextualized an ideological foundation not in conflict with their fundamental Salafi principles to serve as a framework for their interaction with the state. Central to this ideological foundation was the notion that Salafists should approach the state on the basis of "advising, reforming, and changing according to what is beneficent, far from the logic of rebellions and violating authority."[79] As such, the ideological prism through which quietest Salafists perceived their apoliticism was practically more in the form of an intermediary function rooted in political submission to central authorities than total disconnect from politics.

Not only did this Salafi approach to the state obviate a clash with the Syrian hegemonic power in the country, but it also saved Salafists from Syria's dual policy of "divide and conquer" and/or "co-opt or liquidate." In other words, Syrian intelligence did not truly co-opt the Salafists. Yet Syrian intelligence's concern with anti-Syrian Islamists and Christian opposition to Syrian occupation allowed Salafism to grow exponentially in depressed Sunni areas thanks in no small measure to Salafi mobilization structures. These involved informal networks of mosques, religious institutes, social institutions, forums, and *musaliyat* (prayer and discussion places), many of which were established during the Syrian occupation of Lebanon (1990–2005).

Syrian policy in Lebanon, led by their *mukhabarat*, focused on co-opting individuals, groups, and parties in return for political and/or economic spoils. If co-optation did not work, then liquidation of opponents was carried out. The trail of Syria's murderous policy is littered with corpses of ordinary and influential Lebanese, among whom were Druze leader Kamal Jumblat, president-elect Bashir Gemayel, and Mufti of the Republic Hassan Khaled. Conversely, Syria had been to a great extent successful in co-opting many groups and parties, including Islamist ones. Sheikh Sha'ban's Islamic Unity Movement slowly but steadily moved into the Syrian orbit, inched gently by the Iranians. More so, the movement became an ardent supporter of the Islamic resistance. By 1990, President Asad had formulated a strategy premised on supporting the Islamic resistance, spearheaded by Hezbollah. As the Syrian government began to exert more formal suzerainty over Lebanon, it sought to use Hezbollah to pressure Israel for a return of the Golan Heights and to undermine the development of any opposition movement in Lebanon. Thanks to Syria, Hezbollah became the preeminent military and political force in Lebanon, while other parties were forced to disarm and toe the Syrian line. In July 1991, in a largely symbolic but foretelling gesture, Secretary-General of Hezbollah Abbas al-Mussawi, along with members of the party's consultative council, visited Sha'ban in Tripoli. After the meeting, the two Islamist leaders issued a joint statement in which they underscored "the great message of the Islamic resistance in the south and the Intifada in Palestine in the face of dangerous aggressive plans in order to reawaken the Arabic and Islamic *ummah* as a whole."[80] Similarly, Fathi Yakan's Islamic Association followed the same path until Yakan had a falling-out with his colleagues, left the association, and established in 2006 a pro-Syrian, pro-Hezbollah association by the name of Islamic Action Front (see chapter 4). Thanks in no small measure to Syria's gerrymandering of the 1992 parliamentary elections, three candidates of the Islamic Association won, including Fathi Yakan.

As noted, Syrian strategy entailed a divide-and-conquer policy among Lebanon's communities. Notwithstanding President Asad's efforts to cultivate strong relations with the Shi'a community, he was consistently skeptical about the Sunni, Christian, and Druze communities, and he masterfully divided and conquered them. Of particular concern for him was the religious and sociopolitical dynamics of the Sunni community. He was ever apprehensive about any Islamic activism that could threaten his rule in Lebanon.

In addition to co-opting Islamist parties in order to counteract radical Sunni Islamists, the Syrian regime cultivated a strong relationship with a Sufi organization, one that Nizar Hamzeh and Hrair Dekmejian have argued was a middle-class intellectual Sufi protest against political Islamism.[81] The Association of Islamic Philanthropic Projects (Jam'iyat al-Mashari' al-Khayriya al-Islamiyah), commonly known as al-Ahbash, is one interesting and controversial grassroots Islamist organization that does not fit the mold of conventional Islamist movements. It is a Sufi (spiritualist) movement that devoutly follows the teachings of its founder and ideologue Sheikh Abdallah Ibn Muhammad Ibn Yusuf al-Hirari al-Shi'bi al-Abdari, also known as Abdallah al-Habashi, an appellation signifying his Ethiopian origins. Habashi was born in 1920 in al-Hirara, Ethiopia, where he studied Shafi'i jurisprudence and became a mufti. In 1947, the sheikh left for Hijaz, after being expelled from Ethiopia by Emperor Haile Selassie. A year later, he went to Jerusalem and then to Damascus to study with the Rifa'iyya and Qadiriyya Sufi orders. In 1950, he made Beirut his home and was licensed as a sheikh by al-Azhar University's branch in Lebanon.[82]

As explained on al-Ahbash's own internet site, his system mixes elements of Sunni and Shi'a theological doctrines with Sufi spiritualism. Some of their tenets, as publicized on their site and in their journal, *Manar al-Huda*, emphasize Islam's pluralist character and oppose the use of violence against the ruling authorities; accept the legitimacy of Imam Ali (the Shi'a doctrine of legitimacy), and of his sons Hassan and Hussein, as well as uphold the teachings of Hussein's son, Zayn al-Abidin (in this, al-Ahbash set themselves apart from all other Sunni jurists and are closer to Shi'a Islam); defend many Sufi beliefs and practices condemned by Islamists as heresies; reject the ideology and intolerance of Islamist thinkers beginning with Ibn Taymiyah and Ibn Abd al-Wahhab and their contemporary disciples Qutb, Mawdudi, and Yakan; reject the doctrine of *takfir*, which levels the charge of unbelief on Muslims; and oppose the creation of an Islamic order in Lebanon, endorsing the current communal-based political system.[83]

Given al-Ahbash's anti-*takfir* and moderate religiopolitical attitude, it was compellingly logical that the Syrian regime would forge strong relations with the group. On the one hand, the Alawi-dominated Syrian regime would check the power of Sunni Islamist organizations by bolstering al-Ahbash as a mainstream moderate Sunni movement. On the other hand, al-Ahbash's outlook as an Islamist movement coextensive with Lebanonism and Arab nationalism made the movement receptive to Syrian overtures.

In the meantime, the Sunni community emerged from the civil war weak and in a state of disarray. Its traditional leadership had been overshadowed by the militia leaders, who themselves were beaten by the Shi'a forces. The community's spiraling downfall was also affected by the murder of important political and religious figures, such as Sheikh Subhi Saleh, Nazem al-Qadri (a member of parliament), Prime Minister Rachid Karame, and Grand Mufti Hassan Khalid. Its weakness was best illustrated when the Sunnis were excluded from the Tripartite Accord, brokered by Syria in 1985 to end the civil war.[84] No less significant, the mainstay of the religious leadership of the community, Dar al-Ifta', and other Sunni institutions, including mosques, had been affected no less by the damage of the civil war than by attempts by Islamist groups, especially al-Ahbash, to take them over. In addition, Khalid's deputy, Muhammad Rashid Qabbani, had been held back from exercising any effective power to resurrect Dar al-Ifta's paramountcy in the Sunni community because he was not elected as grand mufti until 1996. It was against this background that the Sunni Lebanese (and Saudi) billionaire Rafiq Hariri emerged as the new *za'im* (feudal leader) in Beirut. His reconstruction of the capital and contributions to Sunni Muslim institutions, including Dar al-Ifta', had ingratiated him with many Sunnis who felt that he was reempowering the Sunni community. Significantly, on the surface Syrian authorities maintained a balanced relationship with Hariri; on a deeper level, however, their relationship with him was at best ambivalent. Inasmuch as they needed his political and economic capital to rebuild Beirut under their rule, they frowned on this very same capital that made him potentially too powerful to toe the Syrian line.

It was this multilayered political complexity in Lebanon in general and within the Sunni community in particular, with which the Syrian regime was concerned, that provided the Salafists the sociopolitical and religious breathing space to expand their *da'wa* networks. No sooner had calm been restored to northern Lebanon than Salem al-Shahal established Jam'iyat al-Hidaya wal-Ihsan (Association of Guidance and Charity) in 1987. His son Da'i al-Islam directed the association with the help of his brother Radi al-Islam and his cousin and brother-in-law Hassan al-Shahal. Al-Shahal sought to make the association the representative of the quietest Salafi movement in Lebanon and therefore the "official" framework according to which the objectives of Salafism could be best accomplished. The objectives of the association were to "reform society and build mosques, schools, institutes to teach the Qur'an, and help the poor and the orphans, as well as provide ways for their subsistence."[85] Al-Shahals established branches for the Association in Akkar and Tripoli so that it could be suitably located to fulfill its mission. The Association's Salafist ideology was in harmony with that of the Wahhabi religious establishment in Saudi Arabia, where al-Shahals acquired their religious instruction. In addition to obtaining financial support from wealthy Saudis and Gulf Arabs associated loosely or closely with the Wahhabi religious establishment, the Association received not insignificant support from Jam'iyat al-Bar wal-Ihsan (the Benevolent Charitable Association) in the Arabian Peninsula.[86] In 1996, the Lebanese government, most likely at the behest of its Syrian patron, dissolved al-Shahal's association on the grounds that it incited sectarian hatred in its educational curricula. In response, Da'i al-Islam operated his religious institutions and charitable associations under a new association that was different from the original one only in name.

In the early 1990s, Dr. Hassan al-Shahal split up with his relatives and established in Tripoli a religious institute by the name Da'wa and Irshad (Propagation and Guidance), which had a branch in the village of Sheikh 'Ayash in Akkar.[87] In 1994, he established Jami'yat Da'wat al-Iman wal-'Adl wal-Ihsan (the Association of Faith, Justice and Beneficence), which became the organizational umbrella of his religious institutes and his Salafi mission. In 1993, Salafi sheikh Sa'd al-Din ibn Muhammad al-Kibbi established al-Imam Bukhari Institute in Akkar, the most renowned scientific Salafi institute, which emphasizes the teachings of Imam Bukhari and Sheikh al-Albani.[88] Most graduates of the institute continue their religious training in Saudi Arabia. The Bukhari Institute also supervises the elementary school Madrasat Dar al-Kitab al-Karim al-Dinniyah in the neighborhood of Abi Samra in Tripoli. The Saudi religious establishment has reportedly supported the institute. Many other institutes, such as Al-Amin Institute and Tripoli Institute, were also established. Traditional Sunni urban families have more or less supported these institutes, which have been linked to *masjids* (mosques), forums, charitable organizations, and even universities, forming large Salafi networks, whose social and religious expansiveness served to broaden the popular base of support for Salafists. Certainly, this expansiveness accrued political capital for Salafists despite their apolitical nature.

Moreover, transnational Salafi networks have played a significant role in supporting these various Salafi institutes. According to the Islamic Unity Movement–Command Council, in addition to wealthy Muslims, especially in the Gulf, three Salafi transnational charitable institutes have substantially funded and more or less guided the orientation of Salafists in Lebanon. The Kuwaiti Jam'iyat Ihya' al-Turath al-Islami (the Society for the Revival of Islamic Heritage) had supported sheikh Da'i al-Islam's organization before supporting Sheikh Safwan al-Zu'bi's and Sheikh Nadim Hijazi's institutes, along with other institutes. Until 2001, the Saudi charitable institute Mu'assassat al-Haramayn supported various institutes, including that of Da'i al-Islam. After 2001, most funding of Salafi institutes has been funneled through the Saudi Ministry of Awqaf (religious endowment) and private institutions. Finally, Qatar's Mu'assassat Sheikh Eid al-Thani al-Khayriyah (Sheikh Eid al-Thani Charitable Organization) has also supported Da'i al-Islam's institute and other Salafi organizations.[89] This Saudi, Kuwaiti, and most recently Qatari funding, which increased significantly since the 1980s when Egyptian funding in the form of scholarships and educational grants to al-Azhar University dried up, has helped proliferate Salafi associations and institutes, as well as bolstered their links with Islamist transnational associations.[90] Moreover, Salafists have maintained their independence from the official religious establishment Dar al-Ifta'. This independence has enabled them to operate freely far from the politicking and restrictive supervision of the religious establishment.

No less significant, Islamist organizations and associations with a Salafi tint, such as Fathi Yakan's al-Jinan Association and Sa'id Sha'ban's al-Risala Institute of Legal Studies, only reinforced the work of Salafists. Al-Jinan Association, which was established in 1964 to impart knowledge on the basis of Islamic principles and culture, built Qur'anic schools, nursery schools, elementary schools, and technical schools—even an athletic club—all in Tripoli and northern Lebanon.[91] In 1988, the association founded al-Jinan University in Tripoli which developed into full-fledged university with several faculties and schools under the leadership of Yakan's wife, Dr. Mona Yakan, who passed away in 2013.[92] Subsequently, the university opened a branch in Sidon.[93] The sons of Fathi Yakan, 'Abed and Salem, have presided over the association and the university, respectively. Similarly, Islamic associations that profess moderation and *wasati-yah* (middle-way approach, or centrism), such as Jam'iyat al-Islah al-Islamiyah (the Association of Islamic Reform), have forged personal and institutional links with Salafi organizations. The Association of Islamic Reform, which operates

Tripoli University, Islamic Reform Secondary School, al-Khayrat Mosque, and the Athletic Reform Club, collaborates with Salafi organizations on social, educational, and religious matters.[94] More specifically, Salafists have worked at the association's institutions. For example, Dr. Hassan al-Shahal is a prominent faculty member of Tripoli University's Faculty of Islamic Studies.

Most importantly, at the heart of these informal interconnected networks have lain the informal interpersonal networks of Salafi sheikhs and preachers, who have created informal patronage systems. Through their supervision of mosques, schools, and charitable organizations, they have managed to elicit the support of the poor and the disadvantaged. Some of them have even emerged as miracle preachers. For example, many in the Akkar region have taken their sick family members to see Sheikh Zayd ibn Bakar ibn Zakariya so that he could bestow upon them his convalescent prayers and blessing.[95] Not surprisingly, Salafism found its way to Palestinian refugee camps especially near Tripoli and Sidon. As Bernard Rougier perceptively observed, Salafism, in particular Salafi jihadism, developed in Palestinian refugee camps on account of multiple factors, including not in the least the disillusionment of refugees with the PLO's insolvent policies and discourse. Consequently, Salafi jihadism helped transmute their nationalist struggle into a global jihad waged in defense of the imaginary borders of their identity and authentic Sunni Islam.[96]

Despite several setbacks in 2000 and 2001 (see chapter 4), the growth of Salafi movements was put on display to the shock and surprise of many in Lebanon when Salafists, protesting blasphemy of the Prophet, heavily participated in the riots in Christian East Beirut in February 2006. A majority of Salafi organizations issued a statement under the name of the Salafi Associations in Lebanon, in which they deplored the riots but affirmed that "Salafiyah is neither a political party nor an organization; rather it is a firm scientific school that calls for upholding the [Holy] Book and Sunna according to the correct understanding of the methodology of the righteous Salaf from the companions and followers."[97]

No doubt, this significant proliferation and growth of Salafi movements, which broadened their popular base of support, had fostered additional political capital for the Salafists regardless of the extent to which they adopted apolitical attitudes toward Lebanon's confessional system. Essentially, Sunni politicians and parties needed their support to win elections, and conversely Salafists needed to engage the confessional system to ensure their uninterrupted *da'wa* and to curb what they considered the harmful social and political influence of polytheism, which came to be represented mainly by the ascendance of the Shi'a Islamist party Hezbollah and its alliance with the Syrian regime. Nevertheless, this effort was pursued timidly and inconsistently because the Salafists were not as one, in principle or in practice, over how to engage politics, save the fact they lacked political experience and organization. In the meantime, the advent of al-Qaeda–affiliated Salafism and the development of Salafi jihadism in Lebanon added another layer of complexity to the ideological and practical relationship among Salafists and to the relationship between them and the confessional system and other communities, especially the Sunni community and parties. In sum, the question over what *manhaj* to pursue to engage politics preoccupied and consumed Salafists, sharpening their ideological and practical outlook on society and state.

Notes

1. See Kamal Salibi, "Islam and Syria in the Writings of Henri Lammens," in *Historians of the Middle East*, edited by Bernard Lewis and P. M. Holt (London: Oxford University Press, 1962), 330–42. See also Henri Lammens, *La Syrie: Precis Historique* (Beirut: Imprimerie Catholique, 1921).

2. Yusuf al- Sawda, *Fi Sabil Lubnan* (For Lebanon) (Alexandria: Madrasat al-Farir al-Sina'iyah, 1919), 15. Quote first cited from Asher Kaufman, "Phoenicianism: The Formation of an Identity in Lebanon in 1920," *Middle East Studies* 37, no. 1 (January 2001).

3. Maurice Barrès's concept of nationalism was based on pride in tradition and heritage, patriotic spirit of Catholicism, and geographical determinism as a determinant of the unique national character of France. Barrès's concept was an intellectual fodder to Phoenicianists, who took pride in the glory of their Phoenician heritage, Catholic Maronitism, and the unique national character of Lebanon. Even Corm's title apparently took its inspiration from *La Colline Inspirée*, by Barrès. See Maurice Barrès, *La Colline Inspirée* (Paris: Plon-Nourrit, 1922) and *Le Culte du Moi* (Paris: Plon-Norrit, 1922). See Charles Corm, *La Montagne Inspirée; Chasons de Geste*, 2nd ed. (Beirut: Éditions de La Revue Phenicienne, 1964).

4. See E. P. Hoyek, "Les Revendications du Liban, Memoire de La Delegation Libanaise à la Conference de la Paix," in *La Revue Phénicienne*, edited by David Corm and Son (Beirut: Édition Maison d'Art, 1919).

5. Meir Zamir, *The Formation of Modern Lebanon* (London: Croom Helm, 1985), and Edmond Rabbath, *La Formation Historique du Liban Politique et Constitutionnel* (Beirut: Librairie Orientale, 1973).

6. For the creation of Greater Lebanon and the confessional system, see Robert G. Rabil, *Religion, National Identity, and Confessional Politics in Lebanon: The Challenge of Islamism* (New York: Palgrave Macmillan, 2011), 9–29.

7. On the most comprehensive account of Syria's Arab nationalist politics during the mandate, see Philip Khoury, *Syria and the French Mandate: The Politics of Arab Nationalism, 1920–1945* (Princeton, NJ: Princeton University Press, 1987).

8. See the communiqué addressed to the French high commissioner by the Patriarchate on February 6, 1935, in Rabbath, *La Formation Historique du Liban*, 407–8.

9. Farid el-Khazen, *The Communal Pact of National Identities: The Making and Politics of the 1943 National Pact* (Oxford: Centre for Lebanese Studies, 1991), 10.

10. Ibid., 34–37.

11. See Khoury, *Syria and the French Mandate*, 486–93.

12. See Raghid Solh, "The Attitude of the Arab Nationalists towards Greater Lebanon during the 1930s," in *Lebanon: A History of Conflict and Consensus*, edited by Nadim Shehadi and Dana Haffar Mills (London: I. B. Tauris, 1988), 149–61.

13. Out of a total resident population of 793,396, the Maronites numbered 227,800 (28.8 percent), the Sunnis 178,100 (22.4 percent), and the Shi'ites 155,035 (19.6 percent). The Maronites, being the largest sect, were allocated the powerful office of the president of the republic; the Sunnis, the second largest sect, were allocated the premiership; and the Shi'a, the third largest sect, were allocated the position of speaker of parliament. The distribution of parliamentary seats was set up at a Christian-to-Muslim ratio of 6:5, and government positions were also distributed according to the 6:5 ratio. For the official results of the census, see a copy as it appeared in the official gazette in Rania Maktabi, "The Lebanese Census of 1932 Revisited: Who Are the Lebanese?," *British Journal of Middle Eastern Studies* 26, no. 2 (1999), 223.

14. The celebrated term "Arab Face" was first mentioned in Solh's speech on October 7, 1943, which is considered the formal enunciation of the National Pact. See text of speech in Basim al-Jisr, *Mithaq 1943, Limadha Kan? Wa Hal Saqat?* (National Pact 1943, Why It Was Founded? Did It Collapse?) (Beirut: Dar al-Nahar lil-Nashr, 1978), 485–95. The other celebrated theme, "No East, No West," was emphasized by Khoury while advocating a special relationship with the Arab world. Al-Jisr, *Mithaq 1943, Limadha Kan? Wa Hal Saqat?* 482–84.

15. On Christian movements and currents during this episode in Lebanon's modern history, see Walid Phares, *Lebanese Christian Nationalism: The Rise and Fall of an Ethnic Resistance* (Boulder, CO: Lynne Rienner, 1995), 85–90.

16. For example, the Syrian Social Nationalist Party (SSNP), founded by the Greek Orthodox Antun Sa'ada in the 1930s, advocated Syrian nationalism, as opposed to Arab nationalism. On SSNP ideology, see Labib Zuwiyya Yamak, *The Syrian Social Nationalist Party: An Ideological Analysis* (Cambridge, MA: Harvard University Press, 1966).

17. Georges Naccache, *L'Orient*, March 10, 1949; reproduced in *Un Reve Libanais: 1943–1972* (Beirut: Éditions du Monde Arabe, 1983), 57–58.

18. Hajj Ahmad Darwish, "Al-Salafiyun fi Lubnan: Al al-Shahal Bayna Trablus wal-Shamal" (The Salafists in Lebanon: Al-Shahals between Tripoli and the North), *Al-Shira'*, January 22, 1996.

19. Abd al-Ghani 'Imad, *Al-Harakat al-Islamiyah fi Lubnan: Ishkaliyat al-Din wal-Siyasah fi Mujtama' Mutanawe'* (Islamic Movements in Lebanon: The Ambiguity of Religion and Politics in a Diverse Society) (Beirut: Dar al-Tali'a lil-Tiba'a wal-Nashr, 2006), 314–16.

20. Ibid., 316–17.

21. Khudr Taleb, "Al-Islamiyun fi al-Shamal" (The Islamists in the North), *As-Safir*, July 14, 1998. See also Muhammad Abi Samra, *Trablus: Sahat Allah wa Mina' al-Hadatha* (Tripoli, Lebanon: Square of God and Port of Modernity) (Beirut: Dar al-Saqi: 2011), 115–16.

22. Abi Samra, *Trablus*, 115–16.

23. "Emir" literally means a prince, but in Islamic terms it denotes a Muslim leader reigning over an Islamic community. "Sheikh" is an honorific title given in Islamic milieu, such as Tripoli, to respected scholars of Islam.

24. Author's interview with Sheikh Salem al-Rafi'i, July 19, 2012. The interview took place in his villa in Dedeh next to Tripoli and lasted a couple of hours. Sheikh al-Rafi'i gave a comprehensive account of his experiences in Lebanon and overseas, as well as of his ideological and political views.

25. Darwish, "Al-Salafiyun fi Lubnan."

26. Al-Harakat al-Islamiyah fi Lubnan (Islamic Movements in Lebanon), "Al-Jama'a al-Islamiyah" (Islamic Association), in *Al-Harakat al-Islamiyah fi Lubnan* (Beirut: Al-Markaz al-Arabi lil-Ma'lumat, 2007), 110.

27. Ali Lagha, *Fathi Yakan: Ra'ed al-Harakah al-Islamiyah al-Mu'asirah fi Lubnan* (Fathi Yakan: The Pioneer of the Contemporary Islamic Movement in Lebanon) (Beirut: Mu'assassat al-Risalah, 1994), 24–25.

28. On al-Ikwan in Syria, see Robert G. Rabil, "The Syrian Muslim Brotherhood," in *The Muslim Brotherhood: The Organization and Policies of a Global Movement*, edited by Barry Rubin (New York: Palgrave Macmillan, 2010).

29. For details on the Muslim Brotherhood's doctrine and objectives, see The Information Center of the Muslim Brotherhood in Syria, "Introducing the Muslim Brotherhood, Part One and Two," January 29, 2007, and February 7, 2007, respectively, available at http://www.ikhwansyria.com/index.php?option=com_content&task=view&id=19&Itemid=114.

30. See al-Harakat al-Islamiyah, *Al-Jama'a al-Islamiyah fi Luban*, 111. See also Ibrahim Bayram, "Al-Jama'a al-Islamiyah min Ubad al-Rahman ila al-Intikhabat al-Niabiyah" (The Islamic Association from Ubad al-Rahman to Parliamentary Elections), *An-Nahar*, April 1, 1997. At the time, Kamal Jumblat was the minister of interior. Based on the official license, the founders were Fathi Yakan, Sheikh Faisal Mawlawi, Zuhair al-Abidi, and Ibrahim al-Misri.

31. In 1958, the Islamic Association published a weekly newspaper called *Al-Mujtama'*, which remained in circulation for five years. In 1964, the Islamic Association

began publishing *Al-Shihab* and another weekly by the name *Al-Iman*. In addition, Islamic Association students published a periodical by the name *Al-Tali'a*, which was replaced by *Al-Mujahid.*

32. Lagha, *Fathi Yakan*, 29.

33. In the early 1960s, al-Jama'a, in conjunction with independent Muslim activists, established Jam'iyat al-Tarbiah al-Islamiyah (the Islamic Educational Association), which served as the foundational organization for founding dozens of Islamic pedagogical and technical schools throughout Lebanon under the name Madaress al-Iman (The Faith Schools). Out of these schools emerged Kashafat al-Iman (the Faith Boy Scouts). Then the graduates of these schools helped establish Rabitat al-Tulab al-Muslimin (the Muslim Students League) as the Islamic Association's student organization in Lebanese universities. At the same time, the Islamic Association established the Cooperative Medical Center, which became the nucleus of the Islamic Medical Association. The Islamic Medical Association has supervised a vast network of dispensaries and health centers throughout Lebanon, in particular in Sunni-populous areas and neighborhoods. For information on the Islamic Association's organizations, see its website, www.al-jamaa.org/index.php. See also al-Harakat al-Islamiyah, *Al-Jama'a al-Islamiyah*, 112.

34. See the Islamic Association's website at www.al-jamaa.org/pageother.php?cats mktba=15.

35. Ibrahim Bayram, "Al-Jama'a a-Islamiyah min Ubad al-Rahman ila al-Intikhabat al-Niyabiyah" (The Islamic Association from Ubad al-Rahman to Parliamentary Elections), *An-Nahar*, April 1, 1997.

36. Fathi Yakan, *Al-Masa'la al-Lubnaniyah min Manthur Islami* (The Lebanese Question from an Islamic Perspective) (Beirut: Mu'assassat al-Risalah, 1979).

37. Ibid., 39.

38. Ibid., 40–43.

39. Ibid., 61–62.

40. Ibid., 116–18.

41. Ibid., 116. It is noteworthy that, according to Yakan, administrative confessionalism is synonymous with political confessionalism (political sectarianism) when it comes to the distribution of political and administrative positions in the state on the basis of sectarianism (from the office of the Maronite president to the lowest position in the state).

42. See Yakan's interview with *Al-Diyar*, March 1, 1995, published in Fathi Yakan, *Adwa' 'ala al-Tajribah al-Niyabiyah al-Islamiyah fi Lubnan: Al-'Ida' al-Niyabi 'Ubr al-I'lam* (Lights on the Islamic Parliamentarian Experience: The Parliamentarian Performance through the Media), vol. 2 (Beirut: Mu'assassat al-Risalah, 1996), 93–94.

43. Yakan, *Al-Masa'la al-Lubnaniya*, 127.

44. Ibid., 135.
45. Ibid., 136.
46. Fathi Yakan, *Al-Mawsu'ah al-Harakiyah* (The Encyclopedia of Activism) (Amman: Dar al-Bashr, 1983), 55–56.
47. Yakan, *Al-Mas'ala al-Lubnaniyah,* 22.
48. Lagha, *Fathi Yakan,* 263–64. See also the objectives of the Islamic Association on its website, www.al-jamaa.org/pageother.php?catsmktba=15.
49. Fathi Yakan, *Madha Ya'ni Intima'i lil-Islam* (What Does It Mean Being a Muslim) (Beirut: Mu'assassat al-Risalah, 1977), 73–74, and Lagha, *Fathi Yakan,* 57.
50. Lagha, *Fathi Yakan,* 35.
51. Sayyid Qutb, *Ma'alim fi al-Tariq* (Milestones), (Chicago: Kazi Publications, 1964), 20.
52. Yakan, *Madha Ya'ni Intima'i lil-Islam,* 120–21.
53. Fathi Yakan, *Abjadiyat al-Tasawor al-Haraki lil-'Amal al-Islami* (The Elementary Facts of the Conceptual Movement of Islamic Activism) (Beirut: Mu'assassat al-Risalah, 1981), 154–55.
54. Lagha, *Fathi Yakan,* 65–77.
55. Ibid., 185.
56. See Yakan's interview on al-Jazeera TV, March 16, 2007, excerpts of which were transcribed by the Middle East Media Research Institute (MEMRI), Special Dispatch No. 1518, March 23, 2007.
57. Ibid.
58. Yakan, *Abjadiyat al-Tasawur al-Haraki,* 160–62.
59. Ibid., 164–66.
60. Ibid, 165. See also Yakan's interview with *Al-Diyar,* March 1, 1995.
61. An adaptation of this section on Yakan appeared in Rabil, *Religion, National Identity, and Confessional Politics in Lebanon,* 32–39.
62. 'Imad, *Al-Harakat al-Islamiyah fi Lubnan,* 205. 'Imad's description of Sha'ban's ideology is based on a comprehensive interview Sha'ban gave to *Al-Shira'* in 1984.
63. Ibid., 206.
64. A. Nizar Hamzeh, "Islamism in Lebanon: A Guide to the Groups," *Middle East Quarterly* 4, no. 3 (September 1997), 47–53.
65. 'Imad, *Al-Harakat al-Islamiyah fi Lubnan,* 207.
66. Ibid., 208.
67. Ibid., 209.
68. Muhammad Abi Samra, *Trablus: Sahat Allah wa Mina' al-Hadtha* (Tripoli, Lebanon: The Square of Allah and the Port of Modernity) (Beirut: Dar al-Saqi, 2011), 155.
69. Hanna Batatu, *Syria's Peasantry, the Descendants of Its Lesser Rural Notables, and Their Politics* (Princeton, NJ: Princeton University Press, 1999), 303–7.

70. Ibid., 305.

71. "Harakat al-Tawhid al-Islami," *An-Nahar*, April 4, 1997. See also "Al-Harakat al-Islamiyah fi Lubnan" (Islamic Movements in Lebanon), *Al-Wasat*, January 1, 2000.

72. "Indimam 'Jund Allah' ila Harakat al-Tawhid" (Jund Allah Joins Harakat al-Tawhid), *As-Safir*, April 5, 1983, and Khudr Taleb, "Al-Islamiyun fi al-Shamal: Min Manabir al-Masajid ila al-Maqa'ed al-Baladiyah" (Islamists in the North: From the Pulpits of Mosques to Municipality Seats), *As-Safir*, July 14, 1998.

73. For details, see Abi Samra, *Trablus*, 123–25.

74. 'Imad, *Al-Harakat al-Islamiyah fi Lubnan*, 214–18.

75. Ibid. See also "Hashem Minqara: Free at Last," *Middle East Intelligence Bulletin* 2, no. 8 (September 5, 2000).

76. "Hashem Minqara," and Amnesty International, *Lebanon: Arbitrary Arrests, "Disappearances" and Extrajudicial Killings by Syrian Troops and Syrian-Backed Forces in Tripoli* (AI Index: MDE 24/02/87), February 1987.

77. According to Ali Lagha, Fathi Yakan met President Asad three times, in December 1979, July 1985, and August 1988. President Asad discussed with Yakan Lebanese and Islamic matters, key among them how to deal with and confront Israel's aggression. See Ali Lagha, *Fathi Yakan: Ra'ed al-Harakah al-Islamiyah al-Mu'asirah fi Lubnan* (Fathi Yakan: The Pioneer of the Contemporary Islamic Movement in Lebanon) (Beirut: Mu'assassat al-Risalah, 1994), 31–32.

78. Author's interview with Syrian philosopher Sadek al-Azm, December 15, 2012. This line of thought was also implicit in the author's interview with Salafi sheikh Salem al-Rafi'i, July 19, 2012.

79. "Al-Harakat al-Islamiyah (al-Sunniyah) fi Lubnan" (Sunni Islamic Movements in Lebanon), *Al-Wasat*, January 10, 2000.

80. "Hezbollah wa Harakat al-Tawhid: Da'm al-Muqawamah wa Muwajahat al-'Asr al-Amereki" (Hezbollah and Harakat al-Tawhid: Supporting the Resistance and Confronting the American Era), *As-Safir*, July 7, 1991.

81. See Nizar Hamzeh and Hrair Dekmejian, "A Sufi Response to Political Islamism: Al-Ahbash of Lebanon," *International Journal of Middle East Studies* 28, no. 2 (May 1996).

82. Ibid.

83. See al-Ahbash websites www.aicp.org and www.al-ahbash.org. See also Hamzeh and Dekmejian, "A Sufi Response to Political Islamism."

84. In 1985, the Syrian regime mediated among the three powerful militia leaders to end civil strife and reform the system by eliminating confessionalism. On December 28, 1985, Nabih Berri of the Shi'a party Amal, Druze leader Walid Jumblat of the Progressive Socialist Party, and Elie Hobeika of the Christian Forces signed the Tripartite Accord, laying out the details for ending civil strife

and reforming the system. The agreement emphasized the Arab identity of Lebanon and Lebanese-Syrian special relations. Neither the Sunni leadership nor the Islamists were involved in devising the accord. For details of the agreement, see Markaz al-Tawthiq wal-Buhuth al-Lubnani, *Al-'Alaqat al-Lubnaniyah al-Suriyah: 1943–1985* (Lebanese-Syrian Relations: 1943–1985), vol. 1 (Antilias, Lebanon: Dar al-Nashr wal-Tawthiq, 1986), 500–15.

85. "Al-Harakat al-Islamiyah (al-Sunniyah) fi Lubnan" (Sunni Islamic Movements in Lebanon), *Al-Wasat*, January 10, 2000.

86. Darwish, "Al-Salafiyun fi Lubnan." On May 4, 2005, the U.S. Treasury Department listed the Benevolent Charitable Association as a terrorist-designated organization. See report by Office of Foreign Assets Control, U.S. Department of Treasury, "Terrorism: What You Need to Know about U.S. Sanctions," available at http://www.treasury.gov/resource-center/sanctions/programs/documents/terror.pdf (accessed July 8, 2013).

87. Darwish "Al-Salafiyun fi Lubnan."

88. The Bukhari Institute was founded as a private charitable endowment according to an Islamic legal judgment issued by the Sunni Legal Court in Akkar, which falls under the jurisdiction of the official Dar al-Ifta', on February 24, 1993, under number 72 of File 47. Mufti of the Republic Muhammad Rashid Qabbani, in his letter dated March 11, 2010, consented to the qualification of the institute to teach religious legal studies and offer a certificate of secondary religious studies.

89. Hana' 'Alian, "Al-Tayarat al-Wahhabiyah fi al-Shamal," Islamic Unity Movement–Command Council, available at http://attawhed.org/News/NewsDetails.aspx?NewsID=12368 (accessed August 30, 2013). See also Zoltan Pall, *Lebanese Salafis between the Gulf and Europe: Development, Fractionlization and Transnational Networks of Salafism in Lebanon* (Amsterdam: Amsterdam University Press, 2013).

90. Kuwait dispensed its funding through the Association for the Renewal of Islamic Heritage, whose branch in Lebanon was chaired until 2010 by Salafi sheikh Safwan Zu'bi.

91. For details on al-Jinan Association and its schools and institutes, see its website, www.jinan.edu.lb/main/index.php?id=jinanfoundationar (accessed July 9, 2013).

92. For information on al-Jinan University, see its website, www.jinan.edu.lb/main/index.php?id=rulesar# (accessed July 9, 2013).

93. For information on the university's Sidon branch, see its website, www.jinan.edu.lb/saida/ (accessed July 9, 2013).

94. For details on the Association of Islamic Reform, see its website, www.islahonline.org/News/Details.aspx?NewID=96 (accessed January 1, 2013).

95. See the investigative report on Salafism by the television show *Tahqiq* on MTV, November 11, 2012.

96. Bernard Rougier, *Everyday Jihad: The Rise of Militant Islam among Palestinians in Lebanon* (Cambridge, MA: Harvard University Press, 2007).

97. "Al-Mu'assassat al-Salfiyah Ijtama't wa Nadadat bi Ahdath al-Achrafieh," (Salafi Associations Met and Condemned Disturbances in Achrafieh), *An-Nahar*, February 9, 2006. The statement listed all associations that signed it. The signatories included: Jami'yat Da'wat al-Iman wa Ma'had wa Kuliyat al-Da'wa wal-Irshad (Tripoli); Waqf wa Ma'had al-Imam al-Bukhari (Akkar); Waqf al-Abrar wa Ma'had Trablus lil-'Ulum al-Shar'iyah (Tripoli); Waqf wa Ma'had al-Amin lil-'Ulum al-Shar'iyah (Tripoli); Jam'iyat al-Istijaba wa Waqf al-Istijaba al-Khayri (Sidon and Southern Lebanon); Jam'iyat wa Markaz al-Siraj al-Munir (Beirut); Waqf al-Turath al-Islami (Tripoli); Waqf al-Nour al-Khayri (Sheba' wal-'Arqub); Waqf al-Bar al-Khayri (al-Dinneyeh); al-Markaz al-Islami wa Masjad 'Abd al-Rahman ibn 'Awf (Beka' Majdal 'Anjar); Jam'iyat al-Irshad wa Madrasat al-Ibda' (Akkar); Waqf 'Ubad al-Rahman (Tripoli); Waqf Ihya' al-Sunna al-Nabawiyah (al-Dinneyeh); Dar al-Hadith li-'Ulum al-Shar'iyah (Tripoli); Waqf I'anat al-Faqir (Tripoli); Tajamu' Sanabel al-Khayr (Akkar); Waqf al-Khayr al-Islami wa Masjad wa Markaz al-Aqsa (al-Dinneyeh); al-Waqf al-Islami al-Sunni al-Khayri (Zgharta); Waqf I'anat al-Marda (Tripoli); Waqf al-Furqan lil-Bahth al-'Ilmi (Tripoli); Waqf al-Ahya' fi al-Islam (Tripoli); and Waqf al-Balagh al-Islami (Tripoli).

Chapter Three

The Quietest Salafi Ideology of Sheikh Sa'd al-Din Muhammad al-Kibbi

This chapter explores the ideology of Sheikh Sa'd al-Din Muhammad al-Kibbi, the founder and director of the Salafi al-Bukhari Institute in Akkar. Sheikh Kibbi, in line with Sheikh Abd al-Aziz ibn Abdallah ibn Baz and Sheikh Nasir al-Din al-Albani (both deceased), is a proponent of the quietest Salafi school that predominates the Wahhabi religious establishment in Saudi Arabia. He advances an apolitical attitude to politics and political authority, marked by a legal obedience to the ruler insofar he does not renounce Islam. He, like al-Albani, believes that Muslim society is torn by divisions. He has, therefore, developed the theory of *al-ta'lim wal-tarbiyah* (teaching/instructing and educating) as an integral part of Islam's missionary *da'wa* (call to Islam). He follows the example set by Prophet Muhammad's *da'wa* during the initial stages of Islam, which relied on persuasion rather on jihad. In this respect, Sheikh Kibbi provides an ideological framework intended to show the damage inflicted by *takfir* (excommunication) and jihad on Muslim society and therefore to persuade Muslims not to be lured to the wicked and fallacious philosophy of *takfir*. At the same time, he rejects excommunicating what he calls *takfiri* groups on ideological and practical grounds, for this would lead to further divisions in Muslim society, undercutting his vision of Muslim unity. His theological vision of *tawhid* (unity/oneness of God) underlines a comprehensive Islamic education of Muslims intended to bring about Muslim unity, in accordance with the principles and practice of Islam, as a foundation for creating the true Islamic community.

The Exemplary Islamic Village: The Bukhari Institute

Born in Beirut in 1960, Sheikh Sa'd al-Din Muhammad al-Kibbi received his doctorate in Islamic law/jurisprudence from al-Jinan University in Tripoli in

2002. He taught at several colleges and institutes, including the Islamic University of Abu Bakr in Pakistan (1991–92) and the Institute of the Glowing Lamp (al-Siraj al-Munir) (2010–11) in Lebanon. He established al-Imam al-Bukhari Islamic Law Institute in 1993 on a hilltop in the Akkar region amid three hundred Sunni-majority villages.[1] The Bukhari Institute is recognized as an institute for teaching religious (Islamic) legal studies by the mufti of Lebanon, Muhammad Rashid Qabbani,[2] and as a Salafi institute by the late grand mufti of Saudi Arabia and head of the Council of Higher Ulema, Sheikh Abd al-Aziz ibn Abdallah ibn Baz.[3]

Besides offering Islamic legal studies, the institute offers technical apprenticeship so as to help its students have self-sustaining jobs before and after graduation. Most of their graduates continue their higher learning in Islamic law studies in Saudi Arabian universities, with a particular interest in the Islamic University in Medina. Sheikh Kibbi has used the institute as a means to uphold his vision of creating a true Islamic community. Detractors accuse the institute of being the most dangerous incubator of Salafi-jihadi thought, an accusation ardently refuted by Sheikh Kibbi.[4] In addition to focusing on Qur'anic and legal studies, Sheikh Kibbi has underscored Islamic morality and Islamic education. In fact, the purpose of his curricula can be discerned from the principles he has upheld at the institute and from his vision of the institute as the exemplary Islamic village. Apparently Sheikh Kibbi believes that the institute's mission of teaching Islamic legal studies, along with an Islamic comprehensive education, constitutes an imperative first step toward creating the true Islamic community.

Upon entering the institute, students face a long scroll listing the rules they have to adhere to during their religious and technical training there. The scroll is titled "The Disciplines for Students Seeking Knowledge." The disciplines include the following:

1. True intention about God.
2. The obligation to follow the *manhaj* [way/method] of the pious ancestors in accordance with the Book [Qur'an] and the Sunna.
3. Humility to truth and diminution of sins.
4. Nurturing the honor of the teacher and respecting and appreciating him.
5. Choosing the friend who helps and being cautious of those associated with wickedness.
6. Ensuring the retention of knowledge and writing down the benefits so they don't get forgotten.
7. The intention of acquiring knowledge is work and not bragging or showing off.

8. To seek God the almighty and invoke Him if there is something you cannot understand.
9. To be truthful in your words and cautious about falling in with the liars (impostors).
10. Taking care of your wealth.[5]

Evidently the Bukhari Institute is a center for teaching Islamic legal studies in accordance with the principles of the quietest Salafi school of thought (also referred to as the scientific school), as advocated by Sheikh Nasir al-Din al-Albani, Sheikh ibn Baz, and the partisans of *hadiths*, in particular Imam Bukhari, after whom the institute was named.

The Creed, Ideology, and Ideological Terminology of Sheikh Kibbi

The Salafi school, according to Sheikh Kibbi, "is the Islamic *da'wa* that was transmitted to the messenger of God [Prophet Muhammad] and was recognized [understood] by the Prophet's companions, whose followers, may God have mercy on all of them, embraced. The followers represent the victorious [saved] sect, *ahl al-Sunna wal-jama'a* (partisans of Sunna and the group). The Salafi school has been made known by the school of *ahl al-Hadith wal-Sunna* (partisans of *hadiths* and Sunna), who aggrandized the *hadith* of the messenger of God and had a consensus on the Sunna during a period of time when groups, reported about by the messenger of God, rebelled [against Islam]."[6]

As it turned out, Sheikh Kibbi explains, these rebellions caused the Muslim *ummah* (community of believers) to be divided pursuant to the *manahij* (ways) by which Muslims led their life after the days of Prophet Muhammad and the generation of the companions and their followers. As a result the *khawarij* (those who rebelled) appeared.[7] They killed Uthman (the third rightly guided caliph) and then rebelled against Ali (the fourth rightly guided caliph). They (*khawarij*) leveled the charge of unbelief (*kafaruh*) against Ali and excommunicated him and the companions. The main causes of the division are ignorance, following heretical tendencies and allegorical comparisons of texts, pursuing scholastic theology, and employing weak *hadiths* and false stories about the messenger of God. Correspondingly, a party of scholars and *du'at* (preachers/those who call to Islam) emerged and called for condemning this division over the *manahij*, abandoning reprehensible innovations, and holding onto the *manhaj* of the pious ancestors (*al-salaf al-salih*). By describing these scholars as Salafists and ascribing to them the *manhaj* of the *Salaf*, many mistakenly thought that this was a new party.[8]

For Kibbi, the legal terminology of *Salaf* implies the first three munificent generations in Islam, which include the companions, their followers, and the followers of their followers. The companions are those who met the Prophet, believed in him, and died for Islam. Whereas the followers are those who accompanied the companions, the followers' followers are those who followed them and walked in their footsteps. As such, those who are called Salafists are those who adhere to the *manhaj* of the pious *Salaf*. It follows from this that the Salafist *da'wa* is the reformist school that has become known as the school of *ahl al-Hadith*, which struggles to follow the Sunna and to shun *bid'a* (reprehensible innovation).[9] Whereas the pious ancestors and those who walked in their footsteps are called *ahl al-Hadith* because they held onto the *hadith* of the Prophet and acted on it, *ahl al-Hadith* are also called *ahl al-Sunna wal-jama'a* because they held onto the Sunna and rallied around it in the era of rebellion against Islam. Sheikh Kibbi further explains that Sunna, according to the terminology of theological scholars, implies the *'aqida* (creed) and *manhaj* of the Prophet and his companions. The *ahl* (partisans) who ascribed to the Sunna, held onto it, and unanimously agreed on it are designated *ahl al-Sunna wal-jama'a*. Moreover, they are also called *ahl al-Sunna wal-jama'a* because the designation *ahl al-Sunna* distinguishes them from the partisans of reprehensible innovations and heretical tendencies, while at the same time the term *al-jama'a*, according to the Islamic legal understanding, signifies the saved sect (*al-firqa al-najiyah*).[10]

With regard to creed, Sheikh Kibbi shares with the Wahhabi religious establishment the definition of the Salafist creed. He subscribes to the Islamic terminology of creed as "being the absolute faith in *rububiyat Allah* (Lordship of God), exalted be He, *uluhiyat Allah* (godship of God), His *asma'ihi wa sifatihi* (names and attributes), His angels, books, messengers, day of judgment, divine destiny, all that is confirmed from divine secrets, and the fundamentals of religion and the consensus of the pious ancestors."[11] Since the purpose for which God created mankind is to worship Him alone, the Islamic religion is called the religion of *tawhid* (oneness of God), for "*tawhid* is the greatest duty God imposed cognitively and practically on the worshippers; for whose sake messengers were sent and books were transmitted; and according to which sins are excommunicated, paradise made deserving, and [mankind] saved from the hell."[12] Thus the Salafi school considers *tawhid* to be the noblest objective for which the books were revealed and the messengers were sent to fulfill their revelations. According to Sheikh Kibbi, this *tawhid* is divided into three categories of belief and action. First, *tawhid al-uluhiyah* (oneness of godship) is the *tawhid* that the messengers of God advocated to exclusively confine worship to God alone. Under this broad stipulation, *tawhid al-uluhiyah* may go beyond the basic Salafi principle under which all forms of worship must be directed exclusively toward God. Sheikh Kibbi explains: "When we say confining worship to Him, we don't only mean prayer, almsgiving, fasting, and so on but also all that falls under this term from sayings and actions."[13] For example, all forms of supplication, invocation, prayers, and pleas have to be directed toward God. More so, seeking help is also a form of worship. In sum, according to Sheikh Kibbi, "worshipping is a collective term of all what God loves and approves of esoteric and exoteric sayings and actions."[14]

Second, *tawhid al-rububiyah* (oneness of lordship) is *tawhid* of God in His actions. Sheikh Kibbi explains that "it is the belief that almighty God is the creator and provider of worshippers, who breathes life and death into them, who gives and proscribes, helps and harms, esteems and humiliates, and who acts in the universe as He pleases, glory be to Him, with no associate in all of this. This includes the belief (faith) that He alone has the powers of legislation (making laws)."[15] Finally, *tawhid al-asma' wal-sifat* (oneness of the names and attributes) is the belief that God has names and attributes that are fitting to Him. Sheikh Kibbi explains that "the names of God are endowed, which means that we cannot call God a name that He has not called Himself or the Prophet has not called Him . . . for they are derived [taken] from the Book and the Sunna."[16] He adds that "the names of God are not limited to a specific number according to the Prophet" and that the intent behind the *hadith* that affirms God has ninety-nine names is "about invoking and worshipping God through them, and not about limiting the names of God to this number."[17]

With respect to the attributes of God, they are attributes that are suitable to His almightiness and glory (excellency). They are perfect, sublime, and laudatory attributes, which God Himself and His messenger have described respectively in the noble Book and Sunna. Sheikh Kibbi affirms that "we believe in these attributes in the same way our pious ancestors did, peace be upon them, without *tahrif* (alteration of words), *ta'til* (theological concepts denying God all attributes), *tashbih* (allegorical comparisons), *takyif* (adaptation), and *tamthil* (exemplification)."[18] Taking all this into consideration, Sheikh Kibbi makes the distinction between faith and intellect, whereby the former trumps the latter. He considers that an underlying fundamental of God's attributes lies in the fact that "everything that has been confirmed in the Book and Sunna should be believed and accepted as true even if it contradicts the intellect (mind), for intellect is created, and what is created is limited, and what is limited is incomplete, and what is incomplete does not illustrate the complete truth of the creator."[19]

Clearly, Sheik Kibbi's view of *tawhid* does not, broadly speaking, overlap with that of other Salafists, especially *harakis* (activists) and Salafi jihadists. Sheikh Kibbi has refrained from excommunicating sinners, dissenters, and polytheists. He believes that excommunicating polytheists would place them outside the realm of Islam, and therefore jihad against them would eventually follow. In fact, it has become axiomatic for many Salafists to wage jihad against polytheists once they have been excommunicated. Sheikh Kibbi is evidently concerned about the consequences of excommunication for the *ummah*. He believes that since the *ummah* is not strong enough to wage jihad, excommunicating Muslims for sins, violations, or *shirk* (polytheism) would only further weaken the Muslim society, thereby preventing the creation of a true *ummah* in its formative stage. Sheikh Kibbi perceives the present state of the *ummah* as similar to that which existed during the initial stages of Prophet Muhammad's *da'wa* in Mecca, where he faced serious obstacles from pagans and polytheists but preferred dealing with them through persuasion rather than waging jihad against them. By recognizing his military weakness, the Prophet realized that his mission of *da'wa* would have irrevocably suffered had he waged jihad against them. Thus Sheikh Kibbi, in principle as well in practice, goes to great lengths to demonstrate his vision and to refute what stands in its path.

The *Manhaj* and Vision of Sheikh Kibbi

In principle, the *manhaj* (methodology) of Sheikh Kibbi is about providing the right conditions for helping create his vision of the true *ummah*. Nevertheless, the immediacy of his *manhaj* is associated with the way Muslims need to apply legal rulings and abandon reprehensible innovations. Only in this way can Muslims succeed in placing the mission of Islam *da'wa* on solid grounds and therefore spread it across all corners of the world. Considering this, his *manhaj* is thus premised on contextualizing the methods by which legal rulings and *bid'a* are effected and therefore why they should be applied and abandoned, respectively.

Sheikh Kibbi departs from the point that since the Salafi school seeks to hold on to the *manhaj* of the pious ancestors, it should follow their way in receiving knowledge and legal rulings. Consequently he rejects *taqlid* (emulation) of the four *madhabs* (canonical law schools) without either advocating or opposing *ijtihad* (independent reasoning/interpretation). Rather, he insists on "standing with the truth and proof wherever they are." This line of reasoning jibes with his dogmatic view that the act of worship, which is the main objective of Salafism, is based on knowledge and not on ignorance, which leads to *bid'a*. In this respect, knowledge is recognizing the truth through its proof. For him, this is the knowledge acquired by the companions of the Prophet, which the followers practiced.

It follows from this that Sheikh Kibbi assumes that scholars could be right or wrong. He explains that "since *Ahl al-Hadith* relied on the texts and the consensus, they did not deny employing the correct analogy and opinion."[20] But he cautions that "what *Ahl al-Hadith* reject are the opinions and analogies that violate the texts of the Book and Sunna or the immutable consensus."[21] He supports his case by referencing classical religious scholar Ibn al-Qayim, who said that an opinion has three parts: one undoubtedly wrong, one correct, and one vague (suspicious). The rationale is that Salafists employed the correct opinion, acted on it, and issued *fatwas* (legal opinions / religious edicts) based on it. Certainly, they rejected the wrong one. However, they employed the vague one only under strenuous conditions insofar as it did not violate the texts and the consensus of the companions. Even so, they made accepting or rejecting the vague opinion a matter of choice.[22]

Apparently what Sheikh Kibbi intends to accomplish by bolstering his assumption is not only confirming the precedence of what is evident in the texts of the Qur'an and Sunna to analogies but also upholding the view that Muslims should not heed the sayings of scholars when they contradict the texts. It is on this referential basis that he enjoins rejecting *taqlid* of the four imams and their *madhabs*, while at the same time showering them with respect.[23] Significantly, his rejection of *taqlid* is firmly linked to his concern that the aggrandizement of the four imams could lead to placing their *hadiths* ahead of the Sunna. He even cites sayings of the imams to defend his concern. For example, when Abu Hanifa was asked what he would do if his *hadith* contradicted the Book of Allah, he answered, "Set my *hadith* aside to the Book of God." Then he was asked, "What if it contradicted the *hadith* of the Prophet?" He replied, "Set my *hadith* aside to that of the Prophet." Then he was asked, "What if it contradicted that of the companions?" He answered, "Set my *hadith* [aside] to that of the companions."[24]

The other premise of Sheikh Kibbi's *manhaj* is abandoning *bid'a*. Sheikh Kibbi subscribes to *ahl al-Hadith*'s position of rejecting any accretion to the Qur'an and the Sunna. More specifically, he, like *ahl al-Hadith*, rejects adding by way of religious innovations any belief or act of worship to the Book and the Sunna. *Ahl al-Hadith* believe that God has completed (perfected) the religion of Islam for them and bestowed upon them His blessing. Sheikh Kibbi invokes the Qur'anic Surat (al-Ma'ida: 3) to support his claim. The verse reads: "This day have I perfected your religion for you, completed My favor upon you, and have chosen for you Islam as your religion." It follows from this that Sheikh Kibbi rejects *bid'a* in religion since the Book and the Sunna are divinely complete. He also rejects *bid'a* in religion on the ground that God has rejected what He has not condoned. He also invokes the Qur'anic Surat (al-Shura: 21) to reinforce his claim. The verse reads: "Have they set up such associates of God, who have laid down for them a [religious] way of life, which Allah has not permitted?" Correspondingly, he enjoins the "duty of *al-itba'* [to follow / apply literally the Qur'an and Sunna] and rejecting *ibtida'* [to initiate reprehensible/illegitimate innovations]."[25]

But his rejection of *bid'a* in religion does not necessarily entail refusing certain innovations in terms of *ijtihad*, in what he considers temporal innovations with regard to legal rulings involving the safeguarding of the remaining four of Islam's Five Necessities: life, regeneration, intellect, and wealth.[26]

Taking all this under consideration, it becomes clear that Sheikh Kibbi contextualizes his *manhaj* by theologically emphasizing the right method by which to receive knowledge and reject *bid'a*, all in the interest of delegitimizing what he calls interchangeably *ahl al-ahwa'* (partisans of heretical tendencies/dissenters/ heretics) and *jama'at al-takfir* (*takfiri* groups). This is so because he believes that these groups are harming the mission of Islam *da'wa* by their false beliefs, in particular the *bid'a* of *takfir*, and terrible actions. As a result, Sheikh Kibbi's vision, which rests largely on spreading *da'wa*, will have been aborted if *khuruj* is not curbed. Sheikh Kibbi believes that his vision cannot be accomplished without first advocating *da'wa* through persuasion, in terms of educating and teaching Muslims, to fulfill its objective of coextensively bringing about faith, peace, and Islam, the pillars of the true *ummah*, whereupon all souls submit voluntarily to the revelation of God.[27]

Ahl al-Sunna, Ahl al-Ahwa', and the Regulations of *Takfir*

What is constant in the literature of Sheikh Kibbi is his concern with the potential harm inflicted by *ahl al-ahwa'*, also referred to as *takfiri* groups, on the Muslim community. This does not mean, however, that Sheikh Kibbi has resorted to excommunicating these groups, despite his vehement opposition to them. Instead, he has underscored the theoretical and practical difference between *ahl al-Sunna* and *ahl al-ahwa'* so as to enlighten Muslims about the dreadful consequences of following *ahl al-ahwa'* and therefore to persuade them not to travel the path of falsehood and *bid'a*, which would lead to *takfir* and in turn to jihad. Moreover, he has left the door open to these groups to rejoin the right path of Islam once they have shed their false beliefs. At the same time, he has theologically emphasized the regulations of *takfir* in order to curb, if not cease, its employment as an instrument of change in Muslim society.

Embracing the view that Muslims, especially the youth, are duped by *takfiri* groups into waging jihad on what they consider their enemies within and beyond the Muslim world at a time of great distress in Muslim society, Sheikh Kibbi implores Muslims to act with prudence and awareness and not with ignorance, fanaticism, and capriciousness. He also prods them to listen to the "true" scholars of Islam, and to engage in self-criticism to discover the flaws and failings in Muslim society.[28] He identifies features that distinguish *ahl al-Sunna* from the *takfiri* groups. Among the features of the *takfiri* groups are the following: (1) they contest the knowledge of the *ulema*, accusing them of misunderstanding the present reality of Muslim society; (2) they follow allegorical comparison of texts and specious interpretation of texts; (3) they exaggerate and are pigheaded; (4) they excommunicate and engage in cyclical excommunication (*takfir wal al-takfir al-mutaselsel*), by employing the rule, Who does not excommunicate the unbeliever he is an unbeliever himself; and (5) they sow corruption on earth by inflicting damage on Muslims and disrupting the Islamic *da'wa* under the pretext of jihad and protecting sacred places. They wage jihad under all circumstances, situations, times, and places without considering the harmful and/or favorable consequences of their actions for Muslim society.[29]

Conversely, the features defining *ahl al-Sunna wal-jama'a* include the following: (1) they are fond of the *ulema*, and they respect them; (2) they reject allegorical comparisons, sophistry and anthropomorphization, and they interpret the Qur'an through the Qur'an, the Sunna, and the *hadiths* of the companions; (3) they pursue a middle way in religion and knowledge, far from exaggeration and pigheadedness; (4) they recognize truth and have mercy on mankind, they don't excommunicate except those excommunicated by God and His messenger, and they forgive violations committed on the grounds of ignorance and allegorical comparisons and interpretations; and (5) they believe that jihad in Islam is the purview of the military apparatus of the Islamic state. In this respect, they reject exploiting the ongoing tribulations in the Muslim world as a pretext to incite against political authority and rebel against the ruler. They are patient with the ruler's injustice, and they struggle to offer advice as much as they can.[30]

In underlining the difference between the two parties, Sheikh Kibbi makes his position clear with regard to *takfiri* groups, *takfir*, and political authority. Clearly, he refrains from excommunicating *takfiri* groups, opting instead to forgive their violations on the grounds of ignorance and allegorical comparisons and interpretations. Most important, he attributes the main cause of *takfir* to ignorance. Ignorance could be defined as incomplete knowledge or flawed knowledge and could be caused either by underperforming in acquiring knowledge or by allegorical analogies.[31] Similarly, *ahl al-Ahwa'*, unlike the *ulema*, memorize texts in isolation as to whether they can be applied to present circumstances, and they do not peruse and understand them in relation to the context of the other texts. Hence, according to Sheikh Kibbi, they do not apply the rule that performing a religious duty is linked to the ability of performing it, *fala wajeb ma'a al-'ajz wala muharram ma'a al-darura* (for there can be no duty while helpless [weak] and no prohibition when necessity demands it).[32] He further adds that they "may know this rule, but they ignore it on account of their heretical tendencies and eagerness to carry out military actions."[33] Sadly, they "depict to the Muslim youth that ability is inherent in them and fail to consider the ability of the *ummah* and the collective [good] of society."[34]

Considering that *takfir* is the modern scourge of Muslim society, Sheikh Kibbi stresses *dhawabit* (general rules/regulations) for excommunication. First, the fundamental rule for a Muslim is to remain a Muslim unless he or she consciously renounces Islam. Second, *ahl al-Sunna wal-jama'a* do not excommunicate people for committing violations (sins). Third, excommunication is related to falsehood and disavowal of belief. Sheikh Kibbi subscribes to the *hadith* of Imam Nawawi who said that "the partisans of truth don't excommunicate Muslims for committing sins, and they don't excommunicate *ahl al-hwa' wal-ida'*. [Only] he or she who disavows what is known of the religion of Islam must be judged for his apostasy and excommunicated." And finally, it is proscribed to testify that a certain person is a *kafir* (infidel), for it is a great injustice to bear witness that God will not forgive or have mercy on him or her.[35]

Clearly Sheikh Kibbi restricts *takfir* only to the disavowal of the sources of Islam, while at the same time exposing and offering to forgive the foolhardiness of *ahl al-ahwa'*. His immediate concern is to prevent Muslims from falling in the wrong and calamitous ways of *ahl al-ahwa'*, in the interest of maintaining Muslim unity and strengthening Muslim society first and foremost by transforming it into a more faithful one.

Society, Political Authority, and *Al-Taghyir*

In order to strengthen Muslim society and make it more aware of the dangers threatening it, Sheikh Kibbi focuses on *taghyir* (transforming) Muslim society. He, in principle, considers transformation of society as a comprehensive matter that begins with changing the souls by "burnishing them with Islam, meanings of *tawhid*, and the ways of the Sunna so that they submit voluntarily and not compulsively to the revelation of God."[36] He also believes that worshippers, according to Islamic law, cannot be tasked with what they cannot handle or do. He refers to several Qur'anic verses (including al-Baqara: 286 and al-Talaq: 7) to bolster his claim. For example, Surat al-Baqara *ayat* (verse) 286 reads: "On no soul does Allah place a burden greater than it can bear." Conversely, he avers that the concept of change for *ahl al-Ahwa'* is a partial matter dealing with one aspect of faith. They, unlike *ahl al-Sunna*, see faith as the undivided belief of the heart and not reflected by speech and manifest action. Therefore, they care less about the idiomatic and actionable deviation of people. They are not concerned with nurturing faith and Islamic education, opting instead for intellectual education. This leads them to be inflexible in their condemnation of whom they consider sinners and to perceive that change can only be achieved through violence, including rebelling against the ruler.[37]

This difference in perspective over changing Muslim society becomes salient when transformation is put into practice. The main disagreement, according to Sheikh Kibbi, is that *ahl al-ahwa'* see no benefit in what he considers essential for bringing about change in Muslim society, *al-ta'lim wal-tarbiyah* (teaching/instructing and educating).[38] Rather, change for them is integral to their political program, according only to their own perspective, something Sheikh Kibbi roundly rejects. He emphasizes that as faith weakened in the present Muslim societies leading to sins, *ahl al-ahwa'* considered them to be infidel and *jahili* societies. Consequently they rebelled against these societies and excommunicated and fought the rulers on the Qur'anic grounds that they "did not rule according to what God sent down."[39] This Qur'anic quote is excerpted from Surat al-Ma'ida verse 44: "Whosoever does not rule by what God sent down, they are the *kafirun* (unbelievers)." This quote is widely used by Salafi jihadists, interchangeably called by Sheikh Kibbi as *ahl al-ahwa'* and *takfiri* groups. His opposition to their actions is so critical that he does not even call them Salafi jihadists.

Clearly Sheikh Kibbi stands at a distance from Sayyid Qutb, *haraki* Salafists, and Salafi jihadists. He is more in line with both late Grand Mufti ibn Baz and Nasir al-Din al-Albani. In fact, he references both of them to support his apolitical attitude toward political authority, focusing on *al-ta'lim* and *al-tarbiyah* of Muslim society. Regarding the relationship between the ruler and the ruled, he follows the example set by Sheikh ibn Baz, who said, "Muslims should obey the rulers in *ma'ruf* (beneficence/benevolence) and not in sins, and if they command committing sins, then you don't obey them, but you don't rebel against them."[40] Ibn Baz sanctioned excommunicating and therefore rebelling against a ruler only when he has been proved to have committed a *kufr bawah* (a clear, manifest unbelief).[41] Even so, rebellion should not be carried out if it is going to cause greater harm and corruption (sin). Ibn Baz adhered to a consentaneous legal foundation according to which "it is not permitted to remove evil by [causing] a bigger evil, and evil should be curbed by way of removing or reducing it."[42] In other words, ibn Baz opposed waging jihad against a ruler if it is consequent upon more corruption, instability, and oppression of people. Rather, he enjoined "patience, obedience in benevolence, advising and wishing welfare to the ruler, and struggling to reduce evil and increase good."[43]

Sheikh Kibbi also cites Sheikh Nasir al-Din al-Albani to support his position toward political authority and rebuilding Islamic rule. In fact, Sheikh Kibbi shares with slight variation al-Albani's view that Muslims should emulate how Prophet Muhammad had initially started his *da'wa* in Mecca. Whereas al-Albani enjoined applying his famous theory of *al-tasfiyah wal-tarbiyah* (purification and education; see chapter 1) as a first step to rebuilding Islamic rule, Sheikh Kibbi enjoins applying his theory as a first step to creating the true Islamic community. Notwithstanding al-Albani's interest in cleansing Islam of foreign accretions, the difference between the two theories is more or less minimal because both advocate a comprehensive Islamic education of Muslims. For Sheikh Kibbi, *ta'lim* is broader than pure instruction. Since Islam comprises creed and its duties, revelation and its legal rulings, and morality and its proper conduct, all of which are reflected in the Islamic civilization and order that fashion the Muslim personality, *ta'lim* entails recognizing, understanding, and knowing all of them. In much the same vein, *tarbiyah* is broader than education. Since obeying God obligates adherence to *shari'a* (Islamic law) and moral and ethical Islamic laws, which includes tying the Muslim to his or her ruler or state, these laws are but worshipping laws meant to bring Muslims closer to God. This cannot be possible without a unique *tarbiyah* that nurtures and actualizes the Islamic faith.[44]

Though Sheikh Kibbi's focal point is *al-ta'lim wal-tarbiyah*, he underscores certain conditions to help bring about the change he desires in Muslim society. First, he enjoins achieving unity (*tawhid*) in objectives and means, as part of God's *tawhid*. Second, he stresses fulfilling the duties of faith that go beyond practicing the five pillars of Islam to speech and manifest action. He relies on al-Bukhari's concept that faith "is speech and manifest action that increases and decreases." This means that the duties of faith that are applied by way of speech and manifest action should entail increasing obedience and decreasing sins. Finally, he instructs "achieving strength and being aware of worldly factors." He considers that "formidable strength rests on unity of ranks and word, and absence of contestation and in-fighting." Closely associated with this are two preconditions. First, Muslims should have the ability to recognize the condition of the *ummah* in terms of its weaknesses and strengths and correspondingly apply the rules (policies) that are most suitable. In this respect, Sheikh Kibbi leaves no room for doubt that the process of decision making is reserved only to the ruler and no one else.[45] Next, Muslims should have the aptitude to effect benevolence (beneficence) and to curb corruption. According to Sheikh Kibbi, this can be done through selecting the most appropriate method of *da'wa*. In this instance, the call to God and jihad are legitimized if the purpose is to "bring people out from darkness to light and to remove oppression and establish justice." The legal ways to accomplish this include: (1) guidance and persuasion, as well as encouragement and warning; (2) dialogue and removal of misgivings; (3) application of the Islamic principle "commanding good and forbidding wrong" as understood by the *ulema*; and (4) peacemaking if it is more beneficial to the *ummah* than jihad.[46]

Apropos of *takfiri* groups that wage illegitimate jihad, Sheikh Kibbi considers al-Qaeda and its actions to be most harmful to Islam and Muslims. He perceives al-Qaeda as a military organization whose leaders have grown in *takfiri* schools or have fallen victims to *takfiri* ideologies due to their ignorance, zeal, and stupidity. Therefore, they have turned their guns toward the heart of the Islamic world, killed and weakened Muslims, and reinforced their enemies.[47] He also underscores al-Qaeda's ideological and operational flaws, which include (1) using indiscriminate force that backfired and weakened Islamic *da'wa*, while turning Muslim countries into areas of conflict; (2) causing the collapse of the Islamic Afghan state in its infancy; (3) waging jihad without considering the higher ideals and objectives of Islamic law; and (4) not referring to the senior *ulema* who are most competent to issue *fatwas* and pertinent legal rulings.[48]

Clearly, Sheikh Kibbi, like al-Albani, seeks to indoctrinate and instill in Muslim society the authentic Islamic creed and education, for he considers the chief mission of Islam, *da'wa*, to be endangered by weakness, division, and jihad in the Muslim world. In this respect, he places *ta'lim* and *tarbiyah* before politics, the interest of the *ummah* before the interest of a nation/state, and the interest of the Muslim individual before the interest of the state. This is so with regard to Lebanon and its confessional politics since he considers the Muslims there as part of the *ummah*. In fact, he is reticent in theory and practice about his relationship with other religious communities in Lebanon. Unlike other Salafists, he has not disparaged the Shi'ites as *rawafid* (rejectionists) in Lebanon, nor has he impugned Christians or Christian authority. When asked about his attitude toward Christians, he responded that he has coexisted peacefully and amicably with the Christians of Akkar.[49] For the time being, the focal point of his *da'wa* is to expand what he calls the exemplary Islamic village, as represented by his institute, to as many villages as possible in Lebanon in general and in Akkar in particular. His interest in politics stems from his *da'wa* and application of *al-ta'lim* and *al-tarbiyah*, whose salient objective is to provide a comprehensive education for Muslims and to curb jihad against political authority by Salafi-jihadi organizations, notably al-Qaeda.

Notes

1. For information on Sheikh al-Kibbi, see al-Bukhari's website, www.boukhary.net/ws/index.php/2013-01-26-07-06-55/2013-01-26-07-09-06 (accessed July 12, 2013).

2. See Qabbani's letter of attestation at www.boukhary.net/ws/images/tazkiat/Qabany.png (accessed July 12, 2013).

3. See letter of Grand Mufti ibn Baz dated May 2, 1998, which was addressed to Mufti of Lebanon Qabbani, available at www.boukhary.net/ws/images/tazkiat/IbnBaz.jpg (accessed July 12, 2013).

4. See Sheikh Kibbi's interview with Lebanese television station MTV on November 3, 2012.

5. A visit to the Bukhari Institute on November 12, 2012.

6. Dr. Sa'd al-Din ibn Muhammad al-Kibbi, *Ta'rif al-Bari'ah bi-Manhaj al-Madrasa al-Salafiyah: (Ahl al-Hadith wal-Sunna)* (Introduction of Devoutness [Godliness] through the Methodology of the Salafist School: (Partisans of Hadiths and Sunna) (Tripoli, Lebanon: The Center of Islamic Science Research, 2009), 5–6.

7. *Khawarij* literally means those who went out but actually connotes rebellion.

8. Al-Kibbi, *Ta'rif al-Bari'ah bi-Manhaj al-Madrasa al-Salafiyah*, 6–7.

9. Ibid., 12–13, 16.

10. Ibid., 18–21.

11. Ibid., 23.

12. Ibid.

13. Ibid., 28.

14. Ibid., 29.

15. Ibid., 29–30.

16. Ibid., 30.

17. Ibid.

18. Ibid., 31.

19. Ibid.

20. Ibid., 45–46

21. Ibid., 46.

22. Ibid., 46–47. Sheikh Kibbi frequently inserts Qur'anic verses and *hadiths* to support his logic.

23. The four imams are Abu Hanifa (Nu'man ibn Thabit), Malik ibn Anas ibn Malik, Muhammad ibn Idris al-Shafi'i, and Ahmad ibn Muhammad ibn Hanbal, who founded the four *madhabs*—Hanafi, Maliki, Shafi'i, and Hanbali, respectively.

24. Ibid., 50.

25. Ibid., 57–58.

26. Religion is the fifth necessity.

27. Sa'd al-Din ibn Muhammad al-Kibbi, *Ulama' al-Islam bayn Ahl al-Sunna wa Jama'at al-Takfir* (Muslim Religious Scholars [*Ulema*] between the Partisans of the Sunna and the Groups of Takfir) (Tripoli, Lebanon: Markaz al-Bahth al'Ilmi al-Islami, 2010), 10, and Sa'd al-Din Muhammad al-Kibbi, *Fiqh al-Taghyir bayna Ahl al-Sunna wa Ahl al-Ahwa'* (The Jurisprudence of Change between the Partisans of the Sunna and the Dissenters/Heretics) (Tripoli, Lebanon: Markaz al-Bahth al'Ilmi al-Islami, 2010), 17.

28. Kibbi, *Ulama' al-Islam bayn Ahl al-Sunna wa Jama'at al-Takfir*, 19–20.

29. Ibid., 4–7. See also Kibbi, *Fiqh al-Taghyir bayna Ahl al-Sunna wa Ahl al-Ahwa'*, 18–21.

30. Ibid. (both), 7–9, 17–18, respectively.

31. Sa'd al-Din ibn Muhammad al-Kibbi, *Dhawabit al-Takfir 'Inda Ahl-Sunna wal-Jama'a* (The Regulations [General Rules] of Excommunication for the Partisans of the Sunna and the Group) (Beirut: al-Maktab al-Islami, 1997), 10–11.

32. Kibbi, *Ulama' al-Islam bayn Ahl al-Sunna wa Jama'at al-Takfir*, 60.

33. Ibid., 60–61.

34. Ibid., 61.

35. Kibbi, *Dhawabit al-Takfir 'Inda Ahl al-Sunna wal-Jama'a*, 19–23.

36. Kibbi, *Fiqh al-Taghyir bayna Ahl al-Sunna wa Ahl al-Ahwa'*, 17.

37. Ibid., 18–20.

38. *Al-ta'lim wal-tarbiyah* implies a comprehensive meaning of education in Islam. Whereas *ta'lim* involves instructional and cognitive aspects of education, *tarbiyah* involves physical and emotional aspects of human growth (upbringing).

39. Kibbi, *Fiqh al-Taghyir bayna Ahl al-Sunna wa Ahl al-Ahwa'*, 22–23.

40. Kibbi, *Ta'rif al-Bari'ah bi-Manhaj al-Madrasa al-Salafiyah*, 71–72.

41. *Kufr bawah* include banning the teaching of Islam, destroying mosques, burning copies of Qur'an, and engaging in and promoting *shirk* (polytheism).

42. Kibbi, *Ta'rif al-Bari'ah bi-Manhaj al-Madrasa al-Salafiyah*, 73.

43. Ibid.

44. Kibbi, *Fiqh al-Taghyir bayna Ahl al-Sunna wa Ahl al-Ahwa'*, 40–41.

45. Ibid., 53.

46. Ibid., 62–64. One has to bear in mind that according to Sheikh Kibbi, only the ruler or Islamic state has the right to declare jihad.

47. Kibbi, *Fiqh al-Taghyir bayna Ahl al-Sunna wa Ahl al-Ahwa'*, 27.

48. Ibid., 28–30.

49. See Kibbi's interview with Lebanese TV station MTV, November 3, 2012.

Chapter Four

The Activist (Haraki) Salafi Ideology of Sheikh Zakariya 'Abd al-Razaq al-Masri

This chapter explores the *haraki* (activist) Salafi ideology of Sheikh Zakariya 'Abd al-Razaq al-Masri. Although he shares with the quietest school the basic creedal tenets of Salafism, Sheikh Masri's *haraki* ideology is formulated according to the *manhaj* (methodology) he considers best suited for applying the Prophetic model and implementing *da'wa* (call to Islam). On the one hand, his ideology is rooted in his theological view of mankind, which he divides into believers and unbelievers. On the other, his ideology is guided by the theological mission of uniting the Muslim community in the face of secularism and the adversarial atheistic attitude toward Islam. His creed, religio-political ideology, political program, and vision are formulated with the objective of defeating the unbelievers and safeguarding Muslim society on the individual and collective levels. In this respect, he ideologically justifies Islamic activism and strategies on the grounds of meeting the atheist-secularist challenges and threats posed to his vision of *tawhid al-ummah* (uniting the Muslim community), which is shaped according to the *manhaj* of the *al-salaf al-salih* (pious ancestors). Correspondingly, he justifies a temporary and utilitarian alliance with Christian infidels because the extent of their enmity to Islam is less than that of the atheist and Jewish infidels. This alliance is meant to transform the US-led aggression against Islam under the pretext of the war on terrorism into an "Islamic awakening–US campaign" against atheism, making it in reality an "Islamist-US campaign."[1] In other words, Sheikh Masri entertains a notion that Islamists should temporarily align themselves with Christians, mainly in United States, to combat atheism and Zionism. He devises a universal political program centering on the role of senior religious scholars as overseer of politics in the Muslim world. Relative to this political vision, and in line with his ideological reservation about Lebanon's plural society and confessional system, he instructs Muslims to pledge their allegiance to the country's Muslim religious authority, whereby Muslim engagement in politics would be more about cooperation with non-Muslims on national matters. At the same time, he prescribes Islamic legal rules, including punishments, to safeguard and promote Islamic values and principles. Though his philosophy of *takfir* (excommunication) and jihad is central to his vision of *tawhid al-ummah*, it is legally regulated regarding Muslims and unapologetically directed against non-Muslims. In other words, he, like Salafi jihadists, enjoins jihad against non-Muslim *kuffars* but, unlike Salafi jihadists, limits *takfir* only to Muslims and rulers who consciously renounce Islam. Contrary to conventional wisdom, *haraki* Salafism is born out of a fundamentalist universal outlook that sanctions violent and nonviolent engagement in politics, depending on what is most suitable to Salafism's universal missionary *da'wa*.

Creed and Ideology: The Building and Safeguarding of Islamic *Kayan* (Nature/Character)

Sheikh Zakariya 'Abd al-Razaq al-Masri perceives the Islamic creed as the means by which human beings come to recognize the invisible matters of the *arkan al-iman* (pillars of faith/belief), which were reported by the divine (true) message of God and therefore made immutable and were submitted to without doubt or hesitation. The pillars of faith include the belief in God, His angels, books, "the other day" (day of judgment), and divine destiny.[2] The pillars of faith, the pillars of Islam, and the performance of good deeds (beneficence) constitute the Islamic religion.[3] Whereas the purpose of faith involves the actions of the heart that endorse all that God revealed to Prophet Muhammad from commandments and messages, the purpose of Islam involves the actions of extremities (manifest action of human beings) that practically apply Islamic law.[4] Performance of good deeds involves loyalty in worshipping God alone in both heart and manifest action, whose intent also entails devotion to God so as to be accepted by Him as an act of worship.[5]

This definition of creed as related to Islam is reflected in God's *tawhid*, which Sheikh Masri, like Sheikh Sa'd al-Din al-Kibbi, divides into three categories: *tawhid al-rububiyah, tawhid al-uluhiyah,* and *tawhid al-asma' wal-sifat.* In fact, Sheikh Masri shares with Sheikh Kibbi the basic creedal principles of *tawhid. Tawhid al-rububiyah* (oneness of lordship) implies that God has the power of creation and to attribute any of these powers to other than Him constitutes *shirk* (polytheism). *Tawhid al-uluhiyah* (oneness of godship) implies that all forms of worship must be directed exclusively toward God, resulting in absolute obedience to Him. Any association in worship or worshipping other than God constitute *shirk.* And finally, *tawhid al-asma' wal-sifat* (oneness of the names and attributes) implies the depiction of God with perfect attributes and sublime names, as set forth in the revelation. Any reference of His names and attributes to metaphorical interpretation or anthropomorphism constitutes polytheism.[6]

Nevertheless, Sheikh Masri goes beyond the basic description of *tawhid* to subsume under its three categories, especially under *tawhid al-uluhiyah*, a program of action meant to construct and safeguard the *kayan* (nature/character) of the individual Muslim and the *jama'a* (group). Significantly, the purpose behind Sheikh Masri's program of action is paving the way for *tawhid al-ummah*, which he considers essential for protecting the *ummah* (Muslim community of believers) from the manifold challenges and threats besetting it. Sheikh Masri believes that since God is the creator of mankind, He alone deserves to have exclusive sovereignty or authority. Therefore, God's revelations have become the "guide" of mankind, whereupon no one but God has the authority to *amr wa nahi* (command and proscribe).[7] It follows from this that Sheikh Masri premises the *da'wa* to God's sovereignty as the basis of the relationship between God and mankind, expressed in mankind's total support of and absolute obedience to God's commandments and proscriptions. This is what Marsi also refers to as *tawhid al-uluhiya*.[8] In this respect, it is compulsory to place God and His messenger's commandments above all others and to remove all that violate God's rulings. Mankind, then, need to work to accomplish this within the context of *qudra wa istita'a* (ability and capacity).[9]

Evidently Sheikh Masri's concept of *hakimiyat Allah* (God's sovereignty), which is subsumed under *tawhid al-uluhiyah*, is in line both with that of Sayyid Qutb and with the *tawhid al-hakimiyah* of the Salafi jihadists. Sheikh Marsi, like Salafi jihadists, implicitly deems any government that does not apply God's rulings as un-Islamic. But he, unlike Salafi jihadists, does not anathematize these governments and make them legitimate targets of attack. Rather, he enjoins building and safeguarding the Islamic character as a steppingstone to *tawhid al-ummah*.

Correspondingly, he underscores building and safeguarding the individual and collective character of mankind as the mission of God's revelations, whose objective is to create a Muslim society harmoniously and strongly bonded together.[10] He emphasizes two factors to build the individual character. The first one involves believing in the pillars of faith, which entails (1) believing in God by means of believing in His lordship, godship, and His names and attributes, which, given the fact they are all based on the Qur'an and the Sunna, enlighten the heart and therefore clear-sightedness; (2) believing in His angels and their role in the different stages of mankind; (3) believing in the divine books revealed to the messengers that comprehensively treat the spirit of mankind; (4) believing in the messengers of God who were charged with informing the content of the books to mankind so that they can regulate their activity; (5) believing in the day of judgment, where human beings are judged on the basis of their good and bad actions; and 6) believing in *qadar* (divine destiny) that allows mankind to accept tragedy or joy with patience and humility and therefore enjoy God-inspired peace of mind.[11] Only in this way can the "diseases and moods" of the heart be treated so that human beings can become true worshippers of God and therefore suited to join Muslim society.

The second factor involves adhering to the pillars of Islam, whereby (1) *sha-hada* (testimony that there is no god but God and that Muhammad is His messenger) expresses the belief of the heart in the pillars of faith so that the human being can introduce his belonging to a particular faith, Islam; (2) *salat* (prayer) strengthens the link between the human being and his or her almighty, exalted God and purifies the heart; (3) *zakat* (almsgiving) cleanses the spirit of the human being from parsimony and stinginess so that he or she can partake in the welfare of Muslim society; (4) *sawm* (fasting) reinforces the stamina and determination of the human being to uphold what God has commanded and proscribed; and (5) *hajj* (pilgrimage) reinforces the feeling of brotherly faith that allows the human being to be part of the whole Islamic entity. Adhering to these pillars, according to Sheikh Masri, makes the individual Muslim a human being open to the Islamic group (*jama'a*) and ready to become a healthy cell in the Muslim body.[12]

Simultaneously, Sheikh Masri emphasizes four factors that stem from *shari'a* (Islamic law) to build the character of the *jama'a*. First, he enjoins building the Muslim family, including regulating the relationship between the husband and wife, according to Islamic law. He refers to the Qur'anic Surat (al-Nisa': 34) to uphold his view that men should be the "protectors and maintainers" of women in order to prevent the collapse of the family.[13] He also instructs that children must respect their parents and each other. Likewise, parents should take care of their children and properly guide them. Second, he instructs good neighborly relations, marked by good deeds. Third, he enjoins protecting and visiting relatives, as long as they have not renounced God, in order to prevent wrongdoers from seducing them into wickedness. Finally, he enjoins forging an all-inclusive brotherly Islamic entity according to God's rulings, which specified the relationship among Muslims at the uppermost and foundational levels of society. Believers should obey the ruler in all but violations, and the ruler has to take care of the ruled and not mistreat them. Notwithstanding the fact that the ruled should oppose the multiplicity of rule, the ruled must support and love each other, for Muslims are brothers.

Consequently, by building the individual and collective character of Muslim society, Muslim society becomes strong and united, unimpeded by linguistic, ethnic, geographic, class or whatever discrimination standing in the face of their loyalty to each other.[14]

No less significant, inasmuch as Sheikh Marsi underscores the building of the individual and collective character of Muslim society, he advocates its safeguarding. He emphasizes safeguarding the Muslim individual and society internally and externally. On the internal level, he emphasizes two factors. The first involves applying the Islamic principle of commanding good and forbidding wrong, "whereby 'good' is all that God commanded and 'wrong' is all that God proscribed."[15] The application of this principle, according to Sheikh Masri, protects Muslim society from disintegration and fragmentation. He cites Qur'anic Surat (al-'Imran: 110) to bolster his claim. An excerpt of Surat reads: "Ye are the best of peoples, evolved from mankind. Enjoining what is right, forbidding what is wrong, and believing in Allah." This principle also concerns *taghyir* (changing/transforming) wrongdoers and deviants, whereby change has degrees in importance. The highest is "change by the hand" by those who have the authority, such as the ruler, father, or school director, which enables them to bring about change without incurring *fitna* (strife). Next comes "change by the tongue" by those who are able to illustrate the Qur'an and the evidence of Islam. And finally, there is "change by the heart," which implies staying away from the wrongdoer so that his or her wrong does not in time become in itself a "good."[16]

Sheikh Masri, like many Salafists, also adheres to the Islamic creedal principle *al-wala' wal-Bara'* (confessing loyalty to Muslims and disavowal of non-Muslims). He believes that *al-wala'* (loyalty) depends on loving and supporting Muslim believers, and therefore a believer must not love or support an unbeliever (*kafir*) over a believer. If a believer loves or supports a *kafir* over a believer, then he or she is a hypocrite. However, Sheikh Masri, unlike Salafi jihadists, does not excommunicate hypocrites, believing that God would harshly punish them.[17] Adhering to this principle, according to Sheikh Masri, not only strengthens the bond among Muslims and therefore protects Muslim society but also helps distinguish a believer from an unbeliever.

The other factor involves applying *shari'a* (Islamic law) penalties, which are divided into *hudud*, *qasas*, and *ta'zir*. *Hudud* penalties are applied when the crimes violate public welfare and are punishable by preestablished sentences cited in the Qur'an. They are serious crimes, some of whose preestablished sentences cannot be reduced by a judge or a ruler. Theft is punishable by cutting off the hand of the thief. Adultery is punishable in two ways. If the adulterer is not married, then the penalty is a hundred lashes and one year in prison. If the adulterer is married, then the penalty is a hundred lashes and death by stoning, all carried out in public. Defamation of the honor of either a male or female, mainly through false accusation of adultery or fornication, is punishable by eighty lashes, carried out in public. Highway robbery is punishable by a sentence proportionate to the crime. Although no specific penalties are mentioned, penalties take the form of the offense. For example, if in the act of robbery the victim is killed, then the offender faces a death sentence. Alcohol-drinking is punishable by eighty lashes. And finally, renunciation of the faith is punishable by death.[18]

Qasas penalties are retribution punishments taking the same form as the offense. For example, an offense of murder entails a death sentence to the offender. Sentences of offenses against human life, short of murder, can be commuted by a judge or a ruler. Finally, *ta'zir* penalties are applied to offenses equivalent to misdemeanors. Broadly speaking, the offender has disobeyed God's law and word. Common *ta'zir* crimes include bribery and usury. *Ta'zir* punishments are not specified in the Qur'an and vary according to the gravity of the crime, circumstances, and place.[19]

On the external level, Muslim society can be protected by *da'wa* and jihad in the path of almighty Allah. According to Sheikh Masri, *da'wa* entails introducing Islam to non-Muslims by religious scholars and *du'at*, those who propagate Islam and are well versed in the religion. Sheikh Masri stresses the noble act of *da'wa* by referring to the messengers of God whose mission had been *da'wa*. Moreover, he emphasizes *da'wa* as a call from God to mankind to follow the right path, which will lead to paradise.[20] He also instructs *da'wa* among Muslims, whose purpose is to remind them of what they know. He premises *da'wa* among Muslims on the Islamic principle of "commanding right and forbidding wrong." Sheikh Masri believes that *da'wa* protects Muslim society by confronting the ideas and beliefs of non-Muslims before their introduction into society. He centers his belief in the axiomatic notion that offensive actions are the best defense.[21]

The other external factor Sheikh Marsi advocates to protect the Muslim community is "jihad in the path of Allah." He defines jihad as "the exercise of strength and ability in confronting the *kuffars* (infidels) to spread the religion of God the almighty."[22] He believes that

God has legitimized jihad in order to orient the inherent capacity of mankind in the direction of achieving higher and munificent objectives by transforming this capacity into a propagation of this religion [Islam] to other societies. Human beings, like other creatures, once feeling powerful, seek to impose their creedal, moral, or ethical orientation on others. If that powerful human being is not guided by the revelation of almighty God who orders justice and beneficence, then he/she will use this political, economic, or military power to oppress others and spread his principles among them. This is why God has legitimized jihad for His cause to end the aggressions of those with power and authority against their peoples and against those who are calling them to God. Those with power and authority do so to interdict the arrival of the religion's benevolence to the general public under them.[23]

Sheikh Masri adds that the "purpose of confronting the *kuffars* is to fight them by money, tongue, and spearheads."[24] He bolsters his view by emphasizing that jihad is sanctioned by the Qur'an [Surat al-Saff: 10 and 11] and the *hadith*. Qur'anic Surat [al-Saff: 11] reads: "That ye believe in Allah and His messenger, and that ye strive (your utmost) [*tujahidun*] in the cause of Allah, with your wealth and your persons: That will be best for you if ye but knew." The *hadith* that Sheikh Masri uses in support of his view reads: "The head of the matter [religion] is Islam, its pillar is prayer, and its highest peak is jihad for Allah's cause."[25]

Correspondingly, Sheikh Masri ranks jihad into two categories: intellectual confrontation and military confrontation. The intellectual confrontation entails introducing Islam, its creed, and *shari'a* to non-Muslims and then calling them to Islam. This, according to Sheikh Marsi, must be done by Muslims who are well versed in the creed and laws of Islam, while bearing in mind that the call to Islam should not be compulsory. Nevertheless, if the *kuffars* are barred from the *da'wa*, then the next step will be military confrontation. It follows from this that the mission of this offensive jihad is to remove the leaders of *kuffars* from power so that their peoples can voluntarily and freely decide whether or not to respond to *da'wa* and submit to God.

Taking all this into consideration it becomes clear that Sheikh Masri, like Sayyid Qutb and Salafi jihadists, does not look at jihad as only a defensive strategy. One could safely argue that Sheikh Masri has theologically justified his axiom that the best defense is offensive jihad. This is supported by his view, unlike that of Sa'd al-Din al-Kibbi, that al-Qaeda is an Islamist organization seeking to establish an Islamic state that includes all Muslim countries and therefore is neither a *takfiri* group nor a terrorist organization.[26] However, this does not mean that Sheikh Masri does not underscore defensive jihad. In fact, given the weak state of the Muslim world, defensive jihad is often called upon to protect the realm of Islam. Sheikh Masri views defensive jihad as a legal obligation.[27] Significantly, he adopts a position toward the United States similar to that of the Salafi jihadists. He blames the United States for its unequivocal support of Israel at the expense of the Palestinians and severely censures Washington's policies and actions in Afghanistan, Iraq, Kashmir, Bosnia, and Chechnya, among other places in the Muslim world. He concludes that the United States, under the pretext of the war on terrorism, aims at controlling the wealth of the *ummah* because it does not have enough resources to support its huge industrial development. Therefore, he perceives the struggle between the United States and its allies on one side, and the Islamic awakening as represented by Islamist organizations and groups and Islamists on the other, as a civilizational, social, economic, moral, ethical, and ideological struggle. It is within this context that Sheikh Masri considers the "martyrdom, jihadi operations" against the United States as self-defense operations, sanctioned by all divine revelations.[28]

In sum, Sheikh Masri's vision centers on the *tawhid* of the *ummah* by building and safeguarding Muslim society on the individual and collective levels. He theologically justifies his vision by elaborating and subsuming the concept of *hakimiyat Allah* under the creedal tenet of *tawhid al-uluhiyah*, whereby God's rulings as set forth in the Qur'an and the Sunna form the legal and moral foundation of Muslim society. Though he shares with Sheikh Kibbi the basic Salafi creedal principles, his ideological elaboration of the concept and means that underpin building and safeguarding Muslim society are more in line with radical Islamists and Salafi jihadists. But, he, unlike them, does not use his elaborate theological principle of *tawhid al-uluhiyah* to excoriate Muslim rulers who don't make God's revelation the foundation of their governments. Conversely, he, in much the same vein as Salafi jihadists, supports defensive and offensive jihad, including jihadi operations against what he considers aggressor states, at the forefront of which is the United States. Not surprisingly, his vision of *tawhid al-ummah* has developed as both a response to and growth of his theological and sociopolitical outlook that believers are fighting a fateful battle against unbelievers.

Salafists and Non-Muslims: The Fateful Battle between Belief and Unbelief

Sheikh Masri departs from the theological point that the Qur'an is the most compassionate, unadulterated, complete, timeless, final revelation of God. In fact, he believes that "the religion of Islam is the only relied-upon revelation accepted by almighty God."[29] He affirms that Islam is the religion of God and that whoever follows a different religion will not be accepted by God and therefore will be a loser in the hereafter.[30] He cites the Qur'anic verses [Surat al-'Imran: 18 and 85] to bolster his claim.[31] Correspondingly, he believes that "no one has the right to choose *kufr* (unbelief) over faith, and atheism over *tawhid*; and therefore one needs to be a believer in the religion of Muhammad, the seal of prophets and messengers, whose message has completed the previous divine revelations."[32] Otherwise, he or she must be fought until he or she becomes a believer or dies. He supports this notion by citing a common missionary propagandist *hadith* referred to by Imam Bukhari (and Imam Muslim), in which prophet Muhammad said: "I have been ordered to kill the people until they testify that there is no god except Allah, and that Muhammad is the Messenger of Allah, and they establish prayer and pay the *zakat*. If they do that, their blood and wealth are protected from me save by the rights of Islam. Their reckoning will be with Allah."[33] It is out of this missionary philosophy that, according to Sheikh Masri, the duty of jihad was born to raise the flag of Islam and establish the *hukm* (rule) of God on earth. At the same time, he cautions that only the Islamic ruler has the right to declare jihad unless it is a matter of self-defense.[34]

This is the theological background against which Sheikh Masri divides mankind into two categories: believers and *kuffars* (unbelievers). Broadly speaking, he considers this Manichaean classification, including the ascription of dishonorable epithets to unbelievers, as essential to protect and expand the realm of Islam. Fundamentally, it is, however, the protection and expansion of the realm of Islam that will decide what Sheikh Masri considers the fateful battle between believers and *kuffars*. As such, he concerns himself not only with the ideological aspect of this battle but also with the pursuit of appropriate legal methods and policies that will help resolve the battle in favor of believers. Consequently he elaborates a theological (fundamentalist) scheme, based on what he considers a sober reading and analysis of the Muslim and *kafir* worlds, addressing the ways by which *kuffars* are either brought to Islam or fought.[35]

Sheikh Masri begins by classifying the members of Islam in the interest of increasing and reinforcing the number and unity of believers respectively and therefore the unity and strength of the Muslims. In other words, classification of members of Islam helps change "weak" Muslims into strong devout Muslims, thereby strengthening Islam and believers. He classifies membership in Islam into three categories: Muslims, believers, and hypocrites. First, he defines Muslims as those who testify to the two testimonies (*shahadatayn*): There is no god but God, and Muhammad is His messenger. But these Muslims have varying degrees in adhering to the legal and practical rulings (laws) of Islam, consequent upon the strength or weakness of their faith. Therefore, they can be defined by their devoutness, disobedience, or sinfulness. Those who are devout adhere to the practical laws of Islam, such as performing religious duties and avoiding legal prohibitions. Devout Muslims will be saved from hell and go to paradise if their devoutness is coupled with their true faith. Testimonies by devout Muslims are encouraged and accepted in the Islamic justice system, and devout Muslims should be promoted as exemplary guides to others.[36]

Next, disobedient Muslims are those who adhere to the legal and practical laws of Islam but commit *saghair* (minor prohibitions). For example, a disobedient Muslim does not charge usury, yet he engages in some sort of deceit in his trade. He does not fornicate, yet he lets his eye roam indecently. He is depicted as disobedient so as to encourage him to become devout and to discourage others from walking in his footsteps. Finally, sinful or dissolute Muslims are those who don't abide by all five pillars of Islam, or the obligatory rules, and commit some *kabair al-munhiyat* (serious prohibitions or major sins).[37] Consequently, sinful Muslims are subject to *hudud* or *ta'zir* penalties, depending on the gravity of violation/sin, so as to deter them from repeating their sins and to discourage others from emulating them.[38] For example, renunciation of Islam is punishable by the *hudud* death penalty.

Second, he describes believers as those who believe in Prophet Muhammad and all that was esoterically and exoterically transmitted to him by God. Since belief is an act of the heart, believers adhere to the pillars of faith as revealed to Prophet Muhammad by the angel Gabriel.[39] As such, belief (faith) is the foundation of Islam. Finally, he describes hypocrites as those who embrace *kufr* in their heart but carry out visible actions in conformity with Islam. Hypocrites dissemble in order to profit morally or materially. Sheikh Masri considers hypocrites as the most dangerous members of Islam because it is hardly possible to truly know them. It goes without saying that belonging to Islam is voluntary, whereas disavowing Islam incurs the death penalty.

Conversely, Sheikh Masri classifies non-Muslims into two groups: partisans of divine revelations, known also as people of the Book, and partisans of temporal schools. People of the Book, who are the recipient of divine revelations, are divided into three categories: Jews, Christians, and Zoroastrians. Zoroastrians, unlike Christians and Jews, cannot be considered *dhimmi* (those protected within the realm of Islam if they pay a head tax [*jizya*]), for there is no consensus among the *ulema* as to whether the Zoroastrians are the recipient of a divine book. Nevertheless, the members of these three revelations fall into three conditions. The first relates to the Jews and Christians who submit to the authority of the Muslim ruler and therefore can live as protected people among Muslims. They are called *ahl al-dhimma* (partisans of the protected), and the *'aqd al-dhimma* (protection covenant) concluded with them is fundamentally eternal insofar they do not violate it. Broadly speaking, the covenant with them stipulates that they have to pay the head tax, not defame the Prophet and Islam, not fornicate with or marry a Muslim woman, and not engage in highway robbery. These stipulations, according to Sheikh Masri, are legitimized by God so that *ahl al-dhimmi* can be guided by the righteous ways of Muslims and consequently straighten their deviant ways, which had been caused by their doctored revelatory texts.[40]

The second condition relates to the *kuffars* with whom Muslim authorities temporarily contract an agreement, whose purpose is to serve the welfare of the general public. They include those who enter Muslim countries on an official visa. Muslims can neither deceive nor harm them as long as they do not violate their contract. The third condition relates to those with whom Muslim authorities have no agreement, and therefore they do not submit to Muslim rule. They are called combatant *kuffars*. Muslims should fight them until they submit to the rulings of Islam and the Muslim ruler.[41]

With regard to partisans of temporal schools, Sheikh Masri divides them into two main groups: polytheists and atheists. *Mushrikun* (polytheists) associate worshipping others with God and associate others with God's creation, authority, and revelations. According to Sheikh Masri, even if polytheists believe that there is a God who created this universe, their belief remains false because they associated others in godship and lordship.[42] Despite all proofs about monotheism, polytheists remain at a distance from the truth on account of their flawed intellect and corrupt senses. Correspondingly, Sheikh Masri believes that these polytheists "are of no more use than being fuel for hell."[43] On the other hand, atheists are those who have fundamentally denied the presence of God. They believe in neither a creator nor a revelation. They confine their belief to materialism. They are called communists in the present era. Communism had been represented by the Soviet Union, which collapsed under the hammers of the people's God-given constitution. It is represented now by China, which will have a prominent role in influencing the international political equations. Ominously, Sheikh Masri believes that China has set itself on a collision course with its main rival, the United States. Moreover, he shares an apocalyptic view that the forthcoming ideological world war, in which nuclear and other nonconventional weapons are used, would be totally destructive.[44]

He concludes that polytheists and atheists have no place in Muslim society, even if they pay the head tax. They are like contagious deadly diseases that need to be excised. At the same time, he supports the notion that the recipients of divine revelations should forge an alliance to eliminate the polytheists and atheists. Herein lies the reason behind Sheikh Masri's classification of both believers and *kuffars*. True members of the Muslim faith vary according to devoutness, disobedience, and sinfulness, yet they are all brothers in Islam and have the opportunity to straighten their ways. This can only strengthen the believers and therefore Muslim society in confronting the unbelievers. Yet Sheikh Masri believes that it behooves Muslim society to ally itself with certain *kuffars* from the people of the Book to confront the polytheists and atheists. He believes that *kuffars* have varying degrees of enmity toward Islam and that therefore it is in the general interest of Muslim society to work with those *kuffars* whose enmity to Islam is less than others. He justifies this alliance on the ground that these *kuffars* are after all the recipient of divine revelations and that Muslim society needs all the help it can get to confront the powerful machinations of the polytheists and atheists.[45] In other words, Muslim society has to use all the means possible within its reach to decide the fateful battle against unbelief and consequently establish God's rulings on earth.

No less significant, Sheikh Masri also classifies the *kuffars* from the people of the Book with whom Muslim society can forge an alliance. Whereas he locates the Jews behind the polytheists and atheists as the most formidable enemies of Islam, he considers Christians in all their different denominations as less adversarial to Islam. He even revives and repackages dormant and virulent anti-Semitic charges, spanning the gamut from "killers of Christ" to "the most deceitful of mankind," in order to wrap the Jews with a dark and heavy mantle of *kufr*. This salient anti-Semitism in his discourse is not inseparable from Israel, which he considers as an illegitimate entity.[46] Nevertheless, he maintains his position that although Muslim society should favor concluding an alliance with Christians over Jews, Muslims could conclude an alliance with some Jews but never with polytheists and atheists. This alliance in no uncertain ways implies affecting the truth of Islam or conceding certain loyalty to the *kuffar* allies. In fact, Sheikh Masri stresses that this alliance with *kuffars* is more of a *muhadana* (truce) than a *mudahana* (concession). He defines *mudahana* as a concession of a certain truth made by Muslims to satisfy some demands by *kuffars*, something Muslims will never do. On the other hand, he defines *muhadana* as a truce with the *kuffars* meant to defer the confrontation with them until the time is right. He adds that a truce is only an agreement made by two ideological, essentially different parties to confront a common political or military threat, while at the same time maintaining their own separate entities.

It is this dichotomous, fundamentalist view of mankind, setting believers against unbelievers, together with unbelievers' theological classification in relation to Islam's missionary duty, that informs Sheikh Masri's political outlook and political program.

Al-Masri's Worldview: Atheism, Secularism and the Unity of the *Ummah*

Sheikh Masri considers secularism a new Western convention intended to separate religion from political authority for some and to separate religion from public life for others. He also deems that secular extremism has led some to remove religion from the life of the individual, ban its practice, and malign its principles, creeds, and ethics.[47] Secularism emerged in Europe as a response to the repression of the Christian church, whose leaders sought to maintain their control of the state. They oppressed people and fought development and modernity, all in the name of religion. Striking root in France following the French Revolution, the phenomenon of secularism soon spread across Europe and Russia before arriving on the shores of Egypt in the late nineteenth century. Thanks to Western colonialism, secularism expanded to North Africa and the Levant, where secular parties, such as the Baʿth Party and the Syrian Social Nationalist Party, reinforced this Western invention.[48]

Before long, secularism, according to Sheikh Masri, permeated Arab society partly on account of the media and educational curricula, partly on account of confining religion to mosques, and partly on account of severing religion from the economy, politics, and the legal system. Even religious supervision of personal status laws has been affected by Western laws. Sheikh Masri concludes that colonialism has imposed secularism on the Muslim world, with the result that it has virtually dominated Muslim society by controlling its ideology, economy, bureaucracy, and politics. This domination has continued unabated with Israel's occupation of Palestine and the American occupation of Afghanistan in 2001 and Iraq in 2003. Correspondingly, Sheikh Masri believes that Muslims have the right to intellectually and militarily resist this domination.[49]

Significantly, secularism has developed into an Oriental and Western secularism. The prominent principles of Oriental secularism are denying the existence of almighty God and believing in authority within the purview of the human intellect. Similarly, the prominent principle of Western secularism revolves around national interest and individual self-interest, which constitute the pillars of Western politics, economy, society, and military. Interest precedes all other considerations, including morality and ethics. Western society has no qualms committing all sorts of aggression if its interest is at stake. Not surprisingly, Western and Oriental secularism, under the slogan the end justifies the means, work together to destroy the family, wreck moral values, and spread sexual anarchy, in Sheikh Masri's view.[50]

But according to Sheikh Masri, what the two forms of secularism prominently share is combating Islam by discrediting its creedal beliefs, contesting its legal laws, disfiguring its history, and undermining its values. And the more extreme secularists are, the more they are inimical to religion. In this respect, although Sheikh Masri believes that secularism in both its variants seeks to affect the Muslim personality in order to control it, he makes a stark but nuanced distinction in the degree of enmity and threat that Oriental and Western secularisms pose to Muslim society. He believes that atheism has emerged out of oriental secularism as a response to the cruelty of the "men of the oriental church," a cruelty that exceeded that of the "men of the Western Church."[51] Soon enough, atheism found its political expression in the former Soviet Union and China. Since atheism espoused the greatest inimical attitude toward Islam, Oriental secularism, by extension, posed the most serious threat to Muslim society.

Moreover, Sheikh Masri adds, when the Soviet Union collapsed as a result of both its clash with its people, in particular the Muslims, and its principles that contradicted the harmonious relationship between human instinct and divine religion, Western secularists have tried to reduce the enormity of the confrontation between secularism and human instinct (*fitra*). They have focused on separating religion from political authority without separating religion from public life, emphasizing that secularism does not contradict religion. A person can be both secular and a Christian or Muslim. This logic, according to Sheikh Masri, roundly conflicts with Islam, for the religion obligates the Muslim to submit to God's rulings in all aspects of human life, be they social, political, economic, or judicial.[52] No less significant, Islam, unlike Christianity, promotes science and modernity insofar they serve mankind, as well as encourages commerce, industry, agriculture, among other things, to help mankind build earth. Did not God command mankind to build earth in His Qur'anic Surat [Hud: 61]?[53] On the other hand, what heals the human spirit other than the divine relations? Therefore, secularism has no place in the intellect of the *ummah*, and secularism constitutes *kufr* of God and His blessings.[54]

As a result, secularism has caused the struggle between the Muslim peoples and their governments, which, according to Sheikh Masri, has been reflected by both a security struggle with the internal agents of the secular enemy in the Muslim world and a military struggle with the secular enemy and his agents on Muslim soil. Sheikh Masri cites the struggle between the Syrian regime and the Muslim Brotherhood in the 1980s and the struggle between the Algerian regime and the Islamic Front as ideal examples of the security struggle. He does not hide his doctrinal and political opposition to the Syrian regime. He has pejoratively called it the "Nusayri Socialist Ba'thist" regime of Hafiz al-Asad, in reference to Asad belonging to the heterodox Alawi sect, which had been known until the early twentieth century as the Nusayri sect.[55] By underscoring the doctrinal and intellectual conflict between the secular Syrian regime and the Islamist organization, he luridly details the gory cruelty with which the Syrian regime clamped down on Islamists and their supporters. This opposition toward the Syrian regime has only intensified following the beginning of the Syrian rebellion in March 2011. Sheikh Masri has been vocal in condemning the Syrian regime and active in organizing protests against the Syrian crackdown on protestors. His inflammatory sermons against the Syrian regime, delivered from the pulpit of his Hamza mosque in Tripoli, have become a rallying cry for scores of Salafists and Sunni Muslims in northern Lebanon (see chapter 6).[56] In fact, no sooner had the rebellion begun than Sheikh Masri's mosque became a rallying ground for anti-Syrian and anti-Iranian regime protests. He has railed against Iran for supporting the Syrian regime, accusing Tehran of seeking "to establish a

Persian state in Arab lands and trying to sabotage national unity."[57] Particularly he accused the Syrian regime of being an agent of colonialism and a proponent of secularism. In July 2011, during an anti-Syrian regime demonstration, Sheikh Masri declared that "all communities in Syria and other Arab and Muslim countries need to stand in the face of colonial racism."[58]

Similarly, he has accused Washington, Moscow, and Jerusalem and their agents in the Muslim world of waging a war against the Islamic resistance on Muslim soil. He accused the United States of invading Afghanistan and Iraq in order to put in power secular collaborators and to prevent the founding of Islamic rule there. In this respect, he has supported the Islamic insurgency against American forces in Iraq, claiming that the Iraqi resistance has sought to establish Islamic rule in conformity with the correct Islamic principles, which would be applied to non-Muslims within the context of righteousness and justice.[59]

Given the security and military struggle waged by the secular powers against the Muslim world, Sheikh Masri insists that division among Muslims is legally proscribed. He essentially sees that it has become an obligation for Muslim scholars and intellectuals to formulate, in the shadow of Muslim awakening, a clear political outlook regarding how to deal with the present reality.[60] It is in response to this imperative challenge that Sheikh Masri premises his political vision on what he considers Islam's perception of mankind and its classification (see above). He believes that a change in international political alliances and slogans is necessary to formulate a winning strategy for the Muslim world. He strategizes that "an alliance between the believers and the Western secularists under the slogan of confronting atheism would strengthen Muslims and Islam."[61] He explains that this alliance would obviate Muslims from confronting both Oriental and Western secularism and prevent them from uniting into a single front, thereby provoking despair among Muslims given their present weakness. This new alliance would change the ongoing Western confrontation with the Muslim world, which has been fed by international Zionism and atheist communism, into an alliance between the West and the Muslim awakening against Zionism and Oriental secularism. Whereas the ongoing confrontation is taking place under the slogan of the war on terrorism, the new confrontation would take place under the slogan of the struggle against atheism.[62]

Simultaneously, Sheikh Masri, at one and the same time, cautions that this alliance would come to pass only after the Muslim awakening brings about Muslim unity. Only then, he theologically affirms, as Prophet Muhammad indicated, would the confrontation with Zionism and Oriental secularism take place.[63] He cites a *hadith* by Prophet Muhammad (referred to by Sheikh Abu Daoud) in which the Prophet said, "You [Muslims] will reconcile the *Rum* [Christians] and then fight an enemy behind you." He also refers to a Qur'anic verse and *hadith* in whose interpretation he tries to show that God has preordained the alliance between the Muslims and the Christians against their mutual enemy: the Oriental seculars, represented now by China.[64] Interestingly enough, Sheikh Masri believes that the onset of the battle will take place once China's resources are depleted, whereupon Beijing sends its troops overseas to secure its needed resources, especially from the Middle East. Meanwhile, the United States, influenced by the Muslim awakening, will find that its national interest lies with the Muslim world and not with Israel. This is the strategic battle between the Muslim and Christian societies on one side, and the atheist and Zionist societies on the other, whereupon neither Muslims nor Christians should allow the Zionists to disrupt the equation of the battle.[65] Herein Sheikh Masri reveals again his antagonism toward both Syria and Iran. He cautions that Zionists and their atheist allies would try to disrupt the strategic battle from within the Muslim world by using Iran and Syria, which have been the covert enemies of the *ummah*. Iran and Syria have been deceiving Muslims by their artful dissimulation of Islamic and Arabic slogans.[66]

Sheikh Masri concludes that this strategic battle, whose contours are legally (on the basis of the Qur'an and *hadith*) set in sharp relief, is none other than a jihad in the path of God, in which death is rightfully and truthfully a martyrdom for Allah's cause.[67] What follows and stems from Sheikh Masri's apocalyptic worldview is his political program regarding confessional Lebanon and Muslim society.

Salafism, *Tawhid al-Ummah*, and the Lebanese State

No doubt, Sheikh Masri's aspiration of uniting the *ummah* and imposing God's revelation as the foundation of its rule clashes with the reality of Lebanon as a confessional state comprising eighteen religious communities. No less problematic is Sheikh Masri's theological rejection of temporal rule in his quasi-democratic country of birth, whose president is a Christian.[68] Apparently this poses a conundrum for Sheikh Masri, who believes that Islam comprehensively covers all aspects of life including politics and who rejects the legitimacy of secular states. Yet he does not support rebellion against the ruler, in this instance a *kafir* Lebanese regime. Nor does he fully support the implementation of his theological and actionable concept of *tawhid al-uluhiyah*, which is clearly at odds with Lebanon's reality. Nor is this to say that his upbringing in Lebanon among non-Muslims has affected his creed and beliefs. Some think that it is his long view, coupled with the Islamic precepts of patience and endurance, that define his approach to Lebanese society and politics, while others assume that it is his experience as a former member of the Islamic Association and a close associate of

Fathi Yakan that tempers his approach to politics. Whatever is the case, Sheikh Masri has adopted an original approach to politics in Lebanon, deriving from his overall political program whose objective is Muslim unity. This approach has neither negated his creed nor confined him to the politicized camp of the Islamic Association nor alienated him from the Sunni major political camp, led by the Future Movement. One could argue that it is his commitment to his creed, together with his lack of political experience and/or political legacy, that have thus far defined his approach to politics.

As already mentioned, Sheikh Masri's major objective is to help bring about the unity of the *ummah*, or what he calls *tawhid al-ummah*. This rests on two pillars. The first concerns *da'wa* to loyalty to God (*hakimiyat Allah*) under *tawhid al-uluhiyah*, whereby mankind not only worships God alone but also submits to his creedal and legal rulings. The other concerns *da'wa* to the unity of loyalty to God among those who share an ideological affinity to God, His revelation, and His messenger Muhammad. By loving and championing God and His messenger, this unity at the leadership and popular levels would mold Muslims into one active body in the unity of loyalty to God. Similarly Muslims can neither be a body without a head nor a body broken in parts nor a body with multiple heads.[69]

It is from this theological foundation that Sheikh Masri translates his vision of *tawhid al-ummah* into a political program applicable to both the whole Muslim society and individual states, in this instance Lebanon. The outline of the program revolves around two stages: uniting Sunnis and uniting Sunnis and Shi'ites. The unity of Sunnis must be effected internally on the local level and externally on the international level. Uniting Sunnis on the internal level involves taking several measures. First, all parties, movements, groups, and Islamic dignitaries should be united behind one *marja'* [religious authority/reference to follow), represented by *al-Ifta' fi al-balad* (official religious office for research and religious edicts (*fatwas*) under the supervision of a grand mufti]. This is vital because (1) the mufti is a religious scholar capable of deducing juridical rulings from *shari'a* to address important political, economic, social, and intellectual developments; (2) the *ifta'* is a recognized official institution whose objective is not to replace governments but to improve conditions inasmuch as possible under governmental supervision, in conformity with the political, social, economic, moral, military, and educational teachings of the *shari'a*; (3) the *ifta'* has broad legal powers to establish religious institutions and supervise the religious orientation of private and public schools and mosques; (4) the *ifta'* has the authority to monitor the revenues and expenses of Islamic parties, institutions, and associations so that the sources of revenues and expenditures can be known, all in the interest of total transparency; (5) the mufti has no particular intellectual orientation and stands at an equal distance from all parties and Muslims, thereby breaking the psychological barrier of rivalry, hatred, and suspicion among and between Muslim parties and individuals; and (6) Muslims and Muslim parties and groups are loyal to *ifta'*.[70]

It is on the basis of the last condition that Sheikh Masri outlines his political program regarding Lebanon, including whether or not Muslims should participate in politics. He emphasizes that Muslim loyalty to the *ifta'* in confessional Lebanon obviates Muslim loyalty to the non-Muslim president. Consequently, since Muslim loyalty to *'ifta'* is the highest *marja'* for Muslims, governmental participation becomes permitted. Participation in politics develops into cooperation with others over administering the common matters of the state. Otherwise, Muslim loyalty would be to *kuffars* and secularists, as a result of which Muslim existence would weaken and Muslim rights would be undermined, save the fact that non-Muslims would impose their hegemony over Muslims.[71] Though Sheikh Masri, unlike Fathi Yakan, does not elaborate in painstaking details his political program, he is clearly at one with Fathi Yakan in supporting Muslim participation in Lebanese politics on the grounds of helping Muslims and preventing Christians (and Shi'ites) from imposing their hegemony over Sunni Muslims.

Regarding uniting Sunnis on the international level, Sheikh Masri advances a program of three steps, all meant to strengthen the *ummah* and prevent aggression against it. He proposes establishing an international *'ifta'* council, which includes muftis from all Muslim countries. These muftis would elect a grand mufti who would become the *marja'* and spokesperson of all Muslims in the world. Next, the international grand mufti would form a consultative council, which includes muftis from Muslim countries. This council would be charged in establishing a system dealing with the method by which questions from the *ummah* are presented so that decisions about them can be determined and adhered to. Finally, the international *ifta'* council would establish follow-up committees both to supervise the flow of work and to make sure decisions taken in the councils are implemented in their respective countries and educational and pedagogical committees charged with unifying religious instruction in light of recommendations submitted by local legal *ifta'* committees to the international *'ifta'* council.[72]

With respect to the second pillar of *tawhid al-ummah* that entails uniting Sunnis and Shi'ites, Sheikh Masri recommends that the Shi'ites unite their *marja'*. Once this is accomplished, Sheikh Masri proposes establishing an open forum bringing together representatives from both Sunni and Shi'a *marjas*, who would be charged with establishing creedal and legislative/legal committees. Made up of senior religious scholars from both sects, the creedal committee would examine and specify conditions upon which basis the creedal principles of the *ummah* would be united. In much the same vein, the legal committee would examine and specify conditions according to which legal issues are decided on the basis of the Qur'an and the Sunna and regulations over what matters the two sects can and cannot disagree upon.[73]

Once *tawhid al-ummah* is accomplished, the *ummah* would become like one body in which all its organs work in harmony. This would strengthen Muslim society and uplift it in righteousness and dignity, for it has acted on God's commands. Significantly, Sheikh Masri advises that if the unity between Sunnis and Shi'ites is not concluded, then efforts must continue toward their unity in light of the higher interest of the *ummah* as related to the Qur'an and the Sunna and to prevent the enemies of Islam from exploiting this division.[74]

Clearly, Sheikh Masri's attitude toward Shi'ites does not apply to the Iranian and Syrian regimes. As shown above, he has viscerally opposed both regimes, even before the Syrian rebellion. This opposition has dramatically intensified in tone and protests in the wake of the Syrian rebellion. He has drawn a common thread linking the Iranian regime with China's communism and atheism. In a statement posted on his Facebook page on February 8, 2013, he wrote, "Communist China conceals its defective doctrine in the mantle of the Iranian republic; and Safavid Iran hides its wicked ideology in the mantle of Islamic unity when it enters Arab countries."[75] He has vilified the Iranian regime for supporting Hezbollah's military activities in Syria against the opposition. On May 18, he stated, "The Iranian compass has taken Hezbollah to Homs instead of Jerusalem, where are your minds you Shi'ites."[76] He has also unremittingly pilloried Hezbollah, accusing it, among other things, of murdering children and women in Syria. In a much darker brush, he has painted the Syrian regime into a mad dog committing horrible crimes. In a statement issued by the Council of Ulema of Islamic Awakening in Lebanon, Sheikh Masri wrote, "The Ba'th party, in fighting the innate nature [instinct] upon which God created mankind, and in committing the most horrible crimes and massacres against the Muslim peoples of Syria, Lebanon, and Palestine, has become like a mad dog."[77]

Significantly enough, despite his disparagement of the Iranian and Syrian regimes, he has refrained from leveling the charge of unbelief (*takfir*) on the Shi'ites—that is, excommunicating them. On the matter of jihad and *takfir*, he, unlike some Salafists in Lebanon, has restricted the use of *takfir* in light of what he considers its damaging effect on the *ummah*.

Takfir and Jihad in the Theoretical and Practical Framework of Sheik Masri

Broadly speaking, Sheikh Masri has toed an ideological line on *takfir* similar but not identical to the theological position adopted by the quietest Salafi school. He believes that *shari'a* is strict with respect to matters of *takfir*. He upholds the position that *takfir* on the basis of *ijtihad* (independent religious decision on the basis of the Qur'an and Sunna) could be right or wrong. If the independent judgment is wrong, then it is as if Islam has been charged with *kufr*, and therefore the decision in itself is the *kufr*. Excommunication is not accepted unless it is based on a legal, clear, and immutable text, impervious to doubt.[78] The danger in *takfir* lies in removing the security cover that Islam provides for its sons and daughters. Similarly the expansion of the phenomenon of *takfir* and countervailing *takfir* in the *ummah* would lead to the disintegration of Muslim society, for it would be torn by hatred, revulsion, and strife.[79]

Sheikh Masri distinguishes the believer from the *kafir* on the restrictive basis that a believer is the one who testifies to the *shahadatayn*: There is no god but God, and Muhammad is His messenger. Therefore, one's Islam cannot be invalidated unless he or she commits prohibitions that, according to the revelation, permit describing the believer with *kufr*. According to Sheikh Masri, there are four reasons for *takfir*. First, there is allowing what God has forbidden and forbidding what God has allowed. This constitutes *shirk* in almighty God, for it subordinates God's ruling to one's own. The second is renouncing the pillars of Islam and faith or violating one of the seven major prohibitions.[80] Third, cursing God, His messenger, or His religion. And finally, there is demeaning the symbols of Islam, such as prayer and fasting, as part of defaming Islam.

Nevertheless, describing a believer as a *kafir*, in contrast to a Salafi jihadist, does not automatically lead to jihad against the *kafir* and therefore his or her death. Only by consciously renouncing Islam would a *kafir* be subjected to a death penalty, which would be decided upon only by the ruler.[81] With respect to jihad against non-Muslims, Sheikh Masri justified jihad as shown above on the basis of protecting the *ummah* from the aggressions of its enemies. More specifically, he justified jihadi operations against the United States as defensive ones, yet he identified legal regulations according to which jihad can be waged in the interest of preventing strife and oppression. He specified the following regulations: (1) jihadi operations by the Islamic resistance can be waged against the enemy and its allies, regardless of whether they are civil or military persons, on the occupied land; (2) jihadi attacks by the Islamic resistance targeting the employees of the government of the occupying enemy and its allies can be waged on their soils and on the land of all Muslim states; (3) attacks by the Islamic resistance targeting the civil peoples of the enemy and its allies on unoccupied lands are not permitted, unless they are deemed as last choice necessary means to pressure the enemy to give up its aggression; and (4) attacks by the Islamic resistance targeting the civil peoples and military personnel of the enemy and its allies are not allowed in a neutral, peaceful country.[82] Evidently, Sheikh Masri's view of jihad against what he considers non-Muslim enemies of the *ummah* overlaps with that of Salafi jihadists.

One could safely argue that his view of jihad stems from his nearly ethereal belief that *tawhid al-ummah* is the noblest and most pressing mission of the *ummah*, trumping all other concerns, matters, and considerations in Muslim society. For example, for the sake of *tawhid al-ummah*, he supports a virtually almost impossible cooperation between al-Qaeda and Saudi rulers, since both of them aspire to impose *shari'a* as a foundation of Islamic rule. Clearly he neither considers Salafi-Jihadi organizations as terrorist ones nor idolatrous states as un-Islamic and therefore legitimate targets of attack. Conversely, jihad against non-Muslim *kuffars* is an obligatory missionary objective, even with *kuffar* allies at the right time.

Notes

1. "Sheikh Masri defines Islamic awakening as Muslim activism, led by Islamists, to propagate Islam according to the Qur'an and the Sunna, with the objective of formulating a work plan leading Muslims to truth and uprightness. Accordingly, what sheikh Masri refers to as an 'Islamic awakening-US campaign' is in reality an 'Islamist-US campaign.'" Zakariya 'Abd al-Razaq al-Masri, *Istratijiyah al-Sahwa al-Islamiyah fi Kayfiyat al-Ta'amul ma'a al-'Ilmaniyah al-Sharqiyah wal-'Ilmaniyah al-Gharbiyah* (The Strategy of the Islamic Awakening Regarding How to Deal with Oriental and Western Secularisms) (Tripoli, Lebanon: Markaz Hamza lil-Wala' wal-Bahth al-'Ilmi wal-'Amal al-Islami, 2009), 6.

2. Zakariya 'Abd al-Razaq al-Masri, *Usul al-'Aqida al-Islamiyah: Durus wa Tamarin* (The Fundamentals of Islamic Creed: Studies and Exercises) (Beirut: Mu'assassat al-Risala, 2003), 19–20 and 242–43. According to *hadith*, the pillars of faith were cited by Prophet Muhammad when asked about them by the angel Gabriel. The pillars of faith include the belief in God, His angels, books, "the other day" (day of judgment), and divine destiny.

3. The five pillars of Islam include the *shahada* (testimony), *salat* (prayers), *zakat* (almsgiving), *sawm* (fasting), and *hajj* (pilgrimage).

4. Al-Masri, *Usul al-'Aqida al-Islamiya: Durus wa Tamarin*, 242.

5. Ibid., 15–16, 242.

6. Ibid., 31 and 289. Sheikh Masri considers polytheism in all three instances as the *shirk al-akbar* (greater shirk).

7. Ibid., 53–54.

8. Zakariya 'Abd al-Razaq al-Masri, *Al-Usul wal-Thawabit wa Atharaha fi Wihdat al-Ummah al-Islamiyah* (The Fundamentals and Immutables and Their Influence on the Unity of the Islamic Ummah) (Tripoli, Lebanon: Markaz Hamza li-Wala' wal-Bahth al-'Ilmi wal-'Amal al-Islami, 2006), 49.

9. Ibid.

10. Al-Masri, *Usul al-'Aqida al-Islamiyah*, 55.

11. Ibid., 55–56.

12. Ibid., 57–58.

13. Surat al-Nisa' Ayat 34 of the Qur'an reads: "Men are the protectors and maintainers of women, because Allah has given the one more [strength] than the other and because they support them from their means. Therefore the righteous women are devoutly obedient and guard in the [husband's] absence what Allah would have them guard."

14. Al-Masri, *Usul al-'Aqida al-Islamiyah <al-Islamiyah>: Durus wa Tamarin*, 58–60.

15. Ibid., 65.

16. Ibid., 66–67, 266.

17. Zakariya 'Abd al-Razaq al-Masri, *Al-Qiwa al-Dawliyah fi Muwajahat al-Sahwa al-Islamiyah: Dhawabit Shar'iya fi al-'Amaliyat al-Jihadiyah* (International Powers Confronting the Islamic Awakening: General Rules (Regulations) for Jihadi Operations) (Tripoli, Lebanon: Maktabat al-Iman, 2004), 40–41.

18. Al-Masri, *Usul al-'Aqida al-Islamiyah: Durus wa Tamarin*, 67–69, 266–67.

19. Ibid., 70–71, 267–68.

20. Ibid., 71, 268.

21. Ibid., 268–269, and al-Masri, *Al-Usul wal-Thawabit wa Atharaha fi Wihdat al-Umma al-Islamiyah*, 49–51.

22. Al-Masri, *Usul al-'Aqida al-Islamiyah*, 269.

23. Ibid., 73–74.

24. Ibid., 269.

25. This *hadith* is reported by Sheikh al-Tabrani and authenticated by Sheikh al-Sayuti.

26. Zakariya 'Abd al-Razaq al-Masri, *Istratijiyah al-Sahwa al-Islamiyah fi Kayfiyat al-Ta'amul ma'a al-'Ilmaniyah al-Sharqiyah wal-'Ilmaniyah al-Gharbiyah* (The Strategy of the Islamic Awakening Regarding how to Deal with Oriental and Western Secularisms) (Tripoli, Lebanon: Markaz Hamza lil-Wala' wal-Bahth al-'Ilmi wal-'Amal al-Islami, 2009), 58.

27. Al-Masri, *Al-Qiwa al-Dawliyah fi Muwajahat al-Sahwa al-Islamiyah: Dawabit Shar'iya fi al-'Amaliyat al-Jihadiyah*, 50.

28. Ibid., 96–97.

29. Zakariya 'Abd al-Razaq al-Masri, *Al-Islam wa Huriyat al-Insan* (Islam and the Freedom of the Human Being) (Beirut: Mu'assassat al-Risala, 2001), 35.

30. Ibid.

31. An excerpt of surat al-'Imran ayat 19, which Sheikh Masri cites, reads: "The religion before Allah is Islam (submission to His Will)." The other surat al-'Imran ayat 85, which he also cites, reads: "If anyone desires a religion other than Islam (submission to Allah) never will it be accepted of him; and in the Hereafter he will be in the ranks of those who have lost."

32. Al-Masri, *Al-Islam wa Huriyat al-Insan*, 39.

33. Ibid.

34. Ibid.

35. Ibid., 41–50.

36. Ibid., 51–52.

37. Major sins are seven: *shirk* (polytheism), performing sorcery, committing murder, charging interest (usury), devouring the wealth of orphans, defaming innocent women, and fleeing from the battle.

38. Al-Masri, *Al-Islam wa Huriyat al-Insan*, 54–55.

39. The pillars of faith are: belief in God, His angels, His books, His messengers, other day (day of judgment), and divine destiny.

40. Al-Masri, *Al-Islam wa Huriyat al-Insan*, 63–67.

41. Ibid., 67–68.

42. Ibid., 69.

43. Ibid., 70.

44. Ibid., 71.

45. Ibid., 73–74, 102–9.

46. Ibid., 102–5.

47. Al-Masri, *Istratijiyah al-Sahwa al-Islamiyah fi Kayfiyat al-Ta'amul ma'a al-'Ilmaniyah al-Sharqiyah wal-'Ilmaniyah al-Gharbiyah*, 10.

48. Ibid., 11–12.

49. Ibid., 14–15.

50. Ibid., 16–17.

51. Ibid., 20.

52. Ibid., 21.

53. An excerpt of Surat Hud, ayat 61, of the Qur'an reads: "It is He who has produced you from the earth and settled you therein."

54. Al-Masri, *Istratijiyah al-Sahwa al-Islamiyah fi Kayfiyat al-Ta'amul ma'a al-'Ilmaniyah al-Sharqiyah wal-'Ilmaniyah al-Gharbiyah*, 37–51.

55. Ibid., 53.

56. Author's observation of Sheikh Masri's statements and activity during field trips to Lebanon and through Lebanese media.

57. Antoine Amrieh, "Anti-Syrian Government Demonstration Breaks Out after Friday Prayer in Tripoli," *Daily Star*, July 22, 2011.

58. Ibid.

59. Al-Masri, *Istratijiyah al-Sahwa al-Islamiyah fi Kayfiyat al-Ta'amul ma'a al-'Ilmaniyah al-Sharqiyah wal-'Ilmaniyah al-Gharbiyah*, 60–61.

60. Ibid., 65.

61. Ibid., 68.

62. Ibid., 68.

63. Ibid., 68.

64. Qur'anic Surat al-Rum, ayat 2 and 3, reads:" The *Rum* have been defeated—in a land close by. But they, [even] after [this] defeat of theirs will soon be victorious."

65. Al-Masri, *Istratijiyah al-Sahwa al-Islamiyah fi Kayfiyat al-Ta'amul ma'a al-'Ilmaniyah al-Sharqiyah wal-'Ilmaniyah al-Gharbiyah*, 71–73.

66. Ibid., 72–73.

67. Ibid., 73.

68. Sheikh Masri was born in Tripoli, Lebanon, in 1953. He studied at the Islamic University in Medina and earned his doctorate in Islamic jurisprudence *(fiqh)* from Um al-Qura University in Mecca. He taught *fiqh* and Islamic ideology at the Tripoli University and al-Jinan University in Tripoli and al-Uza'i University in Beirut.

69. al-Masri, *Al-Usul wal-Thawabit wa Atharaha fi Wihdat al-Umma al-Islamiyah*, 49–51.

70. Ibid., 53–56.

71. Ibid., 56.

72. Ibid., 60–62.

73. Ibid., 63–66.

74. Ibid., 68.

75. Sheikh Masri's statement posted February 8, 2013, and available at www.face book.com/dr.zakaria.almassri (accessed July 29, 2013).

76. Sheik Masri's statement posted on May 18, 2013 and available at www.facebook .com/dr.zakaria.almassri (accessed July 29, 2013).

77. The council's statement was issued in Tripoli on February 10, 2013, and posted on Sheikh Masri's Facebook page on February 12, 2013, www.facebook.com/ dr.zakaria.almassri (accessed July 29, 2013).

78. Al-Masri, *Usul al-'Aqida al-Islamiya*, 375–76.

79. Ibid., 376.

80. For pillars of Islam, see note 3. For pillars of faith, see note 2. For major sins or prohibitions, see note 37.

81. Al-Masri, *Usul al-'Aqida al-Islamiya*, 379–80.

82. Al-Masri, *Al-Qiwa al-Dawliyah fi Muwajahat al-Sahwa al-Islamiyah: Dawabit Shar'iya fi al-'Amaliyat al-Jihadiyah*, 109. First cited in Abd al-Ghani 'Imad, *Al-Harakat al-Islamiyah fi Lubnan: Ishkaliyat al-Din wal-Siyasah fi Mujtama' Mutanawe'* (Islamic Movements in Lebanon: The Ambiguity of Religion and Politics in a Diverse Society) (Beirut: Dar al-Tali'a lil-Tiba'a wal-Nashr, 2006), 320–21.

Chapter Five

The Emergence and Ideology of the Salafi-Jihadi Usbat al-Ansar

This chapter traces the emergence of the Salafi-jihadi organization Usbat al-Ansar (the Partisans' League) and examines its ideology. Usbat al-Ansar grew out of and in response to the distressed sociopolitical climate of the Palestinian refugee camps in Lebanon, in particular the Ayn al-Helweh camp in Sidon. Notwithstanding the dismal living conditions in the camps, growing disillusionment with Palestinian nationalism and religio-political mobilization of refugees by religious scholars greatly shaped this climate. Significantly, the concept of jihad as an armed struggle was advanced with the onset of Lebanon's civil war by an Islamist organization that believed Muslim society was under ideological, political, and military assault. This jihadi-based Islamism transformed into Salafi jihadism at the hands of Palestinian Islamists who, unlike the PLO, put up a fight against Israel's onslaught on the Ayn al-Helweh camp in 1982, thereby legitimizing Islamic activism. The ideological transformation of the Usbat gradually developed as a result of both the organization's aim at constructing a distinct Islamist identity and the appeal of Salafi jihadism as an actionable ideology, sanctioned by divine directives. The Usbat acts on its ideology by imposing its fundamentalist view of Islamic creedal principles on Palestinian society and making jihad (armed struggle) a focal point of its militant activism against idolatrous societies and rule. Though it professes to act independently from al-Qaeda, Usbat al-Ansar has supported the violent activities of the Salafi-jihadi organization, including participating in the al-Qaeda–led insurgency against American troops in Iraq.

The Seeds of Jihad in Ayn al-Helweh:
Al-Haraka al-Islamiyah al-Mujahida

Broadly speaking, neither global jihad nor Salafi-jihadi ideology had initially popular traction in Lebanon. Sheikh Abdallah Azzam's call for global jihad in Afghanistan in the 1980s, with the tacit or explicit encouragement of Pakistan, Saudi Arabia, and United States, fell virtually on deaf ears in Lebanon.[1] In contrast to other Arabs, very few Lebanese answered the call and went on to fight the atheist Soviets in Afghanistan. Moreover, the Salafi-jihadi ideology of al-Qaeda had difficulty penetrating the bastion of Salafism in northern Lebanon until the late 1990s. Even then its theoretical and operational appeal had been linked to local and regional considerations that guarded against its proliferation. Nevertheless, the ideologies of jihad and then Salafi jihadism gradually found their way into the Palestinian refugee camps in Lebanon, in particular Ayn al-Helweh refugee camp in Sidon, on account of a combination of local and regional sociopolitical factors that coincided with a Palestinian growing disillusion with Palestinian nationalism, as led by the PLO.

The first notions of jihad, as an armed struggle, can be traced to the emergence of the al-Haraka al-Islamiyah al-Mujahida (the Islamic Jihad Movement) in the Palestinian refugee camp of Ayn al-Helweh. The Arab defeats in the 1967 and 1973 wars and the growing militarization of the Palestinian refugees in confessional polarized Lebanon, together with the mounting call among Islamists that "Islam is the solution," conditioned a significant number of refugees to heed the politicized sermons of religious scholars. Chief among them was Sheikh Ibrahim Ghunaym, who is widely known as the "spiritual father of all Palestinian men of religion."[2] Born in the village of Safuriyya in northern Palestine under the British mandate in 1924, he fled to Lebanon during the 1948 war. He settled in a shanty east Beirut suburb, colloquially known as Maslakh. In the early 1950s, he joined the Naqshabandiyah Sufi order. The autodidactic sheikh then moved to Akkar, before settling in the Palestinian refugee camp of Nahr al-Bared, where he dedicated his time to Islamic teaching, preaching, and guidance of Palestinians. In 1963, he moved to the biggest and most densely inhabited refugee camp in the country, Ayn al-Helweh, where he became a preacher and a teacher at al-Nur Mosque.[3]

Over the years he inspired a group of loyal disciples, who eventually became the champions of radical Islam in the camp and the city of Sidon. Among them were Sheikhs Abdallah Halaq and Jamal Khattab. Sheikh Ghunaym mobilized his students by consistently underscoring the paramountcy of armed struggle in its pure form of jihad against the Zionists. At the same time, Sheikh Ghunaym and his circle of students forged an intimate relationship with Sheikh Hamed

Abu Naser, known as Abu Jihad. Originally from the West Bank, Abu Naser lived in Jordan, where he established contacts with both the Muslim Brotherhood and the PLO before leaving for the Ayn al-Helweh camp in Lebanon. Known for both his military and *shari'a* expertise, Abu Naser also advocated armed struggle against the Zionists and their allies within the context of the growing Islamic activism permeating the Arab world. No less significant, the onset of the civil war in Lebanon in 1975 sharpened the determination of these scholars and students to take a stand against the Zionists, their allies the "Christian crusaders of Lebanon," and atheist communists. It is out of this close clique of embittered and dispossessed Palestinian refugees in Lebanon that al-Haraka al-Islamiyah al-Mujahida was born in 1975. Jihad against Israel and its allies was central to al-Haraka's Islamic activism. According to a statement issued by al-Haraka upon its establishment,

> the duty of jihad was virtually absent in theory as well as in practice, and the majority of the Islamic orientations were preoccupied with the intellectual confrontation and the educational development. They [Islamists] had a negligible presence in the arenas of military confrontation with the Zionist enemy and their Christian crusader allies in the region, at a time secular and leftist units spearheaded the confrontation not out of religious conviction. It was disgraceful for Islamists to be absent from the arena of the battle, while they were at times accused of cowardice and at other times of collaboration and backwardness. Even religion was accused of being the opium of the people.[4]

According to Palestinian Islamist Ra'fat Marah, al-Haraka was driven to ideological, political, and military activism following its scrutiny of the political landscape of the Muslim world. From an ideological standpoint, al-Haraka illustrated that "the enemy of God, from Jews, crusaders, communists, atheists, and governments that do no rule according to what God sent down, are waging a cultural and ideological war against Islam to wipe out Islamic civilization and control Muslim lands." From a political standpoint the organization emphasized that "the Muslim world is subjected to a war of annihilation and to political hegemony by the enemies of God." Finally, from a social standpoint al-Haraka underscored that "our [Muslim] societies have been assailed ideologically, morally and ethically, thereby ripping the Islamic personality on the social, familial, and individual levels. Thus, these societies have to be shaped anew on the basis of Islam, devoutness, and jihad in the path of God."[5]

Correspondingly, al-Haraka focused on "effecting God's worship and establishing an Islamic society," by pursuing its objectives in stages. They included building the "distinguished Islamic personality in its ideological, political, and military totality," "acquiring the *mujahid* organization," and "working to realize the Islamic state and apply *shari'a* in any place of the Muslim world where the causes for its creation have ripened."[6] It is clear from the literature of al-Haraka that it was a forerunner of Palestinian Salafi jihadism. No longer was the Palestinian nationalist cause at the heart of Palestinian activism. The question of Palestine became subsumed under the transnational objective of establishing an Islamic state and protecting the *ummah* (Muslim community).

Meanwhile, the founding members of al-Haraka chose Sheikh Abu Naser as the emir (leader) of the movement, while Sheikh Ghunaym remained its spiritual leader and guide. Initially, al-Haraka participated moderately in the civil war on the side of the PLO and their allies in the Lebanese National Movement against the Christians. But its participation increased dramatically in southern Lebanon following Israel's 1978 and 1982 invasions of Lebanon. In addition to putting up a fight, along with other Islamists, in defense of the Ayn al-Helweh camp during the 1982 invasion, the movement carried out several deadly operations against the Israel Defense Forces (IDF) in 'Adlun, Marji'yun, and Sidon. In 1983, Abu Naser left Lebanon for Jordan under vague circumstances. He was replaced by Sheikh Halaq, who cooperated with the Islamic resistance, which came to be headed by Hezbollah. Significantly, the movement supported the PLO in the early years of the War of the Camps (1984–89) against the Shi'a Amal movement. The War of the Camps had been instigated by Syrian president Hafiz al-Asad, who opposed the PLO's attempt at reestablishing its power in Beirut's Palestinian refugee camps following the organization's evacuation from Lebanon in 1982. The pro-Syrian Amal movement laid a rigorous siege on the camps and fought the PLO there. However, in 1986, Sheikh Halaq suspended al-Haraka's military operations and focused its activities on *da'wa* (call to Islam) and religious and social issues. He later on explained the movement's shift from military activism and the dissolution of its mujahideen on the grounds that

the Palestinian Islamic Movement has become mature [rightly guided]. Its fundamental work in the beginning aimed at liberating Palestine and confronting the Jews. On this basis, we began to work within the framework of the al-Haraka al-Islamiyah al-Mujahida. We carried out a series of military operations against the Jews in Sidon and Ayn al-Helweh camp and against some collaborators. We also participated in some operations led by the faithful Resistance between 1984 and 1985. But in 1986 we terminated the military order of the movement, and the work of its sheikhs and rank and file moved towards the realms of education and propagation through the mosques and cultural institutions. We consider what is required is the use of arms in the right direction against the Jews and to liberate the land from the occupier. Using arms in other places is a great error, for we need to use them only in confronting the Jews.[7]

Apparently, the decision to suspend the military activities of the movement was related, on the one hand, to its concern over being dragged into the struggle for the leadership of the Shi'a community between Hezbollah and the Amal movement and, on the other hand, to the strategy of Syria, which was shared by most Lebanese parties, to control Palestinian activities in Lebanon. Significantly, Sheikh Halaq wholeheartedly supported the Islamic resistance as it developed under the leadership of Hezbollah. No less significant, al-Haraka had little support, if any, from the main Islamist organization in Lebanon, the Islamic Association. At first, the two parties cooperated with each other, especially after the Islamic Association established a headquarters in Sidon and began participating in the Islamic resistance against Israel and the Christians. Nevertheless, the Islamic Association more or less ideologically opposed the creation of another Islamist organization and more so was greatly concerned about the reaction of the Syrian regime to the growing activities of Islamists.[8]

Paralleling these developments, the Iranian revolutionaries, who had been trained by Fatah, the military arm of the PLO, in southern Lebanon, established contacts with Sheikh Ghunaym and al-Haraka leaders that eventually transformed into fairly good relations with the Iranian government in the wake of the triumph of the Iranian Revolution in 1979.[9] In fact, during the mid- to late 1970s, southern Lebanon had become a nodal point connecting Iran and Lebanon, and a hotbed for Islamic activism. It was within the context of Iran's foreign policy in Lebanon to export its revolution there and to establish contacts with religious scholars, including Sunni Islamists, that Sheikh Ghunaym and his movement received support from the Khomeini regime. This support increased in the early 1980s following the fallout between the Iranian regime and the PLO, which supported Iraq in the Iran-Iraq War. This was manifested in Iran's support for institutional networks geared toward spreading Khomeini's vision of Islam. The Iranians, through their embassy in Lebanon, helped found Tajammu' al-Ulema al-Muslimin (the Congregation of Muslim Ulema) in 1982. Bernard Rougier observed that this organization had two objectives: to weaken the role of Lebanon's traditional notables so as to give the religious elites authority over the country's political affairs and to unify the Muslim religious communities in order to reduce sectarian antagonism between Sunnis and Shi'ites.[10] Clearly the rationale behind establishing the Congregation lay in the notion that since sectarianism had catastrophic consequences for Lebanon, it was therefore necessary for the clergy to stake a claim to political authority. After all, Khomeini's revolution was led by *ulema* and premised on the theory of *wilayat al-faqih* (rule by the jurisconsult).

Sheikh Halaq and Sheikh Maher Hammoud, among others, joined the Congregation, whose members eventually emerged as the main proponents of Iranian and, by extension, Hezbollah interests in the refugee camps. Sheikh Halaq grew extremely hostile to the PLO, while at the same time developing a strong loyalty to Iran's brainchild in Lebanon, Hezbollah. He deplored the PLO's policies and actions and emphasized, as Rougier wrote, that Hezbollah had substituted itself for the Palestinian resistance.[11]

It is noteworthy that during Israel's invasion of Lebanon in the summer of 1982, Sheikh Ghunaym was in Tehran participating in an international conference on the dispossessed, sponsored by the Iranian government. He then returned to the Nahr al-Bared refugee camp, where he subsequently helped build al-Quds Mosque with funding from the Iranian embassy.[12] He forged close relations with Sheikh Sa'id Sha'ban, the leader of the Islamic Unity Movement, and throughout the 1990s he ubiquitously supported Hezbollah. Significantly, in 1986 and with Iranian support, Sheikh Ghunaym, along with Sheikhs Halaq, Khattab, Muhammad al-Najmi, and Salim al-Lababidi, established Majlis Ri'ayat al-Shu'un al-Diniyah (the Guardianship Council of Religious Affairs), known by its acronym Murshid. Murshid has sought to socialize Palestinians to the requisites of a vanguard Islamic group, which could serve as the core of al-Haraka's future Islamic community. This involved developing a curriculum of religious studies from the primary level to university level, establishing elementary and secondary schools in the refugee camps, creating schools to teach the Qur'an; constructing and renovating mosques as places for worship and religious instruction, offering scholarships to those who want to pursue religious studies at Islamic universities, and forming a missionary council to educate females.[13] Moreover, in 1989, al-Haraka, in conjunction with Murshid, established Ittihad al-Talabah al-Muslimin (the Muslim Student Union), which, in turn, founded the educational periodical *Al-Hadaya*. The objectives of the periodical included (1) *da'wa to* Islam, abiding by it, and protecting it; (2) fashioning the exemplary student who will adhere to Islam and excel in education and ethical conduct; (3) instilling the spirit of jihad and upholding Islamic causes; (4) supporting just student matters; and (5) confronting Western and secular campaigns against Muslim society.[14]

No doubt, as a result of all these efforts, including unremitting pro-jihad religious sermons by Sheikhs Ghunaym, Halaq, and Khattab, a deep sense of religiosity coupled with a commitment to jihad as an instrument of change began to take root in the Ayn al-Helweh camp. At the same time, the growing perception of the PLO as a corrupt and inefficient organization, together with the formal and informal discrimination of the host country against Palestinian refugees, reinforced the trend of Islamic activism. Usbat al-Ansar grew out of this Islamic climate dawning on the refugee camp.

Al-Nasha' (The Emergence) of Usbat al-Ansar

Among the students of Sheikh Ghunaym who valiantly tried to defend the Ayn al-Helweh camp against Israel's onslaught in 1982 was Hisham Sharaydi. In contrast to the swift collapse of the PLO's defenses in southern Lebanon, including in and around the camp, Sharaydi and other Islamist fighters put up a fight that lasted twenty days in the face of Israel's military juggernaut. Eventually Sharaydi was captured by the IDF and taken to the Ansar detention camp, where he was held for a year and a half. The Ansar camp, in Lebanon's Nabatieh region, was supervised by the IDF and manned by the South Lebanese Army, a Christian-led proxy armed group funded, trained, and equipped by Israel. His detention at the infamous camp only reinforced his Islamic drive and enhanced his Islamist credentials, though he had only a rudimentary religious education. Upon his release, he was welcomed as a hero and appointed preacher at the Masjid al-Shuhada (Martyr's Mosque), near the camp's northern entrance. Apparently, as Rougier perceptively observed, "the resistance that Shaykh Ghunaym's students originally put up provided a durable foundation for the legitimacy of Islamism at Ain al-Helweh."[15] It is this foundation that allowed Sheikh Hisham Sharaydi, along with his supporters, to act on his Islamist beliefs and practices and to try to impose them on the refugees in the camp. His movement Usbat al-Ansar embodied these beliefs and served as a means for their implementation.

Hisham Sharaydi was born in the Ayn al-Helweh camp in 1957. His family hailed from the village of Safsaf, in Galilee, in today's northern Israel. Religion played little role in his upbringing. He temporarily joined both Fatah and then the Popular Front for the Liberation of Palestine. Influenced by Sheikh Ghunaym, he moved in the direction of Islamism. Ra'fat Marah notes that Sharaydi joined the Islamic Association in 1981.[16] Whatever the case may be, he cooperated and worked with both the Islamic Association and the Islamic Tahrir Party in Sidon. Meanwhile, in addition to being inspired and taught by Sheikh Ghunaym, Sharaydi was moved by the Islamist beliefs of Imam Hassan Zaghmut, who introduced him to the ideas of Hassan al-Bannah, the founder of the Muslim Brotherhood.[17] At the time of Israel's invasion in 1982, Sharaydi had a general knowledge of Islam, based, broadly speaking, on the necessity of jihad as an armed struggle and establishing an Islamic state undergirded by Islamic law. Significantly, he adhered to the Islamic creedal principle *al-amr bil-ma'ruf wal-nahi 'an al-munkar* (commanding good and forbidding wrong) as interpreted by a *hadith* related to by Sheikh Muslim: "I heard the Messenger of Allah, may Allah bless him and grant him peace, say, 'Whoever of you sees something wrong should change it with his hand; if he cannot, then with his tongue; if he cannot, then with his heart, and that is the weakest form of belief.'"[18]

Obviously these Salafi concepts—of (1) jihad, (2) establishing an Islamic state, (3) commanding good and forbidding wrong—marked his Islamic activism in the camp and Sidon. Upon being appointed the imam of Martyr's Mosque, he took it upon himself to impose his understanding of "forbidding wrong" in the camp by force more than persuasion on those he believed had committed sins of belief and practice. In fact, his campaign to police by force all that he considered moral and religious transgressions, such as drinking, reckless sexual behavior, provocative dressing, and laxity in performing the five daily prayers, put him at odds with the other forces in the camp, including Fatah.[19] Moreover, he frequently walked the narrow alleys of the camp with his armed group and preached from the pulpit of his mosque always in his fatigues and with an AK-47 in hand. His entourage, which included those who had fought on his side in 1982, such as Ahmad 'Abd al-Karim al-Sa'di, Ahmad al-Khatib, and Ahmad Juma', became known interchangeably as *shabab al-sheikh* or *jama'at al-sheikh* (the men of the sheikh or the group of the sheikh). Fatah grew increasingly alarmed by his gradual but steadily rise to prominence in the camp. Tension between the two parties steadily increased as Sheikh Sharaydi cooperated closely with and fought alongside the Islamic Association, the Islamic Jihad Movement, and Hezbollah against Israel and its allies, the South Lebanese Army and the Christian Lebanese Forces. In 1985, his group heavily participated in the battle of East Sidon on the side of the Islamic resistance against the Christian Lebanese Forces. And in 1990, he took the side of Hezbollah against Fatah in the battle over the control of Iqlim al-Tufah in southern Lebanon.[20]

In the interim, Sharaydi formally established his movement in 1986, naming it Usbat al-Ansar. It is noteworthy that following the brutal Syrian suppression of the Islamic Unity Movement in Tripoli, its members escaped to the Ayn al-Helweh camp, where they rallied around Sharaydi's group, thereby further enhancing his Islamist credentials and power base.

Meanwhile, Fatah's power as the military arm of the PLO continued to weaken in Lebanon. The PLO's attempt at reclaiming its power in Tripoli, Beirut, and Sidon in the 1980s after its forced evacuation from the capital in 1982 was met with harsh resistance by the Syrian regime and its ally, the Shi'a movement Amal. All that remained for the PLO was whatever influence it had in Lebanon's Palestinian refugee camps. Moreover, once preparation for the Madrid peace negotiations had begun, controlling the camps had evidently become vital for the PLO, as the spokesperson of the Palestinians. Not surprisingly, Fatah's attempt to impose its authority throughout the camps, especially in Ayn al-Helweh, clashed with Sheikh Sharaydi's undaunted Islamist power base and opposition to peace talks. Consequently Fatah's chief in the camp, Amin Kayyed, allegedly ordered the assassination of Sheikh Sharaydi, who was murdered in front of his mosque on December 15, 1991. Large crowds, including Sheikhs Halaq and Hammoud, participated in his funeral procession, shouting derogatory epithets at Fatah and its leader.[21] Clearly this completed the process by which the PLO's hegemony in the camps came to an end, while at the same time it manifested the rise of radical Islam in its Salafi-Jihadi variant.

Though a combination of local and regional factors was behind the emergence of Sharaydi's new Islamist movement, the dismal and regressive condition of the Palestinians under the leadership of the PLO cannot be discounted as a major force in engendering the jihadi Islamist variant of Sharaydi's movement. This jihadi variant, whose seeds were planted by the Islamic Jihadi Movement, grew wearing the mantle of Salafism, if only because Salafism offered clear, broad, and definite directives that fostered a strong sense of identity, authenticity, and empowerment for the refugees. Palestinian refugees had been lost in the hodgepodge of vacuous slogans and promises and trapped in the misery of the camps. This intellectually unencumbered Salafism provided the link to and continuity of a glorious past and justified jihad against that which afflicted Muslim society in its present weakened and humiliated state. This link to the past, and the determination with which the members of Usbat al-Ansar sought to restore God's rule on earth and transcend their reality in the refugee camp as part of the saved sect, underscored the ideological foundation out of which Usbat al-Ansar emerged. A statement by Usbat al-Ansar about its emergence emphasized:

We all know the bitter reality that the people had to contend with before and after the collapse of the Islamic caliphate. Ideas of nationalism and patriotism seeped into our Muslim world, and as of recently secularism and communism spread throughout that world. The enemies of Islam exploited this opportunity and spread depravity [sinfulness] throughout the earth, trying to convince the sons of the Islamic *ummah* that the backwardness that afflicted them was the result of their clinging to the religion and the creed. Since the creed of many sons of the *ummah* had weakened, these erroneous ideas and destructive principles were able to find a place among Muslims. Therefore the manifestations of *kufr* and wickedness took different colors and various images . . . in Ayn al-Helweh in Lebanon, where *kufr* and disobedience prevailed, cursing God and His messenger was common, ignorance and degradation of the religion pervaded the minds of the people, the youth drowned in the darkness of sins, and committing major sins was conventional, a noble sheikh stood up carrying the banner of Islam under these difficult circumstances and critical conditions. He enlightened in the *da'wa* to Islam confused hearts and dark alleys. . . . The sheikh and his brothers took off calling to God, commanding good and forbidding wrong, comprehending [applying] the religion of God, preparing the greatest force to terrorize the enemies of God and fight in the path of God in order to restore the rule of God. They pleaded to God to become members of the victorious [saved] sect [community], upon which the messenger of God wished victory.[22]

The Creed, Mission, and Objectives of Usbat al-Ansar

Usbat al-Ansar considers itself a Muslim league abiding by the creed and order of the religion of Islam, for it believes that Islam is the only correct solution to all human problems. Usbat al-Ansar adheres to the basic principles of God's *tawhid* and believes in His *rububiyah* (lordship), *uluhiyah* (godship), and *al-asma' wal-sifat* (names and attributes). Fundamentally, it strives to *tawhid al-rububiyah* by asserting that God has the powers as the Lord of Creation and to attribute any of these powers to other than God constitutes *kufr*. It strives to *tawhid al-uluhiyah* by directing all forms of worship exclusively toward God. Worshipping other than God constitutes *kufr*. And it strives to *tawhid al-asma' wal-sifat* by depicting Him only in the way His revelation described Him. Any depiction other than that literally present in the revelation constitutes *kufr*. Significantly, Usbat al-Ansar also strives to *tawhid* God in its actions, which essentially entail arbitrarily imposing God's rulings, as it understands them, on mankind.[23] The movement believes that God is the sole creator of the universe and that His command is total and absolute for the universal order. Almighty God decides divine destiny and organizes the universe according to what He wants and to what His wisdom determines. Correspondingly, Usbat al-Ansar acts on *tawhid* God in His revelation and in His worship. In this sense, Usbat has broadened the theological concept of *hukm Allah* (God's rule or sovereignty) by subsuming it under both *tawhid al-uluhiyah* and *tawhid al-rububiyah*.[24] Broadly speaking, Salafi jihadists have subsumed God's sovereignty under *tawhid al-uluhiyah*, which allowed them to enforce their views on Muslims' actual practice of worship. Usbat al-Ansar abides by this enforcement and makes clear that there is no revelation other than that of God. It follows from this that His divine legislations (Islamic law) that stem from His revelation constitute the only legal order for mankind. Usbat al-Ansar contends that it "disavows, dislodges, and excommunicates any legislator other than God" and adds, "We desire no god but God, we accept no authority other than His, and we desire no religion other than Islam."[25] Put simply, Usbat al-Ansar considers any regime that does not apply God's rulings to be un-Islamic, and therefore jihad against it is legally and dutifully sanctioned.

It is according to this creedal basis that Usbat al-Ansar defined its mission. The mission specifies that "the Usbat—as a group of Muslims—undertakes to enforce what God has imposed on all believers, from worship, *da'wa* to Him, commanding good and forbidding wrong, preparing jihad in the path of God, and diligent work to restore God's rule on earth."[26] Usbat also deems "that it is obligatory for Muslims to accept [apply] Islam in its totality as God and His messenger commanded." Accordingly, Usbat al-Ansar focuses on the totality of Islamic activism, specifying the following objectives: (1) *da'wa* to almighty God, (2) commanding good and forbidding wrong, (3) preparing and waging jihad in the path of God, (4) working to recover the homeland and the authority that has been violated, and (5) appointing a caliph who will rule according to what God has sent down.[27]

Complementing its mission, Usbat al-Ansar puts a premium on the ideological importance and application of the Islamic principle *al-wala' wal-bara'* (the principle of loyalty and disavowal). Usbat has more or less adopted a version of *al-wala' wal-bara'* similar to Salafist sheikh Muhammad al-Maqdisi's radicalized version. Muslims should not only distance themselves from non-Muslims but also should express their belief in demonstrating their open hatred of and enmity toward *kuffars*, while at the same time supporting their Muslim brethren. Moreover, Usbat enjoins Islamic associations and groups to both cease joining the governments of the *kuffars* and participating in their parliaments under the pretext of Islamic interest, for joining them would only obscure Islamic truth and make the *kuffar* institutions appear credible to people.[28] At the same time, Usbat underscores the importance of unity among Muslims and the exertion of every truthful effort by every truthful Muslim to bring about God's rule on earth. In this respect, Usbat makes clear that it "disavows polytheism and polytheists, *kufr* and *kafirin* (unbelief and unbelievers), and hypocrisy and hypocrites; it also disavows all parties and movements that contravene Islam, and all rulers, along with their assistants, who govern in *kufr*."[29]

In this respect, Usbat unequivocally asserts that it levels the charge of unbelief on tyrants and all ideas that contravene the religion of Islam. Among these ideas are: (1) secularism that separates religion from the state, which is *kufr* because Islam addresses all matters, be they on the individual, societal, or state level; (2) democracy that implies rule of the people by the people, which is *kufr* because only God almighty has legislative powers; (3) socialism that denies the presence of a creator, which is *kufr* because God is the creator; (4) nationalism that implies a belonging to a certain ethnic community that fights in the interest of only the nation, which is *kufr* because Islam indiscriminately supports all believers, regardless of race and origin; and (5) patriotism that implies the love of and belonging to a fatherland, meaning the interest of the fatherland precedes religion and divine law, which is *kufr* because Islam enjoins the love and support of believers, regardless of their fatherlands.[30]

Evidently, Usbat does not consider the Palestinian cause to be a priority of its comprehensive mission. Belonging to a certain nation does not imply a priority for the movement. Palestine and all other Muslim states, which are considered violated, are equitably included in Usbat's Muslim homeland that needs to be recovered. Usbat indicates that its activism lies in the actionable restoration of the stolen caliphate and the imposition of God's rule. Its motto is a call to "cooperation among Muslim mujahideen in order to lift the banner of no god but God and Muhammad is His messenger."[31] It is not surprising, then, that Usbat had supported the insurgency in Iraq as a priority of its jihad in the path of Allah, and one should not be astonished if Usbat would support future jihad in any Muslim country or against any group, ruler, or individual deemed *kafir*.

The Praxis and Terror of Usbat al-Ansar and Its Offshoot

Sharaydi was succeeded by his closest aide, Muhammad Abd al-Karim al-Sa'di, known as Abu Muhjin.[32] Abu Muhjin, like his predecessor, was not deeply versed in religious education, and his family hailed from the same village of Safsaf. In addition to continuing Sharaydi's effort to curb the power of Fatah during the 1990s, Abu Muhjin's organization, in an attempt to assert its radical Salafi ideology, carried out a number of attacks on Christian religious targets and liquor stores in Sidon. In fact, it was mainly under the leadership of Abu Muhjin that Usbat al-Ansar fully articulated its Salafi-jihadi ideology. Usbat issued its major statement about its emergence and ideology on March 30, 2004. Its Salafi ideology and legal outlook under the leadership of first Sharaydi and then Abu Muhjin gradually developed under the guidance and supervision of Sheikhs Usama Amin al-Shahabi and 'Imad Yassin. Significantly, the more the movement matured ideologically, the more it moved away from Iran and Hezbollah's orbit of activism. Moreover, Abu Muhjin, more than his predecessor, tried to project an independent identity of Usbat by extending the scope and breadth of its adherence to the Salafi-jihadi principles, "commanding right and forbidding wrong" and "loyalty and disavowal." It is within this context that he expanded the militant activism of Usbat within and beyond the camp of Ayn al-Helweh.

Before long he became involved in a power struggle with other extremist groups over the control of the region of Sidon in general and the camp in particular. In 1995, his group allegedly assassinated Sheikh Nizar al-Halabi, the leader of al-Ahbash, whose group had been supported by Syria to either co-opt or curb the power of Islamists. No less significant, Usbat considered al-Ahbash's ideology and work to be a distortion of Islam and a perversion of the Qur'an. Lebanese authorities arrested scores of defendants and executed three members of the group for their participation in the plot. They also issued death sentences in absentia against several members of Usbat al-Ansar, including Abu Muhjin. Other defendants were sentenced to various prison terms, and another participant in the murder, Yasir Izzat Saud, was sentenced to death, but his sentence was later commuted.[33] Since then, Abu Muhjin has disappeared from public view, and de facto leadership of the organization passed on to his brother, Tareq al-Sa'di, known as Abu Tarik. Nevertheless, the organization continued with its extremist pattern. In 1999, the group, avenging the murder of Sharaydi, assassinated Amin Kayyed and his wife. Moreover, in June 1999, the group allegedly assassinated three Lebanese judges and the chief prosecutor for southern Lebanon at the Justice Palace in Sidon, in revenge for the execution of three of their colleagues. In 2000 and 2001, acting on the principle of commanding right and forbidding wrong, Usbat engaged in various terror activities in the camp and Sidon.

Oddly enough, Usbat denied any involvement in any violent action, yet it asserted its legal right, which emanates from the revelation, to act on forbidding wrong.[34] Despite the outrage the killings evoked and the strict measures enforced by the Lebanese army to restrict the movement of Usbat al-Ansar's members outside the camp, the organization managed to hit the Russian embassy in Beirut with rocket-propelled grenades and engage in armed skirmishes with the Lebanese army, which was staking out the camp. One daring incident with the army stood out. On July 11, 2002, while a unit from the Lebanese army was monitoring the movement of members of Usbat near the camp, they opened fire on the unit killing three soldiers.[35] Michel Suleiman, then the commander of the army, gave an ultimatum to Usbat to give up Badi' Hamadah, the main culprit in the attack, and rigorously cordoned off the camp. Concerned about a deadly conflagration with the army, religious scholars including Jamal Khattab and Mahir Hammoud managed to persuade Usbat to deliver Hamadah to the army. He surrendered to the army on July 16, 2002, and Lebanese authorities executed him. Apparently the decision to give up Hamadah further deepened the divisions within Usbat.[36] Nevertheless, the group remained active in establishing practical and operational contacts with Islamist and Salafi-jihadi organizations, including al-Takfir wal-Hijra in northern Lebanon and al-Qaeda.

Reports about al-Qaeda supporting Usbat al-Ansar and establishing a foothold in the camp have ominously circulated in Lebanon. Undoubtedly, members of the group traveled to Iraq to participate in the jihadi insurgency there.[37] The group took pride in this participation by regularly announcing the names of jihadists who died in Iraq, and *muezzins* (those who call for prayers) around the camp, especially in the Usbat's Tawari' Mosque, celebrated these announcements.[38] Hazem al-Amin even reported that potential suicide bombers were taken to the Ayn al-Helweh camp for training.[39] In January 2006, Lebanese authorities announced the arrest of an al-Qaeda cell composed of Lebanese, Jordanians, Palestinians, and Saudis, suspected of planning to carry out terror attacks throughout Lebanon.[40] Acting on a tip by the FBI, Lebanese authorities arrested Assim Hammoud on April 27, 2006, who was suspected of planning an attack on the PATH commuter rail lines that carry tens of thousands of people between New York and New Jersey each day. Maj. Gen. Ashraf Rifi, then commander of Lebanon's Internal Security Forces, was quoted by the *Washington Post* as saying that "Hammoud was recruited to al-Qaeda in 2003 by a Syrian who later took him twice to Lebanon's largest Palestinian refugee camp, Ain al-Hilweh, for weapons training."[41]

For sure, the ease with which dozens of jihadists left the camp for Iraq despite close surveillance by the army pointed to Syrian complicity in making Lebanese authorities turn a blind eye to the movement of members of Usbat al-Ansar and other minor Salafi-jihadi organizations in the camp. Concerned about a potential US attack on Syria and about the creation of a Pax Americana in the region following the US invasion of Iraq in 2003, the Syrian regime tried to undermine American occupation and efforts in Iraq. It was an open secret that the Syrian regime allowed many jihadists from across the Arab world to travel to Damascus International Airport, from which buses would transport them to the border town of Abu Kamal in preparation for their exit to Iraq.[42] In fact, the implications of the US invasion for Syrian policy in Lebanon entailed Syrian, and by extension Lebanese, dilution of the heretofore policy of rigorously controlling Islamist movements in Lebanon. This obviously encouraged jihadi activism in Lebanon, which was manifested not only in the growing contacts between Salafi-jihadi organizations in Lebanon and al-Qaeda but also in the emergence of an organization inspired by, and affiliated with, al-Qaeda—Fatah al-Islam (see next chapter).

In fact, Usbat al-Ansar denied any operational link with al-Qaeda, yet it commended the organization's work in defending the *ummah* and supported its methodological jihad against occupation and the enemies of Islam. Responding to the US State Department's inclusion of Usbat al-Ansar as an al-Qaeda–affiliated terrorist organization on its terrorism list, Usbat spokesperson Sheikh Abu Sherif stated:

> Usbat al-Ansar confirms that it has no organizational relationship with Osama bin Laden and its decision making is independent. Yet, there are stronger links than organizational links with all Muslims. They are the links of religion and creed. As such, we declare that it is the duty of the Muslim *ummah* to unite in confronting the crusader campaign, supported by the Jews.[43]

Meanwhile, this support of and participation in the insurgency in Iraq did not bring a rapprochement or joint operational planning between Usbat and Hezbollah. Usbat had maintained a cautious and ambivalent approach to Hezbollah, partly because it preferred not to be involved in the infamous shift of confessional alliances that mark Lebanese politics and partly to avoid being dragged into an open confrontation with the army or military intelligence in southern Lebanon, both of which include pro-Hezbollah senior officers. The relationship between the two groups took a dramatic turn when a Hezbollah commander, Ghaleb 'Awali, was allegedly murdered by an Usbat splinter group, Jund al-Sham, in 2004. Jund al-Sham categorically denied any responsibility, and as usual accusatory fingers were pointed to Israel. Only following the May 2008 seizure of West Beirut by Hezbollah did Usbat publicly emphasize its attitude toward Hezbollah and its patrons, Iran and Syria.

During the course of communications between Hezbollah and Usbat in the wake of the May seizure of Beirut, which was initiated by Hezbollah as a damage-control measure in regard to its relations with Sunni groups and the Sunni community at large, Usbat underlined three positions vis-à-vis the Party of God. First, Usbat admitted that it had a deep and fundamental creedal problem with Hezbollah. Second, it stressed that it had reservations about the Iranian-Syrian project to control Lebanon, to which Hezbollah is a party. And finally, it said it appreciated Hezbollah's military efforts and sacrifices in confronting Israel.[44] Related to these positions, Usbat, though it expressed its grievances against the Syrian regime for keeping it the target of arbitrary accusations and harassment, underscored that it has no intention of militarily targeting Syria, for its priority is to confront the United States and Israel. Similarly, though it expressed its reservations about Iran's policy, Usbat asserted that if it found itself compelled to choose between the American or Iranian projects in the region, it would confront the American project. Significantly, in spite of its ideological assertive attitude, Usbat stated that it would not level the charge of unbelief on the Shi'a in general and on Hezbollah in particular.[45]

It is likely that this latter attitude of Usbat played a role in inviting the charge by some extreme members of the movement that its leadership had lapsed into "moderation." Reports from the rumor mill in southern Lebanon have supported this charge on the grounds that Usbat has been generally quiet since 2008. On closer examination, however, this charge of moderation is misleading. For one, the charge has been leveled by its members who feel that Usbat's leadership has been slow in trying to curb Shi'a ascendancy in the state. More specifically, Usbat has maintained heretofore a cautious policy regarding all parties in Lebanon, in large part on account of political polarization and heightened sectarianism in the country following the murder of former prime minister

Rafiq Hariri in 2005. Usbat, like other Palestinian parties in Lebanon, fears that the only common political denominator among almost all Lebanese parties is disarming Palestinians under the pretext of national unity.[46] In other words, Usbat is worried about falling victim to the treacherous politics in Lebanon, all in the name of national unity. No less significant, factionalism among and between Palestinians has more or less made Usbat attentive to concerted efforts undertaken by major political parties with the help of highly respected religious scholars, such as Khattab and Hammoud, to maintain calm in the refugee camps at a time of charged political polarization in Lebanon.

Nevertheless, this concern should not be construed as a step in the direction of moderation. On the one hand, Lebanese armed forces have to a great extent clamped down on occasional efforts by Usbat al-Ansar and its offshoot Jund al-Sham to expand their area of operations beyond the camp. On the other, Lebanese authorities have concluded provisional truces with Usbat in return for its intelligence cooperation on al-Qaeda operatives in the camp. Moreover, military intelligence has maintained close surveillance of Salafi jihadists and radical Muslims, especially following the rebellion in Syria in 2011. Notwithstanding the groundswell of Sunni support for the rebellion in Syria, Salafists and Islamists, regardless of their nationality, have rallied around charismatic Salafi scholars opposed to the Asad regime, such as Sheikh Ahmad al-Assir, who mobilized Sunnis to support and/or participate in jihad against the Syrian regime (see chapter 8). Reportedly, former members of Jund al-Sham and Usbat-al-Ansar have been at the forefront of this jihadi mobilization, training members of al-Qaeda–affiliated Jabhat al-Nusra, which has emerged as a strong Salafi-jihadi organization within the Syrian opposition. According to Nasser Sharara, "The ex-members of Fatah al-Islam and Jund al-Sham got on with the task of training and organizing Golani's men [in reference to the leader of Jabhat al-Nusra]. Within a few months they managed to improve al-Nusra Front's performance and organization, turning it into the most formidable armed faction in Syria and an important front for al-Qaeda's global jihad."[47]

Similarly, in response to a question as to whether Usbat al-Ansar would someday give up its weapons as part of an amnesty by Lebanese authorities, Abu Sherif stated: "Weapons are part of this religion. Our stances are not temporary. They emanate from the revelation of God. As such, we are confronting the American-Zionist project, and we will not make a concession on this."[48]

Notes

1. Born in the West Bank in 1941, Sheikh Abdallah Azzam is celebrated among many Arab Muslims for mobilizing Arab mujahideen to fight the Soviets in Afghanistan.

He pursued religious studies in the Department of Shari'a at Damascus University and subsequently went on a fellowship to al-Azhar University in Egypt, where he received his doctorate in Islamic jurisprudence in 1973. He taught for few years at Jordan University, where he supervised the university's youth sector for the Muslim Brotherhood, before leaving for Saudi Arabia in 1981 to teach at King Abd al-Aziz University in Jeddah. There he met his student Osama bin Laden and forged a consequential relationship with Sheikh Kamal al-Sananiri, a member of the Muslim Brotherhood, who encouraged him to join and better organize the mujahidin movement in Afghanistan. Consequently, he obtained a teaching position at Islamabad Islamic University, where he set up contacts with Afghan mujahideen. Significantly, he advocated jihad in Afghanistan as an obligation for all good Muslims, while repeatedly declaring that every Muslim had a moral and financial obligation to participate in jihad. In 1984, he founded Maktab al-Khadamat (Service Bureau) for Arab mujahideen in Peshawar, which served as a nodal point for welcoming, training, and equipping Arab volunteers before sending them off to Afghanistan. Initially, Saudi Arabia funded Azzam's efforts as part of its support of a global jihad against the Soviets in Afghanistan. In November 1989, Azzam, along with his two sons, was killed in a car bombing in Peshawar. For details on Sheikh Azzam, see Gilles Kepel, *Jihad: The Trail of Political Islam*, trans. Anthony F. Roberts (Cambridge, MA: Belknap Press of Harvard University Press, 2002), 144–47, and on his ideology, see Abdallah Azzam, *Jihad Sha'b Muslim* (The Jihad of a Muslim People) (Beirut: Dar Ibn Hamza, 1992).

2. Bernard Rougier, *Everyday Jihad: The Rise of Militant Islam among Palestinians in Lebanon*, trans. by Pascale Ghazaleh (Cambridge, MA: Harvard University Press, 2007), 44.

3. Ra'fat Fahd Marah, *Al-Harakat wal-Qiwa al-Islamiyah fi al-Mujtama' al-Filistini fi Lubnan: al-Nasha', al-Ahdaf, al-Injazat* (The Islamic Movements and Forces in the Palestinian Society in Lebanon: Emergence, Objectives, and Accomplishments) (Beirut: Markaz al-Zaytuni Lil-Dirasat wal-Istisharat, 2010), 164–65.

4. Ibid., 164.

5. Ibid.

6. Ibid.

7. See Sheikh Halaq's statement in "Al-Haraka al-Islamiyah al-Mujahida," *Al-Mustaqbal*, March 3, 2000.

8. Marah, *Al-Harakat wal-Qiwa al-Islamiyah fi al-Mujtama' al-Filistini fi Lubnan*, 165–66.

9. Many future leaders of the Iranian Islamic Republic received training in Lebanon's Palestinian camps. Among them were Muhammad Ghazani, the future oil minister; Ayatollah Ali Janati, who had taken part in several Fatah operations against Israel; Ayatollah Ruhollah Khomeini's sons, Mustafa and Ahmad; and Ayatollah

Hussein-Ali Montazeri's son Muhammad. See Fouad Ajami, *The Vanished Imam: Musa al-Sadr and the Shi'a of Lebanon* (Ithaca, NY: Cornell University Press, 1986), 224, and Rougier, *Everyday Jihad*, 28. Among those who also came to Lebanon from Iran was Mustafa Shamran, who helped Imam Sadr found Amal and train its members. Two other important figures who came to Lebanon regularly and then became Iranian ambassadors to Syria are Ali Muhtashami and Muhammad Hassan Akhtari. These two figures played a significant role in founding and supporting Hezbollah. See Akhtari's interview with *Ash-Sharq al-Awsat*, "Akhtari: Hezbollah, Hamas wa al-Jihad Abna' Shari'youn lil-Thawra al-Iraniyah," (Akhtari: Hezbollah, Hamas and [Islamic] Jihad are Legitimate Sons of the Iranian Revolution), May 14, 2008. For more details, see Waddah Sharara, *Dawlat Hizb Allah: Lubnan Mujtama'an Islamiyan* (The State of Hezbollah: Lebanon a Muslim Society), 3rd ed. (Beirut: Dar al-Nahar, 1998).

10. Rougier, *Everyday Jihad*, 32.

11. Ibid., 41.

12. Ibid., 45.

13. Ibid., 58–59; Marah, *Al-Harakat wal-Qiwa al-Islamiyah fi al-Mujtama' al-Filistini fi Lubnan*, 168; and "Al-Haraka al-Islamiyah al-Mujahida," *Al-Mustaqbal*, March 3, 2000.

14. Marah, *Al-Harakat wal-Qiwa al-Islamiyah fi al-Mujtama' al-Filistini fi Lubnan*, 168.

15. Rougier, *Everyday Jihad*, 46.

16. Marah, *Al-Harakat wal-Qiwa al-Islamiyah fi al-Mujtama' al-Filistini fi Lubnan*, 173.

17. Abd al-Ghani 'Imad, *Al-Harakat al-Islamiyah fi Lubnan: Ishkaliyat al-Din wal-Siyasah fi Mujtama' Mutanawe'* (Islamic Movements in Lebanon: The Ambiguity of Religion and Politics in a Diverse Society) (Beirut: Dar al-Tali'a lil-Tiba'a wal-Nashr, 2006), 323.

18. Ibid. See also the missionary statement of Usbat al-Ansar on its website, http://alqasem.arabblogs.com/nashah/index4.html (accessed August 2, 2013).

19. Marah, *Al-Harakat wal-Qiwa al-Islamiyah fi al-Mujtama' al-Filistini fi Lubnan*, 180.

20. Ibid., 190–91; 'Imad, *Al-Harakat al-Islamiyah fi Lubnan*, 323; and Rougier, *Everyday Jihad*, 48–49.

21. Ibid. (all).

22. See the statement on the emergence of Usbat al-Ansar on its website, http://alqassem.arabblogs.com/nashah/index2.html (accessed August 3, 2013).

23. See Usbat al-Ansar's definition of its creed on its website, http://alqassem.arabblogs.com/nashah/index1.html (accessed August 4, 2013).

24. *Hukm Allah* is synonymous with *hakimiyat Allah* in the sense that God's sovereignty, or His rule, is exclusive.

25. See Usbat al-Ansar's definition of its creed on its website, http://alqassem.arab blogs.com/nashah/index1.html (accessed August 4, 2013).

26. See Usbat's mission on its website, http://alqassem.arabblogs.com/nashah/index4 .html (accessed August 4, 2013).

27. Ibid.

28. See Usbat al-Ansar's understanding of the principle of loyalty and disavowal on its website, http://alqassem.arabblogs.com/nashah/index3.html (accessed August 4, 2013).

29. Ibid.

30. See Usbat al-Ansar's website, http://alqassem.arabblogs.com/nashah/index1.html (accessed August 4, 2013).

31. See introductory statement of Usbat on its website, http://alqassem.arabblogs .com/nashah/index.html (accessed August 4, 2013).

32. Gary C. Gambill, "Ain al-Hilweh: Lebanon's 'Zone of Unlaw,'" *Middle East Intelligence Bulletin* 5, no. 6 (June 2003).

33. "Halabi's Killer Gets Sentence Commuted," *Daily Star*, July 28, 2000. For complete details on the assassination of Sheikh Halabi, the names of the defendants, and the sentences issued against them, see Court of Justice, Assassination of Sheikh Nizar Al-Halabi, decision no. 1/1997, January 17, 1997, available at the Special Tribunal for Lebanon's website, www.stl-tsl.org/en/documents/relevant -law-and-case-law/relevant-case-law/terrorism-cases/court-of-justice-assassination -of-sheikh-nizar-al-halabi-decision-no-1-1997-17-january-1997 (accessed August 8, 2013).

34. For details on the Usbat's terror activities and accusations and the sentences levied against the movement's members by the Lebanese government, see Marah, *Al-Harakat wal-Qiwa al-Islamiyah fi al-Mujtama' al-Filistini fi Lubnan*, 183–86.

35. See details of the incident in *An-Nahar* and *As-Safir*, July 8, 2002.

36. Divisions within Usbat al-Ansar began following the assassination of its leader Sharaydi. The first split was led by Sheikh 'Imad Yassin, who felt that Abu Muhjin was not the right choice for succession. The next split took place when the son of Sharaydi, Abdallah, claimed himself to be the rightful successor. He was passed over on account of his youth, as he was then only twenty years old, and because his Islamic education was weak. Subsequently Abdallah founded his own Salafi-jihadi movement, Usbat al-Nur, in 2002. The other split took place when Muhammad Ahmad Sharqiyah, known as Abu Youssef, a Palestinian refugee from the Nahr al-Bared camp in northern Lebanon, moved to the Ayn al-Helweh camp in 1989. He joined Usbat al-Ansar, and later on, following the death of its leader, he established Jund al-Sham (Soldiers of Bilad al-Sham). Members of Usbat al-Ansar joined his new movement. Abu Youssef emphasizes two objectives for Jund al-Sham: establishing God's revelation (Islamic law) as set forth in the Qur'an, Sunna, and the

opinions of previous scholars, and jihad in the path of God, whereby preparation is made to fight the enemies of God, the United States, Israel, and those attacking Muslims. Jund al-Sham established its headquarters in Ta'mir, an area adjacent to the camp. See 'Imad, *Al-Harakat al-Islamiyah fi Lubnan*, 324–25, and the investigative report by Subhi Yaghi, *An-Nahar*, October 29, 2004.

37. See Gambill, "Ain al-Hilweh: Lebanon's 'Zone of Unlaw.'"

38. See Thair Abbas, "Al-Qaeda in Lebanon," *Ash-Sharq al-Awsat*, March 19, 2006.

39. See Hazem al-Amin's report in *Al-Hayat*, January 26, 2006, first cited by 'Imad, *Al-Harakat al-Islamiyah fi Lubnan*, 329.

40. "Tawqif Shabaka lil-Qaeda fi Lubnan" (Arrest of an al-Qaeda cell in Lebanon), *As-Safir*, January 13, 2006.

41. See Spencer S. Hsu and Robin Wright, "Tunnel Plot Suspects Linked to Al-Qaeda," *Washington Post*, July 11, 2006. See also Hsu and Wright, "Plot to Attack N.Y. Foiled," *Washington Post*, July 8, 2006.

42. For details on Syrian complicity in supporting the insurgency in Iraq, see Robert G. Rabil, *Syria, the United States, and the War on Terror in the Middle East* (Westport, CT: Praeger Security International, 2006), 140–60.

43. See statement of Sheikh Abu Sherif in "Usbat al-Ansar," *As-Safir*, September 26, 2001.

44. Marah, *Al-Harakat wal-Qiwa al-Islamiyah fi al-Mujtama' al-Filistini fi Lubnan*, 182.

45. Ibid., 182–83.

46. For detailed analysis of Islamism and confessional politics in Lebanon, see Robert G. Rabil, *Religion, National Identity, and Confessional Politics in Lebanon: The Challenge of Islamism* (New York: Palgrave Macmillan, 2011).

47. Nasser Sharara, "Al-Nusra Front in Lebanon," *Al-Akhbar*, February 25, 2013.

48. Marah, *Al-Harakat wal-Qiwa al-Islamiyah fi al-Mujtama' al-Filistini fi Lubnan*, 193.

Chapter Six

Salafism, Confessional Politics, and Shi'a Ascendancy

Al-Infitah (Opening Up) or the Rise to Rebellion?

This chapter surveys the end of the civil war in Lebanon and the emergence of the Second Republic under the trusteeship of Syria. It examines the Islamist parties' *infitah* (opening up) to the political system, focusing on whether or not Hezbollah (the Party of God) would transform into a conventional party. At the same time, it scrutinizes Syrian policy in Lebanon and the Lebanese-Syrian relationship against which Hezbollah emerged as the preeminent political and military power in the country, to the chagrin of other parties including the Sunni leadership represented by late former prime minister Rafiq Hariri and the Salafists. It also investigates the setbacks and opportunities Salafists faced under Syrian hegemony, exposing in the process their operational and ideological links to both Salafi jihadism and Salafi transnational networks. The chapter then examines the background against which Hariri was assassinated and Beirut was overtaken by Hezbollah, and analyzes the implications of these developments for Lebanon's politics, communal relations, and Salafism's ideology and praxis. Special attention is paid to the *infitah* of the quietest Salafi school to Hezbollah, which exposed not only the ideological and political incongruities and differences among Salafists but also the depth of Salafism's grievances and simmering hostility toward the Shi'a Islamist party.

The End of the Civil War: The Taif Agreement and Syrian Hegemony

By the late 1980s, the civil war in Lebanon had broken down into intra- and interdenominational conflicts. The Christian Lebanese Forces, led by Samir Geagea, had fallen out with the Maronite president Amin Gemayel, a former leader of the Phalange Party and older brother of late president Bashir Gemayel, founder of the Lebanese Forces. The Shi'ite Amal movement, which had barely concluded its brutal campaign against the PLO in the Palestinian refugee camps, had begun an armed struggle with the Shi'a Islamist party Hezbollah for the control of the Shi'a community, especially in southern Lebanon. And whatever little power the Sunni community had following the defeat of its PLO foot soldiers, first by Israel and Syria and then by Amal, collapsed under the military weight of Hezbollah and Amal in West Beirut. The community frayed politically at the seams under the yoke of Syria's (and its proxies') subjugation and internal fragmentation. Significantly, in 1988, when the term of President Gemayel neared its end, he, unable to present to the Lebanese parliament an agreed-upon list of presidential hopefuls as mandated by the constitution, appointed Gen. Michel Aoun to head an executive cabinet until a president was elected.[1] Pro-Syrian deputies disapproved of Aoun's appointment, regarding it constitutionally illegitimate, and lent their support to the government of Prime Minister Salim al-Hoss. At the time, Lebanon witnessed two authorities: one formal, led by Aoun and exercising its authority over the Christian area, the other de facto and pro-Damascus, led by Hoss and extending its authority over the areas under Syrian control.

In March 1989, General Aoun proclaimed a "liberation war" against Syria. His war was to take the form of an *intifada* against Syria similar to that of the Palestinians in the West Bank.[2] Syria responded by shelling the Christian area and imposing on it a sea-and-land blockade, especially East Beirut. In view of the constitutional impasse and the escalation of hostilities, and at the urging of Saudi Arabia, Lebanese deputies left for the city of Taif in Saudi Arabia. At the meeting there, the Lebanese deputies, with the intercession of Arab delegates from Saudi Arabia, Algeria, and Morocco, and under pressure from Syria, managed to introduce significant amendments to the Lebanese constitution. The new version of the constitution became known interchangeably as the Document of National Understanding and the Taif Accord. In addition, over Aoun's objections, the deputies elected Elias Hrawi president, whom Aoun refused to recognize. On August 21, 1990, the Lebanese parliament approved the constitutional amendments introduced by the Taif Accord, which were signed into law by President Hrawi on September 21.

General Aoun opposed the Taif Accord as a Syrian scheme to whittle away at Maronite power and called on the Lebanese Forces to stand by him in order to meet the Syrian challenge. Contemplating the surge of Maronite support for Aoun, the Lebanese Forces, in addition to considering Aoun's liberation war against Syria to be political suicide, reckoned that under the pretext of meeting the Syrian challenge, Aoun was paving the way for dismantling them. Deadly hostilities broke out in Christian East Beirut between the Lebanese Forces, commanded by Geagea, and Aoun's forces. Remarking on Aoun's losing battles with

Syria and the Lebanese Forces, Karim Pakradouni wrote: "The General lost the 'liberation war' against Syria because it was bigger than him, and he lost the 'eastern battle' [East Beirut] against the Lebanese Forces because he considered it smaller than him."[3]

It was against this background that Iraq rocked the region by invading Kuwait in early August 1990. The United States needed Syria's help in forming the international and Arab anti-Iraq coalition to extract Iraq from Kuwait. On October 13, the Syrian army, along with a unit of the Lebanese army under the Command of Col. Émile Lahoud, launched an all-out attack on Aoun's forces. The Syrian air force intervened for the first time in the history of the Lebanese conflict and bombed Aoun out of the presidential palace. Within hours, East Beirut, the last bastion of Lebanese opposition to Syria, fell. Obviously, the United States had yielded to Asad's demand for total hegemony over Lebanon as a price for bringing Syria into the US-led anti-Iraq coalition. No less significant, a by-product of the war was the launching of the Madrid Peace Conference, with Syrian participation.

The collapse of East Beirut and the emergence of a "new Lebanon," the Second Republic, under Syrian hegemony expedited the implementation of the Taif Accord.[4] The agreement was divided into three parts: General Principles and Reforms (political and other reforms), Extending Lebanese Sovereignty over All Lebanese Territories, and Liberating Lebanon from Israeli Occupation.

The document stated that Lebanon is a free, sovereign state, and a definitive homeland to its citizens ("sons"); and that Lebanon is Arab in identity and affiliation ("belonging"). The thrust of political reforms revolved around conferring equal powers to the three high posts in the land. Executive power was transferred from the president to the Council of Ministers, which would set the general policy of the state, draft bills and decrees, take the necessary measures for their implementation, and supervise the activities of all state agencies. The president would name a prime minister on the basis of consultations with the speaker of the Chamber (Parliament). He could attend a meeting of the council but without the right to vote.

The Chamber was enlarged to 108 members, divided equally between Muslims and Christians and apportioned according to sect. Being the legislative authority, the Chamber would exercise full control over government policies and activities. The speaker's term was increased to four years. The electoral law would be based on the province (governorate) in light of cross-sectarian representation.

Political confessionalism (sectarianism) would be abolished in phases, set by a national committee, but in the meantime all posts in the civil service, with the exception of the top three, would be accorded on the basis of competence. Other reforms included administrative decentralization. The other two sections dealt mainly with (a) building the armed forces to shoulder their responsibilities in confronting Israeli aggression; (b) dismantling all militias; (c) implementing United Nations (UN) Resolution 425, which calls for strict respect for the territorial integrity of Lebanon, the withdrawal of Israel from all Lebanese territory, and the creation of the UN Interim Force in Lebanon (UNIFIL); and (d) taking the necessary measures to liberate all Lebanese territory from Israeli occupation. The Taif Accord also provided that Syrian forces shall assist the legitimate Lebanese forces in establishing the state's authority within a period not exceeding two years and that the two governments shall decide on the future redeployment of Syrian forces. With regard to Lebanese-Syrian relations, the accord underscored that "Lebanon, which is Arab in identity and affiliation, is bound by fraternal, sincere relations to all Arab states and has special relations with Syria that draw their strength from the roots of kinship, history and common internal interests."[5] In other words, Lebanon, under the pretext of special relations, had become an appendage to Syria, given the latter's preponderant power.

Admittedly, it is true that the Taif Accord introduced major reforms, yet confessional representation dominated the new system as the new distribution of power was an expression of a confessional formula. Augustus Richard Norton remarked that "the accord effectively concedes the futility of any serious attempt to expunge political sectarianism in Lebanon, at least for the foreseeable future. (It bears recalling that the unwritten 1943 pact also was not intended to institutionalize political sectarianism.) The accord leaves no doubt that, rhetoric aside, confessionalism is here to stay for some time to come."[6]

Meanwhile, in line with the Taif Accord's emphasis on the Lebanese-Syrian special relations, the Syrian and Lebanese presidents signed the May 20, 1991, Treaty of Brotherhood, Cooperation, and Coordination and the September 1, 1991, Lebanon-Syria Defense and Security Agreement, which institutionalized Syrian trusteeship (occupation) over Lebanon.[7] Before long, with Syrian prodding, parliamentary elections were scheduled for summer 1992, after a hiatus of two decades.

Islamism and the Lebanese State: Hezbollah and al-Jama'a Islamiyah's *Infitah* and Lebanonization

The upcoming parliamentary elections posed a challenge to both Sunni and Shi'a Islamist parties. For the Jama'a Islamiyah (Islamic Association), led by Fathi Yakan, the challenge was more about legally justifying its decision to participate in Lebanon's politics. The Jama'a had already dabbled with politics in the early 1970s but had neither justified in Islamic legal terms its participation nor formulated a political program. It is noteworthy that it was then the only organized

Islamist party and faced an insignificant challenge from Salafists who had been mainly interested in *da'wa* and reestablishing their popular bases following their subjugation and harassment by Syrian intelligence. Sheikh Da'i al-Islam al-Shahal, for example, returned to Tripoli following an itinerant stay in Sidon and other areas far from the watchful eye of Syrian intelligence. He focused mainly on *da'wa* and on expanding the network of charity and educational institutions established by his father Salem. At the center of these institutions was Jami'yat al-Hidaya wal-Ihsan (the Association of Guidance and Charity), which was supported by Saudi Arabia's largest charity institution, Mu'assassat al-Haramayn. Moreover, a significant number of activist Islamists had decided to wait out Syrian hegemony in Lebanon.

Notwithstanding the fact that Fathi Yakan had already ideologically paved the path for the *infitah* (opening up) of his party to Lebanon's confessional system, he subordinated its decision to participate in the upcoming election to an Islamic legal study by the Islamic Association. The study, *The Islamic Legal Justifications to Enter the Elections Battle*, which was released on August 9, 1992, recommended that the association participate in the parliamentary elections. The study based its findings on the following:

1. It considered parliamentary work as a method of *hisbah*[8] (accountability) and a pulpit for those who "command good and forbid wrong," (*al-amr bil-ma'ruf wal-nahi 'an al-munkar*), especially on the basis of *hisbah* that relies on change through the tongue and not force. All Muslims are required to carry out this duty to achieve the principles of Islamic law, safeguard social life, and protect people from moral deviation.
2. To participate in parliamentary sessions does not mean approving any legislative position contradicting Islamic law. A deputy can object, provide an alternative, criticize, or boycott the session. This means that the principle of participation rests with the position and the practice. If the practice is religiously legitimate with the objective of rightly informing legislations and reforming the system, then it is a duty to do so.
3. To participate in parliament sessions is a gateway to *da'wa* (the call to Islam) in Islam and to propagate its beliefs and principles through dialogue and conversation.
4. To participate in parliament activities is to provide opportunities to realize peoples' interest and block vices and to achieve a balanced economic development.[9]

Along with these justifications, the study underscored that "its participation would fill the void left by the downfall of the various leftist currents, which until recently monopolized political decisions in the name of Muslims, let alone enhance the nationalist and jihadi feeling to stand up to the projects of West-ernization and to the hegemony and domination practiced by the international system and the oppressive powers in the world."[10]

To be sure, the legal justification to participate in Lebanon's confessional poli-tics was close to Yakan's ideology, which was mainly premised on the necessity of improving the welfare of the Muslim society and confronting the Zionists and their allies (see chapter 2). Apparently the priority Yakan had put on under-mining Christian influence in the state and confronting the Zionists coincided with Syria's policy of reducing Christian power to insignificance in Lebanon and of maintaining Syria as the vanguard of Arab nationalism by way of its *nidal* (struggle) and *sumud* (steadfastness) against Israel.[11] This partly explains the reorientation of Yakan and his organization in the direction of Syria's national security policy in Lebanon and the region. In fact, the Islamic Association's 1992 parliamentary elections program was virtually written by Syria's Ba'thist pen. The program underscored that the association's "Project of Liberation, Reform and Change, perceived Lebanon as an undivided part of the Arabic *ummah*, where Arab existence provides the strategic depth to Lebanon." The program also asserted that the Zionist project has posed the biggest threat to the *ummah* (Islamic community) and Lebanon, for it was able to rape Palestine and vaga-bondize its people.[12] Before long, his political subservience to the Syrian dik-tat in Lebanon paid off in the parliamentary elections. Three members of the Islamic Association won: Fathi Yakan for northern Lebanon in Tripoli, As'ad Harmouch for northern Lebanon in al-Dinniyah, and Zuhair al-'Abidi in Bei-rut. It goes without saying that mainly pro-Syrian candidates could win under the Syrian occupation of Lebanon.

Conversely, Hezbollah's *infitah* to Lebanon's confessional system entailed not only an ideological transformation but also a social transformation according to which Lebanon's political system and national identity would be defined by the Islamic resistance.

Initially the Islamist party was extremely wary and concerned about both the upcoming elections and the resulting impending change in the system and the ramifications of the implementation of the Taif Accord for its jihadi organiza-tion. Hezbollah tried to create a political bloc opposing the accord but to no avail. Most political forces in Beirut supported the Taif Accord and were toeing the Syrian line. Eventually Hezbollah made a distinction between its political and military opposition and opted not to stand in the way of the Taif Accord's implementation, beginning with the deployment of the Lebanese army in Bei-rut.[13] This calculated, pragmatic decision was the outcome of several meetings between the party leadership and President Asad on one side and the Lebanese government on the other. In dealing with the Taif Accord—and by extension the sponsor of the accord, Syria—Hezbollah based its decision-making process on what it called *al-thawabit* (immutable fundamentals/principles) and *maslaha* (interest). Foremost among the *thawabit* was the absolute enmity to Israel, while *maslaha* was an expression of common denominators with other parties under the "heading" of *thawabit*. The party leadership saw that Damascus was the only Arab state confronting Israel, even after it had attended the Madrid Peace Conference. And it saw that the two (Damascus and Hezbollah) had a common interest in forcing Israel from Lebanon.[14] Simultaneously, the defense and agriculture ministers (Muhsin Daloul and Albert Mansour) held a few meetings with the party leadership in which they decided to create coordination committees to preempt problems. Most important, Hezbollah's decision not to confront the government of the Second Republic lay in the understandings with President Asad and the government that its freedom of action would not be restricted nor its resistance against Israel obstructed.[15] Nevertheless, according to Hassan Fadlallah, it was the vision of President Asad that governed the development of Hezbollah-Syrian relations, as he was careful to nurture the resistance against Israel.[16]

But if dealing with the Taif Accord reflected some kind of a qualitative jump from rejectionism and radicalism to some sort of accommodation, it was the decision over whether to participate in the political system and the upcoming elections that would test political flexibility and maturity. Participation in the elections was essentially an admission of the legitimacy of the political system that the organization was so adamant about abolishing. This decision entailed an evaluation of Hezbollah's religio-political ideology in relation to its evolution into a vigorous social movement. On February 16, 1985, Hezbollah issued an open letter that introduced the party and declared its ideological, jihadi, political, and social visions.

The open letter was orated by Sayyid Ibrahim Amin al-Sayyid.[17] Guided by Ayatollah Khomeini's political ideological view, it dichotomized the world into the oppressed and the oppressors, and presented the Party of God as the party of the oppressed, supporting the struggle of all the oppressed. It identified the members of Hezbollah as the sons of the *ummah*, whose nucleus had been established by the Iranian Revolution. They abide by the wise and just command represented by the guardianship of the jurisprudent (*wilayat al-faqih*). Correspondingly, the open letter specified the identity of the party as an *ummah* not confined to Lebanon but tied to all Muslims. It stated that "we in Lebanon are neither a closed organizational party nor a narrow political framework. Rather, we are an Ummah tied to the Muslims in every part of the world by a strong ideological-doctrinal, and political bond, namely Islam, whose message God completed at the hands of the last of His prophets, Muhammad."[18]

As such, the party considered itself an indivisible part of the Islamic nation readily prepared, on the grounds of religious duty (*wajib shar'i*) and in light of the decisions of *wali al-faqih* (just jurisconsult/jurisprudent), to confront all that befalls Muslims. It identified the United States as the first root of vice and underscored the unremitting attack on Muslims waged by America's NATO allies and Israel, the Zionist entity in the holy land of Palestine. It denounced the Zionist-Phalangist cooperation and specified three objectives in Lebanon: expelling the Americans and their allies, submitting the Phalangists to a just power and bringing them to justice for their crimes, and allowing Lebanese to determine their political future and the form of their government, though enjoining them to choose Islam, which is alone capable of guaranteeing justice and liberty for all. It called for the establishment of the Islamic state (*al-dawla al-Islamiyah*) in Lebanon, on the basis of free choice and not force. Correspondingly, it condemned the Lebanese political system, even censuring any opposition that does not demand changing the very foundation of the system. Significantly, it called for the obliteration of Israel, rejecting any form of negotiation, settlement, proposal, or treaty with the Zionist entity. It appealed for a broad Islamic participation in the Islamic resistance, stressing the continuity of martyrdom and jihad until the Zionists evacuate the occupied lands, as a first step in the right direction to wipe them from the face of the earth.[19]

Therefore, the decision prefigured a definition of a political vision expressed in a political program, which, in turn, provoked an extensive internal debate in the party. Hezbollah set up a committee, made up of the party's leadership, to assess whether or not the party should participate in Lebanon's political system. Deputy Secretary-General of Hezbollah Naim Qassem explained that the committee could not address the question of legitimacy, since it was the prerogative of the *wali al-faqih*, Ayatollah Ali Khamenei, Iran's supreme leader. Nevertheless, the committee comprehensively addressed other matters related mainly to the question as to whether a readjustment of the party's religio-political program would affect the resistance.[20]

The committee perceived that participation has significant advantages, chief among them using the parliament as a political podium to take care of the resistance and its matters, drafting legislation to benefit the livelihood of people and oppressed areas, and granting Hezbollah official recognition from the Lebanese parliament, thereby conferring on the resistance official and popular legitimacy. In addition, given that the party linked its participation in the elections to a candid declaration about maintaining the priority of resistance, the committee saw that there is no need for concern that such participation would have a negative bearing on resistance activity. Instead, elections constitute an additional capital supporting the resistance.

The committee also pointed out disadvantages to parliamentary representation, chief among them (a) the difficulty of having a precise popular representation on account of the system's confessional-based allocated number of representatives, which renders representation in the parliament more political than numerical, and (2) the enactment of laws contradictory to *shari'a* (Islamic law), despite their opposition by Hezbollah's deputies. Based on the above deliberations, the committee voted in favor of parliamentary participation, not only as an interest but also as a necessity.[21] This was harmonious with Hezbollah's total vision for defending the affairs and interests of people in the political realm and not in conflict with the priority of jihad for liberation. Subsequently, the committee presented its findings to Ayatollah Khamenei and requested from him a legal opinion (*istifta'*) on the legitimacy of participating in the elections, which he authorized and supported (*ajaza wa ayyada*).[22] Immediately thereafter, the party began drafting its political program and on July 3, 1992, announced its participation in the elections. This marked the *infitah* (opening up) of Hezbollah to Lebanon's political system.

But this *infitah* was not only made possible by the blessing of Ayatollah Khamenei. Ayatollah Muhammad Hussein Fadlallah played a crucial role in nudging the Islamist party toward what he termed "Lebanonization" of the Islamist movement in Lebanon, a term that became synonymous with *infitah*. He supported Hezbollah's engagement of Lebanon's political system as a means for the Islamist movement to electorally legitimize itself and to realize transitional goals without even confirming the legitimacy of the system. Such Lebanonization, he explained, had to heed the unique circumstances of confessional Lebanon and the particular condition of the Maronites. He also emphasized that Hezbollah should enter the electoral arena if only for the sake of Islamic legitimacy in Lebanon, which dictates the formation of a parliamentary party. This is not to say that the Islamists have embraced the parliamentary system, but parliament does provide a forum where they can express their views and urge others, if not to adopt those views, at least to be more accommodating toward them.[23]

Interestingly enough, Lebanonization as a term and concept has taken a political dimension far from its original meaning, leading to a confused reading of Hezbollah's intentions and policies. Hezbollah's entry into Lebanon's political arena has raised questions about the future of the Islamist party. Some scholars, such as Augustus Richard Norton, Hala Jaber, Judith Palmer Harik, A. Nizar Hamzeh, and Magnus Ranstorp, have argued in slightly different versions that Hezbollah's Lebanonization process would in due time transform the Islamist party into a conventional political party, shedding both its jihadi character (especially vis-à-vis its struggle with Israel) and its long-term ideal of an Islamic regime and state.[24] This line of reasoning has become a sort of biblical mantra following Israel's withdrawal from southern Lebanon in summer 2000, in spite of the fact that it was refuted by the party itself. Brushing aside the notion of making political concessions in return for political and administrative positions, Qassem sarcastically observed that "the repeated talks about the Lebanonization of Hezbollah and its admission into the internal political life is but another title of the necessity to abandon its fundamentals and the priority of resistance, and to stop fighting Israel and surrender its weapons and the reasons for its power."[25]

Essentially, Lebanonization of Hezbollah has been at the heart of the political process to support Hezbollah's jihad and resistance. In fact, this process did not begin until the party was sure about its sociopolitical and military power in the Lebanese milieu and no longer concerned about the cost of its politicization at the expense of its resistance role. As Qassem asserted: "The introduction [identity] of Hezbollah, which has been fashioned in a way so as to interrupt the debate and resolve the relationship between the [party's] jihadi and political aspects, is that 'the movement of Hezbollah is a jihadi movement whose primary objective is the struggle [jihad] against the Zionist enemy,' and 'the clever and sagacious political jihad can and should be the buttress and pillar of this jihadi movement.'"[26]

This inseparable "organic" link between Hezbollah's political and jihadi organizations was apparently ignored by the various aforementioned scholars of the Islamist party. Arguably, this oversight rested with the desire of the scholars to project an image of Hezbollah consistent with its pragmatic transformation into a political party far from the stigmatization of terrorism. But in so doing, they obfuscated and/or misread the true reality of Hezbollah, as a jihadi movement commandeering political jihad, to use Qassem's terminology. Interestingly, the party underscored the values of resistance as a foundation out of which *mujtama' al-muqawamah* (resistance society) would be forged. In this respect, Hezbollah has been keen on transforming Lebanese society into a resistance society as part of its Islamist resistance project, whereby the society at large would be integrated into the resistance. In expounding the way in which the rest of society should integrate with the Resistance, Qassem asserted: "Resistance for us is a societal vision in all its dimensions, for it is a military, cultural, political and informational resistance. It is the resistance of the people and the *mujahideen*, it is the resistance of the ruler and the *ummah*, it is the resistance of the free consciousness anywhere. As such, we have always called for building the society of resistance. Not one day have we accepted a group of resistance, because the society of resistance bears continuity, whereas the performance of the group of resistance is circumstantial.[27]

Clearly, Hezbollah's *infitah* and Lebanonization are more about supporting the party's resistance and redefining Lebanon's national identity in the interest of both Hezbollah's jihad and changing the country's political system. Expectedly, Fathi Yakan supported the Islamic resistance, as led by Hezbollah, and made this support a priority of his political program.

For Syria, the *infitah* and Lebanonization of the Islamic Association and Hezbollah had a complete different dimension.

Syrian Suzerainty and Lebanonization

The Islamic Association's *infitah* was an opportune policy for Syria because it was trying to help Lebanon build its state institutions under its suzerainty. Accordingly, the Syrian regime needed political allies to participate in the political system so as to give it a legitimate cover and to act as a barrier against the emergence of an anti-Syrian coalition. Moreover, being ever wary about Islamists since their rebellion in Syria and Tripoli, the Syrian regime placed a premium on co-opting Islamists and donning the mantle of piety. The Islamic Association under Yakan provided the Syrian regime a proxy force both within the country's system, especially the parliament, and within the realm of Sunni Islamism. Consequently, Yakan, along with other Sunni sheikhs such as Sa'id Sha'ban of the Islamic Unity Movement, emerged as the main proponents of Syrian interest in Lebanon. It is noteworthy that Sunni sheikhs in southern Lebanon, such as Jamal Khattab and Mahir Hammoud, had also emerged as proponents of Iranian interests, and by extension of Syrian interests, in Lebanon.

Conversely, the *infitah* and Lebanonization of Hezbollah had a completely different dimension for Syria, related no less to Damascus's national security than to Hezbollah's utilitarian political and military jihad. As the Syrian government began to exert more formal suzerainty over Lebanon, it sought to use Hezbollah both to pressure Israel for a return of the Golan Heights and to undermine the development of any opposition movement in Lebanon. Such objectives were difficult to reconcile. How could Syria help to build Lebanon's state institutions and support Hezbollah's military role? President Asad established rules to govern the relationship between the state, the Lebanese political forces, and Hezbollah, which the Syrian intelligence chief in Lebanon would oversee:

1. Pro-Syrian officials would staff Lebanese state institutions and the army.
2. The cabinet of ministers would exclude any anti-Syrian official, and Damascus would retain effective veto power over sensitive government portfolios such as the ministries of the interior, defense, and foreign affairs.
3. The Syrian chief of intelligence in Lebanon would oversee elections and gerrymander districts to control them.

4. Hezbollah would take the lead on military operations against Israel but enjoy the implicit political support of the Lebanese government. Whereas Hezbollah would pursue armed resistance, the Lebanese government would resist by politically supporting Hezbollah.

5. Unless otherwise approved by Damascus, Hezbollah would limit its operations to the Israeli-occupied "security zone" in southern Lebanon.

6. Neither Hezbollah nor the state could use force against the other, with Damascus the arbiter in disputes.

7. Lebanese political parties could pursue their objectives so long as they did not conflict with Syrian policies.

8. Absent Damascus's approval, no political party could use external forces to advance a political agenda.

9. While Damascus would supervise Hezbollah's operations against Israel, Hezbollah could decide the timing within windows specified by Damascus.

10. Hezbollah could capitalize on its resistance role and financial assistance from Iran to advance its political agenda but could not do so at the expense of pro-Syrian parties such as Amal.[28]

This new framework became the backdrop against which Hezbollah evolved militarily, organizationally, and politically. In other words, thanks to Syria, Hezbollah became a preeminent military and political force in Lebanon, while other parties were forced to disarm and toe the Syrian line. Oppositional figures were either co-opted, exiled, imprisoned, or liquidated.[29]

On the surface, the *infitah* of Hezbollah and the Islamic Association pointed to a new era of communal cooperation in Lebanon. Most Lebanese were happy the civil war was over. On closer examination, however, segments of the Sunni and Christian communities felt that the war had ended at their political expense, given the fact that they were not content with Syria's political arrangement that pronouncedly favored Hezbollah. In fact, many Islamists, especially Salafists, were unhappy with Syria's occupation of Lebanon and support of Hezbollah. Although Salafists did not overtly oppose the Syrian regime and its allies in Lebanon, they capitalized on two developments to indirectly accumulate political power. In the early 1990s, the Syrian regime focused on removing all vestiges of Christian opposition. Though the Lebanese Forces supported the Taif Accord and its implementation, they grew increasingly critical of Syria's calculated strategy to control Lebanon's Second Republic. Samir Geagea, the leader of the Lebanese Forces, was found guilty of ordering political assassinations and sentenced to life in prison. He was the only warlord to face trial and go to prison. Other Christian leaders, including former president Gemayel and General Aoun, had already been forced from the country. No less significant, the Syrian regime had been keen to balance its relationship with the Second Republic's first prime minister, Rafiq Hariri, who was Saudi Arabia's point man in the country, against that with its allies, mainly Hezbollah, which was supported by Iran. After all, it was essentially a Saudi Arabian–Syrian sponsorship of the Taif Accord that guaranteed its success. Supported by Saudi Arabia, Hariri, a dual citizen of Lebanon and Saudi Arabia, and a business tycoon close to the royal family of al-Saud, had taken the initiative in reconstructing Beirut and virtually dominating the internal politics of Lebanon. Consequently, the Syrian regime was hard pressed to supervise and reconcile what had been infamously referred to in Lebanon's political circles as the emergence of Hong Kong under Hariri and the emergence of Hanoi under Hezbollah. Not surprisingly, it was for all practical purposes this irreconcilable link in Syria's dual policy in Lebanon that preoccupied the Syrian regime before it broke down with the murder of Hariri in 2005. This preoccupation, together with Syria's attempt at eliminating Christian opposition, provided the Salafists the maneuvering room to proliferate and grow into large, informal networks of missionary, charitable, and educational institutions, supported by Salafi transnational organizations in the Gulf.

Nevertheless, this growth, though partly fueled by funds from the Gulf, notably from Saudi Arabia, and by an identity crisis further intensified by Syria's Ba'thist discourse and support of Hezbollah's jihad and sociopolitical program, experienced a rough-and-tumble path that marked Salafism's self-image at one and the same time as the saved sect and the dispossessed community.

The Emergence of al-Takfir wal-Hijra and the Iraqi War: Setbacks and Opportunities

The assassination of al-Ahbash leader Sheikh Nizar Halabi in 1995 by Usbat al-Ansar redrew the attention of Lebanese and Syrian authorities to Islamist movements, especially Salafists. As mentioned in the previous chapter, scores of Usbat al-Ansar members and supporters were arrested and some of them sentenced to death and life in prison. Significantly, the state campaign against Salafists took a social and national-identity dimension. In his opening statement against the defendants, state attorney Nasri al-Maalouf demanded that the "defendants should be punished not only for homicide but also in order to abolish a school of thought that sought to distort our history and undermine our country's reputation and national coexistence."[30] It is against this background that Lebanese authorities censured Da'i al-Islam al-Shahal's organization Jami'yat al-Hidaya wal-Ihsan. In 1996, Lebanese authorities accused the Salafi organization of inciting sectarian hatred and ordered its closure, virtually causing its collapse. No doubt, its closure was more about the general crackdown on Salafists than concerns about national identity and history. After all, Sheikh Halabi was close to the Syrian regime and supportive of Syrian policy in Lebanon.

This setback for the mainstream, generally quietest movement of al-Shahal took another dramatic turn with the emergence in northern Lebanon of a radical Islamist organization with connection to al-Qaeda. To be sure, Usbat al-Ansar had been closely associated with this radical Islamist organization, al-Takfir wal-Hijra. This group has its ideological origins in the movement founded in the 1960s in Egypt by an agricultural engineer named Shukri Mustafa. The ideology of this group goes beyond the common ideological denominator of Islamist organizations of creating an Islamic state ruled by *shari'a* and adhering to a strict Salafi interpretation of the Qur'an. The group, similar but not identical to Salafi-jihadi groups, believes that much of the world is heretical and consequently enjoins its members to purify the world of *kuffars* (infidels). As a result, the group is known for perpetuating violence against those it considers *kuffars*, including those Muslims who do not live according to true Islam.

Al-Takfir wal-Hijra was reportedly established in Lebanon in 1997 by Bassam al-Kinj, also known as Abu-Aisha. Family and friends of Kinj appear to constitute a significant number of this group. In addition to believing in the aforementioned ideology, the group opposed Lebanon's confessional system and Syria's hegemony over Lebanon. According to Amnesty International, prior to their clash with the Lebanese army in 2000, members of the group set up a couple of annual encampments in Jurud al-Dinniyah, an area east of Tripoli in the north of Lebanon, to offer Islamic teaching and training in the use of arms.[31] Reportedly Kinj fought alongside Osama bin Laden, during the 1980s in Afghanistan against the Soviets. During his 1998 stay in Peshawar, Pakistan, he forged close relationships with a number of Islamists, who later on formed the leadership nucleus of al-Takfir wal-Hijra.

In 1990, while working as a taxi driver in Boston, Kinj befriended Raid Hijazi, who was later indicted by Jordanian authorities for his involvement in plotting to bomb tourist targets in Jordan during the millennium celebrations.[32] In 1996, Kinj decided to return home to Lebanon, whereupon he established Al-Takfir wal-Hijra. According to Étienne Sakr, Kinj split the organization into three regional branches: a northern Lebanon branch, which he led; a Beirut branch led by a member of the Akkaoui family; and a Beka' branch led by Qasem Daher. Kinj received financial support from associates of bin Laden to establish and arm his organization.[33] Moreover, Kinj's Takfir wal-Hujrah received moral and military support from Usbat al-Ansar, which guided a number of radical Islamists to the training camp of the radical organization in Jurud al-Dinniyah.

In early January 2000, the group clashed with the Lebanese army, which had increased its presence in and around Tripoli following a series of bomb attacks on Greek Orthodox churches in October and November 1999 in the city. Heavy fighting initially took place in 'Asun, then spread to Jurud al-Dinniyah and Kafr Habbu. It is noteworthy that the battle in 'Asun had begun in al-Shahal's radio station building, where members of Takfir wal-Hujrah had taken refuge. Lasting for eight days, the clashes claimed the lives of eleven soldiers, five civilians, and twenty-eight members of the group, including Kinj. The incident had regional and international repercussions because many of those arrested were foreign nationals, including Chechens, Pakistanis, and Afghanis. In July 2000, Mount Lebanon Criminal Court indicted 120 men, dozens of them in absentia, "for their alleged connection with the Dhinniya clashes" and charged them several months after their arrest on various counts of "attacking internal state security," according to the Amnesty International report.[34]

The incident of al-Dinniyah brought to the fore of public opinion the fact that al-Qaeda affiliates and members had found their way into northern Lebanon's susceptible landscape, thanks no less to the rundown condition of the area than to the Salafists' missionary activities, especially al-Shahal's. In fact, Lebanese authorities arrested members of the dissolved Jami'yat al-Hidaya wal-Ihsan for their connection to al-Takfir wal-Hujrah, and Da'i al-Shahal fled to Saudi Arabia to escape prosecution.[35] Subsequently al-Shahal issued a statement in which he affirmed that the activism of his group is religious, educational, and propagandist, and that the armed group that had taken refuge in his radio station building had essentially stormed the building by force.[36] Though al-Shahal, along with other Salafists, denied any connection to al-Takfir wal-Hujrah, it was hardly possible for him to deny the ramifications of his missionary discourse for the mobilization of the youth of northern Lebanon. Initial investigations into the background of those arrested revealed that most of the leaders of the radical organization were foreigners and had participated in jihad in Afghanistan among other places. However, most of the rank and file came from impoverished areas in Tripoli and northern Lebanon. Interestingly, some members hailed from Bab al-Tabbaneh in Tripoli, the most densely impoverished quarter of Tripoli and the bastion of Salafism.[37] It was there that the Islamic Unity Movement had risen and fallen. Its brutal suppression there at the hands of the Syrians and their allies had been kept fresh in the collective consciousness of al-Tabbaneh residents, partly in consequence of the daily harassment meted out to them by Syrian loyalists in the state and partly in consequence of the daily reminder of Salafi sheikhs that Islam was under attack by *kuffars*. High unemployment among the youth and poor social services by the state only reinforced the belief among them that jihad was necessary to withstand the internal and external assault on

Islam. Correspondingly, many from those impoverished areas migrated to Jurud al-Dinniyah to join Kinj's group in the hopes of participating in jihad. Radwan al-Sayyid perceptively explained this phenomenon:

> The various Islamic organizations share one background that underscores that Islam has been a target not only of serious threats consequent upon modernity, but also of conspiratorial threats plotted by international Zionism and international "crusaderism," or Christian extremism. However, the behavior of these organizations is different. Conventional organizations deem that the confrontation with this reality should be carried out peacefully in terms of educational, political, and informational activity, as well as by cooperating internationally with Islamist organizations. Conversely, the patience of these youth [members of al-Takfir wal-Hujra] has run out on account of this constant educational [missionary] and emotional mobilization. Therefore, this phenomenon broadens not only in Lebanon, but also in Egypt, Pakistan, Indonesia, and among Muslim communities in Europe and the United States. As a result, these groups that desire direct action split from the conventional groups and rally around charismatic leaders under whose authority they wage jihad.[38]

Notwithstanding the state policy of restricting and monitoring the movement of Salafists, they faced another setback in the wake of the September 11 terror attacks on the United States. Washington put pressure on the Gulf regimes to close those charitable organizations with links to al-Qaeda and to monitor the transactional charity activities of their citizens. As a result, most of the funding of Salafists from the Saudi Mu'assassat al-Haramayn dried up.[39] Clearly, al-Shahal's network and informal patronage structure suffered the most. Nevertheless, this significant decrease in financial support from Saudi Arabia led Salafists to seek other sources of revenue, relying principally on the contacts they established with like-minded colleagues during their studies in Gulf universities. Eventually these contacts constituted integral parts of transnational networks of Salafists espousing similar ideologies. Broadly speaking, two main networks have become associated with the quietest and *haraki* (activist) Salafi schools of thought. Significantly, the quietest-oriented Kuwaiti Jam'iyat Ihya' al-Turath al-Islami (Society for the Revival of Islamic Heritage), along with wealthy Gulf individuals from Saudi Arabia and Kuwait, has supported the network of quietest Salafists, and the activist-oriented Qatari Sheikh Eid Charity Organization, along with wealthy Gulf individuals, has supported the network of *haraki* Salafists.[40] The Saudi government has continued to support the quietest Salafi network through the Ministry of Religious Endowments and private institutions.

This led to two developments. Da'i al-Islam al-Shahal's heretofore predominant network and position within the broad Salafi movement in Lebanon gradually gave way to multiple bases of Salafi influence. Next, al-Shahal slowly but steadily moved from his father's quietest school of thought in the direction of the *haraki* school, though he has not admitted being a *haraki.*

Parallel to these developments, the US invasion of Iraq and the subsequent insurgency there against American troops not only helped Salafists deepen their transnational connections but also helped Salafists in Lebanon to resume their missionary activities, including participating in the jihad against Americans in Iraq. Clearly this was made possible as part of a Syrian strategy to undermine US efforts and the occupation of Iraq. The czar of this covert policy in Lebanon was none other than Syria's intelligence chief there, Rustum Ghazale, who had succeeded Ghazi Kanaan in 2002. Ghazale supervised *al-khuruj ila al-Iraq* (jihadi exit to Iraq) from his headquarters in Majdal Anjar, near the Syrian border. Broadly speaking, Ghazale allowed Salafists to mobilize Sunni youth and then guide them with the help of transnational Salafists to Syria, where they joined cells of jihadists preparing to enter Iraq.[41] Notwithstanding the participation of Usbat al-Ansar in the jihad in Iraq (see previous chapter), the case of Mustapha Darwish Ramadan offers a nuanced insight into the participation of Lebanese Salafists in the insurgency against American troops in Iraq under the supervision of Syrian intelligence.

Born in Beirut but of Kurdish descent, Ramadan married a woman from Majdal Anjar, where he settled before leaving for Denmark. It was there that he established contacts with radical Muslims across Europe, and he eventually joined a Kurdish Sunni radical organization, Ansar al-Sunna, with roots in northern Iraq. Reportedly, Ramadan's initial contacts with Abu Mus'ab al-Zarqawi, the leader of al-Qaeda in Iraq, had been set up by Ansar al-Sunna.[42] Ultimately Ramadan went back to Majdal Anjar in 2003, where he disseminated his radical ideology and underscored the importance of *takfir* and jihad. Soon enough, he attracted a core of young loyalists who followed his lead to Iraq to wage jihad against the infidel Americans. Assuredly, Ramadan's jihadi activism in Majdal Anjar and nearby villages would not have taken place in the first place had it not been for Syrian endorsement. After all, this area was the stronghold of Syrian intelligence. Within a year, Ramadan, known then as Abu Muhammad al-Lubnani, emerged as a key member of an al-Qaeda–affiliated organization, Ansar al-Islam, and a close aide to Zarqawi. His reputation preceded him as a propagandist for jihad in Iraq and a fearless jihadist who organized many suicide bombings, which wreaked havoc there. He was eventually killed, along with his son Muhammad, in 2005. His storied jihad in Iraq attracted much attention in Lebanon and the West to the displeasure of Syrian intelligence. Moreover, the death of other jihadists from Majdal Anjar in Iraq confirmed to Western intelligence and some Lebanese intelligence officers their premonition that Syrian intelligence in Lebanon act as the conduit for jihad in Iraq from Lebanon, among other places.[43] Syria's complicity in jihad in Iraq was further corroborated when a Lebanese jihadist, Ismail Khatib, who had acted as an intermediary between Ramadan and Salafists in Lebanon, passed away under suspicious circumstances in the custody of Lebanese authorities in the Beka'. Khatib and other Salafists, some of whom were from Majdal Anjar, had been arrested on various terrorism charges in 2004. Some Lebanese officers pointed their fingers to Syrian intelligence as the party behind the death of Khatib, if only because the latter could have revealed the extent to which Syrian intelligence had been involved in the insurgency in Iraq.[44]

Similarly, an account of the process of *khuruj* to Iraq through Syria was given by a Saudi defendant Fahd al-Yamani, known as Faisal Akbar, who was arrested by Lebanese authorities following the murder of former prime minister Rafiq Hariri in February 2005. Akbar's account was included in the interrogative report on jihadi activities that was submitted by the chief of the information branch at Internal Security, Wissam al-Hassan, to Lebanon's military court on May 9, 2006. Akbar detailed:

> Usually, we welcome jihadists from Lebanon after being nominated by individuals who had joined the group [*jama'a*]. These are activists who had pledged their allegiance [*bay'ah*] and are trustworthy. Upon their [jihadists] arrival from Lebanon to Syria, they would be taken to a place we call hosting place [*madafah*]. Neither the address of nor the way to *madafah* would be known to them. The details are called the secure movement measures. Thereafter, jihadists submit to a security course. Then they would be taken to Iraq if the circumstances of their transportation are appropriate. Otherwise, they would stay in the *madafah* until the opportune moment to enter Iraq. In the meantime, jihadists pledge allegiance to the emir, whereupon they would abide by the activism of the *jama'a*. A jihadist has the right to append stipulations to his pledge of allegiance on the condition he would be a fighter or martyr. He can specify his stipulations including fighting only the Americans.[45]

Not surprisingly, the covert Syrian policy to support the insurgency in Iraq played out in favor of indirectly expanding the networks of Salafists in Lebanon, whose principal activism remained focused on missionary and educational activities. As we have seen (chapter 2), Salafi organizations have mushroomed in Lebanon, and as confessional politics in the country returned to their time-honored role of forging confessional electoral alliances, Salafists have inadvertently accumulated political power in the form of representing compact communal groups, mainly in Tripoli and the Akkar region. The vote of these groups has virtually become essential to secure the election of a predominant Sunni bloc in the parliament and by extension a Sunni-led coalition government. Though Salafists, generally speaking, had no common ideological or economic interest in the leadership of Rafiq Hariri, they eventually forged with him a utilitarian relationship. This relationship was more in the form of a marriage of convenience intended mainly to fend off arbitrary Syrian policies and actions against them and to curb the ascendant power of Hezbollah. In this respect, committed as he was to rebuilding Beirut as the Hong Kong of the Middle East, Hariri was sufficiently receptive to the concerns of Salafists, for they overlapped with his own concerns about how to finesse Syria's power and curb Hezbollah's growing political and military influence in Lebanon.

Hezbollah: A Red Line

Bolstered by Saudi support and enormous wealth and an international network of powerful actors, Prime Minister Hariri set out to rebuild Beirut and mark his legacy on Lebanese politics since his election to the premiership in 1992. Many Lebanese saw in the rising political clout of Hariri a Saudi-Syrian endorsement to rebuild and secure Lebanon. Hariri would not have been considered a candidate to the premiership without Syrian approval. And since Syria participated in the peace conference, his candidacy was perceived to be a step in the direction of preparing Lebanon (and Syria) for peace with Israel. Nevertheless, he had to walk a fine line, balancing his economic and political programs with those of Syria and Hezbollah. In fact, he was not happy with President Asad's arrangement that strongly favored Hezbollah as a political and military party, at the expense of all other parties in Lebanon. He, in conjunction with other political figures, tried to drive a wedge between Syria and Hezbollah under the pretext of securing stability in the country. Hezbollah's military activities in southern Lebanon threatened Hariri's grand plan for Beirut.

Before long, Hariri's premonition was confirmed. In response to Hezbollah's rising attacks on the Israel Defense Forces and its proxy force the South Lebanese Army, including launching Katyusha rockets on northern Israel, Israel launched a week-long military operation, code-named Operation Accountability, into southern Lebanon on July 25 to curb the power of Hezbollah and to provoke a mass exodus toward Beirut as a means to put pressure on the Lebanese government to secure its border with the Jewish state. Israel's chief of staff, Ehud Barak, declared that the Lebanese government should disarm Hezbollah so that Israel would not do it.[46]

The operation was wide in scope, causing much human and material destruction, let alone a large number of internally displaced citizens.[47] It also threatened not only the stability of Lebanon but also the stability of the region and the collapse of the peace process. Consequently, the United States and France tried to broker a cease-fire as a stepping-stone to stabilizing southern Lebanon under governmental control. Washington pursued two concurrent policies, one with Damascus and the other with Beirut. US secretary of state Warren Christopher negotiated with President Asad and Syrian foreign minister Farouq al-Shara the appropriate measures to stop the confrontation. Out of these talks emerged a plan according to which Hezbollah would continue its resistance in the Israeli-occupied buffer zone but would desist from launching rockets into Israel, providing that Israel would not target civilians.[48] Once the parties involved (Israel, Hezbollah, Lebanon, and Iran) approved the plan, hostilities stopped in the evening of July 31, 1993. Significantly, the "July Understanding" was born in the form of an oral, tacit understanding of the new rules of engagement.

On the other hand, Christopher had negotiated a secret agreement with President Hrawi and Prime Minister Hariri to the effect that the United States would support the redeployment of the Lebanese army to southern Lebanon, including the area under the control of UNIFIL, to secure peace along the border with Israel.[49] In fact, a series of actions undertaken by the Lebanese government revealed its collaboration with Washington without Syrian knowledge.

On the first day following the end of hostilities, the cabinet held an extraordinary session in which it decided to deploy the army in the operational area of the UNIFIL forces. The United Nations approved the cabinet's decision the same day, though it had objected to this decision in the past. The next day, President Hrawi convened a meeting of the Defense Supreme Council, in which he questioned, without mentioning Hezbollah, the presence of "armed men" in areas where the army had clear orders to prevent any armed presence. He accused the army command of being "scandalously lax" in executing its clear orders in the south, Iqlim al-Tufah, and the western Beka'. He added, "We are with the resistance, but we cannot accept a resistance that would compromise the state and does not coordinate with the army."[50]

Prime Minister Hariri strongly approved the position of the president and declared that "we are all nationalists, we appreciate the army's role and its importance, but it must execute orders and not be lenient with anyone," and added that "the government is ready to bear the responsibility for the resistance on the condition that it does not exceed its bounds and keep its objectives within the interest of the state, without compromising it."[51] Consequently the Council decided to stop recognizing licenses to carry and ship arms unless they were referred to the Defense Ministry for approval or suspension. According to Karim

Pakradouni, a former minister and former head of the Phalange Party, "the summary of this meeting was that the president and the prime minister were in agreement that the army does not implement the directions given to it and does not confront Hezbollah members. Both hold [Commander of the Army] Émile Lahoud responsible for this condition and accuse him of indulging the resistance, and think that he is covertly coordinating with Damascus."[52]

This marked the beginning of an apprehensive and troubled relationship between Hariri and the future president of Lebanon. In any event, following a pointed communication between Hariri and Lahoud, the latter refused a request by a U.N. delegation to send the army to the south and prepared himself to resign from his post. The flurry of these drastic events took Damascus by surprise and confirmed Hezbollah's suspicions and concerns. Immediately thereafter, the political deputy of Secretary General of Hezbollah Hassan Nasrallah, Hajj Hussein al-Khalil traveled to Damascus to discuss the unfolding events and was surprised to know that the Syrian leadership knew about them from the media. No sooner, President Asad made a call to his Lebanese counterpart and conveyed his unhappiness and refusal to any concession affecting the Resistance. No sooner had the call ended than Lebanese authorities began blaming each other; and, most importantly, suspended all decisions regarding the Resistance and sending the army to southern Lebanon. In fact, they began clamoring for supporting the Resistance and coordinating with Syria.[53] Moreover, President Asad called on Lahoud to visit him in Damascus, where he expressed his gratitude for Lahoud's nationalist stance. The intent of the visit was not lost on Hrawi or Hariri. Lahoud stood in Asad's favor, and that spoke volumes about the fact that the commander of the army had become in Lebanese parlance "untouchable."[54]

Clearly, Hezbollah was a red line for the political establishment, led by Hariri. However, Hezbollah grew wary about Hariri's motives and plans regarding its military arm, which were frustrated by Syria. But as the political and military power of Hezbollah grew, other parties, including former Hezbollah allies such as the Progressive Socialist Party and Amal, rallied around Hariri to curb Hezbollah's political power as represented in the state. Damascus, supervising the whole political scene, had to walk a fine line, balancing its support of Hezbollah with its support of other pro-Syrian parties. All this came into the open in the 1996 parliamentary elections, which were regarded in Lebanon as the battle to cut down Hezbollah to size. As the 1996 elections approached, Hezbollah found itself the target of Hariri and his allies and even its own erstwhile allies. Nabih Berri of Amal was not ready to give Hezbollah its fair share of number of candidates in a joint slate for the elections. Hariri defined the elections as a "battle between moderation and extremism" and declared that he would not cooperate with extremists.[55] Even Druze leader Walid Jumblat broke his alliance with Hezbollah, which went back years. A day before the elections, he railed against the resistance and its actions. Hezbollah's parliamentary deputy, Muhammad Ra'd, asserted that "government [*al-sultah*] seeks to reduce the presence of the resistance in the parliament."[56] Bayram Ibrahim, writing in the Lebanese daily *An-Nahar*, captured the essence of the battle to cut down Hezbollah to size: "As such Hezbollah faces a merciless war from three active factions. It has become clear that this war targets 'clipping' the wings of the bird that has developed and grown in a way overshadowing the others, causing them discontent and anxiety."[57]

Hezbollah took on the challenge and threatened to enter the battle of elections either singly or in alliance with Sunni Islamists, independents, and leftists. Berri and Nasrallah exchanged sharp statements, which intensified the politically charged climate. Both groups mobilized their allies. The Islamic Association in Sidon, the Syrian Social Nationalist Party–Higher Council, the Communist Party, and former Speaker of the House Kamil al-As'ad supported Hezbollah. The Ba'th Party, the Syrian Social Nationalist Party–Ali Qanso, and Hariri allies supported Amal. With tension escalating, many feared renewed fighting between the two Shi'a parties. It was at this juncture that Nasrallah was called to Damascus, whereupon his party joined a coalition list with Amal, and the "merciless war" came to an end. Hezbollah (and supporters) won ten seats. Hezbollah's submission to a joint list with Amal demonstrated time and again Syria's arbitrary power but also the political limits that not only Hariri but also pro-Syrian allies had to observe.

Subsequently, Hezbollah entered the 2000 parliamentary elections battle riding the wave of victory of forcing Israel from Lebanon. The parties that had tried to cut it down to size in the 1996 elections either entered into coalition lists with or supported Hezbollah's candidates. Hezbollah (and supporters) won twelve seats. Though Hariri had a landslide victory, especially in Beirut, his frustration with Syria and Hezbollah's independent activities, especially those related to its resistance, only grew stronger. On the other hand, the Islamic Association's fortunes sank to a new low, losing even its sole parliamentary seat in northern Lebanon.

The defeat of the Islamic Association was related no less to its diminishing popular base than to its unequivocal support of Hezbollah under the leadership of Fathi Yakan. As already mentioned, Yakan had made supporting the Islamic resistance a priority of the association's political program. This eventually did not sit well not only with Salafists but also with the rest of the leaders of the association, who grew critical of Yakan's orientation. Eventually Yakan left the association. Meanwhile, Salafists had few, if any, options regarding parliamentary elections. Notwithstanding the fact that they had neither a political party nor legal sanction of their participation in the elections, they had to choose between implicitly supporting pro-Syrian allies, such as Rashid Karame and the Islamic Association, or implicitly supporting Hariri's party. With little fanfare, they more or less supported the latter, moved mainly by their grievances against Syria and reservations about Hezbollah. This subtle apolitical attitude began to change following the murder of Hariri and the resultant assertive stances Salafists had begun to display.

The Implications of Hariri's Assassination for Salafists: *Al-Infitah* or Rise to Rebellion?

The year 2000 marked a new phase in Hezbollah's development and its relationship with Syria and with other parties and communities in Lebanon. Israel's unilateral withdrawal from the south of Lebanon in May 2000 enhanced Hezbollah's stature in the Arab world in general and Lebanon in particular but undercut the legitimacy of the Syrian presence. No longer could Syria justify its presence in Lebanon on the grounds of protecting the country from Israeli aggression. Past whispers about the need for Syria to redeploy its forces soon transformed into vocal calls demanding Syrian redeployment. It was none other than the spiritual leader of the Maronite Church, Patriarch Nasrallah Sfeir, who led this new campaign against Syrian presence in Lebanon. On September 20, 2000, from Bkirki, the seat of the Maronite patriarch, the Council of Maronite Bishops released a statement in the form of a "call to all whom it may concern in and outside Lebanon to participate in the rescue." The call began by stating that the situation in Lebanon had reached such a crisis that it had become a matter of obligation to speak the truth without any reservation. Called the Bkirki statement, it underscored that (a) Israel had withdrawn from southern Lebanon and the time had come for the Syrian army to redeploy in Lebanon in preparation for its full withdrawal in accordance with the Taif Accord, (b) the talk over the possibility of civil strife was superficial unless someone intended to fuel it, (c) the presence of the Syrian army next to the presidential palace, a symbol of national dignity, distressed the Lebanese, and (d) Lebanon was no longer sovereign in the shadow of a hegemony that included all organizations, agencies, and administrations whereby many Lebanese were in Israeli and Syrian prisons.[58]

The Bkirki statement not only broke the taboo against public criticism of Syria but also challenged Syrian rule in Lebanon. Consequently, though Israel's withdrawal from Lebanon was certified by the United Nations, Syria and Hezbollah sought to legally justify their resistance against Israel by maintaining certain territorial claims to territories occupied by Israel. With Syrian encouragement, the Lebanese government staked a claim to Lebanese sovereignty over disputed border areas, mainly the mountainous Shebaa Farms and the hills of Kfarshouba.[59]

Meanwhile, President Asad passed away on June 10, 2000, after thirty years in power. His son Bashar assumed power. Though Bashar sought to observe the rules governing Syria's relationship with Lebanon and Hezbollah, he enhanced Hezbollah's political status and power not only by receiving Nasrallah warmly in Damascus but also by supplying Hezbollah with sophisticated weapons, including some from Iran. This rapprochement accelerated after the United States launched military operations against Iraq in March 2003, shattering the regional order. In response to all these developments, Hariri's relationship with Syria and its allies steadily deteriorated.

Meanwhile, encouraged by the rapid unfolding of events in the region, many Lebanese sought to reclaim their country from Syrian occupation. The Lebanese question was placed on the international stage with the American-French cosponsorship and successful passage of UN Security Council Resolution 1559, which called for Syria to withdraw from Lebanon and for Hezbollah to be disarmed.[60] Meanwhile, while Damascus sought to extend the mandate of pro-Syrian president Émile Lahoud, former Lebanese prime minister Rafiq Hariri and Druze leader Walid Jumblat began to rally anti-Syrian politicians.[61] It was at this critical juncture in Lebanese-Syrian relations that Hariri was assassinated on February 14, 2005, sparking mass protests—the Cedar Revolution.

The swiftness with which the opposition not only blamed Syria but also held the Lebanese government responsible (even bluntly asking it not to participate in Hariri's funeral procession) attested to the new political climate dawning on Lebanon and the determination of the opposition to confront and overthrow Syria's authority in Lebanon.[62] In a dramatic shift of Sunni political attitude, Sunni Muslims, including Salafists, held a broad communal meeting chaired by Mufti Muhammad Rashid Qabbani, in which they issued a statement condemning the assassination of Hariri and insisting that "the murder of the martyr Prime Minister Rafiq Hariri targeted the existence, role, and dignity of Muslim Sunnis." They added that "they would not be satisfied with deploring this crime . . . and they have had enough injustice and that patience could no longer be born."[63] Hezbollah issued a statement that the heinous crime was aimed "at destabilizing Lebanon and planting discord among its people."[64] Amal stated that the "Zionists are behind the crime, aiming at creating turmoil."[65]

As the clamor for Syria's withdrawal from Lebanon became irrevocable, President Asad of Syria delivered a speech before the Syrian parliament on March 5, 2005, in which he stated that Syrian troops would withdraw first to the Beka' Valley then to the border in compliance with Resolution 1559 and the Tai'f Accord.[66] Shortly thereafter, in a show of solidarity with Syria, Hezbollah and other Syrian allies called for a peaceful demonstration on March 8 in Beirut to rally support against what they called "foreign intervention." Shedding his initial neutral stance following Hariri's assassination, Hezbollah's secretary–general, Hassan Nasrallah, affirmed that the demonstration was to "denounce Resolution 1559, to show thanks, loyalty and appreciation to the Syrian leadership, people and army for its achievements in Lebanon."[67] He ominously added that "the resistance will not give up its arms because Lebanon needs the resistance to defend it even if I am optimistic that Israel will soon withdraw from the Shebaa Farms."[68]

But Hezbollah (and Syria) apparently underestimated Lebanese frustration with the pro-Syrian order in the country and eagerness for freedom and democracy. Reacting to Hezbollah's show of force and solidarity with Syria, approximately 1.5 million Lebanese took to the streets on March 14, clamoring for freedom and calling for Syria's swift withdrawal. It was the largest demonstration in Lebanon's history, not only eclipsing that organized by Hezbollah but also hastening the collapse of the Syrian order in Lebanon. Meanwhile, a report by a fact-finding mission sent to Beirut by UN secretary-general Kofi Annan to look into Hariri's assassination was released by the international organization. The report stated that: "After gathering the available facts, the Mission concluded that the Lebanese security services and the Syrian Military Intelligence bear the primary responsibility for the lack of security, protection, law and order in Lebanon. . . . It is also the Mission's conclusion that the Government of Syria bears primary responsibility for the political tension that preceded the assassination of former Prime Minister Mr. Hariri."[69]

President Asad criticized the UN report, saying that "it is a report of political character when I was expecting a report of a technical-criminal nature."[70] However, implicated in the assassination and under growing international pressure, the Syrian regime set a date for its withdrawal from Lebanon. In a joint news conference meeting with Syrian foreign minister Farouq al-Shara in Damascus, UN envoy Terje Roed-Larsen announced Syria's commitment to withdraw all its military and intelligence forces from Lebanon by April 30.[71] On May 23, UN Secretary General Annan stated that "a United Nations mission has verified that Syrian troops and security forces have fully withdrawn from Lebanon."[72]

Syria's withdrawal brought to an end three decades of Syrian dominance in Lebanon, ushering in a new era for the country full of promises but fraught with danger as the country polarized around two camps taking their names after the pro- and anti-Syrian demonstrations on March 8 and March 14, respectively. At the same time, Saad Hariri inherited the political mantle of his father and has come to lead the major party in the March 14 camp, the Future Current, also known as the Future Movement. Broadly speaking, most Sunni forces, including Salafists, rallied around Hariri's Future Current, with the notable exception of Fathi Yakan. Yakan believed that "the assassination of Hariri via this huge, calculated, and sophisticated explosion leaves no doubt that those who have an interest in implementing UN Security Council Resolution 1559 should be accused, at the forefront of which are the United States and Israel." He added that "whoever accuses Syria of the crime of assassination is either a paid agent or lacks intellect, thought, and common sense."[73] Yakan's unequivocal support of Syria and Hezbollah, and his critical attitude toward the late Rafiq Hariri and then his son Saad, further deepened the rift between him and the leadership of the Islamic Association, especially with Sheikh Faisal Mawlawi, Abdallah Babeti, and As'ad Harmouch.

Significantly, the murder of Hariri reinforced the trends within the broad Salafi movement, whereupon on the one hand some heretofore apolitical Salafists contended that they could no longer stay aloof from politics in light of the ongoing systematic marginalization of the Sunnis, on the other hand most Salafists who had been forced to live overseas began to return home and claim influential positions within the Sunni community. Leading this movement toward political engagement was Dr. Hassan al-Shahal, who established the first Salafi political bureau, under the name the Islamic Political Bureau.

The Islamic Political Bureau was born out of several Salafi meetings in which senior religious scholars explored the idea of fashioning under the sanctity of Islamic jurisprudence a legal and political framework to serve as a means of guidance for the people.[74] According to Dr. al-Shahal,

> the purpose of establishing the bureau is to keep abreast of the political conditions that Lebanon goes through on a daily basis and to take legal political stances in light of what is happening in the country. It is no longer acceptable to marginalize the role of the partisans of the Sunna after what happened. Lebanon cannot arise anew without an active, influential, and principal role for this sect. On the basis of this departing point, the bureau took and issued several stances and communiqués respectively to accomplish its objectives, including supporting the office of the prime minister, which will confirm that it will not become a lightning rod for every political crisis storming the country.[75]

Commenting on the implication of the assassination of former prime minister Hariri for the Islamic situation in Lebanon, Dr. al-Shahal stated that "the most important thing that resulted from the assassination of the leader Hariri is the feeling of hollowness among Sunni Muslims and that they are targeted. This is not the first time a Sunni dignitary of this magnitude has been assassinated.

This has led Sunnis to summon each other to find a way to gather their ranks and unify their word at the level of the whole country from its north to its south."[76]

This feeling of marginalization and being under attack has been a common thread in the social fabric of the Salafi community. Nevertheless, the murder of Hariri, whose position as prime minister represented the epitome of Sunni power following the civil war, has mobilized many Salafists, including the quietest Salafists and those in the mainstream who stood in the middle between the quietest and activist Salafists. This, however, did not lead Dr. al-Shahal to excommunicate the Shi'ites. Rather, he welcomed cooperation between and among all Islamic groups, with the exception of al-Ahbash, for, according to him, their ideology rests on the principle of *takfir* of all who do not adopt their ideology and methodology. He also expressed hope that Shi'a-Sunni tension would not devolve into sectarian strife. Significantly he called, in the name of the Islamic Political Bureau, for a complete national reconciliation. Interestingly enough, it was within his *infitah* (opening up) to other communities as part of his efforts for national reconciliation that he called for the release of the leader of the Lebanese Forces' Samir Geagea, along with all other political prisoners, including those Salafists arrested in Majdal Anjar and Jurud al-Dinniyah. No less significant, al-Shahal asserted that "Salafists are looking forward to participating in parliamentary elections, making alliances with whom they see in harmony with their Islamic orientation."[77]

Obviously, this *infitah* to the political system in Lebanon entailed neither the formation of a political party nor the formulation of a comprehensive political program. It was mainly about engaging the political system by way of supporting the candidates most willing to support the Sunni community and whose programs are harmonious with the Salafi orientation. Moreover, this *infitah* entailed the initiation of an Islamic legal process that would guide Muslims and make sure legislations do not violate Islamic law. No less significant, this *infitah* under the pretext of national reconciliation paved the way for an agreement with Hezbollah, something many Salafists, as we shall see, could not fathom. Nevertheless, the *infitah* to the Shi'a community was also instigated by two other developments.

Dr. al-Shahal's *infitah* to Lebanon's various communities, especially the Shi'a one, was supported by Sheikh Hassan Abdallah, the director of the Administrative Council of the Congregation of Muslim Ulema. Sheikh Abdallah, along with other *ulema* (religious scholars) from the congregation, saw that the rapid unfolding of events from the withdrawal of Syrian troops to the murder of Hariri, which might result in international pressure on the resistance, necessitated a concerted effort by Muslims to prevent sectarian strife. He explained:

We were greatly shocked the moment the crime of assassinating president [*sic*] Hariri took place. The first implications of the murder for confessionalism were very bad. We were worried that this horrible crime would be exploited by those who don't want the well-being of the Muslim community to provoke sectarian strife. We convened long meetings to establish a foundational framework for engaging the upcoming period, for we were totally convinced that the situation in Lebanon before the assassination of Hariri is no longer the same after his death. As such there should be a practical movement to prevent strife within the Muslim arena.[78]

It was against this background that the congregation sponsored a large Sunni-Shi'a meeting at the headquarters of the UN Educational, Scientific, and Cultural Organization in Beirut, followed by meetings with Mufti of the Republic Qabbani, Shi'a spiritual leader Abd al-Amir Qabalan, former prime ministers Salim al-Huss and Rashid al-Sulh, Speaker of the House Nabih Berri, Secretary-General of Hezbollah Sayyid Hassan Nasrallah, and senior Shi'a religious scholar Sayyid Muhammad Hussein Fadlallah. Sheikh Abdallah found common concerns among the Shi'a and Sunni communities, on the basis of which he devised points of cooperation that included confronting all non-monotheistic ideas that defile Islam in order to provoke strife among its sons and daughters and convening conferences, under the name "Islamic Unity in Confronting Takfir," to discuss the issue of *takfir* and its Islamic scientific principles.[79] The meetings also underlined the common concern about the American and Israeli designs to strike at Islamist movements, especially those that supported the liberation of Palestine.

These rapprochement efforts, undertaken mainly to prevent sectarian strife but also to protect the resistance, coincided with local and regional Salafi ideological reservations about sectarian strife. These ideological reservations were expressed by Sheikh Safwan al-Zu'bi, the representative in Tripoli of the Kuwaiti organization Jami'yat Ihya' al-Turath al-Islami (the Society for the Revival of Islamic Heritage). Sheikh Safwan al-Zu'bi espoused the main tenets of the quietest school of Salafism. He promulgated his ideas in Lebanon, supported by the transnational network of Salafists that orbited the realm of the institution al-Turath al-Islami. In the aftermath of the Gulf War and the reclamation of Kuwait from Iraq's occupation, the institution, under both internal pressure and appeasement from Kuwaiti authorities, radically transformed its *haraki* Salafi ideology into a quietest ideology. Kuwaiti authorities have been concerned about politicized Islamists who would dare challenge their rule. Correspondingly, they favored and supported the quietest Salafi trend in the institute until it became the hallmark of al-Turath al-Islami.[80] Thereafter, the institute, funded mainly by the Kuwaiti state, promulgated its ideology by supporting a transnational network of Salafi organizations that espoused its quietest school of thought. Reflecting the ideas of his major sponsor, Sheikh Safwan al-Zu'bi, the head of the Waqf al-Turath al-Islami (the Islamic Heritage Endowment), viewed *haraki* Salafi ideology and activism as detrimental to Muslim society in general and to Lebanese society in particular. He believed that *haraki* Salafists have used a perilous sectarian discourse in order to mobilize Sunnis and to enhance their own standing in the community. He, like Dr. Hassan al-Shahal and Sheikh Sa'd al-Din al-Kibbi, shared the view that *takfir* of Muslims is *takfir* in and of itself, for it wreaks havoc on Muslim solidarity. No less significant, he believed in the application of the Islamic creedal principle *hisbah* (commanding right and forbidding wrong) only in terms of persuasion, leaving the final say for "charging wrong" to the ruler.[81]

Sheikh Safwan al-Zu'bi's concerns acquired an urgent immediacy following the Salafi rebellion of Fath al-Islam in the Nahr al-Bared refugee camp in the summer of 2007 and Hezbollah's seizure of West Beirut in the summer of 2008 (see next chapter). He believed that the reputation of Salafists had been tarnished, whereupon people misconstrued Salafism for militancy, and that Sunni-Shi'a sectarian strife would befall Lebanon if no serious attempts were made to pacify the raw emotions in both communities within the context of a sober, scientific intercommunal dialogue. Obviously, Sheikh Safwan al-Zu'bi's concerns coincided with those of Dr. al-Shahal and Sheikh Abdallah. In fact, these concerns had become, broadly speaking, the common foundational inclinations for *da'wa* for the quietest school of thought in Lebanon.

As a result of the *infitah* and the concerns more or less engendering it, Salafists, led by Dr. al-Shahal and Sheikh Safwan al-Zu'bi, signed a memorandum of understanding with Hezbollah on August 18, 2008. The memorandum was signed by Dr. al-Shahal for the Salafists and by Sheikh Ibrahim Amin al-Sayyid, the head of Hezbollah's Political Council, for the Shi'a Islamist party. The text of the memorandum was orated by Sheikh Abd al-Ghafar al-Zu'bi, the political consultant of the Islamic Heritage Endowment. Concluded with the objective of organizing the relationship between Salafists and Hezbollah and reducing sectarian tension, the memorandum included the following provisions:

1. Departing from the point that it is forbidden to shed Muslim blood, we forbid and condemn any attack by a Muslim group against another. In the event that a group has been assaulted, it has the right to resort to all legitimate means to protect itself.

2. To refrain from inciting and polarizing the public because this leads to discord, whereupon the decision-making process is moved from the hands of the wise people to the hands of hypocrites and the enemies of the Islamic nation.

3. To confront the American-Zionist project, which strives to provoke strife and further divide what has already been divided and fragmented.
4. To strive to eliminate the *takfir* thought among Sunnis and Shi'ites.
5. In the event Hezbollah or the Salafists come under implicit or explicit cruel attack by internal or external parties, each group has to stand as firmly as possible by the other.
6. To establish a committee comprising senior clerics from the Salafi *da'wa* and Hezbollah to discuss controversial matters and confine disputes to the committee, thereby preventing their transition to the street.
7. Each party has the right to freedom of belief and neither party has the right to impose its ideas and legal Islamic opinions on the other.
8. The two parties believe that the purpose of understanding is to prevent strife among Muslims and to strengthen civil peace and coexistence among all Lebanese.[82]

Following the oration of the understanding, Dr. al-Shahal affirmed that it was a step in the right direction in light of the dangerous situation consequent upon what happened in Beirut and that had the situation remained the same Lebanon would have burned in the fire of sectarian strife. He also acknowledged that "political reference within the Sunni community has been left to the Future Current" and asserted that "we have not embarked on such a step without coordinating with them [Future Current], and had they objected we would not have taken this step, for its fate would be failure."[83]

No sooner had the ink dried on the memorandum than a fierce campaign was launched by Sheikh Da'i al-Islam al-Shahal to nip the memorandum in the bud. He furiously called for its abolition. He asserted that the broad Salafi current throughout Lebanon rejected the memorandum, which was sponsored and signed by the Islamic Heritage Endowment that had neither representation nor significant influence among Salafists. He claimed that the memorandum was no more than an endeavor by Hezbollah to divide Sunni ranks in general and Salafi ranks in particular, in an attempt to refurbish the image of the organization of Hezbollah following the calamitous events in Beirut. He asked, "Why did the memorandum did not address the weapons of the opposition in the north and the arms sent to the opposition parties? Why it did not provide a solution for the case of Ba'l [Jabal] Muhsin with the Sunnis of Tripoli? Whence come the weapons to Ba'l Muhsin? What's the position regarding the Sunni creed? What's the position regarding Beirut?"[84]

Da'i al-Islam al-Shahal's furious reaction reflected to a large extent the fury and anger of the Sunni "street" toward Hezbollah, which intensified under Syrian occupation and peaked in the aftermath of Hezbollah's blatant seizure of

West Beirut. Apparently Dr. al-Shahal and Sheikh Safwan al-Zu'bi, along with other members of the quietest school, had not gauged the depth of this anger. Even the leader of the Future Current, Saad Hariri, who avoided making direct comments about the memorandum, rushed his aide and parliamentary deputy Samir al-Jisr to deny publicly the notion that the Future Current had adopted the memorandum.[85] Coming under immense pressure from the Sunni political establishment and Salafists, Dr. al-Shahal and Sheikh Safwan al-Zu'bi swiftly froze the memorandum. Commenting on the memorandum, Sheikh Safwan al-Zu'bi stated that it had eliminated the crude image of Salafism, prevented strife, and had encountered no legal or popular objections. He wistfully added that the Salafists had concluded a national conciliatory agreement with international repercussions, and that the Future Current had wasted an opportunity to sponsor this agreement with all its dimensions.[86]

Actually, the reaction of the Sunni community in general and the nonquietest Salafists in particular had been the outcome of years of marginalization, oppression, and entrapment of many Sunnis in the hermetic crucible of Salafism's religio-political discourse of mobilization. It was the outcome of the discrepancy between the belief of the Salafists that they represented the saved sect and their palpable feeling of hollowness and weakness. It was their rise to rebellion against Hezbollah and the symbols of the confessional system that contravened their ideology and outlook. In fact, Da'i al-Islam had already set his mind on rebelling against Hezbollah before the memorandum was signed. In the aftermath of Hezbollah's takeover of Beirut, he issued a "call to arms" to Sunni youths and stressed, "We have the right to defend ourselves and this does not make us a radical group as some media and politicians are saying."[87] Sheikh Bilal Dokmak, another Salafi leader in Tripoli, descriptively concluded that "Beirut has fallen quickly because there were no real committed fighters there." He added that "Salafists have always been against Hezbollah's arms, because they are only fighting Israel to liberate Lebanese land. We believe that one should fight Israel in the name of Allah, and never stop [even] if all the land is liberated."[88]

As internal and regional developments continued to unfold before the dismal eyes of Salafists, the rise to rebellion soon transformed into a jihad for a glorious cause in Bilad al-Sham—a "Greater Syria" that includes Lebanon.

Notes

1. The United States, Israel, Syria, and Lebanese Christians and Muslims all preferred different candidates. Frustrated, President Gemayel appointed General Aoun. I sat in on a meeting with President Gemayel, Archbishop Elia Elia of the Catholic Orthodox Church, and Maronite Chairbishop Joseph Lahoud at the

Sheraton Commander Hotel in Cambridge, Massachusetts, in September 1991, during which Aoun's appointment was discussed.

2. Karim Pakradouni, *La'nat Watan: Min Harb Lubnan Ila Harb al-Khalij* (Curse of a Fatherland: From the Lebanese War to the Gulf War) (Beirut: Trans-Orient Press, 1992), 205.

3. Ibid., 219.

4. For the text of the Taif Accord, see *An-Nahar*, August 22, 1990. For an analysis of the accord, see Fida Nasrallah, *Prospects for Lebanon: The Question of South Lebanon* (Oxford: Centre for Lebanese Studies, 1992), and Joseph Maila, *The Document of National Understanding: A Commentary* (Oxford: Centre for Lebanese Studies, 1992).

5. Ibid.

6. Augustus Richard Norton, "Lebanon after Ta'if: Is the Civil War Over?," *Middle East Journal* 45, no. 3 (Summer 1991), 461.

7. Robert G. Rabil, *Embattled Neighbors: Syria, Israel, and Lebanon* (Boulder, CO: Lynne Rienner Publishers, 2003), 130–32.

8. *Hisbah* connotes the accountability to obey the religious and moral instructions of Islam, which include financial and social matters.

9. See the full text of the Islamic Association's study in Fathi Yakan, *Adwa' 'ala al-Tajribah al-Niyabiyah al-Islamiyah fi Lubnan: Al-ida' al-Niyabi bayn al-Mabda' wa al-Tatbiq* (Lights on the Islamic Parliamentary Experience in Lebanon: The Parliamentary Performance between Principle and Practice) (Beirut: Mu'assassat al-Risalah, 1996), 179–98.

10. Ibid.

11. For the ideology of the Ba'th Party under president Hafiz al-Asad and the imprint of his personality cult on Syria's domestic and foreign policies, see Robert G. Rabil, *Syria, the United States, and the War on Terror in the Middle East* (Westport, CT: Praeger Security International, 2006), 1–33.

12. Al-Jama'a al-Islamiyah (Islamic Association), "Al-Barnamej al-Intikhabi li-Murashihi al-Jama'a al-Islamiyah" (The Electoral Program of the Islamic Association's Candidates), August 1, 1992, in Fathi Yakan, *Adwa' 'ala al-Tajribah al-Niyabiyah al-Islamiyah fi Lubnan: Al-ida' al-Niyabi bayn al-Mabda' wa al-Tatbiq* (Lights on the Islamist Parliamentary Experience in Lebanon: The Parliamentary Performance between Principle and Practice) (Beirut: Mu'assassat al-Risalah, 1996), 209.

13. Hassan Fadlallah, *Al-Khiyar al-Akhar: Hezbollah: Al-Sirah al-Zatiyyah wa al-Mawqaf* (The Other Choice: Hezbollah's Autobiography and Stance) (Beirut: Dar al-Hadi, 1994), 109–17.

14. Ibid., 142–43.

15. Ibid., 116.

16. Ibid., 148. See also Naim Qassem, *Hizbullah: Al-Manhaj, al-Tajribah, al-Mustaqbal* (Hizbullah: The Curriculum [Program], the Experience, The Future), 6th ed. (Beirut: Dar al-Hadi, 2009), 152–54.

17. See the open letter's text in Fadlallah, *Al-Khiyar al-Akhar*, 184–13. An English translation of the letter is available in Joseph Alagha, *The Shifts in Hizbullah's Ideology: Religious Ideology, Political Ideology, and Political Program* (Amsterdam: Amsterdam University Press, 2006), 233–38.

18. Ibid.

19. For an excellent analysis of the open letter, see Alagha, *The Shifts in Hizbullah's Ideology*, 115–48.

20. Qassem, *Hizbullah: Al-Manhaj, al-Tajribah, al-Mustaqbal*, 333–34.

21. Ibid., 335–38.

22. Ibid., 338–39.

23. Shaykh Muhammad Hussayn Fadlallah and Mahmoud Soueid, "Islamic Unity and Political Change: Interview with Shaykh Muhammad Hussayn Fadlallah," *Journal of Palestine Studies* 25, no. 1 (Autumn 1995), 67–69.

24. Richard Augustus Norton, "Hizbullah: From Radicalization to Pragmatism?" *Middle East Policy* 4, no. 4 (January 1998); Magnus Ranstorp, "The Strategy and Tactics of Hizballa's Current Lebanonization Process," *Mediterranean Politics* 3, no. 1 (1998); Judith Palmer Harik, *Hezbollah: The Changing Face of Terrorism* (London: I. B. Tauris, 2004), 51–52, 73–78; Hala Jaber, *Hezbollah: Born with a Vengeance* (New York: Columbia University Press, 1997), 205–14; and A. Nizar Hamzeh, "Lebanon's Hizbullah: From Islamic Revolution to Parliamentary Accommodation," *Third World Quarterly* 14, no. 2 (1993). Marlin Dick, writing in *Middle East Report Online*, emphasized that Hezbollah behaves more and more like a Chicago political machine than a branch of the Iranian Revolutionary Guards. Marlin Dick, "Hizballah's Domestic Growing Pains," *Middle East Report Online*, September 13, 2010, www.merip.org/mero/mero091310.html.

25. Qassem, *Hizbullah: Al-Manhaj, al-Tajribah, al-Mustaqbal*, 352.

26. Ibid., 113.

27. Naim Qassem, "Kayfa Yankharet Baqi al-Mujtama' fi al-Muqawamah?" (How Does the Rest of Society Integrate with the Resistance?), *An-Nahar*, June 8, 2007.

28. Harik, *Hezbollah: The Changing Face of Terrorism*, 43–52, and author's discussions with senior members of the Phalange Party, the Lebanese Forces, and Lebanese analysts throughout the 1990s.

29. An adaptation of this section appeared in Robert G. Rabil, *Religion, National Identity, and Confessional Politics: The Challenge of Islamism* (New York: Palgrave Macmillan, 2011), 72–73.

30. Court of Justice, Assassination of Sheikh Nizar Al-Halabi, decision no. 1/1997, January 17, 1997, available at the Special Tribunal for Lebanon's website, www .stl-tsl.org/en/documents/relevant-law-and-case-law/relevant-case-law/terrorism -cases/court-of-justice-assassination-of-sheikh-nizar-al-halabi-decision-no-1-1997 -17-january-1997, 8 (accessed August 9, 2013).

31. See Amnesty International, *Lebanon: Torture and Unfair Trial of the Dhinniyyah Detainees,* AI Index: MDE 18/005/2003.

32. See Joshua L. Gleis, "National Security Implications of Al-Takfir Wal-Hijra," *Al-Nakhlah* (Spring 2005).

33. Étienne Sakr (Abu Arz), "Syria and the Islamist Movements in Lebanon," *The Guardians of the Cedars National Lebanese Movement,* February 23, 2003.

34. See Amnesty International, *Lebanon: Torture and Unfair Trial of the Dhinniyah Detainees.*

35. Among those arrested in al-Dinniyah was Sa'id al-Shahal, the son of Hassan al-Shahal and grandson of Da'i al-Shahal. See Abd al-Ghani 'Imad, *Al-Harakat al-Islamiyah fi Lubnan: Ishkaliyat al-Din wal-Siyasah fi Mujtama' Mutanawe'* (Islamic Movements in Lebanon: The Ambiguity of Religion and Politics in a Diverse Society) (Beirut: Dar al-Tali'a lil-Tiba'a wal-Nashr, 2006), 312–13.

36. Ibid., 313.

37. "Khabiran fi al-Dirasat al-Islamiyah Yuhalilan 'majmu'at al-Dinniyah'" (Two Experts in Islamic Studies Analyze the al-Dinniyah Group), *An-Nahar,* January 12, 2000. See also Manar al-Huda al-Husseini, "Man Hum Jama'at al-Takfir wal-Hujra" (Who Is the Group al-Takfir wal-Hujra), *Al-Usbu' al-'Arabi,* January 17, 2000.

38. Radwan al-Sayyid, "Khabiran fi al-Dirasat al-Islamiyah Yuhalilan 'majmu'at al-Dinniyah'" (Two Experts in Islamic Studies Analyze the al-Dinniyah Group), *An-Nahar,* January 12, 2000.

39. For more details on the connection of Lebanese Salafists with transnational networks and charitable organizations, see Zoltan Pall, *Lebanese Salafis between the Gulf and Europe: Development, Fractionalization and Transnational Networks of Salafism in Lebanon* (Amsterdam: Amsterdam University Press, 2013), 52–54.

40. Ibid., 53.

41. Author's interview with a retired army brigadier general in Lebanon, July 15, 2012. On Syria's covert policy of supporting jihad in Iraq, see also 'Imad, *Al-Harakat al-Islamiyah fi Lubnan,* 336. For details on jihadi operations in Iraq and Lebanon, see Fida' 'Itani, *al-Jihadiyun fi Lubnan: Min "Quwat al-Fajr" ila "Fath al-Islam"* (Jihadists in Lebanon: From al-Fajr Forces to Fath al-Islam) (Beirut: Dar al-Saqi, 2008), 131–92.

42. 'Imad, *Al-Harakat al-Islamiyah fi Lubnan,* 336; Bilal Y. Saab and Magnus Ranstorp, "Securing Lebanon from the Threat of Salafist Jihadism," *Studies in Conflict*

and Terrorism 30, no. 10 (2007), 835; and Fawaz A. Gerges, *Journey of the Jihadist: Inside Muslim Militancy* (Orlando, FL: Harcourt, 2006), 273–77.

43. Author's interviews with a senior Lebanese officer on July 5, 2006, and with a retired Lebanese brigadier general on July 15, 2012. Moreover, the author held discussions with senior members of the Lebanese Forces who relayed similar versions of Syrian complicity in and supervision of jihad in Iraq from 2005 to 2008. Among those who were killed in Iraq in 2005 were Hassan Sawan, Ali al-Khatib, and Muhammad Abu Nuh.

44. It is noteworthy that by this time Lebanon's intelligence agencies had competing loyalties. Broadly speaking, Internal Security had been supported by Rafiq Hariri as a bulwark against the prominent power of military intelligence, some of whose members leaned toward Hezbollah and Syria. For a nuanced different view, see 'Itani, *al-Jihadiyun fi Lubnan*, 133–34, 141. Significantly, some of the officers who accused Syria of supporting jihad in Iraq have postulated that the 2012 and 2013 suicide bombings against Syrian intelligence headquarters that claimed the lives of individuals close to the Asad family were carried out by some of the same jihadists who were once supported by the Syrian regime.

45. 'Itani, *Al-Jihadiyun fi Lubnan*, 147.

46. *Haaretz*, July 27, 1993.

47. According to various reports, the operation caused the death of dozens of Lebanese, the destruction of approximately six thousand homes, and the displacement of a quarter of a million Lebanese from the south. See various Lebanese newspapers, August, 1993.

48. Hassan Fadlallah, *Harb al-Iradat: Sira' al-Muqawamah wa al-Ihtilal al-Israili fi Lubnan* (The Battle of Wills: The Struggle of the Resistance and Israel's Occupation in Lebanon) (Beirut: Dar al-Hadi: 2009), 171–72.

49. Ibid., 171; Qassem, *Hizbullah: Al-Manhaj, al-Tajribat, al-Mustaqbal*, 163–64; and *Al-Hayat*, August 3, 1993.

50. Karim Pakradouni, *Sadmah wa Sumud: 'Ahd Emile Lahoud (1998–2007)* (Shock and Steadfastness: The Era of Emile Lahoud [1998–2007]), 2nd ed. (Beirut: All Prints Distributors and Publishers, 2009), 25.

51. Ibid.

52. Ibid., 27.

53. Fadlallah, *Harb al-Iradat*, 174–75.

54. Pakradouni, *Sadmah wa Sumud*, 29–30.

55. "Al-Hariri fi 'Ayn al-Tinih: Bayna al-Tataruf wa al-I'tidal" (Hariri in 'Ayn al-Tinih: Between Extremism and Moderation), *An-Nahar*, August 21, 1996.

56. "Ra'd: Al-Sultah Tasa' ila Tahjim Hudur al-Muqawanah fi al-Majlis," *An-Nahar*, August 21, 1996.

57. Bayram Ibrahim, "Al-Janub wa al-Bika' ba'd Intikhabat Baabda! Hal Tanjah Siyassat Tahjim Hezbollah?" (The South and the Beka' after Baabda Elections! Will the Policy of Cutting Down Hezbollah Succeed?), *An-Nahar*, August 21, 1996.

58. See the full statement in *As-Safir*, September 21, 2000.

59. Gary C. Gambill, "Syria and the Shebaa Farms Dispute," *Middle East Intelligence Bulletin*, May 2001. See also Robert G. Rabil, *Embattled Neighbors: Syria, Israel, and Lebanon* (Boulder, CO: Lynne Rienner Publishers, 2003), 271–72.

60. UN Security Council Resolution (UNSCR) 1559, September 2, 2004.

61. *Daily Star* (Beirut), January 29 and February 3, 2006. For details, see Rabil, *Syria, the United States, and the War on Terror in the Middle East,* 168–81.

62. See *An-Nahar*, February 15 and 16, 2005.

63. See Mufti Qabbani's statement in *As-Safir*, February 15, 2005.

64. Ibid.

65. Ibid.

66. SANA (Syrian Arab News Agency) translated the speech into English and posted it on its website. See www.sana.org/english/headlines/5-3/Assad's%20speech.htm. For the original Arabic text, see *Al-Hayat*, March 6, 2005.

67. See *Daily Star*, March 7, 2005, and *An-Nahar*, March 7, 2005.

68. Ibid.

69. See Peter FitzGerald, *Report of the Fact-Finding Mission to Lebanon Inquiring about the Causes, Circumstances, and Consequences of the Assassination of Former Prime Minister Rafiq Hariri* (25 February–24 March 2005), United Nations Security Council, March 24, 2005. Interestingly, the report stated that, according to testimonies, in a meeting between President Assad and Hariri in Damascus, "Mr. Hariri reminded Mr. Assad of his pledge not to seek an extension for Mr. Lahoud's term, and Mr. Assad replied that there was a policy shift and that the decision was already taken. He added that Mr. Lahoud should be viewed as his personal representative in Lebanon and that 'opposing him is tantamount to opposing Assad himself.' He then added that he [Mr. Assad] 'would rather break Lebanon over the heads of [Mr.] Hariri and [Druze leader Walid] Jumblat than see his word in Lebanon broken.'"

70. Adnan El-Ghoul, "Assad Slams UN's Report on Hariri Assassination," *Daily Star*, March 31, 2005.

71. See *An-Nahar*, April 4, 2005.

72. "Syrian Forces Have Verifiably Been Withdrawn from Lebanon, Annan Says," UN News Service, May 23, 2005.

73. Qassem Qassir, "Al-Harakat al-Islamiyah fi Lubnan ba'da Istishhad al-Hariri wal-Insihab al-Suri," (The Islamic Movements in Lebanon in the Aftermath of Hariri's Martyrdom and Syria's Withdrawal), *Al-Mustaqbal*, May 11, 2005.

74. Ibid.

75. Ibid.

76. Ibid.

77. Ibid. Dr. al-Shahal underscored the importance of Salafi voting power by highlighting the growth, expansion, and influence of Salafi institutions. He cited the following institutes: the Institute of Propagation and Guidance; al-Amin Institute; the Institute of Imam Bukhari; and the Tripoli Institute. Then he mentioned that Salafists now had a significant number of mosques throughout Tripoli, Akkar, al-Miniyeh, and northern Lebanon, plus institutes and dispensaries for the caring of orphans and sick people. He mentioned that Salafists now had a presence in Sidon and Beirut, where major institutes have been established. Chief among them are the Islamic Endowment Institute, which was established in Beirut, and the Islamic Remedy Association, under the leadership of Sheikh Nadim Hijazi, which was established in Sidon. The association has several centers, including a school, mosques, orphanages, and civil defense facilities.

78. Ibid.

79. Ibid.

80. For excellent details on the Jami'yat Ihya' al-Turath al-Islami, see Pall, *Lebanese Salafis between the Gulf and Europe*, 79–95.

81. Kudr Taleb, "Salafiyun Yabhisun 'an Tashih al-Sura . . .Waqa'u fi Kamin al-Takhwin," (Salafists Seeking to Correct the Image . . . Fall in the Trap of Treason), *As-Safir*, August 22, 2008.

82. See text of memorandum of understanding in "Hezbollah wal-Tayar al-Salafi Yuwaqi'an Wathiqa Tafahum Laysat Muwajahah Dud Ahad" (Hezbollah and Salafist Current Sign a Memorandum of Understanding Directed against No One), *As-Safir*, August 19, 2008.

83. Ibid.

84. "Da'i al-Islam al-Shahal Yarfud al-Wathiqah: Muhawalat Ikhtiraq Fashila min Qibl Hezbollah" (Da'i al-Islam al-Shahal Rejects the Memorandum: A Failed Penetration Attempt by Hezbollah), *As-Safir*, August 19, 2008.

85. "Al-Jisr: Al-Mustqbal Lam Yataban al-Wathiqah" (Al-Jisr: The Future Did Not Adopt the Memorandum), *As-Safir*, August 19, 2008.

86. Taleb, "Salafiyun Yabhisun 'an Tashih al-Sura."

87. Hanin Ghaddar, "A Rising Threat?" *Now Lebanon*, May 23, 2008.

88. Ibid.

Chapter Seven

The Sunni Leadership and Salafism

Political Expediency and Self-Denial

This chapter examines the confessional politics of the Future Movement and their implications for the Sunni community, in particular the Salafists. Marked by compromise and political horse-trading, the movement's confessional politics entailed making bargains with both Hezbollah and Salafists, not in the least for maintaining the leadership of the country and leading the Sunni community. However, both bargains soon collapsed on account of domestic and regional dynamics, involving the political fallout of the July 2006 war and the 2008 seizure of Beirut. At the same time, it is true Hezbollah's arms secured for the party political victories; nevertheless, they also hastened its demonization by Salafists. The chapter also examines the relationship between Saad Hariri and the Salafists, exposing in the process the lack of vision of his leadership consequent upon its ambivalent approach to Salafists and its self-denial about both its weakness and their political potential.

Confessional Politics at Work: The Hallmark of Political Compromise

The collapse of the Second Republic created a political vacuum, sparking a sectarian struggle for political power. In fact, this struggle initially began when the pro-Syrian government of Omar Karame resigned and pro-Syrian and opposition forces haggled over the composition of a new government whose mandate was mainly to oversee the parliamentary elections set to begin in late May 2005. Following marathonic hours of wrangling, a new government was born in April reflecting a delicate balance of sectarian power distribution. However, given the politically charged atmosphere and the rapid erosion of Syrian power, Saad Hariri's Future Movement (also known as the Future Current) obtained two important cabinet positions—the interior and justice ministries—which were essential for overseeing the elections and leading the probe into former prime minister Rafiq Hariri's assassination.[1] The birth of the new government did not mitigate the polarization of Lebanese politics. But this polarization, unlike that recently over Syria, was now over the elections, including choosing an electoral system and forging alliances, all in the interest of staking a claim to political power in the new parliament. This claim to power blurred the lines between the pro-Syrian March 8 camp, led by Hezbollah, and the anti-Syrian March 14 camp, led by the Future Movement. Inasmuch as the Future Movement had been interested in leading and shaping the new republic, Hezbollah had been concerned about UN Security Council Resolution 1559, part of which calls for its disarmament. The political cover and legitimacy of Hezbollah that Syria had institutionalized in the political system tumbled with the collapse of the Second Republic. The group recognized that it could become a target of the international community, led by the United States, and therefore sought to be an integral force, if not the power broker, in both the executive and legislative institutions of the state. Consequently, it pursued a dual policy of co-opting other communities in the name of national unity and making the elections both a referendum for its role as a resistance movement and a means of showing its political strength. At the same time, Hezbollah secretary general Hassan Nasrallah defiantly refused disarmament and urged political reconciliation in Lebanon by reaching out to Christian factions, which had been among the most vocal in calling for Hezbollah to surrender its weapons.[2]

Among the Druze, Progressive Socialist Party (PSP) chief Walid Jumblat was concerned about his community's numeric weakness, which, absent broad communal electoral alliances, would lead to a sclerotic political representation. Consequently, he solidified his alliance with Saad Hariri and more or less mended his relations with Hezbollah. Following long hours of horse trading, Jumblat, Hariri, and Nasrallah struck a deal to base the upcoming parliamentary elections on the 2000 electoral law.[3] This would allow the parties to shape the emergence of the new political order and enable Hezbollah to undermine the candidacy of any politician calling for its disarmament. This was the background against which the quadripartite alliance (Hezbollah, Amal, the PSP, and Future Movement) was born. More specifically, as implied by Deputy General Secretary of Hezbollah Naim Qassem, the alliance was about allowing Hariri's Future Movement and Jumblat's PSP a majority in the parliament in return of a guarantee that neither the resistance nor its weapons would be touched.[4]

Christians were taken aback by Jumblat's maneuvering, prompting the League of Maronite Bishops to issue a statement on May 12 condemning the electoral law: "In light of this law, the Christians can elect only 15 MPs out of

64 while the others, almost 50 MPs, are elected by Muslims."[5] Nevertheless, Christian factions decided not to boycott the elections for fear of prolonging the parliament's pro-Syrian character. Christian ranks were further shaken by the defection of Gen. Michel Aoun, who had recently returned to Lebanon after fifteen years of exile. In disagreement with the mainstream Christian factions, Aoun created his own electoral lists and party, the Free Patriotic Movement (also referred to as Free Current), even allying himself with pro-Syrian politicians.

Meanwhile, many Salafists were not happy with the quadripartite alliance. Although their political influence on the country's confessional system had been negligible, a significant number of Salafists, even from the quietest school, decided following the murder of Hariri to partake in the elections. Yet, as we have seen in the previous chapter, they had few options and opted to support Hariri's Future Movement. Significantly, what placated the Salafists' infuriation with Hariri's arrangement with Hezbollah was the promise to release scores of Salafi defendants arrested as part of the government's crackdown on the al-Dinniyah and Majdal Anjar Salafi groups. Many defendants had not been taken to trial despite the fact that they had been detained for years. This coincided with the Future Movement's plan to emerge as the leading political force in the Sunni community and in Lebanon as a whole. Riding a wave of nationalist fervor, it began a process of forging political alliances with all groups and parties based in the most part on confessional expediencies and politics, favoritism, and Hariri largesse, the very instruments of Lebanon's confessional system. Essentially, this meant seeking support from the Salafi popular bases in northern Lebanon to undermine pro-Syrian political forces there, mainly the leadership of Omar Karame in Tripoli. Correspondingly, at the urging of Hariri's Future Movement, President Émile Lahoud, in late July 2005, signed two amnesty laws approved by parliament in favor of releasing the leader of the Christian Lebanese Forces, Samir Geagea, and dozens of Salafists involved in the al-Dhinniyah clashes. Obviously this was a reconciliatory measure meant to improve Christian-Muslim relations and Hariri-Salafist relations in northern Lebanon, especially following the 2005 parliamentary elections in which Hariri's Future Movement partnered with Geagea's Lebanese Forces and received Salafi support.[6]

Actually this marked the first time Salafists had competed with each other in order to project the power of their popular electoral base. Furthermore, it was an open secret that Saudi Arabia, followed by Qatar and Kuwait, had injected a significant amount of money in the run-up to the elections through their transnational Salafi organizations. The rumor mill buzzed with news that Saudi Arabia had invested so much cash in the election campaign that diaspora Lebanese were given free tickets to come to Lebanon and vote for the Future Movement. This influx of cash in the electoral machine compelled some parties to stay out of the elections altogether. Notwithstanding the fact that the Islamic Association did not win any seat in the 2000 parliamentary elections, it decided to boycott the 2005 elections on the grounds that, according to its statement, "foreign interference has increased and the financial role has become a significant factor in the electoral process."[7]

Not surprisingly, Saad, Jumblat, Nasrallah, and Aoun emerged as the uncontested leaders of their respective communities. The biggest upset was Aoun's victory in Mount Lebanon (North Metn and Jbeil-Keswran) and Beka' (Zahleh), where his lists won out over almost all mainstream and historic Christian candidates. Subsequently, in late July 2005, the Future Movement–led new government of Fouad Siniora issued a statement declaring its domestic and foreign policy positions. An outcome of compromise, the statement did not mention UN Resolution 1559 while at the same time confirming the government's abidance by international law. In reference to Hezbollah, the ministerial statement emphasized that "the government considers the Lebanese resistance a truthful and natural expression of the national right of the Lebanese citizen to liberate his land and defend his dignity in the face of Israeli threats, ambitions, and aggressions and to work to resume the liberation of Lebanese land."[8]

The Demonization of Hezbollah: The July War and the Takeover of Beirut

The political climate of compromise ushered in by the quadripartite alliance rapidly dissipated as sectarian tension heightened in light of Hezbollah's adamant position to keep its jihadi infrastructure and weapons outside the purview of national dialogue. Parallel to the ongoing tension, in early February 2006 a mob, protesting a Danish newspaper's publication of cartoons of Prophet Muhammad, stormed Christian East Beirut to set the Danish embassy on fire. On their way, they vandalized shops, cars, and churches, shocking and horrifying the population. Many Salafi organizations issued a joint statement deploring the violence and asserting their peaceful *da'wa*. Similarly, in a symbolic gesture to try to contain Christian-Muslim ill feelings, Secretary General of Hezbollah Hassan Nasrallah and Gen. Michel Aoun met at Mar MeKhayel (Saint Michael) church in Shiah, a Beirut suburb across the "Green Line" that had divided the city during the civil war, and signed a ten-point memorandum of understanding dealing with consensual democracy, electoral law, building the state, the missing during the war, security, Lebanese-Syrian relations and protection of Lebanon.[9] On the question of Lebanese-Syrian relations, the memorandum recommended four measures to establish mutual and sound relations: (1) asserting the Lebanese identity of Shebaa Farms, (2) delineating the Lebanese-Syrian border, (3) calling on the Syrian state to cooperate with the Lebanese state to find out the fate of Lebanese detainees in Syrian jails, and (4) establishing diplomatic relations between the two countries.

These measures had been for the most part comparable to the demands of the Maronite Church and had guided the policies of the March 14 forces. However, regarding the resistance and its weapons, the memorandum suggested that the Lebanese people should assume their responsibilities and share the burden of protecting Lebanon, safeguarding its existence and security, and protecting its independence and sovereignty by (a) liberating the Shebaa Farms from the Israeli occupation, (b) liberating the Lebanese prisoners from Israeli prisons, and (c) protecting Lebanon from Israeli threats through a national dialogue leading to the formulation of a national defense strategy.[10]

No sooner was the memorandum announced than it was vilified by some and hailed by others. No doubt, the memorandum was close to a political coup de grace for the March 14 forces, as it sowed discord among their ranks and structured a new configuration of alliances. The shift of the Free Patriotic Movement (or Free Current) from March 14 forces to March 8 forces greatly benefited Hezbollah. According to Naim Qassem, the memorandum "specified the mechanism by which to deal with the weapons of the resistance as part of a comprehensive national defense strategy, establishing the foundation for dialogue about the resistance and its weapons instead of the logic of UNSC 1559."[11] No less significant, Qassem attested that "the memorandum gave Hezbollah a wide nationalist extent through the Christian community, a principal pillar for the resistance and independence of Lebanon, and dispelled the scare campaign about Hezbollah directed at the Christians."[12]

For the March 14 forces, the memorandum was most unfortunate, for it gave Hezbollah political cover and drove a wedge between Christians. But according to an outside observer, the Arab philosopher Sadek J. al-Azm, "the memorandum prevented Christian-Shi'a antagonism and alienation, especially now that the Shi'a community has become the largest one in Lebanon. At the same time, the Maronites have become the glue, sustaining national coexistence, as they are on an equal distance from all other communities."[13] This, of course, did not sit well with the *haraki* Salafists, who deplored not only the agreement but also the naive and weak policies of Hariri's Future Movement that inadvertently sustained what Salafi sheikh Salem bin 'Abd al-Ghani al-Rafi'i described as the "arrogant power of Hezbollah and its illegal weapons."[14]

It was against this background that the 2006 July war between Hezbollah and Israel erupted. From the moment Hezbollah sparked hostilities with Israel on July 12 with a cross-border raid, Lebanon's multicommunal society was torn by divergent views on Hezbollah. The hostilities ended on the basis of a seven-point plan introduced by Prime Minister Siniora and according to UNSC Resolution

1701, which increased the number of the United Nations Interim Force in Lebanon (UNIFIL) troops in southern Lebanon and called for the dismantling and disarming of all militias. Despite the destruction wrought upon both Lebanese infrastructure and Hezbollah's members, the group's secretary general, Hassan Nasrallah, declared a "divine" victory. He called for a national unity government and a new electoral law, asserted that the resistance had dealt a blow to American Middle East strategy, and took pride in his relationship with both Syria and Iran.[15] Iran and Syria rode the wave of Hezbollah's Pyrrhic victory.

Many Lebanese believed that their country had become an arena for settling regional scores between Israel and the United States on one side and Iran and Syria on the other, with Hezbollah fighting Iran's war. Criticism of Hezbollah slowly but steadily surfaced, not in the least by *haraki* Salafists who had become assertive in their belief that Hezbollah is an Iranian party and that, according to Salafi sheikh Zakariya 'Abd al-Razaq al-Masri, "Iran and Syria are hypocritical states" that "are counted on the surface as part of the *ummah* [Muslim community], [but] they are intrinsically the enemy of the *ummah* putting forward Arabic and Islamic slogans in its square that call for [Muslim] unity and liberation of Jerusalem only to deceive the naive people about their real intentions and secret connections."[16]

Paradoxically, Fathi Yakan, in sharp contrast to his former Salafi colleagues, maintained his unequivocal support of Hezbollah. At the same time, his disputes with the leadership of the Islamic Association had already become irresolvable. In August 2006, he declared the establishment of a new Islamist organization under the name Jabhat al-'Amal al-Islami (Islamic Action Front). It included a number of pro-Syrian Islamists and Islamist organizations, including the secretary-general of the Islamic Unity Movement–General Secretariat, Sheikh Bilal Sha'ban, the son of the late leader of the Islamic Unity Movement, and Hisham Minqara, a former commander of the movement. Commenting on the establishment of the new movement, Yakan stated: "God willed it that the birth of the Islamic Action Front had taken place during unprecedented circumstances, amidst a vile and vicious American attack on Lebanon, Palestine, and Iraq. This imposes on the Front responsibilities and exceptional obligations whose preparations are unprecedented so as to make the performance, role and readiness of the movement marked by a jihadi pulse."[17] He also criticized those who have doubted the role of Hezbollah, by emphasizing that "the Islamic resistance in Lebanon has triumphed in confronting the Israeli army, and if it should achieve more military victories it would change not only the Lebanese equation, but also all regional and international equations."[18]

Before long, the polarization of Lebanese society took a dramatic turn for the worse in the shadow of a wave of assassination of anti-Syrian figures.[19]

The pro-opposition Shi'a ministers (and a Greek Orthodox minister) resigned from the cabinet in the belief that the government would no longer be legitimate without the representation of the Shi'a community. The government did not resign. Instead, it formally asked the United Nations to proceed with the international tribunal to investigate the murder of former prime minister Rafiq Hariri and his colleagues. Meanwhile, Damascus and Tehran continued transporting weapons to Hezbollah and replenishing its arsenal—in violation of UN Security Council Resolution 1701.[20] It was at this critical juncture that Lebanese authorities moved to confront a new jihadi organization called Fatah al-Islam, which became the focal point of an uprising in the Nahr al-Bared Palestinian refugee camp in May and June 2007. The human and material cost of the battle against Fatah al-Islam had been staggering. The Lebanese army lost dozens of soldiers, scores of Salafi jihadists were killed and arrested, the refugee camp was destroyed, and its population was uprooted.

The astounding sacrifices of the army and the defeat of the radical group breathed into the country a patriotic fresh air. Inspired by the government's triumph and a renewed confidence by a large segment of the population, the government deepened its investigation into the assassination of anti-Syrian figures and representatives of political movements. Moreover, the government was taken aback by a new trend whereby senior intelligence and army officers had become targets of assassination.[21]

Meanwhile, a president was yet to be elected, even though the term of Émile Lahoud ended in November 2007, and the contending parties engaged in an escalatory discourse of "treason," which further intensified political polarization. Moved no less by the surge of patriotism than by international support, the government took two decisions that sparked civil strife. On May 5, 2008, the government decided to remove airport security chief Brig. Gen. Wafiq Shuqeir over his alleged links to Hezbollah and to consider a private communications network set up by Hezbollah illegal and unconstitutional, something that amounted to criminalizing the Islamist party and exposing its senior cadres.

Nasrallah immediately responded by describing the government's decisions a "declaration of war" and asserting his readiness to use force to protect the "weapons" of Hezbollah.[22] He followed by ordering a swift military onslaught on West Beirut. The pro-government groups were no match for Hezbollah's well equipped and -trained fighters. Saad Hariri and Walid Jumblat were put virtually under house arrest. Hariri's television station was taken off the air and his *Al-Mustaqbal* newspaper headquarters destroyed. The fighting then expanded to some Druze areas in the Chouf and Mount Lebanon and to the northern city of Tripoli. Hezbollah, though sustaining a number of casualties, clearly asserted its military prowess.

An Arab diplomatic delegation led by the foreign minister of Qatar, Sheikh Hamad bin Jassem al-Thani, traveled to Beirut and held intensive meetings with Lebanese leaders to defuse the crisis. On May 15, pending the launch of a national dialogue in Doha, the government reversed its two decisions in "the view of the higher national interests." Consequently, the fighting ended.

The major parties and groups met in Doha, and an agreement was reached that gave the opposition almost all of its demands including a veto power in a national unity government, adoption of the *qada'* (district) for the electoral law, and election of Commander of the Army Michel Suleiman as president. Though the Doha Agreement provided for upholding the sovereignty of the state throughout Lebanon, it did not address the question of Hezbollah's weapons.[23] No doubt Hezbollah scored a political victory, embodied in the Doha Agreement and by the sheer virtue of the fact that the government reversed its decisions. Nevertheless, the fact that Hezbollah used its weapons against Lebanese groups debunked its myth of itself as a resistance movement beyond the pale of Lebanon's Byzantine politics.

Consequently the party was sharply criticized by the spiritual leaders of both the Sunni and Druze communities, save by members of its own sect.[24] The sharpest rebuke and criticism, however, came from the Salafists, who considered the seizure of Beirut as another assault in the relentless campaign of Hezbollah against *ahl al-Sunna* (partisans of the Sunna). Salafists throughout northern Lebanon took to the streets in protest against Hezbollah's takeover of the city, chanting "death to the party of Satan" while clenching their fists in the air.[25] Leaflets circulated in Beirut denouncing and condemning the Shi'ites and Hezbollah as *kuffars* (infidels/unbelievers) and *rawafid* (rejecters/deserters, a derogatory term for Shi'ites used by many Salafists). Ominously, the anathematization of Hezbollah has become a fixture in Friday sermons across many Salafi mosques in northern Lebanon. The mood of Salafists was reflected by Sheikh Bilal Dokmak: "The resistance mask has fallen, and the 'Party of Satan' was targeting the Sunnis and not the majority leaders."[26]

Most ominously, the demonization of the Shi'ites in general and of Hezbollah in particular has become a byproduct of the country's deep polarization, part of which has involved the volatile dynamics of the Sunni milieu consequent upon the Hariri-Salafist ambivalent relationship.

The Ambivalent Hariri-Salafist Relationship: Between Political Expediency and Self-Denial

The Hariri-Salafist relationship, which had been distinguished as a marriage of convenience, gradually transformed into an ambivalent relationship. At the heart of this transformation lay the frequent emergence of hybrid Salafi jihadi organizations that more or less warped the already schizophrenic relationship between Lebanese authorities and the Salafists. More specifically, the Future Movement's assumption of power in 2005 following the collapse of the Second Republic had introduced new dynamics to the Hariri-Salafist relationship, paradoxically affected no less by the need of the Future Movement for the sizable voting blocs of Salafists than by the desire of Hariri to stay at arm's length from Salafi jihadists and their supporters within the Salafi realm. Moreover, the rivalry and double loyalty of some members of the Internal Security Force (ISF) and Military Intelligence added another layer of complexity to this incongruous relationship, turning it into what a Sunni observer called the most blighted ambivalent relationship.

The structural aspects of this transformation partly lay in the confessional system that apportions governmental positions on a confessional basis and partly in late prime minister Rafiq Hariri's effort to establish a highly sophisticated internal security apparatus owing its loyalty to the Sunni leadership. Likewise, the time-honored hallmark of compromise of confessional politics militated against any concerted effort to remove pro-Syrian and pro-Hezbollah loyalists from the apparatuses of the state, especially its army and intelligence service. Add to this the paranoia regarding everything Sunni Islamist that had been embedded in the bureaucracy during years of Syrian occupation. The cumulative effect of these factors politicized and polarized the system along the country's lines of political and sectarian divisions. Consequently Saad Hariri's relationship with the Salafists had a governmental dimension that promoted ambivalence.

Essentially the salient features of this transformation began to appear during and after the elections of 2005. True, Hariri reached out to Salafists to undermine his opponents in northern Lebanon. In reality, however, he had but the Salafists to turn to due to the fact that the Islamic Association and traditional Sunni politicians boycotted the elections. As communal polarization deepened in the country, Hariri tried to maintain Sunni solidarity, which in turn partly hinged on Salafi support. It is noteworthy that the Islamists had splintered after Fathi Yakan established the Islamic Action Front as an umbrella organization for Islamists and Islamist organizations, including the Islamic Unity Movement, whose opposition to Hariri and his party had hardened. Expectedly, Hariri boosted his support for Salafists by providing financial resources and services to areas where they preponderated and to events sponsored by them. The highlight of his support for Salafists clearly transpired when he provided transportation to Sunnis in northern Lebanon, co-led by Salafi sheikhs Da'i al-Islam and Raed Hlayhel, to participate in the demonstration in Beirut in February 2006 protesting the Danish cartoons blaspheming the Prophet. Nevertheless, Hariri, at least in public, continued to shy from exposing his support of Salafists, even though converging interests brought them closer together.

In addition, on the surface the outbreak of the 2006 Hezbollah-Israel conflagration exposed communal unity in the face of Israel's aggression. On a closer examination, however, the conflagration revealed the depth of Sunni wariness of Hezbollah.[27] The notion that the Sunni community needed to take certain sociopolitical and military measures to adjust to the dawning reality of Hezbollah's preponderance in the country began to congeal across many sectors of the Sunni community. In the fall of 2006, Salafists, encouraged by Salafi transnational institutions based in Saudi Arabia, Kuwait, and Qatar, began holding meetings to draw a plan of common objectives, with the purpose of protecting the Sunni community and reinforcing the Sunni leadership, led by Hariri's Future Movement. At the same time, then former deputy Khaled al-Daher, a close associate of Hariri and the Islamists, established the al-Liqa' al-Islami al-Mustaqil (the Independent Islamic Gathering) to rally various Islamists and Islamist groups under the ceiling of one group committed to defending the Sunni community. The Gathering included, among others, Salafi sheikhs Bilal Baroudi and Zakariya al-Masri, Sheikh Fawaz al-Agha, and a former leader of the Islamic Unity Movement, Kan'an Naji. The purpose for which the Gathering was established was to counteract Hezbollah's hegemony in the state and on "the street." This became evident in the aftermath of Hezbollah's seizure of Beirut when Daher issued a statement in which he called for the establishment of al-Muqawamah al-Islamiyah al-Wataniyah fi Lubnan (the Nationalist Islamic Resistance in Lebanon) to defend Lebanon against what he termed "the gangs that belong to Iran," in reference to Hezbollah.[28]

It is hardly possible that these initiatives had taken place without the collaboration and support of Hariri. Enough circumstantial evidence led one to conclude that Hariri had been actually reinforcing Sunni solidarity under his leadership with the help of Salafists. The individuals leading the initiatives, such as Da'i al-Islam and Daher, had become the subject of Hariri's support and funding. And the country most involved in supporting the initiatives was none other than Saudi Arabia, Hariri's regional patron. No less significant, Hariri had charged ISF head Brig. Gen. Ashraf Rifi (along with Daher and Ahmad Fatfat) with organizing the Future Movement's relationship with the Salafists. This is not to say that Hariri had condoned Salafi-jihadi terrorist activities in Lebanon. In fact, the Future Movement–led Siniora government arrested several Salafi-jihadi networks with links to al-Qaeda.[29] But, at the same time, it refrained from confronting the Salafi-jihadi organization Jund al-Sham when it expanded its operations and seized the Ta'mir neighborhood adjacent to the Ayn al-Helweh camp in 2005. Bahiya al-Hariri, aunt of Saad and a Future Movement parliamentary deputy, preferred to engage in dialogue with the jihadi organization. Apparently Hariri supported the Salafists so long as they did not act as al-Qaeda's proxy in Lebanon, setting aside the fact that Salafi-jihadi organizations need not be al-Qaeda's affiliates or proxies to carry out their "messianic" terrorism. Nor has he questioned the ideological and practical nuances in the relationship between Salafi jihadists and *haraki* Salafists, many of whom essentially do not consider Salafi-jihadi organizations as terrorist ones. As long as he was explicitly not involved in the activities of Salafi jihadists and some *harakis*, he maintained his party's, though not his personal, relationship with Salafists. This ambivalent policy transpired when Fatah al-Islam rebelled against the Lebanese army in May 2007.

Fatah al-Islam was formally established in the Palestinian refugee camp of Nahr al-Bared near Tripoli in November 2006. The founder of Fatah al-Islam, Shaker al-Absi, issued a statement in which he affirmed that his group had split from the pro-Syrian Fatah al-Intifada and declared the establishment of Fatah al-Islam. Raising the Salafi black flag, he declared that he was bringing religion to the Palestinian cause. He described the organization as a Palestinian national liberation movement whose orientation follows the "methodology of 'no god but God.'" He defined himself and his organization "as part of this people and of this *ummah* that bears the *ummah's* aspirations and pains and that they firmly believe that they will not accomplish the goals of the *ummah* without carrying on the religion [Islam]. This is us, Fatah al-Islam."[30] He also set the immediate objective of Fatah al-Islam as "fighting the Jews and their supporters in the Zionist crusader West."[31]

Al-Absi, a Palestinian, had been known for his complicity in al-Zarqawi's murder of an American diplomat in Jordan, Laurence Foley, in 2002. Jordanian authorities sentenced him to death in absentia. He escaped to Syria, where he was reportedly imprisoned for three years for his links to al-Qaeda in Iraq. Upon his release, he rejoined Fatah al-Intifada and reportedly resumed his cooperation with al-Qaeda, mainly helping Arab jihadists enter Iraq. Al-Absi disputed this narrative and averred that he was arrested in Syria for an attempt to carry out an operation in the Golan Heights and that he and his group have no affiliation with al-Qaeda.[32] Be that as it may, al-Absi was dispatched to Lebanon in 2006 by the deputy chief of Fatah al-Intifada, Abu Khaled al-Umla. He moved to the al-Baddawi refugee camp in northern Lebanon, where he had a falling-out with his organization. He relocated to the Nahr al-Bared refugee camp, where, shortly thereafter, he seized the headquarters of Fatah al-Intifada and declared the birth of his organization.

The immediate reaction of the March 14 camp in general and the Future Movement in particular was that this new jihadi movement was the creation of

Syrian intelligence. Soon afterward, on November 29, 2006, the Future Move-ment's daily, *Al-Mustaqbal*, published an article based on the interrogation of two Syrian defendants arrested by Lebanese authorities for planning terrorist attacks in Lebanon, that accused President Bashar al-Asad of Syria and his intel-ligence services of charging Fatah al-Islam with carrying out terrorist attacks in Lebanon, including assassinating thirty-six Lebanese dignitaries and targeting UNIFIL forces in southern Lebanon, all under the cover of al-Qaeda.[33] When on February 13, 2007, a day before the second anniversary of Rafiq Hariri's murder, members of Fatah al-Islam attacked two commuter buses in the Chris-tian town of 'Ayn 'Alaq, resulting in the death of three Lebanese and over twenty injured, the March 14 forces issued a statement the next day accusing Syrian intelligence of being behind the murders. The statement maintained that a ter-rorist group led by the Syrian Mustapha Sayo had been apprehended by Leba-nese authorities, whereupon its members confessed to their connection to Syrian intelligence, which had ordered them to carry out the attack as part of a plan to destabilize Lebanon.[34] Conversely, the Syrian regime consistently claimed that Lebanon had become a seductive area for al-Qaeda's operatives after the with-drawal of its troops from the country. Even investigative journalist Seymour Hersh postulated that March 14 leaders had encouraged the growth of Fatah al-Islam as a countervailing force to Hezbollah.[35]

Be that as it may, the Siniora government did not take any action to arrest al-Absi or the members of his group, despite the fact that he was wanted by Jordanian authorities, even after the 'Ayn 'Alaq incident. In fact, al-Absi made a mockery of the Lebanese judicial system by welcoming visitors into the camp and giving interviews to the media, including the *New York Times*. In his inter-view with the *Times* in March 2007, al-Absi admitted that "he shared al-Qaeda's fundamentalist interpretation and endorsed the creation of a global Islamic nation." When questioned about killing Americans in Iraq, he said that "we have every legitimate right to do such acts, for isn't it America that comes to our region and kills innocents and children? It is our right to hit them in their homes the same as they hit us in our homes."[36] That same month, Ashraf Rifi, respond-ing to a question as to whether an al-Qaeda organization existed in Lebanon, stated "that al-Qaeda's presence in Lebanon is a false al-Qaeda," implying that it was a Syrian creation.[37] In the meantime, reports circulated that a significant number of Arab militants had entered Lebanon via Beirut's international airport with the knowledge of Lebanon's security apparatus. Fida' 'Itani wrote that many Salafi associations, encouraged by their Saudi and Kuwaiti supporters, rallied together to "confront the Shi'a flow." He listed several Salafi organizations, such as the Islamic Union, the Islamic Heritage Endowment, and the Islamic Center Endowment, that worked hard to harness Sunni power.[38] Hilal Khashan observed that "the Hariri assassination amounted to a coup that blunted the Saudis' thrust into Lebanon and reaffirmed the preeminence of the Syrian-Hezbollah entente. Riyadh's response came in the form of arming Tripoli's Salafists so as to allow them to stand up to Hezbollah."[39] In fact, in an interview with French television station France 24 in early May 2007 in which he was asked about Fatah al-Islam and about weapons being smuggled into Lebanon to extremists, Prime Minister Siniora responded: "No doubt there are reports revolving around their [Fatah al-Islam's] connections to some Syrian intelligence apparatus. Others have been arrested with links to al-Qaeda. This matter needs to be followed through. But it is a grave mistake to depict the matter as a problem linked to al-Qaeda. . . . And we call upon the Syrians to bear their responsibilities in regulating the border and interdicting people sneaking into and weapons smuggled into Lebanon."[40]

At last the Siniora government decided to move against members of Fatah al-Islam following a bank armed robbery (their third) near Tripoli on May 19. The ISF tracked the robbers to a safe house in Tripoli, and in the wee hours of the next day they unsuccessfully raided the place. Both the government and the ISF failed to notify the army unit stationed next to Nahr al-Bared about the botched raid, thereby exposing them hours later to a bloody reprisal by Fatah al-Islam, in which twenty-two soldiers were murdered. The massacre of the soldiers horrified the public and united it in encouraging the government to clamp down on Fatah al-Islam. Public outrage apparently compelled Salafists and Salafi-jihadi organizations Usbat al-Ansar and Jund al-Sham to withhold their support of Fatah al-Islam. The battle, which relentlessly raged until the Lebanese army controlled the demolished camp on September 2, resulted in the deaths of 170 Lebanese soldiers, 47 Palestinian civilians, and 200 members of Fatah al-Islam. Approximately 200 militants were arrested. Ironically, al-Absi, along with approximately 150 members of Fatah al-Islam, managed to escape. In the meantime, Lebanese authorities raided suspicious safe houses in Tripoli, chief among them a building in the Abi Samra neighborhood, the stronghold of Sheikh Da'i al-Islam al-Shahal. Reportedly the building, where a group of militants led by Nabil Rahim had taken refuge, belonged to Da'i al-Islam. Al-Shahal denied any connection to the group or to the safe house, but he admitted to knowing Rahim. Rahim had been under surveillance by Lebanese and Saudi authorities for his alleged association with al-Qaeda. Defending Rahim, al-Shahal explained that "Rahim's group and other Sunni militants were arming themselves either in anticipation of a possible security vacuum after the Syrian withdrawal . . . or to fulfill what they see as a religious duty to have weapons." He added that "they [Rahim's group] chose to fight to the death rather than be captured and suffer torture. Some youths have come out of detention bruised and beaten, even though they did nothing. This makes people extremists."[41]

Eventually a clear picture emerged of Fatah al-Islam on the basis of extensive interrogations and evidences. Members of Fatah al-Islam had connections to al-Qaeda, and even though the organization claimed to be Palestinian, its members were in the majority Lebanese and foreigners. Chief among the leaders of Fatah al-Islam, besides al-Absi, had been the deputy commander of the organization, Shihab al-Qadour, known as Abu Hraira, and Shahin Shahin. Al-Qadour had been arrested as a youngster by Syrian authorities during their suppression of the Islamic Unity Movement in Tripoli in the 1980s and was a well-known militant with strong ties to al-Qaeda. He was killed by Lebanese authorities in Tripoli in 2007. Shahin was none other than the son of al-Qaeda founder Osama bin Laden, Sa'd Osama bin Laden.[42] In his statement on Fatah al-Islam and the crime of 'Ayn 'Alaq, Cassation Court judge Sa'id Mirza reported that Fatah al-Islam aimed at disrupting Lebanon's society through sabotage and bombings, with the objective of creating a charged sectarian and denominational climate. He also stated that the organization aimed at confronting the Lebanese government because it was implementing the project of the United States in Lebanon and attacking UNIFIL forces in southern Lebanon because they were occupying Muslim land.[43] At the same time, on February 18, 2008, military judge Rashid Muzher issued his accusatory decision in which he revealed that armed Salafi groups in Lebanon had links to Usbat al-Ansar, al-Qaeda, and Fatah al-Islam. He stated that armed Sunni groups had tried to carry out terrorist acts under the slogan of supporting the Sunnis and defending them during any future crisis. He also accused Salafi sheikhs Muhammad Bassam Hamoud, Nabil Rahim, Zuheir Issa, Adnan Muhammad, and Hussam al-Sabbagh of creating these groups, which, among other things, welcomed foreign nationals, especially Saudis, to train them on the use of weapons and bombs. He also emphasized that Sheikh Adnan Muhammad had used his position as imam of the Hamza mosque in the al-Qibbi neighborhood in Tripoli to whip up the interest of the youth in jihad and the necessity to prepare to support *ahl al-Sunna*.[44]

This episode clearly shows that transnational networks of Salafists and al-Qaeda had indeed established contacts with Salafists and militants in Lebanon, which offered a permissive security setting. Out of these contacts emerged Fatah al-Islam and other Salafi-jihadi cells. This is neither to say that the Syrian regime or the Future Movement had no connection with them nor that the Future Movement or the Syrian regime controlled their decision. The reality is in the middle of this gray area. The Future Movement has supported Salafists within the context of reinforcing Sunni solidarity and its leadership of the Sunni community and created a counterbalance to Hezbollah. Gulf countries, especially Saudi Arabia, played a significant role in encouraging Hariri and his Future

Movement to allow Salafists to regroup into armed units as a counterweight to Iran's armed proxy in Lebanon, Hezbollah. Clearly notwithstanding its support of Sunni solidarity under its leadership, Saudi Arabia, the patron of Hariri, has supported Salafists for ideological and regional considerations, anchored in the kingdom's religious policy of propagating its quietest Salafi school and in the kingdom's strategy of offsetting Iran's projection of regional power. Conversely the Syrian regime had indeed supported some Salafists with the objective of destabilizing Lebanon in general and undermining the Future Movement–led government in particular, which had supported the creation of the special international tribunal for investigating the Rafiq Hariri's murder.

It is mainly within the context of these layers of complexity that the ambivalent relationship between Saad Hariri and the Salafists should be understood. One also has to pay attention to certain changes in local and/or regional conditions or settings that may affect the dynamics of the relationship. Drastically two seminal local and regional developments had taken place that affected the Sunni milieu in general and the Hariri-Salafist relationship in general, further deepening the ambivalent character of the relationship.

Hezbollah's seizure of West Beirut had far-reaching implications for the Sunni milieu and Hariri's confessional politics. On the regional level, Saudi Arabia had temporarily suspended its support for an armed Salafi militia. Hilal Khashan observed: "The ease with which Hezbollah managed to defeat Hariri's al-Mustaqbal militia in Beirut in 2008 convinced the Saudi leadership that they could not rely on northern Lebanese Salafis, who formed the backbone of the prime minister's militia, to serve as a countervailing military force to Hezbollah. They have thus curtailed most of their military assistance and contented themselves with promoting as-Salafiya al-Ilmiya [quietest or scientific Salafiyah], or official Salafi, that eschews involvement in politics."[45]

Saudi Arabia was not alone in limiting its funding to the quietest school of Salafism. It is noteworthy that after September 11 terrorist attacks, almost all Saudi aid to Salafists has been funneled through the Ministry of Religious Endowments and a number of private associations.[46] Kuwait and Qatar followed suit through their respective Salafi organizations, the Society for the Revival of Islamic Heritage and Sheikh Eid Charity Institution. Toeing the Saudi line, Hariri funneled a significant amount of cash to the quietest Salafi organizations. But his support of Salafists had been part of a strategic plan intended to solidify his leadership of both the Sunni community and the March 14 camp, with the objective of preparing to win a majority in the 2009 upcoming parliamentary elections. Correspondingly, he set about forging a better relationship with Samir Geagea of the Lebanese Forces and trying to create a leadership in northern Lebanon loyal to him.

The background against which he decided to create a leadership in the north lay not in the factionalism of Salafists but in his inability to control them. This was put on display when Salafists of all stripes demonstrated in al-Nour Square, Tripoli, in August 2008, protesting the detention without trial dozens of Salafists. Salafi sheikhs, together with the families of the detained, vocally and angrily blamed Hariri for what they considered a gross miscarriage of justice of the rights of the very Salafists who supported him. When Future Movement leader and parliamentary deputy Mustapha Alloush tried to address the protestors, he was forcefully pulled aside and prevented from talking. To the surprise of Alloush and other Future Movement members, Salafi sheikhs and Islamists who professed their political loyalty to Hariri stood by and did nothing to defend Alloush. On the contrary, they raucously echoed the frustration of the demonstrators. Chief among the Salafi sheikhs who took the stand in the public court of Salafism and lambasted the government was none other than Sheikh Daʾi al-Islam, who asserted:

> We are the sons of the Sunni sect, and we feel that we have been oppressed for tens of years. The time has come to lift this oppression and prejudice against our children and to call upon the responsible officials to rise to the level of rightful responsibility and to not discriminate between the sons of the single country. Lebanon can comprise all, but it comprises none if it does not include our sons. We are the supporters of peace, light and [divine] guidance, and let no one think that light is our only path, for we will defend ourselves against anyone who targets us. We have come to support the oppressed in the prisons. This is the first step. But the end shall be pride and dignity. We call for the release of all prisoners because they are oppressed.[47]

Feeling somehow betrayed by his Salafi allies, he focused on shaping a leadership broad enough to include various Islamist and Salafi currents, whose loyalty to him could not be contested. In this respect, he also felt such a leadership would eventually marginalize independent or hostile Salafists to the point that they might revise their political stance or adopt neutrality. Correspondingly, he supported the Independent Islamic Gathering, under the leadership of Khaled al-Daher of the Islamic Association, as a spearhead of this broad leadership. His rationale had been to bring closer to him the moderate Islamist movement as a counterweight to the ideologically diverse Salafists, some of whom were already part of the Gathering. In this way he would rally around him a broad Islamist bloc, led by a close ally, which would neutralize or induce independent or undecided Salafists to eventually support him. Eventually, following lengthy discussions and negotiations with Hariri's Future Movement that came close to falling through, the Islamic Association, which had boycotted the previous elections, agreed to support the Future Movement's candidates in the Rashaya–Western Beka', Sidon, and Tripoli electoral districts in return for including the Islamic Association's candidates Imad al-Hout and Khaled al-Daher in the Future Movement's lists in the Beirut III and Akkar electoral districts, respectively.[48] Eventually al-Daher again became a deputy and has emerged as the most vocal force against Hezbollah and Syria.

At the same time, Hariri improved his relationship with the Lebanese Forces (and the Phalange Party) as a bulwark against Hezbollah and its ally in the March 8 camp, General Aoun's Free Current. But this alliance had been forged around labyrinthine negotiations over electoral lists with the objective of getting the highest number of votes. In consequence, some high-profile political figures of the Cedar Revolution (among them Samir Franjieh, Misbah al-Ahdab, Mustapha Alloush, and Ghatas Khoury) found themselves excluded from the alliance's main list or relegated to less favorable electoral districts. As such, Hariri's list in Tripoli included Najib Mikati, Muhammad Safadi, and Samer Saade.[49]

As it turned out, Hariri's strategy eventually failed because it lacked a political vision and was mainly based on tenuous alliances, the hallmark of the infamous shifting alliances of Lebanon's confessional politics. Mikati and Safadi defected from Hariri's camp, and charismatic Salafi sheikhs, such as Salem al-Rafi'i, Zakariya al-Masri, and Raed Hlayhel, have emerged as the most powerful mobilizing forces in northern Lebanon and have contested Hariri's political leadership. Needless to say Hariri's weakness as a leader has become the butt of jokes and pejorative terms by Salafists.[50] No less egregious to the new Salafi leadership of northern Lebanon and other majority-Sunni areas was the fact that the Hariri government had issued a ministerial statement that bore a striking similarity to the 2005 ministerial statement regarding the resistance. Article six of the statement read:

> Departing from its responsibility to safeguard Lebanon's sovereignty, independence, unity, and territorial integrity, the government affirms the right of Lebanon, its people, its army, and its resistance [Hezbollah] to liberate or retrieve Shebaa Farms, Kfarshouba Hills, and the Lebanese part of the Ghajar village, to defend Lebanon in confronting any aggression, and to uphold its riparian rights by all legitimate and available means. The government affirms its adherence to UNSC Resolution 1701 in all its provisions and also affirms its effort to unify the stance of Lebanese by agreeing on a comprehensive national strategy, determined by national dialogue, to protect and defend Lebanon.[51]

Also a product of compromise, the statement sought to reconcile the government's adherence to Resolution 1701 with its right and that of the resistance to defend Lebanon and liberate its territories. In other words, this government, like previous ones, legitimized Hezbollah's military arm as a national resistance and not a militia to be disbanded as called for by UNSC Resolutions 1559 and 1701. For the Salafists, the ministerial statement was another slap in the face. The tragedy was that Hezbollah's much-trumpeted equation of the resistance—as reflected by the "sacrificial tripod" of people, army, and Resistance—has been at the very heart of the Salafists' opposition to the Shi'a Islamist party.

The other development that shook the Sunni community unfolded with the collapse of the Hariri government that preceded the eruption of the Syrian rebellion, which thrust Lebanon into uncharted waters of charged sectarian Islamism, ripping apart the very social fabric of the country.

Notes

1. The formation of the government was as follows: (1) Najib Mikati, prime minister, Sunni, close to President Émile Lahoud and Syria; (2) Elias Murr, deputy prime minister and defense minister, Greek Orthodox, close to President Lahoud; (3) retired general Hassan Saba', interior minister, close to the Hariri family; (4) Ghassan Salameh, minister of education and culture, Catholic, close to the Hariri family (he declined the nomination); (5) Mahmoud Hamoud, foreign minister, Shi'a, close to President Lahoud and Speaker of Parliament Nabih Berri; (6) Damianos Kattar, minister of finance and economy, Maronite, close to Mikati; (7) Adel Hamieh, minister of public works and displaced, Druze, close to both Druze leaders Walid Jumblat and Adel Arslan; (8) Alain Tabourian, minister of Telecommunications, youth, and sports, Armenian, close to President Lahoud; (9) Judge Khaled Kabbani, minister of justice, Sunni, close to the Hariri family; (10) Bassam Yamine, minister of energy and industry, Maronite, close to Suleiman Franjieh; (11) Charles Rizk, minister of information and tourism, Maronite, close to President Lahoud; (12) Mohammad Khalifeh, minister of public health and social Affairs, Shi'a, close to Berri; (13) Tarek Mitri, minister of environment and administrative development, Orthodox, close to President Lahoud and Mikati; and (14) Trad Hamadeh, minister of labor and agriculture, Shi'a, close to Hezbollah.
2. Hezbollah secretary general Hassan Nasrallah has consistently defied mounting international pressure to disarm his party. Addressing a rally in southern Lebanon during elections, he threatened to "cut off any hand that reaches out to our weapons because it is an Israeli hand." In addition, he warned that the "resistance has more than 12,000 rockets that can target northern Israel at any time." See *As-Safir*, May 26, 2005.

3. The 1990 Taif Accord, the constitutional compromise that ended the civil war, offered an imperfect compromise between democracy and sectarian peace. The agreement gave equal parliamentary representation to Muslims and Christians, divided proportionally between the two religions' various denominations. Under Syrian pressure, the legislature was later enlarged from 108 to 128 seats, with 64 Christian representatives (34 Maronite, 14 Greek Orthodox, 8 Greek Catholic, 5 Armenian Orthodox, 1 Armenian Catholic, 1 evangelical Protestant, and 1 candidate representing various "minorities," including Jews) and 64 Muslim representatives (27 Sunni, 27 Shiite, 8 Druze, and 2 Alawi). Using a system still in place today, voters were assigned to electoral districts originally drawn around Lebanon's six administrative regions, requiring candidates to appeal to a broad cross section of religious communities in order to win office. Candidates generally run as members of a list for their district. In the 1992 and 1996 elections, Damascus gerrymandered certain districts to benefit pro-Syrian candidates. In the 2000 elections, the Taif provisions were entirely ignored, and the country was divided into fourteen electoral districts. Overseen by Ghazi Kanaan, then-chief of Syrian intelligence in Lebanon, this division created districts that favored pro-Syrian candidates, bringing together unconnected areas with vast demographic differences. In particular, such gerrymandering joined areas containing denominations of one sect with large areas containing a single majority denomination of another sect. This practice helped dilute anti-Syrian votes, mainly from Maronites. For example, less than half of the 64 Christian representatives were elected from Christian-majority districts; most came from areas annexed to larger Muslim districts, essentially elected by Muslim votes. See Robert G. Rabil, *Religion, National Identity, and Confessional Politics: The Challenge of Islamism* (New York: Palgrave MacMillan, 2011), 90–93.

4. Naim Qassem, *Hizbullah: Al-Manhaj, al-Tajribat, al-Mustaqbal* (Hizbullah: The Curriculum [Program], the Experience, the Future), 6th ed. (Beirut: Dar al-Hadi, 2009), 238.

5. See "The Maronite Statement" in full in the *Daily Star*, May 12, 2005.

6. See *An-Nahar*, July 27, 28, 2005, and *As-Safir*, July 27, 2005.

7. "Al-Jama'a al-Islamiyah: Al-Intikhabat E'adat Intaj lil-Waqe' al-Qadim" (Islamic Association: The Elections Repeated Production of the Past Reality), *As-Safir*, June 6, 2005.

8. See "The Ministerial Statement of the Government of 'Reform and Revival,'" *As-Safir*, July 26, 2005.

9. For an English translation of the memorandum, see "Full English Text of Aoun-Hezbollah Agreement," *Ya Libnan*, February 9, 2006, http://yalibnan.com/site/archives/2006/02/full_english_te.php.

10. Ibid.

11. Qassem, *Hizbullah: Al-Manhaj, al-Tajribat, al-Mustaqbal*, 242.

12. Ibid., 243.

13. Author's interview with Professor Sadek J. al-Azm, November 9, 2009.

14. Author's interview with Salem bin 'Abd al-Ghani al-Rafi'i, July 19, 2012.

15. Nasrallah's speech was aired on the party's television station Al-Manar on September 22, 2006 and was carried over by Lebanese Broadcasting Corporation International.

16. Zakariya 'Abd al-Razaq al-Masri, *Istratijiyah al-Sahwa al-Islamiyah fi Kayfiyat al-Ta'amul ma'a al-'Ilmaniyah al-Sharqiyah wal-'Ilmaniyah al-Gharbiyah* (The Strategy of the Islamic Awakening Regarding How to Deal with Oriental and Western Secularisms) (Tripoli, Lebanon: Markaz Hamza li-Wala' wal-Bahth al-'Ilmi wal-'Amal al-Islami, 2009), 72. This belief has been shared by a significant number of Sunnis, even before Hezbollah's seizure of West Beirut in 2008. Author's discussions with a number of Sunnis, including Islamists from Tripoli, in 2006 and 2012.

17. "Tashkil Jabhat al-'Amal al-Islami fi Lubnan" (Establishing the Islamic Action Front in Lebanon), *Al-Mustaqbal*, August 3, 2006.

18. Ibid.

19. In 2005, political and intellectual figures critical of Syrian interference in Lebanese politics, including Samir Kassir, George Hawi, and Gebran Tueni, were murdered. Parliamentary deputies and Phalangist leaders Pierre Gemayel and Antoine Ghanem were murdered in 2006 and 2007, respectively.

20. On February 8, 2007, Lebanese authorities detained a truck transporting weapons to Hezbollah, which confirmed that the weapons belonged to it but reiterated its right to fight to liberate "the remainder of occupied territories." See *An-Nahar*, February 9, 2007.

21. The departure from the pattern established in February 2005 by Rafiq al-Hariri's killing is exemplified by the car-bomb assassination of the army's chief of operations, Brig. Gen. François Haj, in East Beirut in December 2007. The same month, Samir Shehadeh—the head of an intelligence unit closely involved in the UN-led investigation—was wounded by a roadside bomb south of Beirut. He was replaced by Wissam Eid, who was killed in January 2008.

22. Nasralallah's speech was published by *Al-Intiqad*, May 8, 2008.

23. See the text of Doha Agreement in *As-Safir*, May 22, 2008.

24. Robert Rabil, "Hizbullah and Lebanon: The Curse of a State," *OpenDemocracy*, May 21, 2008.

25. Pictures of Salafists protesting against Hezbollah flashed across major media outlets, including LBCI, on May 8, 9, and 10, 2008.

26. Hanin Ghadar, "A Rising Threat?" *Now Lebanon*, May 23, 2008.

27. See Robert G. Rabil, "Trust Allah, Not Nasrallah: The Hezbollah Crisis Reshapes Lebanese Politics," *PolicyWatch No. 1134* (Washington, DC: Washington Institute for Near East Policy, August 2, 2006).

28. "Al-Liqa' al-Islami al-Mustaqil Yu'lin min Trablus Tashkil Muqawamah Dud al-'Isabat al-Tabi'a li-Iran" (The Independent Islamic Gathering Declares from Tripoli the Establishment of a Resistance against Gangs Belonging to Iran), *As-Safir*, May 12, 2008.

29. On January 13, 2005, the government arrested thirteen individuals from various backgrounds who admitted to supporting al-Qaeda in Iraq under the leadership of Abu Mus'ab al-Zarqawi; on January 16, the government arrested a group that sponsored in the name of al-Qaeda an attack on an army post in Sidon; in late December 2005, the government arrested a jihadi cell linked to Abu Musa'b al-Zarqawi, which launched Katyusha rockets into Israel; and on March 3, 2006, the government arrested a group planning the murder of Hezbollah's leader, Hassan Nasrallah. Qassim Qassir, "Tanzim al-Qaeda fi Lubnan Bayna al-Awham wal-Haqiqa" (The Organization of al-Qaeda in Lebanon between Illusions and Facts), *Al-Mustqbal*, January 18, 2007.

30. See Shaker al-Absi's interview with Salah al-Ayubi, *Al-Hayat*, January 6, 2007. See also *As-Safir*, November 28, 2006.

31. "Munshaqun min Fatah al-Intifada Yu'linun Fatah al-Islam" (Secessionists from Fatah al-Intifada Declare Fatah al-Islam), *Al-Mustaqbal*, November 28, 2006.

32. Shaker al-Absi's interview with Salah al-Ayubi, *Al-Hayat*, January 6, 2007. See also *An-Nahar*, March 16, 2007.

33. "Al-Asad Yursel Irhabiyyin ila al-Baddawi wa Burj al-Barajinah li-Ightiyal 36 Shakhsiya Lubnaniya" (Al-Asad Sends Terrorists to al-Baddawi and Burj al-Barajinah to Assassinate 36 Lebanese Dignitaries), *Al-Mustaqbal*, November 29, 2006.

34. "Hadiyat 14 Azar: al-Qabd 'ala Shabaka Suriya Nafazat Jarimat 'Ayn 'Alaq" (The Gift of March 14: The Arrest of a Syrian Network That Carried Out the Crime of 'Ayn 'Alaq), *Al-Mustaqbal*, March 14, 2007.

35. Seymour M. Hersh, "The Redirection: Does the New Policy Benefit the Real Enemy?," *New Yorker*, March 5, 2007.

36. Souad Mekhennet and Michael Moss, "New Face of Jihad Vows Attacks," *New York Times*, March 16, 2007.

37. Fida' 'Itani, *Al-Jihadiyun fi Lubnan: Min "Quwat al-Fajr" ila "Fath al-Islam"* (Jihadis in Lebanon: From al-Fajr Forces to Fath al-Islam) (Beirut: Dar al-Saqi, 2008), 289.

38. Ibid., 292–93.

39. Hilal Khashan, "Lebanon's Islamist Stronghold," *Middle East Quarterly* 18, no. 2 (Spring 2011), 87.

40. See transcription of Siniora's interview in *Al-Mustaqbal*, May 9, 2007.

41. Rhym Ghazal and Hani M. Bathish, "Fatah al-Islam Snipers Claim Two Lebanese Soldiers as Fighting Rages On," *Daily Star*, June 26, 2007.

42. Lebanese authorities killed al-Qadour while he was entering the Abi Samra neighborhood, reportedly to meet Rahim.

43. "Mirza Yubdi Mutala'atahu fi al-Qadiya wa Yatlub al-I'dam lil-'Absi wa Akharin" (Mirza Delivers His Reading of the Matter and Demands the Execution of al-Absi and Others), *Al-Mustaqbal*, February 19, 2008.

44. "Qarar Yakshuf 'an Majmu'at Salafiyah Musalaha fi Lubnan Murtabita bi Usbat al-Ansar, Tanzim al-Qaeda wa Fatah al-Islam" (A Decision Reveals the Association of Armed Salafi Groups in Lebanon with Usbat al-Ansar, Al-Qaeda Organization and Fatah al-Islam), *Al-Mustaqbal*, February 19, 2008.

45. Khashan, "Lebanon's Islamist Stronghold."

46. Hana' 'Alian, "Al-Tayarat al-Wahhabiyah fi al-Shamal," Islamic Unity Movement–Command Council, http://attawhed.org/News/NewsDetails.aspx?NewsID =12368 (accessed August 11, 2013).

47. Ghassan Rifi, "Ghadab al-'Ailat wal-Mu'tasamin Yanfajir Bi-Wajh Alloush wal-Sakitin Tiwal al-Futra al-Madiyah" (The Anger of the Families and Demonstrators Explodes in the Face of Alloush and Those Who Kept Silent during the Past Period), *As-Safir*, August 9, 2008.

48. "Jamaa Islamiya Proposes Future Movement Election Swap," *Now Lebanon*, June 1, 2009, www.nowlebanon.com/Print.aspx?ID=91712. For an extensive review of the elections, see "Legislatives 2009," *L'Orient–Le Jour*, June 9, 2009.

49. Najib Mikati, a Sunni, ran on Hariri's list as an independent; Muhammad Safadi, a Sunni, ran on Hariri's list as a member of March 14; and Samer Saade, a Christian, ran on Hariri's list as a member of March 14 who belonged to the Phalange Party. See "Legislatives 2009," *L'Orient–Le Jour*, June 9, 2009.

50. Salafists, including Sheikh Ahmad al-Assir, have called Saad Hariri *wazwaz*, a funny but derogative colloquial term implying that he is a small, light bird.

51. See the political and economic sections of the ministerial statement in *As-Safir*, November 27, 2009. The complete text of the statement is available at the Lebanese government's website, www.pcm.gov.lb/Cultures/ar-LB/Pages/default.aspx.

Chapter Eight

Salafism, the Divided House, and the Syrian Rebellion

Jihad in the Path of Allah

This chapter examines the implications of the Syrian rebellion for Lebanon. It probes the background against which the intervention of the Future Movement, Salafists, and Hezbollah in the Syrian conflict developed. It pays special attention to the strategic battle of Qusayr, in which Hezbollah's overt military intervention helped shift the tide of the civil war in favor of the Syrian regime. But, at the same time, the intervention provoked a widespread condemnation from renowned religious scholars and Salafists, who issued *fatwas* (religious edicts) making jihad in Syria an Islamic legal obligation. The chapter then surveys the ramifications of *takfiri* (excommunicative) *fatwas* for communal coexistence and intrarelational dynamics among Salafists. It exposes the power of mobilization of *haraki* (activist) Salafists but also Salafists' factionalism and fractionalization.

Pan-Arabism, the Syrian Regime, and the Syrian Rebellion

Years after the outbreak of the popular uprising in Syria in March 2011, Damascus has continued its slow and steady descent into sectarian strife. Ominously, atrocities—including massacres, suicide bombings, aerial bombings and shelling of civilian areas, and kidnappings—have become regular occurrences in Syria. The ramifications of sectarian strife in Syria have fueled simmering political and sectarian tensions in Lebanon, potentially causing a new sectarian conflagration with dire consequences for the region. Meanwhile, the international community has remained woefully divided as to how to put a stop to the violence in Syria, while at the same time being gripped by incongruous notions about the scope and breadth of the crisis. At the heart of this gloomy crisis are layers of complexity linking sectarian grievances and concerns to regional and international

213

geostrategic considerations. Damascus has stood at the epicenter of a regional struggle that may well shape the new political contours of the Middle East.

What started as a rebellion against the repressive and oppressive Syrian Alawi-dominated regime, in tune with the popular uprisings in the Arab world, has evolved into a struggle equating the survival of the regime with that of the minority Alawi community (and other minorities). Conversely the rebellion has evolved into a struggle against Iranian and Shi'a assertion of regional predominance, tightly linking Syria to the evolving Arab politics, as influenced by the Arab popular uprisings, and to the ongoing shifts in the Saudi- and Iranian-led regional axes of powers that have resulted from the withdrawal of US troops from Iraq. All of this has rekindled revanchist impulses associated no less with sectarian than Islamist-nationalist considerations and grievances on the local and regional levels.

True, the Alawi-dominated regime of the late Hafiz al-Asad and his son Bashar, the current president, has adopted the strident Ba'thist nationalist discourse; nevertheless, it has pursued domestic and regional policies all in the interest of regime security and, by extension, Alawi hegemony over the state. Syrian troops initially entered Lebanon in 1976 on the side of the Christian camp against the National Movement camp and its PLO foot soldiers. The Syrian regime supported Tehran in the 1980–88 Iran-Iraq War against a brotherly Arab and Ba'thist Baghdad. At the same time, the Alawi regime used pan-Arabism as an ideological tool not only to transcend tribal and sectarian differences in Syria but also to wrap itself in the mantle of Arab nationalism's legitimacy to win over the majority Sunni community. The regime thus has defined itself as the defender of Arab rights, first against an aggressive Israel and then against an imperial United States.[1] As of late, the Syrian regime has supported an Islamist-nationalist discourse that coincided with its support of Hezbollah, both as a resistance movement and as a central aspect of its relationship with Iran. Meanwhile, the regime institutionalized its levers of power on the basis of an Alawi preponderance in the state and an uneasy alliance between the Alawi military and the Sunni merchants of Damascus and Aleppo.

But after so many adjustments by the Asad regime to the realities of power, coupled with chronic corruption and oppressive rule at home, what remains of the ideological mantle of the Syrian regime except its fallacy and bankruptcy?

The regime recognizes that the veneer of its legitimate rule has worn out. This partly explains its unwillingness to substantively reform Syria's political structure, thereby relying more on the Alawi-led state apparatus to maintain its survival. Moreover, the regime understands no other language but violence to communicate with its polity. In fact, violence has marked the very history and development of the Ba'thist regime. No less significant, the rise of rural Alawi officers to power in Syria's urban centers has only reinforced the link between the regime and the Alawi community. Alawi perennial reservations about Sunni power in general and Sunni political Islam in particular, which can be traced to Alawi social sycophancy and servility to the mainly Sunni political establishment prior to Syria's independence, have not dissipated. It was not out of an altruistic naïveté that Bashar al-Asad's grandfather, Suleiman al-Asad, petitioned the Léon Blum government in 1936, when Syria was under the French mandate, to express Alawi aspirations for independence separately from Sunnis in Syria. It was not also out of a sacrosanct belief in pan-Arabism that Alawi officers met Alawi dignitaries, shortly after the abortive Nasserite coup of July 18, 1963, to lay foundational plans for the future establishment of an Alawi state with the city of Homs as its capital and to encourage Alawi young men to enlist in the armed forces.[2] In much the same vein, it was not a political aberration that the regime, at the height of its vulnerability in the aftermath of the US invasion of Iraq, not only maintained the principal role of the Ba'th Party in the state but also began to arm and train what came to be infamously known now in Syria as *al-shabiha* (the thuggish ghosts of the regime), who have been behind most of the atrocities committed against the opposition. Thus it is hardly feasible to draw a distinction between Bashar and the regime or, at the moment, to separate the regime from the Alawi community. It is not unreasonable to assume that the regime has already drawn emergency plans to establish a minoritarian state.

The Syrian Regime and Regional Dynamics

No doubt the US invasion of Iraq in 2003 helped bring Iran (and Hezbollah) and Syria closer together. Feeling threatened by Washington, Tehran and Damascus cooperated to undermine US efforts in Iraq and prevent the creation of a Pax Americana in the region.[3] The 2006 war between Hezbollah and Israel only reinforced this alignment of forces that King Abdullah of Jordan notoriously called the Shi'a crescent, linking Shi'a Iran, via Baghdad and Damascus, with Hezbollah's Shi'a stronghold in West Beirut. The seizure of West Beirut by Hezbollah in 2008 only intensified the polarization of Lebanon's sectarian politics and sectarianism. Tensions between the pro-Western, pro-Saudi camp, led by Saad Hariri's majority Sunni Future Movement, and the pro-Iran, pro-Syria camp led by Hezbollah have not only manifested in sharp sectarian discourses but also in skirmishes in Lebanon's major cities, especially in Beirut and Tripoli. All along Damascus has maintained its political and military support of Hezbollah to the chagrin of Sunnis and other members of Lebanon's confessional groups.

Likewise, Tehran has continued to support its Syrian ally, partly guided by the geostrategic belief that it can ill afford the loss of the Syrian regime as a regional ally and a nodal point for its projection of power and deterrence strategy against Israel. Similarly, Hezbollah, Iran's proxy militia, has also been driven by the conviction that a regime change may put the Islamist party far out on a limb by severing its overland weapons supply from Tehran and denying the party Syria's strategic depth. Hassan Nasrallah, secretary-general of Hezbollah, has consistently supported the regime and accused the United States and Israel of conspiring to topple it. In his Martyr Day's Speech on February 16, 2012, Nasrallah asserted that "we stand by the Syrian regime. Can anyone say that the Syrian regime is not a rejectionist regime and did not support the resistance in Palestine, Lebanon, and Iraq? The regime in Syria has stood in the face of the US-Israeli project in the region. . . . Is it not strange that an alignment of the United States, the West, and moderate Arab states was formed along with al-Qaeda to bring down the Syrian regime?"[4]

Consequently the Iranian Revolutionary Guards and Hezbollah's militants have initially expanded their logistical operations in Syria in order to protect the regime. Alternatively, Saudi Arabia, Qatar, and Turkey have supported the rebels. Ankara played a key role in helping to establish the Syrian National Council and the Free Syrian Army. Mecca and Doha, besides supporting a motley of Islamist and Salafi groups, have allegedly been behind smuggling weapons to Syria. Lebanese authorities have intercepted several trucks and ships laden with weapons destined to Syria.[5]

The Paralysis of the International Community

Meanwhile, Western and regional efforts to put a stop to the violence in Syria and force Bashar from power have been stymied by Russia and China, which have vetoed UN Security Council resolutions calling for punitive actions against the Syrian regime. Moreover, several meetings by the so-called Friends of Syria, which included Western and Arabic countries, failed to come to a unifying position regarding the Syrian crisis. During the course of an Arab League summit in Baghdad in late March 2012, Iraqi prime minister Nouri al-Maliki railed against Arab calls for arming the opposition, asserting that "the Syrian President Bashar Assad's regime will not fall and attempts to overthrow it by force will aggravate the crisis in the region. . . . We reject any arming [of Syrian rebels] and the process to overthrow the regime."[6]

It was against this schism in international and Arab ranks that former UN secretary-general Kofi Annan brokered his six-point plan to stop the violence and initiate a political process to address the aspirations and concerns of the Syrian people. Sadly enough, the plan was flouted by parties to the conflict but more egregiously so by the Syrian regime. In fact, sectarian strife has deepened and spilled over into Lebanon's combustible landscape. Fighting along sectarian lines between pro- and anti-Syrian-regime groups has frequently erupted in Tripoli and Beirut. In May 2012, eleven Lebanese men returning from a Shi'a pilgrimage in Iran were kidnapped in northern Syria. The families of those kidnapped, frustrated by the paralysis of the Lebanese government, began organizing sit-ins, which at times turned into violent confrontation in the streets. Meanwhile, sectarian massacres in Syria have increased with the rise of the power of Salafi jihadists.[7]

Portentously, the trend of violence has become the norm in Syria. The regime has dug in its heels, casting aside concerns about potential international intervention or punitive actions. Motivated no less by sectarian concerns and survival than by Iranian (and by extension Iraqi and Lebanese) and Russian political and military support, the regime, at a maximum, has been fighting to maintain its authority over Syria's urban centers and, at minimum, has been trying to demarcate the borders of an Alawi-led minoritarian state. The opposition, despite its chronic disunity, has kept fighting the regime's forces, trying to secure with regional support havens from which to expand its area of operations. With sectarian violence unabated and spilling over into Lebanon, the tacit communal understanding that civil strife will have collective disastrous consequences has eroded. Serious local and regional sectarian and strategic considerations, partly fueled by sectarian Islamism, have thrust Lebanon into a state of morbid communalism.

The Assassination of Wissam al-Hassan and the Rise of *Haraki* Salafists

The massive car bombing in East Beirut on October 19, 2012, brought Lebanon to the brink of full-blown sectarian warfare. Evoking fresh memories of the assassination of former prime minister Rafiq Hariri in February 2005, the bombing in Achrafieh targeted the Sunni head of the information branch in Lebanon's Internal Security Force (ISF), Brig. Gen. Wissam al-Hassan, heightening simmering Shi'a-Sunni tension. Moreover, the assassination went beyond the established pattern of murdering security officers associated with the UN-led investigation of Hariri's murder. Essentially it bore the complex hallmarks of Hariri's murder in that it was apparently meant to affect internal and regional realignment of forces. More specifically, the terrorist act revealed a web of terrorist and intelligence networks sharing a broad regional strategy not necessarily in line with domestic concerns.

On the surface, the murder of al-Hassan may be looked at as falling in line with the established pattern of assassinating security and military officers. In December 2007, Brig. Gen. François Hajj, the army's chief of operations, was murdered by a car bomb in East Beirut. The same month, Samir Shehadeh, head of an intelligence unit closely involved with the Special Tribunal for Lebanon (STL) investigating the murder of Hariri, was wounded by a roadside bomb south of Beirut. He was replaced by Wissam Eid, who was killed in January 2008. In the meantime, al-Hassan had managed to turn the ISF into a highly professional and sophisticated apparatus in step with the domestic and regional developments sweeping the area. Significantly, he transformed the apparatus, which had been established by Hariri as a pro-Sunni organ, into an independent organization far from the penetration and influence of Hezbollah and its political allies grouped in the March 8 camp. Nevertheless, he tried to maintain a balanced relationship with Hezbollah and its allies by sharing sensitive information dealing with the security of the Islamist party. He was behind the uncovering of a number of Israeli espionage cells in Lebanon targeting Hezbollah. At the same time, he maintained a professional relationship with Prime Minister Najib Miqati, who had led the pro-March 8 cabinet since the collapse of the Hariri government.[8] But despite this cooperation with Hezbollah and Miqati, he remained steadfast in supporting the primary mandate of the STL to hold trials of those accused of killing Rafiq Hariri and more than twenty others in 2005.

This matter became of great concern for Hezbollah in late June 2011 when the STL indicted four suspects, two of whom were members of Hezbollah. One of them was Mustapha Badreddine, the brother-in-law of Imad Mughniyah, who led the jihadi apparatus of Hezbollah before being murdered in Damascus in 2008. Correspondingly, al-Hassan walked a fine line between cooperating with Hezbollah on matters dealing with its security and assisting the STL. This delicate stance contrasted sharply with that of his colleagues who were either murdered or injured for their singular involvement in the STL. Nonetheless, the raging strife in Syria and its sectarian ramifications for Lebanon upended the delicate balance in the relationship between the ISF and Hezbollah that al-Hassan had established. True, Lebanon had, in principle, pursued a policy of "disassociation" regarding the Syrian crisis; nevertheless, this policy, in practice, had been all but turning a blind eye to Lebanon's two major antagonistic political camps supporting either the Syrian regime or the Syrian opposition.

Backed by Saudi Arabia, the March 14 forces, led by Hariri's Future Movement, has vocally supported the Syrian opposition and provided a tacit political and security cover for anti-Syrian groups, especially the Salafists. But this support should not be mistaken for a leadership role. The murder of al-Hassan, which followed the eruption of the Syrian uprising, confirmed the death of Hariri's plan to uphold his leadership in northern Lebanon. To be sure, he has been the political leader who could barely control the Salafists upon whose support his leadership hinged. Northern Lebanon, especially Tripoli and Akkar, has emerged as a hub for anti-Syrian activities. Armed groups (and weapons) flowed into Syria, spearheaded by Salafists. Makeshift hospitals and security zones were established, both inaccessible to the Lebanese army, to accommodate Free Syrian Army rebels.[9] When in May 2012 Lebanon's General Security arrested Islamist Shadi Mawlawi on the grounds he was providing material support to Syrian rebels, deadly clashes and demonstrations erupted in northern Lebanon, forcing the government to release Mawlawi and as a result to reveal its appalling weakness. The organizer behind the demonstrations was the charismatic Salafi sheikh Salem bin Abd al-Ghani al-Rafi'i, who has been rallying a critical mass of angry Sunnis unabashedly asserting their power through sit-ins and occasional spurts of violence.[10]

Thanks no less to his charisma than to his fiery, religiopolitical, anti-Syrian regime, and anti-Hezbollah sermons delivered from the pulpit of his al-Taqwa Mosque in Tripoli's Bab al-Tabbaneh neighborhood, Sheikh al-Rafi'i has established himself as a powerful mobilizing figure in the Sunni community. He has railed against the injustice and oppression committed by Lebanese governments against Salafists. Though he lambasted Hezbollah for its malicious campaign against the Sunnis, his confrontational and critical rhetoric spared very few from the political leadership of the Sunni community. Ironically, his discourse, which focused on the oppressed, bore a strong similarity to that of late Shi'a imams Musa al-Sadr and Ayollah Ruhollah Khomeini.[11] His incendiary rhetoric and populist activism, along with those of other *haraki* Salafi sheikhs such as Zakariya al-Masri and Raed Hlayhel, created a charged political climate that the government has had little ability to mollify. Critically, the Miqati government completely conceded whatever remained of its legitimacy when the prime minister himself ordered the release of Mawlawi and welcomed him with open arms. His release only emboldened Mawlawi to defiantly continue his military activism, supporting the Syrian rebels in both Syria and Lebanon. Eventually, in March 2013, Mawlawi was indicted, along with nine Salafists, by Lebanese authorities on the ground that "he belonged to an armed group and al-Nusra Front with the intention of carrying out terrorist acts and transferring weapons and bombs between Lebanon and Syria."[12]

Before long, the weakness of the government, together with the charged political climate and the Future Movement's tacit support of the Syrian opposition, had rekindled the deep-seated tension between the Sunnis of Bab al-Tabbaneh and the Alawis of Jabal Muhsin. Occasional skirmishes between the two parties have turned into virtually existential battles, acting out the Syrian sectarian conflagration on the dilapidated streets of Tripoli. Most glaring has been the reemergence of an anti-Syrian regime network of Salafi-jihadi groups with connections to al-Qaeda and other jihadi groups in Syria. Chief among the leaders of this network have been Sheikh Nabil Rahim and Sheikh Hussam al-Sabbagh, who had both been indicted by Lebanese authorities for terrorist acts. Despite the warrant for his arrest, Sabbagh has overtly led the fight against the Alawis in Jabal Muhsin and supported the jihadists in Syria, including reportedly fighting alongside the notorious al-Nusra Front, which had been designated as a terrorist organization by United States.[13] Ironically, not only have the Lebanese authorities declined to arrest them, but they also have negotiated with them as part of a selected group of political and religious figures in Tripoli to help secure stability in the city.[14]

Furthermore, reports circulated in Lebanon about a retired colonel, Amid Hamoud, overtly helping the Free Syrian Army with weapons and funds, as well as coordinating with Islamic extremists and Future Movement members to fight in Syria.[15] All of this has not gone unnoticed by Hezbollah, which blamed the Future Movement and its allied apparatus, the ISF, for allowing such actions in contravention of the government's purported policy of "disassociation." Certainly Hezbollah has faulted al-Hassan for being implicitly complicit in the efforts undertaken by the Future Movement and Salafists to support the Syrian uprising. After all, according to Hezbollah, is not the ISF the apparatus charged with keeping Lebanon at an arm's length from the Syrian crisis?

Conversely, Hezbollah has not acted as an idle bystander. Initially the Shi'a Islamist party had vocally and logistically supported the Syrian regime, while at the same time denying any military involvement in Syria's conflict. However, enough circumstantial evidence and reports had pointed to a calibrated military involvement by Hezbollah in the Syrian conflict. As it turned out, Hezbollah fighters had been killed in Syria and their bodies brought home to be buried as martyrs. In early October 2012, a Hezbollah commander, Ali Hussein Nassif, was killed in Syria. Though Secretary-General of Hezbollah Hassan Nasrallah scoffed at media reports claiming that thousands of Hezbollah fighters had trekked to Syria to support the regime, he confirmed that Nassif was killed in a Syrian border area as a martyr. Nasrallah explained that Nassif, along with other Hezbollah members, had died defending Lebanese-majority villages inside Syria, along Lebanon's border. He added that these villages had approximately thirty thousand Lebanese residents, some of whom were members of Hezbollah who had taken up the defense of their homes against continuous assaults by Syrian rebels.[16]

Taking all this into consideration, and on the basis of past patterns of assassinations, one may conclude that the death of al-Hassan was most likely orchestrated by Syrian intelligence and Hezbollah to undermine the growing power and independence of the ISF, sever the intelligence link between a highly intelligent and capable security officer and anti-Syrian activists within the ranks of the Future Movement and Salafists, and undercut the STL investigation.

On close examination, however, the timing, logistics, and target of the assassination raise questions about why Hezbollah would carry out such a terrorist act in a country torn by extreme impulses of sectarianism and communal polarization. Immediately after the assassination, deadly clashes erupted between anti-Syrian-regime Sunnis and pro-regime Shi'ites throughout Lebanon, especially in Beirut and Tripoli. Even the Grand Serail, the official residence of the prime minister, came under attack by Sunni extremists, including Future Movement members. Nasrallah himself has consistently exhorted his followers not to be dragged into civil warfare with Sunnis. Moreover, Hezbollah issued a statement following the assassination strongly condemning this act of terrorism. So why would Hezbollah carry out an assassination that could plunge Lebanon into civil strife at a time when the Islamist party had been facing internal and external pressure? If the past civil war in Lebanon is any guide, neither Hezbollah nor the Future Movement stand to benefit from civil strife. This begs the questions as to whether Lebanon's internal affairs have become irrevocably linked to regional developments and whether the members of Hezbollah have become the special foot soldiers of the Syrian regime.

In fact, since May 2011, the Syrian regime has tried to depict the uprising as the work of terrorists and to expand the crisis beyond Syria's borders into Lebanon. It has consistently instigated sectarian tension in northern Lebanon, not infrequently bombing Lebanese areas along the Syrian border, causing civilian deaths. Significantly, the regime has tried to pit the Lebanese army against the Salafists in Akkar, a Hariri and Salafi stronghold. Deadly clashes have consistently erupted between the Alawis of Jabal Muhsin and Salafists of Bab al-Tabbaneh in Tripoli. And, no less significant as it further heightened the tension between Lebanese army units and Salafists in Akkar, a wave of mutual kidnappings between pro- and anti-Syrian-regime supporters swept Akkar in summer 2012. This tension reached a breaking point in May 2012 when Sheikh Ahmad Abdel-Wahed, a Salafi preacher opposed to the Syrian regime, and his companion Hussein al-Mereb were shot dead at a Lebanese army checkpoint in the village of Kuwaikhat in Akkar. Future Movement parliamentary deputies and Muslim sheikhs condemned the army and the government, and Salafists launched violent antigovernment riots throughout Akkar and Tripoli. Northern Lebanon was pulled back from the precipice of civil war by Prime Minister Miqati. Miqati arrested the officers charged with the shooting, though they were later on released, and virtually appeased the Salafists by further recognizing and legitimizing their power. Salafists redoubled their efforts to support the rebellion in Syria, and as Sheikh Rafi'i declared before many of his supporters outside his mosque, "the rebellion has moved to Lebanon."[17] His was also a rebellion against Hezbollah, the status quo, and the leadership of the country, especially that of the Sunni community.[18]

In August 2012, the ISF arrested former deputy and cabinet minister Michel Samaha for planning terrorist attacks in Lebanon. Preliminary investigations revealed that Samaha was acting at the behest of Syrian intelligence chief Ali Mamlouk to help carry out bombings in Akkar in order to create civil strife between Sunnis and Alawis on one side and Salafists and the Lebanese army on the other.[19] Apparently, as the power of Salafists grew in Lebanon amid heightening sectarian polarization, the assassination of al-Hassan supposedly by the Syrian and Iranian regimes could have actualized their plan to drag Lebanon into an open civil war. The centrality of al-Hassan in the Sunni community made such a scenario possible, given the fact that some powerful Salafists are devoutly anti-Shi'a and anti-Syrian-regime. No less significant, Salafists, especially *harakis*, resent the present political and military balance of power in Lebanon, which they consider favors Hezbollah and its allies, thanks no less to Hezbollah's weapons than to Hariri's weakness as a political leader. As Sheikh Salem al-Rafi'i asserted, "Hariri does not really act to check the power of Hezbollah, and he does not allow us to do so, but we will soon act regardless of Hariri and his party's position."[20] Moreover, Sheikh Rafi'i, along with many Sunnis, has firmly believed that Iranian Revolutionary Guards were behind the planning of the assassination. Tehran had already made it clear to Arab and international parties that it would not forsake the Syrian regime even if the whole world rallied against it. Al-Hassan's family has shared Sheikh Rafi'i's belief. In an angry gesture contrary to traditional protocols, al-Hassan's widow refused to accept the Iranian ambassador's condolences or shake his hand following the funeral procession.

Apparently one could argue that al-Hassan's assassination was the result of a conflation of regional and international developments linking the rivalry between Saudi Arabia and Iran to Arab and Western countries' concern about Tehran's nuclear program and to the Syrian regime's attempt to export its crisis to Lebanon. Strategically the assassination of al-Hassan was seemingly intended to usher a violent realignment of forces into the region, with the objective of granting Tehran and its allies in Syria and Lebanon a say in redrawing the political borders of the rump minoritarian "state" taking shape under the Asad regime. Only in this way can Iran and Hezbollah maintain the lifeline of their strategic and "organic" alliance through Syria. This soon became clear with the battle of Qusayr and its ramifications for Salafists, Syria, Lebanon, and Tehran. Notwithstanding the human tragedy consequent upon the massive bombing, the tragedy in Lebanon, as reconfirmed to me by a retired Lebanese general, was that the main political actors have surrendered their nationalist decisions to their regional patrons. For the Salafists, the Syrian rebellion, and its extension in Lebanon, has become the subject of a jihad in the path of God and for a glorious cause.

The Strategic Battle of Qusayr: Shifting the Tide of the Battle

The relentless expansion of the Syrian civil war, despite a staggering human and material cost, has clearly shown that the solution of the crisis has gone beyond Syrian hands. The international community has been far behind reading the political map of the region and the swift changes reshaping it since the removal of the Iraqi Ba'thist regime. At the heart of these changes, coinciding with regional popular uprisings, have been attempts at shaping a new regional order, in which an assertive, Shi'a Iran has been counteracted by conservative Sunni powers backed by the West. The latest manifestation of this jockeying for power was the strategic battle for Qusayr in Syria in May 2013. In contrast to their recent muted involvement in Syria, Iran and Hezbollah's heavy military intervention there not only shifted the tide of the battle in favor of the regime but also derailed the plan of the Syrian opposition to constrict the Asad regime and cut it off from Lebanese Shi'a border areas and the heartlands of Homs and Damascus. It was no easy feat for Hezbollah to overtly intervene in the Syrian conflict and make itself a target of the Sunni world, especially the Salafists.

Hezbollah's decision to intervene revealed Iran's regional strategy. Hezbollah, at the behest of its patron, had entered the battle for three interrelated reasons: (1) to maintain the viability of the Iranian-led rejectionist axis by securing and expanding the territorial connection of Tehran and West Beirut, particularly the area connecting Qusayr with Lebanon's Baalbek-Hermel region; (2) to deny Israel the capacity to undermine Hezbollah as an Iranian proxy/deterrent force by depriving it of its Syrian strategic depth before defanging it in a future war; and (3) to step up to the challenge, as dictated by regional developments, to transform itself into a political and military regional power shaping the new order in the Middle East.[21] Closely related to these objectives has been the prospect that the deeper Iran and Hezbollah are involved in Syria, the deeper their influence over the Syrian regime will be.

It is no coincidence that Hezbollah secretary-general Hassan Nasrallah declared in May 2013 "that the Syrian opposition and its supporters can neither topple Damascus nor overthrow the regime." And, in contextualizing the crisis within the framework of a clash between a *takfiri* American axis and a resistance axis, he asserted that Hezbollah would not allow the Syrian regime to be defeated. He explained:

In Syria now there are no longer a popular uprising or reform matters. We believe that the control of armed groups [Salafi jihadists] over Syria or over certain Syrian provinces adjacent to Lebanon constitutes a grave danger for Lebanon and for all Lebanese. . . . Those who fight in Syria are an extension of the Islamic State of Iraq that killed scholars and bombed mosques. . . and churches. This organization prided itself on carrying out five thousand suicide missions. . . . The *takfiri* mind excommunicates others for whatever reason. . . . Syria is the back of the resistance and its support, and the resistance cannot stand idly by. . . . We are between two axes: the *takfiri*-Western-American axis, which destroys the present and future and refuses any political solution . . . and the other, which has a clear position on the Palestinian cause and the resistance and seeks dialogue.[22]

Then, in a speech delivered on June 14, Nasrallah asserted that "the party will not change its position . . . we will be where we should, for what we began in taking responsibility for we shall continue doing until the end."[23] Put simply, Hezbollah implied that it would partake in the forthcoming decisive battles over Damascus, Homs, Aleppo, and their countrysides to help the Syrian regime reclaim and impose its authority over a wide geostrategic territory.

This overly ambitious, and dangerous, involvement by Hezbollah has undoubtedly cost the party, the antagonists, and the Syrian and Lebanese people a staggering number of casualties, deepening the deadly spillovers, especially in Lebanon. On the one hand, this attests to the high strategic value Hezbollah and Iran have attached to creating a sphere of influence in the region. Whether by accident or design, the Shi'a Islamists have been asserting their power in the historical Sunni capitals of Umayyad Damascus and Abbasid Baghdad. Only in this way do they believe they can set their imprint on the politics of the region, for they consider the Arab Gulf nations a spineless body sheltering itself in the cloak of US power and hiding behind their *takfiri* Salafi jihadists. On the other hand, Hezbollah has added fuel to the already inflamed sectarian Islamism permeating Lebanon and the region and has indirectly reinforced the power of Salafists at the expense of an already weakened Sunni leadership.

The Islamic Legal Obligation of Jihad in Syria: Jihad in the Path of Allah

Religious scholars and politicians condemned Iran and Hezbollah for their military involvement in Syria. *Fatwas* (religious edicts) by well-known scholars were issued calling on Sunnis to go to Syria and participate in the jihad there, which has become a glorious cause. For Islamists throughout the world, Hezbollah has turned from the party of Satan in Lebanon into the party of Satan in the Sunni world. Renowned sheikh Youssef al-Qaradawi, the head of the International Union of Muslim Ulema, once an admirer of Nasrallah, harshly rebuked him and his party. Remarking on Hezbollah's intervention in Qusayr, he sarcastically declared: "[Years ago], I defended Hassan Nasrallah who called his party the Party of God. It is the party of tyranny and Satan. . . . They call him Nasr Allah [supporter of God]; he is the supporter of tyranny, oppression, and deceit; he came to kill the partisans of the Sunna [in Syria]. . . . Now we know what these Iranian Shi'a want." Then, urging every able Muslim to leave for Syria to help his Syrian brothers, he insisted that "it is required from the partisans of the Sunna to stand against them [Iranians and Hezbollah]."[24] Al-Qardawi's stance was immediately echoed by the grand mufti of Saudi Arabia, Sheikh Abd al-Aziz ibn Abdallah ibn Muhammad al-Sheikh: "We call upon the rulers and scholars to take effective measures to deter this odious sectarian party and those behind it from this aggression. It has been revealed beyond any doubt that this party is a seditious party."[25]

The reaction in Lebanon was no less acerbic. Many Salafists roundly condemned Hezbollah, indelibly marking it as the party of Satan. They also deplored the government for its weakness. Convening a news conference in his office in Tripoli to address the implication of Hezbollah's military intervention in the Syrian crisis, Sheikh Da'i al-Islam al-Shahal declared:

> We have used all that we can from causes to prevent our country from
> . . . war. The knife has reached our neck, and we will not wait until we are
> slaughtered anew. If the state does not immediately carry out its duty to
> deter Hezbollah from intervening in Syria and using its influence in the
> state and the army in its own interest, it should declare its inability to pro-
> tect our sons and itself. The party has killed the legitimacy of the state. . . .
> We declare the necessity to prepare to confront the occupation of Lebanon
> by the Safavid project through the readiness of every Sunni family and
> Sunni youth to defend our targeted creed and our homes and honor.[26]

No doubt al-Shahal's statement intended to evoke raw emotions about the much-trumpeted Hezbollah-Iranian deadly threat besetting the Sunni community, but it also implicitly legitimized the growing militarization of the Salafists at the expense of the state's dwindling authority. Related to this widespread militarization had been the call for arms in defense of Qusayr and Syria by Salafi sheikhs and institutes. In fact, Salafi sheikh Ahmad al-Assir's fatwa preceded Syria's and Hezbollah's final offensive on Qusayr in May. On April 22, Sheikh al-Assir, the controversial imam of Bilal bin Rabah Mosque in Abra, Sidon, delivered a sermon in which he stated: "Nasrallah and his *shabiha* have taken the decision to enter into these areas [Qusayr] in order to massacre the oppressed people there. . . . There is a religious duty on every Muslim who is able to do so . . . to enter into Syria in order to defend its people, its mosques, and religious shrines, especially in Qusayr and Homs." Assir added that joining the fight in Homs is "especially a duty for the Lebanese because Lebanon provides the only gateway" into central Syria.[27] In much the same vein, Sheikh Rafi'i declared that "supporting the rebellion in Syria is a jihad and a legal [Islamic] obligation."[28] Responding to Hezbollah's intervention in Syria, Sheikh Rafi'i addressed his followers at al-Taqwa Mosque: "As Hezbollah is sending fighters to defend minority Shi'a areas as it claims, we will also send men and arms to our Sunni brothers in al-Qusayr."[29]

Similarly, on June 1, 2013, the Institute of Muslim Religious Scholars, a Salafi Sunni organization, issued a fatwa that stated: "It is the duty of the Muslims, especially of the clerics, the youth and the wealthy, to help their brethren [the rebels in Al-Qusayr] through every kind of jihad: with words, money, medical assistance and fighting. . . . Each [of us must help] according to his ability." The fatwa warned Muslims that "if they neglect to help their brethren in Syria, they will incur Allah's wrath and also allow the 'Safavid-Iranian' plan to take over Lebanon."[30]

Making jihad in Syria an Islamic legal obligation radically transformed Sunni-Shi'a relations in the region in general and in Lebanon in particular. Lebanon's political and confessional divisions have become inextricably linked to those in Syria. Significantly, simmering ideological tensions and communal grievances, expressed in sectarian Islamism, have become part of the collective consciousness of both the Sunni and Shi'a communities. This has inadvertently reinforced the consolidation of both Sunni and Shi'a identities exclusively from each other and, in turn, increased the emotional national distance between the two communities in a country already bedeviled by a weak national identity. President Michel Suleiman tried to salvage communal harmony by attempting to bring the major parties to endorse, in practice and principle, the country's policy of disassociation from the Syrian conflict. Reportedly Lebanon's major parties agreed to what came to be known as the Baabda Declaration of Disassociation. But the swift developments consequent upon reciprocal acts of violence, reflected in resumed violence between the Salafists of Bab al-Tabbaneh and the Alawis of Jabal Muhsin, car bombings in Sunni-majority Tripoli and the Shi'a stronghold al-Dahiyeh in West Beirut, and random confrontations throughout Lebanon, doomed the president's effort to failure. Before long, Hezbollah's parliamentary deputy, Muhammad Ra'd, stated that the "Baabda Declaration was stillborn."[31] No less significant, parliamentary deputy Tamam Salam, who was charged by the parliament in April 2013 with creating a new coalition government to assume power from the caretaker government of Miqati, has heretofore failed to bring together the principal protagonists.

Meanwhile the country has fallen hostage to two jihadi camps whose visions have become diametrically opposed to each other. The Hezbollah jihadi camp has considered its intervention in Syria to be essential to maintaining its power and has sought to keep its weapons outside the purview of national dialogue. Seeing an American-Zionist conspiracy against the Syrian regime, it has indiscriminately lumped together supporters of the Syrian opposition as *takfiris*. The other, Salafi camp—led mainly by the *harakis* and jihadists—has blasphemed the Shi'a in general and Hezbollah, Iran, and the Syrian regime in particular, denouncing them as *takfiris*, associating them with Satan, and therefore deeming them to be deserving of death. Ominously the two camps have become inextricably linked to regional axes of power and transnational networks adamant about supporting their own ideological and political stances, further deepening the divide between the two camps in Lebanon.

It is within this context of mutual *takfir* and obligatory transnational jihad that the country's veneer of stability has been shattered. On August 15, 2013, a powerful car bomb ripped through al-Dahiyeh in an apparent attack on the party. The carnage left twenty-two dead and over two hundred injured. This was the second attack in the last forty days on the Hezbollah stronghold. In a tape released by an unknown group calling itself the "Brigade of Aisha," masked men claimed responsibility for the attack, pledging to stage more against the Shi'a militia. One stated: "This is the second time that we decide the time and place of the battle. . . . And you will see more, God willing. . . . Hassan Nasrallah is an agent of Iran and Israel and we promise him more and more [attacks]."[32]

The next day, Nasrallah delivered a speech in which he condemned the bombing but soothed the unnerved general public by affirming that the bombing would not thrust Hezbollah into civil war. Nevertheless, he sent a stern message to the Salafists, which had chilling overtones for the public in general. Referencing Salafi jihadists and those who oppose Hezbollah, he cautioned: "You stupid people, read our experience during the last thirty years with Israel. Our response to any bombing of this kind will [lead to the condition] that if we have a thousand fighters in Syria, then they will become two thousand, and if they are five thousand, they will become ten thousand, and if the day has come for me and Hezbollah to go to Syria, we will go."[33]

Before long, on August 23, two car bombs exploded outside two Sunni mosques in Tripoli as many worshipers were just finishing prayers, killing dozens of people, wounding hundreds, and deepening sectarian apprehensions throughout the country. On closer examination, the bombs clearly targeted

Salafi sheikhs Salem al-Rafi'i and Bilal Baroudi, imams of the al-Taqwa and al-Salam Mosques, respectively, where the bombs had been placed. Sheikh al-Rafi'i had made jihad in Syria an Islamic obligation for Sunnis, and Sheikh Baroudi had been constantly censuring Hezbollah and the Syrian regime.[34] Many parties and groups deplored the heinous attack, including Hezbollah. But accusatory fingers were immediately pointed to Hezbollah. Accusing Hezbollah of the attack and referencing the recent speech of Nasrallah, Deputy Khaled al-Daher declared, "The Tripoli bombing is a translation of Nasrallah's speech."[35] Contrary to al-Daher's incendiary statement, the Islamic National Gathering, which includes among its members Sheikh Rafi'i and Sheikh Baroudi, issued a statement that called the residents of Tripoli to be patient, sober, and strong.[36]

Sunnis in general and Salafists in particular were apprehensive of the attack on their city and of targeting the *haraki* sheikhs, who had to a great extent succeeded in mobilizing many Sunnis through their incendiary religiopolitical and sectarian Islamist discourse. Nevertheless, although it is true that their support of the rebellion in Syria and criticism of the government's neglect of their areas have ingratiated them with many in the Sunni community, their *takfiri* and jihadi statements and rhetoric have made them more or less indistinguishable from the Salafi jihadists. Many Sunnis and quietest Salafists have frowned upon the *haraki* Salafists, explicitly blaming them for exploiting sectarian tension for their own ulterior motives and for deepening factionalism and divisions among Salafists and within the Sunni community.

Factionalism and Fractionalization within Salafism and the Sunni Milieu: The Divided House

In early 2013, a group of, broadly speaking, quietest Salafists established al-Liqa' al-Salafi fi Lubnan (the Salafi Gathering in Lebanon) in Tripoli to deal with the implications of the Syrian rebellion for Lebanon, including (a) the rise of sectarian tension, (b) widespread of anarchy and weapons in Tripoli, Akkar, and other Sunni-majority areas, and (c) misconceptions about and grave divisions among Salafists that tarnished the image of Salafism. The group included the sheikhs Safwan al-Zu'bi, director of the Brotherhood Society, Muhammad Khudr, director of the Islamic Club for Propagation and Dialogue, Bassam al-Musri, and Rami al-'Uwayk.[37] Apparently the concerns that the Salafi Gathering in Lebanon was alarmed about were similar to those that led Sheikh Safwan al-Zu'bi to sponsor the Hezbollah-Salafist agreement in 2008. These concerns had become most pressing as *haraki* Salafists intensified sectarian tension and Sunni divisions in order to claim leadership roles in the Sunni community and to influence its religious and political positions. Of great concern to the Salafi Gathering had been *takfiri fatwas* and extremist statements against both Shi'a and Sunnis issued by Salafi sheikhs Salem al-Rafi'i in Tripoli and Ahmad al-Assir in Sidon.

In addition to making jihad in Syria a legal obligation, Sheikh al-Rafi'i, during the course of his religious lecture on the rulings of jihad in his al-Taqwa Mosque, enjoined his followers to be prepared and ready, "for the great battle is coming soon, and it is about truth against deceit to raise the banner of Islam." He portentously added that "there are more dangerous enemies than Hezbollah and Amal, and they are of our own skin who sit with us and eat from our munificence. They are from the partisans of the Sunna who are conspiring against us and against our country and are preparing themselves to fight us."[38] And he concluded on a macabre note that "if the battle begins, we will not initiate it in Jabal Muhsin, or with Hezbollah and Amal but with those who betray God and His messenger and call themselves sheikhs of the partisans of the Sunna."[39] Sheikh al-Rafi'i was referring to the Islamic Unity Movement and al-Ahbash, whom he considered pro-Syrian and pro-Hezbollah and thus traitors living in the abode of the faithful.

Sheikh al-Rafi'i's dangerous and radical statements did not take place in a political intracommunal vacuum. In fact, tension between some Salafists on one side and the Islamic Unity Movement and al-Ahbash on the other had been rising in Tripoli. Following the assassination of ISF chief al-Hassan in October 2012, an armed group attacked the center of the Islamic Unity Movement in Abi Samra, Tripoli, and murdered Sheikh Abd al-Razaq al-Asmar, who had tried to pacify the angry mob, which was accusing the movement of being an ally of Hezbollah.[40] Reportedly, Sheikh Bilal Sha'ban, leader of the Islamic Unity Movement, has not made his position clear about the Syrian crisis. He is reported to have taken the nonaligned position of standing with the Syrian people, something Salafists consider as implicit support for the Syrian regime. A few months later another member of the Islamic Unity Movement was allegedly killed by Salafists.

In March 2013, Sheikh al-Rafi'i harshly censured former prime minister Saad Hariri, secretary-general of the Future Movement Ahmad Hariri, and mufti of Tripoli and North of Lebanon Malik al-Sha'ar. He publicly attacked them for accusing the Salafists of splitting up the Sunni community. In an interview, Ahmad Hariri accused Sheikh al-Rafi'i and Sheik al-Assir of "virtually being instruments for Hezbollah that have been used to destroy the country."[41] He also disparagingly added that "Salafists don't employ [peaceful precepts of] religion. . . . The high-pitched discourse of these movements serve the other party [Hezbollah], which keeps getting stronger. The latter exploits this picture to justify keeping its weapons."[42] In much the same vein, Mufti al-Sha'ar disapprovingly claimed that the "voice of Salafists in Tripoli is louder than their real size

. . . [, for] their presence does not exceed one per cent of the [population] of the city."[43] And he added that "the Salafi project in northern Lebanon has no roots, and its capabilities are not local, for the money is not domestic but is imported from abroad, and they move beyond their means."[44] Responding to their accusations, Sheikh al-Rafi'i delivered a fiery speech at his mosque in which he accused Ahmad of giving the political cover to the army to strike at Salafists, called on his followers not to recognize the authority of the mufti, and blasted Saad Hariri for escaping to France and leaving the Sunni community.[45]

Meanwhile, Sheikh al-Assir had been raising sectarian apprehensions in Sidon to levels unseen in the history of the embattled state. A self-proclaimed religious authority, he presented himself as the guardian of Sunni interests and blasted not only Hezbollah for being an agent of Iran that sought to establish Ayatollah Khomeini's clerical rule in Lebanon but also the political leadership of the Sunni community for being corrupt and kowtowing to Hezbollah.[46] He organized a sit-in in the city, disrupting the life of many of its residents. He even instigated a broad Sunni-Shi'a confrontation when he called on Hezbollah in November 2012 to remove posters commemorating Ashura, the holiest holiday for Shi'ites in which they revere the martyrdom of Imam Hussein, the grandson of Prophet Muhammad. From the pulpit of his Bilal Bin Rabah Mosque, he threatened, "Our goal is to bring down the party of assassins. . . . The banners of Iran's party . . . will be raised over my dead body."[47]

Sheikh al-Assir's statements and actions grew bolder and more abominable by the day, alienating most of Sidon's political leaders. In addition to issuing a *fatwa* calling on Sunnis to wage jihad in Syria, he randomly deployed his gunmen in the city, who clashed with supporters of Hezbollah. It was under these apprehensive conditions that in early June 2013, Sheikh Maher Hammoud (imam of the Quds [Jerusalem] Mosque in Sidon and a supporter of Hezbollah) and Salafi sheikh Ibrahim al-Braidi (imam of the Islamic Unity Mosque in the Beka' town of Qub Elias, a close friend of Sheikh Hammoud, and an advocate of a peaceful solution in Syria) barely escaped assassination when assailants opened fire on them while they were heading to their mosques.[48] Many in Lebanon implicitly blamed the *haraki*-led campaign to rid the Sunni community of what the *harakis* considered the dangerous traitors among them. On June 23, Sheikh al-Assir's gunmen attacked a Lebanese army checkpoint in Abra, a stronghold of al-Assir and where his mosque is located. The attack, which claimed the lives of two officers and fourteen soldiers, prompted a decisive response from the Lebanese army, which subdued al-Assir's militia and forced him into hiding.[49]

All along, although Mufti of the Republic Muhammad Rashid Qabbani had been trying to reconcile the antagonists within the community and prevent Sunni-Shi'a discords, he came under attack by most of the political leaders of the community. There has been an ongoing attempt to put the official Sunni religious establishment Dar al-Ifta', over which the mufti presides, under the control of the political leadership. Mufti Qabbani has been adamant about keeping secular leaders as distant as possible from Dar al-Ifta' and its Islamic Legal Council, which handles the personal-status laws, affairs, and *awqaf* (religious endowments) of the community.[50]

It was within this dreadful context that the Salafi Gathering in Lebanon had invigorated its efforts to address the grave developments unfolding within the community and to present a better image of Salafism. According to members of the Gathering, they sought to distinguish themselves from other Salafists and uncover the true face of Salafism. They believed that some Salafists had deviated from the true ideology by issuing extremist and *takfiri fatwas*, such as the *fatwas* for jihad without regulations and for supporting the rebellions against Arab regimes.[51] Clearly, although their position stemmed from their concerns about the grave developments besetting the Sunni community, their position was a sheer reflection of the ideology of their quietest school of Salafism. The Gathering launched an intracommunal dialogue and an interfaith dialogue with the other communities in the country. They met with various political and religious leaders and affirmed the importance of stability, revealing that their efforts were supported by senior Salafists in Saudi Arabia who were close to the ruling family. In their meeting with former prime minister Omar Karame, the two parties agreed on "the necessity to anchor security and stability in Tripoli and Lebanon, considering this as a priority, because the arms of anarchy are no less dangerous than the arms of terrorism, for they are used daily and therefore they contribute to the fragmentation of society."[52]

The efforts of the Gathering did not only draw the ire of *haraki* Salafists but also that of those who consider themselves mainstream Salafists, such as Da'i al-Islam al-Shahal. He had moved from the quietest school, established early on by his father, Sheikh Salem, in the direction of the *haraki* school, yet he has not considered himself a *haraki*. Sheikh Da'i al-Islam accused the Gathering of being penetrated by Lebanon's intelligence apparatus, which guided some of their efforts. He has rejected the accusation that Salafi sheikhs have exploited sectarian tension in order to support their leadership and the Syrian rebellion. He asserted that "we carry weapons to defend ourselves only, and we support the rebels inside Syria but reject armed formations for them in Lebanon. Nevertheless, taking away the arms in Tripoli is linked to removing them from the rest of the country."[53]

As it turned out, the efforts undertaken by the Gathering impelled Salafists to address the evident ideological and political divisions within their ranks. Aware of the grave developments bedeviling their community and ranks, Salafists of all stripes, broadly speaking, have been concerned that the multiplicity of their factions has kept them fractious and divided. Consequently and as a result of multiple initiatives, on March 17 more than seventy Salafi sheikhs of different ideological backgrounds met at the Dhi Nurayn (Two Lights) Mosque in Ras al-Nab', Beirut, with the avowed objective to "put the Salafi house in order."[54] This constituted the largest Salafi gathering ever, in which they decided to address internal Salafi affairs and provide a prudent framework for dealing with the army and Lebanese authorities. In this respect the participants, who considered themselves the founding members of this large assembly, decided to establish an administrative committee and a scholarly council. The former was tasked with monitoring the unfolding developments in the country and convening to discuss what actions should be taken in response to them. The latter was tasked with drawing up a strategy and a vision for the Salafists and adopting Islamic legal positions regarding the developments. Commenting on the broad outline of the vision to organize the "Salafi house," Sheikh Ihab al-Banna said that the vision "would be based on patriotic principles in harmony with the doctrines of the Salafi school of thought."[55]

Significantly, both the administrative committee and the scholarly council included Salafists of different ideological backgrounds. The Committee included representatives of the different regions in Lebanon. It comprised Sheikh Raed Hlayhel and Sheikh Salem al-Rafi'i for Tripoli, Mufti Zayd Bakar Zakariya for Akkar, Sheikh Rab' Haddad for Beirut, Sheikh Ahmad 'Amoura for southern Lebanon, and Sheikh Hassan Abd al-Rahman for the Beka'. The scholarly council comprised Sheikh Dr. Sa'd al-Din al-Kibbi, Sheikh Salem al-Rafi'i, Sheikh Zakariya al-Masri, Dr. Adnan Amamah, Dr. Ahmad al-Mazuq, Dr. Hassan al-Shahal, Sheikh Da'i al-Islam al-Shahal, and Sheikh Jihad al-Zughbi.[56]

Motivated by their desire to unite and stand as the guardians of the Sunni community, Salafists look to a *hadith* by Prophet Muhammad that "the hand of God is with the group" as the overriding principle to surmount their factionalism. Yet resentments, grievances, and ideological disagreements among them soon surfaced. No sooner had the Salafi assembly concluded a couple of meetings than Sheikh Da'i al-Islam complained that he was invited to the largest gathering of Salafists without even being consulted about its aims. Before long, recriminations and counterrecriminations resumed among Salafists. *Haraki* Salafists resumed their defiance of the Sunni leadership, criticism of the state, and opposition to quietest Salafists, with their discourse reaching a high sectarian Islamist pitch following the suppression of Sheikh al-Assir's movement and the botched assassination attempts on Sheikh al-Rafi'i and Sheikh Baroudi in Tripoli.[57] An activist Islamist in Tripoli observed that the "ideological and political factionalism among the Salafists are so deep that their attempts at unity amidst the dire developments befalling the country are surely doomed to fail." He gloomily added, "The battle is long." [58]

Notes

1. For details on the regime's policies and political discourse, see Robert G. Rabil, *Embattled Neighbors: Syria, Israel, and Lebanon* (Boulder, CO: Lynne Rienner, 2003), 10–38.
2. Matti Moosa, *Extremist Shiites: The Ghulat Sects* (Syracuse, NY: Syracuse University Press, 1987), 301.
3. For details, see Robert G. Rabil, *Syria, the United States, and the War on Terror in the Middle East* (Wesport, CT: Praeger Security International, 2006), 139–208.
4. See Nasrallah's speech in *Al-Intiqad*, February 17, 2012.
5. For example, on April 27, 2012, the Lebanese army intercepted a Sierra Leonean ship with weapons aboard that originated in Libya and were bound for Syria. See "Khoury Thanks Lebanese Army for Seizing Syria-bound Arms shipments," *Daily Star*, May 5, 2012.
6. Al-Maliki's statement was issued on April 1, 2012. See "Syrian Regime Will Not Fall," *Daily Star*, April 1, 2012.
7. Neil MacFarquhar, "U.N. Security Council Issues Condemnation of Syria Attack," *New York Times*, May 27, 2012.
8. Hariri's government collapsed in January 2011 after it lost its majority in the parliament following the withdrawal of Druze leader Walid Jumblat from Hariri's coalition in the March 14 camp.
9. The author's findings are based on a field-research trip in northern Lebanon in June and July 2012 and on extensive discussions with former and current officials in the Lebanese army and intelligence apparatus.
10. Ahmad al-Ayubi, a former member of the Islamic Association, director of the Hay'at al-Sakinah al-Islamiyah (Islamic Devout Council), and a confidante of Sheikh al-Rafi'i, has been advising Sheikh al-Rafi'i on how to mobilize the Sunnis effectively but without violently disrupting the relative peace in Tripoli. Interview with al-Ayubi, July 19, 2012.
11. Author's lengthy interview with Sheikh al-Rafi'i on July 19, 2012.
12. Abd al-Kafi al-Samad, "Shadi al-Mawlawi Yatahada al-Dawla" (Shadi al-Mawlawi Defies the State), *Al-Akhbar*, March 16, 2013.
13. Misbah Ali, "Who Is Sabbagh: A Look into the Life of the Sheikh and Fighter," *Daily Star*, January 15, 2013, and Nader Fawz, "Tripoli, Lebanon: Salafis Make Their Move," *Al-Akhbar*, May 21, 2012.
14. "Al-Mustaqbal Yuhaded bi Harb Shamila fi al-Shamal" (The Future [Movement] Threatens a Total War in the North), *Al-Akhbar*, June 5, 2013.

15. Radwan Martada, "Exclusive: The Man behind Hariri's Secret Army," *Al-Akhbar*, October 25, 2012.
16. See Hassan Nasrallah's speech in October 2012 on Hezbollah's Al-Ahed News website, www.alahednews.com.lb/essaydetails.php?eid=66629&cid=149 (accessed August 20, 2013).
17. Sheikh Rafi'i's statement was carried on most Lebanese television stations, including LBC, July 10, 2012.
18. Author's interview with Sheikh Rafi'i, July 19, 2012.
19. "Tawqif al-Ramz al-Barez lil-Asad Yuthir al-Zuhul" (Arrest of Asad's Prominent Symbol Provokes Shock), *An-Nahar*, August 10, 2012. See also Hanin Ghaddar, "Lebanon's First Defection from Assad," *Now Lebanon*, August 14, 2012.
20. Author's interview with Sheikh al-Rafi'i, July 19, 2012.
21. Robert G. Rabil, "Syria Part of an Aggressive Iranian Strategy," *The National Interest*, June 18, 2013.
22. See Nasrallah's speech on Hezbollah's Al-Ahed News website, www.alahednews.com.lb/essaydetails.php?eid=76648&cid=149 (accessed August 13, 2013).
23. See Nasrallah's speech on Hezbollah's Al-Ahed News website, www.alahednews.com.lb/essaydetails.php?eid=77944&cid=149 (accessed August 15, 2013).
24. Muhammad al-Makki Ahmad, "Al-Qardawi: Mashayekh al-Sa'udiyah al-Kibar Kanu Andaj Mini Li'anahum 'Arifu Hezbollah 'ala Haqiqatahu" (Al-Qardawi: Senior Saudi Sheikhs Were More Mature than I Because They Knew the Truth of Hezbollah), *Al-Hayat*, June 1, 2013.
25. "Mufti al-Sa'udiyah Yad'u ila Rad' Hezbollah al-Taifi al-Muqit" (The Mufti of Saudi Arabia Calls for Deterring the Odious Sectarian Hezbollah), *Al-Mustaqbal*, June 8, 2013.
26. "Al-Shahal: Lan Nantazer Dhabhana min Jadid" (Al-Shahal: We Shall Not Again Wait Our Slaughter), *Al-Mustaqbal*, June 6, 2013. It is noteworthy that the intimation of the Safavid project not only referenced the Iranian project but also cast a pejorative term onto the Shi'a doctrine. Many Salafists believe that the doctrine of Twelver Shi'a Islam is replete with reprehensible innovations introduced during Safavid rule (1502–1736) and therefore consider the adherents of Shi'a Islam to be *kuffars*. For details on how Salafists perceive the creed of Shi'ism, see the Salafist website Almoslim, www.almoslim.net/node/185609 (accessed July 10, 2013).
27. "Lebanese Sunni Cleric Calls for Jihad to Aid Syrian Rebels against Hezbollah," Al-Arabiyah (television station), April 23, 2013.
28. Radwan Murtada, "Al-Rafi'i Yumahid li-Tard al-Khawarij min Trablus" (Al-Rafi'i Paves the Way for Expelling the Rebels from Tripoli), *Al-Akhbar*, March 20, 2013.
29. Rakan al-Fakih, "Lebanese Salafists Call for Jihad in Syria," *Daily Star*, April 23, 2013.

30. The English translation of the fatwa was cited in its entirety in E. B. Picali and H. Varulkar, "Lebanon Openly Enters Fighting in Syria," *MEMRI*, June 13, 2013.
31. "Hezbollah Yan'i I'lan Baabda Rasmiyan" (Hezbollah Announces the Death of Baabda Declaration Officially), *Al-Mustaqbal*, August 15, 2013.
32. "Unknown Group Claims Responsibility for Beirut Bombing," *The Majalla*, August 16, 2013.
33. See Nasrallah's speech on Hezbollah's Al-Ahed News website, www.alahednews .com.lb/essaydetails.php?eid=81839&cid=149.
34. Ghassan Rifi, "Al-Risala Wasalat . . . wal-Madina 'Asiyah 'ala al-Fitna" (The Message Has Arrived . . . and the City Defies Strife), *As-Safir*, August 24, 2013.
35. Ibid. Deputy al-Daher appeared on many television stations and repeated his accusatory statement.
36. Ibid.
37. Abd al-Kafi al-Samad, "Salafiyun Yarfidun al-Tataruf: Al-Sa'udiyah Tad'amuna" (Salafists Reject Extremism: Saudi Arabia Supports Us), *Al-Akhbar*, March 15, 2013.
38. Radwan Murtada, "Al-Rafi'i Yumahid li-Tard al-Khawarij min Trablus" (Al-Rafi'i Paves the Way for Expelling the Rebels from Tripoli), *Al-Akhbar*, March 20, 2013.
39. Ibid.
40. Ibid.
41. Radwan Murtada, "Al-Rafi'i: al-Hariri Harab wa-Tarakna" (Al-Rafi'i: Hariri Escaped and Left Us), *Al-Akhbar*, March 30, 2013.
42. Ibid.
43. Ibid.
44. Ibid.
45. Ibid.
46. The author monitored Sheikh al-Assir's statements throughout the months of June and July 2012. Al-Assir was interviewed or quoted on an almost daily basis by Lebanese television stations, including LBC and MTV.
47. Amal Khalil, "Salafi Sheikh Livid over Saida Ashura Posters," *Al-Akhbar*, November 12, 2012.
48. "Pro-Hizbullah Imam Escapes Assassination Attempt in Sidon," *Naharnet*, June 3, 2013; available at http://www.naharnet.com/stories/en/85442 (accessed August 7, 2013).
49. See *An-Nahar*, *As-Safir*, and *Al-Mustaqbal*, June 24 and 25, 2013. It is noteworthy that neither Salafi organizations in the Ayn al-Helweh refugee camp nor Hamas and Palestinian Islamic Jihad in southern Lebanon had come to the rescue of Sheikh al-Assir. Notwithstanding their support of the Syrian opposition, the Salafi organizations Usbat al-Ansar and Jund al-Sham and Palestinian Islamist organizations have refrained from taking a side in Lebanon's confessional politics or fighting.

Broadly speaking, they share the concern that they may fall victim (or scapegoat) to Lebanon's confessional politics. In addition, Iran has supported Hamas until very recently and Islamic Jihad in Lebanon, making them careful about disrupting their relationships with Hezbollah. In fact, following the removal of Egyptian president Muhammad Morsi from power in July 2013, Hamas has been making an effort to improve its relationship with Hezbollah, which deteriorated following Hamas's public support of the Syrian opposition. Lebanon's rumor mill has it that Secretary-General Hassan Nasrallah has thus far declined Hamas's requests for an audience with him. Nevertheless, political observers in Lebanon believe that Hezbollah will resume its cooperation and coordination with Hamas.

50. Qassim Qassim, "Azmat Dar al-Fatwa: 'Azl Qabbani Laysa Matruhan" (The Crisis of Dar al-Fatwa: Isolating Qabbani Is Not Considered), *Al-Akhbar*, March 18, 2013.

51. Al-Samad, "Salafiyun Yarfidun al-Tataruf: Al-Sa'udiyah Tad'amuna."

52. Ibid.

53. "Da'i al-Islam al-Shahal li-al-Nahar: Salafiyu Trablus Mukhtarakun wa-Ajhiza Amniyah Tuharik Ba'dahum" (Da'i al-Islam al-Shahal to al-Nahar: The Salafists of Tripoli Are Penetrated by Security Apparatus That Stirs Some of Them), *An-Nahar*, July 23, 2013.

54. Radwan Murtada, "Al-Salafiyun Yalimun Shamlahum: Narfud al-Takfir" (Salafists Rally Together: We Refuse Takfir), *Al-Akhbar*, March 30, 2013.

55. Ibid.

56. Ibid.

57. One day after the deadly bombings in Tripoli, the Council of Muslim Ulema met at the house of Sheikh al-Rafi'i in Dedeh and issued a statement, which was read by the mufti of Akkar, Sheikh Zayd Bakar Zakariya. It emphasized that the Asad regime was behind the strife that reached Tripoli, al-Sham (in reference to [mythical] historical Greater Syria, which included Lebanon). It demanded that (1) the ministry of defense and the command of the army perform their duty in ensuring security, (2) the apparatus of the interior ministry dismantle the security "pockets" allied with the Asad regime, (3) the judicial system and security forces hasten their investigations to find out the identity of the culprits, and (4) the militia of Hezbollah immediately pull out its members from Syria. For the full text of statement, see the news website Mideast Observer, www.mideastobserver .com/v/19404 (accessed August 25, 2013).

58. Author's interview with a former leader of the Islamic Association and a member of the March 14 forces on July 10, 2012.

Conclusion

The emergence and development of Salafism in Lebanon are the product of a combination of domestic factors that intersected sociopolitical and ideological regional changes. This is also the case of the transnational Salafi movement. Marked by a weak national identity and a quasi-democratic system, Lebanon offered a congenial setting for Salafism to grow. Yet Lebanon's plurality and confessional system have posed a constant challenge to Salafists, many of whom have been trying to cope with the realpolitik of confessional politics and regional meddling in the affairs of the state. Since its establishment as a missionary *da'wa* (call/propagation to Islam) movement in the 1940s, Salafism has grown into a heterogeneous movement bonded by creedal tenets. Nevertheless, it is divided over ideologies, especially over the *manhaj* (methodology) of Salafism in relation to politics. This book explores three schools of Salafism—quietest, activist, and Salafi-jihadi—which are, more or less, in line with the transnational networks of Salafism whose roots go back to the theological and ideological development of Salafism in Saudi Arabia. In this respect, Salafism in Lebanon has inherited the incongruities, ambiguities, and tensions that marked the various schools of Salafism. True, Salafism in Lebanon may be considered an extension to transnational Salafism; nevertheless, Salafism in Lebanon has developed within a domestic context heavily influenced by regional ideologies and politics. This book demonstrated that the quietest, activist, and Salafi-jihadi schools of Salafism have developed their *manhaj* largely as a growth of, and response to, domestic and regional ideological, socioeconomic, and political transformations and tribulations.

The fiasco and bankruptcy of Arab nationalism fed the growth of Islamism, which, in turn, transformed into a unique "Lebanonized" form of Islamic activism combining extreme ideological impulses and political pragmatism. It lends moral and/or practical support to the Islamic resistance and jihad against what it considers to be the "enemies of Islam." Yet it professes to be an Islamist movement supporting nonviolent political activism.[1] One would argue that the Islamic Association has become a conventional party. Although it has worked to defend the interest and values of the Sunni community, it has become subservient to the realities of confessional politics that are infamously marked by horse-trading compromises revolving around political and economic spoils. Significantly, the Islamic Association has not insignificantly shaped the Islamist outlook of many activist (*haraki*) Salafists. Another consequential development for Salafism has been related to the rise and fall of the Islamic Unity Movement. I still vividly remember hearing about the movement when I was serving in the Red Cross in Beirut in the heyday of the civil war. Then it came as a shock to me: How could a puritanical movement emerge in the land of secularism, decadence, and pluralism? Later on I knew it was a hybrid Salafi movement. Were the tribulations and chaos of civil war the main causes of its emergence? In hindsight, the ideological, socioeconomic, and political fault lines that provoked the emergence of the Islamic Unity Movement are still at play today. I would further argue that these fault lines are now deeper.

Essentially the ideological climate in Lebanon has been torn by an identity crisis and by a clash of visions. Whereas Hezbollah has promoted the construction of an identity based on the centrality of the resistance as a societal movement, the Future Movement, leading the March 14 camp, has forsaken Arab nationalism as an ideology in the interest of advocating a symbolic Lebanon-first policy, practically in tune with Saudi foreign policy.[2] Notwithstanding the fact that the civil war has taken a heavy toll on the Sunni community, the murder of former prime minister Rafiq Hariri has driven the community into a severe predicament affected by the identity, political authority, and religious crisis facing Sunnism in Lebanon. Representing the political leadership of the community, the Future Movement was unsuccessful in constructing a national identity to supersede its historic emotional attachment to Arab nationalism. Rather, moved by the political ambition to maintain its leadership of the Sunni community as an aspect of its political aspiration to lead Lebanon, the Future Movement has attempted to create a political consciousness based on political mobilization against the Syrian regime and Hezbollah. This has created dynamics in the Sunni community that the Salafists exploited and the Future Movement could not control.

Next, the political authority, besides being weakened by a leadership represented by Saad Hariri (who has appointed himself a leader-in-exile), has broken up into political fragments thanks in large measure to the Future Movement's attempt at enfeebling some of the traditional leaderships of the community. The collapse of the Syrian order in Lebanon, together with the eruption of the Syrian rebellion, has underscored the ideological and political bereavement of a Sunni movement in denial of the deep crisis transforming its community. This has been reflected by the Future Movement's inability to create and sustain a loyal leadership in northern Lebanon and by its inability to confront the political and military shrewdness of Hezbollah. No less significant, the religious authority of the community, as represented by the official religious establishment of Dar al-Ifta', has come under significant stress partly because the political leadership has sought to control Dar al-Ifta' and partly because Salafists have kept their networks of mosques, institutes, and charity organizations outside the purview of the religious establishment.

These are some of the fault lines that offered Salafists political opportunities to expand their political and religious popular bases. In essence, however, Salafism, despite its ideological incongruities and tensions, has offered an identity based on authentic Islam and a comprehensive way of life premised on the glorious Prophetic model, as practiced by Islam's pious ancestors (*al-salaf al-salih*). Theirs was a return to the pristine nature of Islam, purged from the reprehensible alien accretions and theological innovations that debilitated and divided the *ummah* (Muslim community). No wonder Salafism continues to appeal to the Sunni downtrodden and oppressed in Lebanon on account of its authenticity and individual and collective empowerment.

Paradoxically the Future Movement has pursued an ambivalent policy toward the Salafists that left it at the mercy of the very Salafists it wanted to control. In fact, the leadership of the Future Movement has more or less hinged on the support of Salafists and their popular bases. Yet this leadership has naively maintained the belief that Salafists cannot affect the religious and political orientation of the community. Former parliamentary deputy and member of the leadership of the Future Movement Dr. Mustapha Alloush informed me that "Salafists cannot change the politics of the Sunni community, and their religious and sociopolitical influence on the community will remain insignificant given the secular and urban nature of the overall Sunni community."[3] This belief, expressed in slight variations by religious scholars, politicians, and scholars, has become a self-serving platitude, further obscuring the view, and obfuscating the understanding, of Salafists.[4] More disturbing has been the notion among non-Sunni politicians in the March 14 camp that the true danger in Lebanon is Hezbollah and not the Salafists.[5] Even a respected journalist told me in colloquial satirical Lebanese: "Salafists are not smart and can be manipulated; Hezbollah is the problem and the threat."[6] The problem with this line of thinking is that it reinforces the endemic naive and simplistic belief that Salafists can be controlled and could not affect the social fabric of the nation. This is not to say that Hezbollah's resistance policies and actions do not pose a real threat to Lebanon as a state and to communal coexistence. The tragedy in Lebanon is that the country has become stuck between two jihadi movements reinforcing themselves vis-à-vis each other at the expense of the majority.

In fact, Salafists have benefited from this naive belief and its attendant policies. The Future Movement has already weakened all other Sunni political leaderships in the country and has failed to unite Islamist movements such as the Islamic Association, al-Ahbash, and the Islamic Unity Movement, leaving the Salafists as the hinge onto which the Future Movement pegs its leadership. As such, it has implicitly and explicitly continued at its own detriment to deal with Salafists as instruments of political and military influence against its rivals within the Sunni community and within the country at large. At the same time, it has ingenuously expected political subservience from Salafists without offering them a political cover in times of tension, all in the name of communal solidarity and national unity. Conversely, Salafists have grown bolder and more assertive, contesting the leadership not only of the Future Movement but also that of the state on the local and national levels.

Sheikh Salem al-Rafi'i asserted to me that "Hariri's leadership has failed to confront Hezbollah, to provide political cover to us [Salafists] in time of need, or to support viable projects for our depressed areas, and still he expects us to follow them [the Future Movement] like sheep." He averred: "Hariri does not know how to lead' and he does not let us lead."[7] Ahmad al-Ayubi, an advisor to Sheikh al-Rafi'i and former Islamic Association member, angrily stated: "This whole leadership should be uprooted. I will not be surprised if the people rebel against them and rush to their houses and forcefully bring them down to the street in their pajamas."[8]

Meanwhile Salafists have exploited the growing sectarian tension in the country to enhance their standing. They used their informal networks—which spanned the gamut from informal interpersonal relations, to patronage networks, to institutes and mosques—to mobilize Sunnis along sectarian lines. Concomitantly Salafists employed religiopolitical rhetoric and discourse to agitate their collective memory of oppression, marginalization, and suffering at the hands of the Syrians and their allies in Lebanon. *Haraki* Salafists have led this campaign of mobilization that soon found its expression in supporting the rebellion in Syria. Critically, the rebellion in Syria has become inseparable from Lebanon. In principle they consider Lebanon and Syria to be part of Bilad al-Sham (Greater Syria), and they call Tripoli, Trablus of al-Sham (Tripoli of Greater Syria).[9] In practice, the rebellion in Syria has become an uprising not only against the Syrian regime and its Shi'a allies Hezbollah and Iran but also against the political order in Lebanon. Salafi transnational networks led by Saudi Arabia and Qatar have injected this campaign with cash and weapons. Although Saudi Arabia and Qatar have supported the propagation of their respective quietest and activist schools of Salafism in Lebanon, they have been united in supporting *haraki* and some "active" quietest Salafists against the Syrian regime, such as Sheikh Da'i al-Islam al-Shahal.[10] Notably, Saudi Arabia has perceived its proxy fight against the Syrian regime as a matter of national interest. Notwithstanding the Sunni-Shi'a sectarian divide, the Saudis have not only seen an Iranian regional expansion of power but also Iranian proxies encircling their borders. They have been preoccupied with the "Shi'a crescent" extending from Tehran to Beirut and perceive Syria to be the nodal point of this axis that needs to be broken. It is an open secret that Saudi Arabia has been at the forefront of countries supporting the Syrian opposition and pushing for a US military strike against the Syrian regime.[11] Even if the conflict in Syria were to be ended, Saudi Arabia would most likely continue supporting Salafists in Lebanon as a counterweight to Iran's proxy in Lebanon, Hezbollah.

Significantly, Salafist grievances against the Shi'ites and Hezbollah have drastically intensified following Hezbollah's overt military intervention in Syria. They have permeated the Friday sermons in Salafi mosques. *Haraki* Salafists, such as Sheikh al-Rafi'i and Sheikh Zakariya al-Masri, have attracted hundreds and at times thousands to their highly charged religiopolitical sermons. This sectarian Islamist mobilization has frequently turned into military confrontations between Sunnis and Shi'a on one side and Sunnis and Alawis on the other. Broadly speaking, religious and political leaderships from both the Sunni and Shi'a communities have thus far called for restraint. Bearing in mind the collective memory of the civil war, they have tacitly shared the understanding that a sectarian strife in Lebanon would be collectively disastrous. The mufti of the Republic, Muhammad Rashid Qabbani, has consistently called on Lebanese not to be dragged into sectarian strife. He has also consistently deplored violence in both communities.[12] Even Secretary General of Hezbollah Hassan Nasrallah cautioned following the bombing in West Beirut in August 2013 that "bombings and murders will not affect our will and will not drive us to fall in the trap of sectarian strife."[13]

Nevertheless, this restraint has actually become hostage to sectarian polarization as the Syrian conflict continues to spill over into Lebanon. Whereas politicians have sounded the alarm about the growing number of Syrian refugees in Lebanon, Salafists have redoubled their efforts to support the Syrian opposition and to undercut Hezbollah's military intervention on the side of the Syrian regime.[14] Strategically, the victory of Hezbollah and the Syrian army in the battle of al-Qusayr has allowed them to control most of the northern and northeastern Lebanon-Syria border, with the exception of some Sunni-majority border towns in Lebanon such as al-'Arsal. As a result, most overland shipments of arms and movement of jihadists into Syria from Lebanon have been more or less curbed. In response, Salafists, including Salafi jihadists with links to al-Nusra Front and other al-Qaeda affiliate organizations, have increased their presence in Sunni-majority border towns and have been streamlining and stepping up their military efforts.[15] This jihadi mobilization has been, in fact, sanctioned and promoted by *fatwas* (religious edicts) from renowned religious scholars, further deepening sectarian tension in the region. Facing these multiple challenges, the state, though adopting a policy of "disassociation," has been either reluctant or too paralyzed by sectarian considerations to impose its authority.

To be sure, the Lebanese army has been targeted in border areas, especially in 'Arsal, reportedly by Salafi jihadists. Some observers noted that targeting the army in 'Arsal in late May 2013 bore the hallmarks of the Salafi-jihadi attack on the army in the Palestinian refugee camp Nahr al-Bared in 2007, with the objective of driving Lebanese authorities out of these areas.[16] Similarly, the army has refrained from extending its authority over tension areas in the hinterland of Ba'albek where al-Qaeda affiliate groups, namely al-Nusra, have fought with Hezbollah.[17] Nevertheless, Lebanese authorities have arrested al-Qaeda members on charges of transferring bomb-making material, including chemical components, to Syria with the cooperation of radical groups from the Palestinian refugee camp of Ayn al-Helweh.[18] Clearly these activities are not random, and they point to a growing cooperation among Salafists in northern Lebanon, Salafi-jihadi groups in Ayn al-Helweh camp, and al-Qaeda–affiliated groups in Syria, namely al-Nusra Front. More specifically, the continuous arrest and indictment of al-Qaeda affiliate groups in Lebanon demonstrate an interlinkage of Salafi and Salafi-jihadi transnational networks at work in confronting Hezbollah and the Syrian regime. In July 2013, the military charged six alleged members of al-Nusra Front with "forming an armed gang in order to conduct terrorist acts in Lebanon."[19] In the same month, two Palestinians from Ayn al-Helweh were arrested in connection to smuggling arms to 'Arsal.[20] In the meantime, members of Salafi-jihadi organizations in Ayn el-Helweh Jund al-Sham and Usbat al-Ansar have joined al-Nusra Front and the Islamic State of Iraq and al-Sham to fight the regime in Syria.

As this book has shown, Salafists will certainly continue to accumulate military and political power so long as sectarian tension and political conflict plague Lebanon. Significantly, while the often-repeated axiom that Salafists are not monolithic and therefore cannot be lumped into one category is qualifiedly true, it is misleading in the sense that, besides few quietest Salafi sheikhs, most Salafists of all stripes have in some ways mobilized their community against Hezbollah and the Syrian regime. Most importantly, *haraki* Salafi sheikhs have emerged as the drivers and executors of this mobilization, which has fulfilled its logical end in waging jihad in the path of Allah in Syria and, by extension, in Lebanon. Correspondingly, as this book revealed, the developmental trajectory of Salafists across the spectrum, from apoliticists to transnational jihadists, has demonstrated the factionalism of Salafists. Nevertheless, it also points to the singleness of purpose with which they have accumulated power through both their apolitical and activist approach to politics under the pretext of protecting the Sunni community (*ahl al-Sunna*).

No doubt Salafists have already emerged as the foot soldiers of the Sunni community. Moved no less by a strong sense of being the subject of oppression than by a conviction of being the "saved sect" and the guardians of Islam, they have successfully claimed a stake to power, regardless of their *manhaj* in relation to politics. The definition of power in Lebanon has always been relative to political influence and sheer military assertiveness. No community should fathom this self-evident truth more than the Sunni community. Its communal and political history in modern Lebanon underscores this reality. The eviction of the PLO from Beirut in 1982 deprived the Sunnis of a prominent political role during the civil war. In addition, the murder of former prime minister Rafiq Hariri deprived the community of the political courage to lead after the civil war. I cannot fail to make the analogy as to how the Phalangists, like Salafists now, had controlled and led the Christian camp during the civil war, despite the fact that they did not have a Christian parliamentary majority. They asserted themselves as the guardians of the Christian community, much of which followed them willingly or not. This has also been the case with the other major assertive Islamist or secular powers in Lebanon. Thus, the Future Movement should neither be surprised nor shocked when Salafists impose their will on the Sunni community.

The book has also tried to remove the veneer of misconception that intentionally or unintentionally wrapped Salafism as a peaceful missionary *da'wa* movement. It demonstrates that *haraki* Salafists have sought power without recoiling from qualifying the use of violence in theory and practice. Essentially, Sheikh Zakariya al-Masri dichotomized mankind into believers and unbelievers and sanctioned jihad against non-Muslim unbelievers. His vision of temporary alliances with Christians as people of the Book is premised on a deferred jihad to be carried out at the appropriate time. He has anathematized Hezbollah and the Iranian and Syrian regimes, as well as supported jihad in Syria. Sheikh Salem al-Rafi'i, considered as the leader of the *haraki* Salafi school, has not only made jihad an Islamic legal obligation for Muslims in Syria but also anathematized nonaligned and pro-Syrian Sunnis in Lebanon, implicitly calling for their murder. No less significant, *haraki* and even "activist" quietest

Salafists, such as Sheikh Da'i al-Islam al-Shahal, have called for arms against Hezbollah and other enemies of Islam and have implicitly and explicitly supported Salafi jihadists. Correspondingly, this book demonstrates that *haraki* Salafists have advocated violent political activism, be it through sit-ins, demonstrations, armed confrontations, and/or jihad, when the need arises. This is not to say that these *haraki* Salafists constitute the majority of Salafists. The book makes clear that quietest Salafists frown upon the ideology and praxis of *haraki* Salafists and Salafi jihadists, yet they have thus far failed to make the qualified political jump to *infitah* (open up) to other communities, especially to the Shi'a community because many Salafists have opposed Hezbollah. In fact, they have placed themselves in a predicament. They have maintained their apolitical attitude; however, in practice they have half-heartedly engaged the system under the pretext of defending the Sunni community. In fact, neither the quietest nor the activist Salafists have established a political program or a party. This book also indicates that Salafists have turned into Salafi jihadists under the influence of charismatic preachers or emirs (Islamic leaders) to partake in jihad against oppression and injustice.

No less significant, this book shows that Salafism, as a fundamentalist ideology separating the believers from unbelievers, poses an ideological and practical threat to Lebanon's plural society and to the region. Although Salafists share basic principles but have divergent and even contradictory ideologies and tendencies, they share a collective identity based on creed and a mission to purge Islam from foreign accretions and to create an ideal Islamic community. Regardless as to whether they are quietest, activist, or Salafi-jihadi, they have collectively consolidated a Salafi identity, increasing the emotional distance between them and the rest of the population. Their political engagement thus far, though still in its inchoate stage, does not intimate an ideological transformation of Salafism into a conventional party. Rather, Salafists have formulated ideologies and acted on policies that imply an inverse adaptation to the system, whereby the system would be transformed to cope with the theory and practice of Salafism. This is not to say that Salafism would emerge as the preeminent political bloc or the preeminent power in Lebanon capable of a radical transformation of the system. Salafi factionalism and lack of political experience and legacy would militate against their preeminence. But this is far from saying that Salafists, such as Sheikhs al-Rafi'i, al-Masri, al-Shahal, Ahmad al-Assir, and Raed Hlayhel, would not emerge as the de facto leaders of the Sunni community, potentially affecting communal harmony by affecting Sunnism in Lebanon. The power of these Salafi leaders does not lie only in their ability to mobilize their community and face off Hezbollah but also in the identity, political authority, and religious crisis engulfing Sunnism in Lebanon.

True this study has ethnographic and anthropological limitations, yet it has tried to offer a comprehensive ideological and political view, not in isolation from the social and economic factors affecting Salafism as a social and religious movement. Traveling throughout northern Lebanon and Tripoli one cannot fail but notice the rural-urban societal divisions that mark the social landscape. Poor villages dot the northern landscape, and segregated neighborhoods displaying wealth in contrast to extreme poverty mark Tripoli. I vividly remember the trips I used to take as a child with my family to Tripoli. My late father loved the mouthwatering sweets of Tripoli and the city's historical landmarks and prom-enades that blended smoothly with its modernity. Alas, my vivid collection of Tripoli starkly collides with my present view of the city. It is no coincidence that Salafism has grown in the very depressed and marginalized neighborhoods of al-Qibbi, Abi Samra, and especially Bab al-Tabbaneh. Additionally, I could not separate the hinterlands of Tripoli from the city I remember. The constant migration from rural areas to Tripoli has created some kind of a belt of misery where neighborhoods on the margin of the city have grown so much in density and space, with the result of transforming Tripoli into a virtual rural city. This has provided an uninterrupted link between Sunni-majority villages, Akkar, and Tripoli, which made me better understand Sheikh Sa'd al-Din al-Kibbi's effort to expand his ideal Islamic village all the way to Tripoli, where he created a Salafi elementary school.

But if any symbol can bolster my argument that Salafism has now emerged as a prominent ideological and political driver of the Sunni community, it is the huge silver sculpture of the word "Allah" in al-Nour (Light) Square in Trip-oli. Originally the square was named after proindependence political figure Abdul Hamid Karame (1890–1950), whose statue stood in its center until it was blown up during the civil war in 1975. The name was changed to Nour Square by the Islamic Unity Movement in the early 1980s, when they replaced Karame's statue with the sculpture. Underneath it an inscription reads "Tripoli the Fortress of Muslims Welcomes You." Significantly, two black Salafi flags flutter behind the sculpture. This square has become some sort of a vocal outlet of Salafists, where they usually gather after Friday prayers to air their grievances. Neither the city nor political leaders have been able to restore Karame's statue or the square's original name, or even remove the flags, despite repeated requests by many in the city. The square has thus typified the power of Salafists, which emblematically rested on the Islamic Unity Movement's symbolic projection of *tawhid Allah* in the fortress of Muslims. In fact, the square is also known as Allah Square. Salafists, in principle, shun this designation, for it misrepre-sents God the creator. However, Salafists, in practice, have been adamant about maintaining Allah Square as it stands, for it symbolically reflects their creedal tenet of *tawhid* Allah and their political view that Allah's rulings are supreme on earth. More important, their insistence on keeping the sculpture and making it the center of their activities signifies a defiance of political authority and a confirmation that they are the "saved" and "victorious" group—in contrast to the "others," whose future is hell.

Notes

1. For an English translation of the "Political Vision" of the Islamic Association in Lebanon 2010, see Robert G. Rabil, *Religion, National Identity, and Confessional Politics in Lebanon: The Challenge of Islamism* (New York: Palgrave Macmillan, 2011), 153–60.

2. For a detailed analysis of Hezbollah's identity construction, see Joseph Alagha, *Hizbullah's Identity Construction* (Amsterdam: Amsterdam University Press: 2011). See also Rabil, *Religion, National Identity, and Confessional Politics in Lebanon*, 62–70.

3. Author's interview with Dr. Mustapha Alloush on July 18, 2012.

4. Mufti of Tripoli and North Lebanon Malik al-Sha'ar claims that the "voice of Salafists in Tripoli is louder than their real size . . . [for] their presence does not exceed 1 percent of the [population] of the city." And he adds that "the Salafist project in northern Lebanon has no roots, and its capabilities are not local, for the money is not domestic but is imported from abroad, and they move beyond their means." See Radwan Murtada, "Al-Rafi'i: al-Hariri Harab wa-Tarakna" (Al-Rafi'i: Hariri Escaped and Left Us), *Al-Akhbar*, March 30, 2013. Bernard Haykel, broadly speaking, described the *harakis* as Salafists who advocate nonviolent political activism. See Bernard Haykel, "On the Nature of Salafi Thought and Action," in *Global Salafism: Islam's New Religious Movement*, ed. Roel Meijer (London: Hurst, 2009), 48. Zoltan Pall wrote that Salafists in Northern Lebanon "do not constitute a large mass movement but can rather be seen as a learned vanguard that possesses widespread religious authority among a relatively extended base of followers." See Zoltan Pall, *Lebanese Salafis between the Gulf and Europe: Development, Fractionalization and Transnational Networks of Salafism in Lebanon* (Amsterdam: Amsterdam University Press, 2013), 99.

5. Author's discussions with Christian politicians and activists associated with the March 14 camp throughout June and July 2012.

6. Author's interview with a Lebanese Christian journalist on July 8, 2012.

7. Author's interview with Sheikh al-Rafi'i on July 19, 2012.

8. Author's interview with al-Ayubi on July 19, 2012. Similar statements by Ayubi were aired on Lebanese television stations. See, for example, his interview with LBCI's Bassam Abu Zayd, *Nharkoum Said*, December 11, 2012.

9. See the statement of the Council of Muslim Ulema on August 25, 2013, on the news website Mideast Observer, www.mideastobserver.com/v/19404 (accessed August 25, 2013).

10. In principle, Sheikh al-Shahal subscribes to the quietest Salafi school. Although he considers himself a mainstream Salafist, in practice he has moved closer to *haraki* Salafism.

11. Following the August 2013 use of chemical weapons by the Syrian regime in al-Ghouta, where approximately fourteen hundred Syrians died, Saudi Arabia consistently pressured the Obama administration to strike at the Syrian regime. For insights into Saudi views on Syria, see the statement of Saudi foreign minister Prince Saud al-Faisal during the Arab League Summit in Cairo in September 2013, in which he urged the international community to take the necessary steps to deter the Syrian regime from committing violence. See *Al-Arabiya*, September 2, 2013, http://english.alarabiya.net/en/News/middle-east/2013/09/01/Saudi-FM -Syria-doesn-t-want-a-political-solution-.html (accessed September 3, 2013).

12. For example, immediately after the deadly bombing in the stronghold of Hezbollah in West Beirut in August 2013, Sheikh Qabbani condemned the act of terrorism and called Muslims not to be dragged to sectarian strife. He stated that the bombing "has neither connection to religion nor to the values and principles of Islam. . . . It is the act of criminal hands from the outside and inside [the country], whose purpose is one: provoke a sectarian strife between the Shi'ites and the Sunnis to fulfill Israeli objectives." See Sheikh Qabbani's statement in *An-Nahar*, August 16, 2013.

13. See Hassan Nasrallah's speech on Hezbollah's Al-Ahed news website on August 16, 2013, www.alahednews.com.lb/essaydetails.php?eid=81839&cid=149 (accessed September 10, 2013).

14. According to a statement by the UN Security Council on July 10, 2013, it was "gravely concerned at the dramatic influx of refugees fleeing violence in Syria, now totaling over 587,000 Syrian refugees and an additional 65,500 Palestinian refugees in Lebanon." See UN Security Council SC/11056, July 10, 2013, www .un.org/News/Press/docs/2013/sc11056.doc.htm. Some politicians in Lebanon estimate the number of Syrian refugees at about 900,000. Author's discussion with a head of a political party on September 12, 2013.

15. Ghassan Rifi of the daily *As-Safir* reported that the jihadi mobilization of Sunnis in Tripoli and northern Lebanon to fight in Syria has now included female activists. He detailed that an all-female jihadi brigade, called the Brigade of al-Naser Salah al-Din, was established in northern Lebanon in cooperation with Lebanese groups who have been fighting with the al-Nusra Front in Syria. Ghassan Rifi, "Tashkil Liwa' Salah al-Din al-Nisai' fi al-Shamal" (The Formation of the Female Salah al-Din Brigade in the North), *As-Safir*, September 14, 2013.

16. Hiyam al-Qusayfi, "Ikhraj al-Jaysh min 'Arsal Ba'd Trablus" (Driving the Army out of 'Arsal after Tripoli), *Al-Akhbar*, May 29, 2013.

17. Haytham al-Mussawi, "Ruqa't al-Tawatur Tatase': Trablus Tashta'el wal-Nasra fi Jurud Ba'albek" (Tension Area Widens: Tripoli Is on Fire and al-Nasra in Hinterland of Ba'albek), *Al-Akhbar*, May 3, 2013.

18. See excerpts of the indictment of al-Qaeda members by military judge 'Imad al-Zayn in Muhammad Nazal, "Mutafajirat wa Mawad 'Kima'iyah' min Ayn al-Helweh ila Suriya" (Detonations and Chemical Components from Ayn al-Helweh to Syria), *Al-Akhbar*, March 21, 2013.

19. "Six Men Charged for Plotting Terror Acts in Lebanon," *Daily Star*, July 19, 2013.

20. Ibid.

Glossary

ahl al-Sunna wal-jama'a	Followers (partisans) of the tradition of the Prophet and of the community/group (congregation of believers).
ahwa'	Heretical tendencies.
al-Ahbash	Organization of Islamic philanthropic projects.
al-amr bil-ma'ruf wal-nahi 'an al-munkar	Commanding good and forbidding wrong (also called *hisbah*).
al-Dahiya	Beirut's southern suburbs and the stronghold of Hezbollah.
al-Da'wa Party	A Shi'a Islamist party initially founded in Iraq.
al-firqa al-najiyah	The saved sect. Also called *al-ta'ifa al-mansura*: the victorious sect.
al-Jama'a al-Islamiyah	The Islamic Association.
al-salaf al-salih	Pious ancestors. The first three generations of Muslims who included the companions (*Sahaba*) of the Prophet (570–632), their followers, and the followers of the followers, the last of whom died around 810.
al-wala' wal-bara'	Loyalty to God and Muslims and disavowal of non-Muslims.
Amal	Shi'ite party and militia founded by Imam Musa al-Sadr and now led by Nabih Berri.
amr ma'ruf	Common knowledge.
'aqida	Religious creed.
arkan al-iman	Pillars of faith/belief.

'asa	Defy; rebel; oppose; revolt.
ayatollah	Literally means "sign of God." An honorific title for a leading Shi'a Muslim scholar.
bay'a	An oath of allegiance to a ruler/leader.
bid'a	Illegitimate or reprehensible innovation.
CIA	US Central Intelligence Agency.
dar al-harb	Abode of war.
dar al-Islam	Abode of Islam.
da'wa	Islamic propagation; call to Islam.
dawlah	State.
DFLP	Democratic Front for the Liberation of Palestine.
dhawabit shari'iyah	Islamic legal safeguards.
dhimmi	Christians and Jews protected under Islamic rule.
din	Religion.
DOD	US Department of Defense.
du'at	Preachers; those who propagate Islam. *Du'at* is plural of *da'iya*.
EU	European Union.
faqih	Jurisprudent or jurisconsult, who is an authority on *fiqh*.
fasiq	Godless; wanton; dissolute.
fatwa	Religious edict.
fiqh	Religious jurisprudence.
fitna	Strife.
fusd	Wicked; corrupt; depravity.
fusq	Sinfulness; moral depravity; viciousness.
GCC	Gulf Cooperation Council.
hadith	Traditional accounts of the sayings and doings of Prophet Muhammad. They are made up of two parts: the names of the transmitters (*isnad*) and the text (*matn*). The *hadith* make up the Sunna.
hajj	Pilgrimage.
hakimiyah	Sovereignty. *Hakimiyat Allah*: Sovereignty of God (and exclusive to God).
halal	Permissible; allowed; lawful.
Harakat al-Tawhid al-Islami	The Islamic Unity Movement.
haraki	Activist.
haram	Prohibited; forbidden; unlawful.
harfi	Literal.

hawa	Desire; craving; caprice.
Hezbollah	The Party of God.
hijra	Emigration.
hizbiyah	Party politics; "partyism" that leads to allegiance to others than God.
hisbah	Accountability for the application of the religious and moral instructions of Islam, which covers financial and administrative matters. See also *al-amr bil-ma'ruf wal-nahi 'an al-munkar*.
hukm	Islamic legal ruling.
huseiniyah	Shi'ite religious centers named after Imam Hussein, which also serve as mourning houses and social centers.
'ibada	Worship.
IDF	Israel Defense Forces.
ijma'	Consensus of scholars of one or more schools of jurisprudence. Salafists refer to *ijma'* as the consensus of pious ancestors.
ijtihad	The application of an intellectual effort to make a religious decision on the basis of independent reasoning.
Imam Hussein	Grandson of Prophet Muhammad martyred at the battle of Karbala, Iraq, in 680 CE.
iman	Faith.
imtiyazat	Prerogatives.
infitah	Opening up.
istishhad	Martyrdom.
itba'	According to; to follow/apply literally the Qur'an and the Sunna.
Jabhat al-Amal al-Islami	The Islamic Action Front.
jahili	Derives from *jahiliyah* and connotes idolatry.
jahiliyah	The age of ignorance before God's message to Prophet Muhammad.
jihad	Literally "struggle." Broadly speaking, it is the struggle of Muslims to reform the self and/or one's community. It also refers to a war waged in defense of Islam, a war that could be offensive and/or defensive.
jizya	Head tax that *dhimmi* were required to pay to an Islamic state for protection.

juhud	Unbelief; disavowal.
jumud	Stagnation.
kayan	Nature; character.
khawarij	Term meaning "those who rebelled," which Salaf-ists use to damn/curse their opponents. Based on "Kharijites," the name of a sect that emerged during the dissension after the assassination of thirdly guided caliph Uthman in 656. Kharijites seceded from the majority of Muslims and advocated the excommunication of other Muslims for acts of minor unbelief.
khuruj	Literally "to get out"; rebellion against a ruler.
kufr	Unbelief. Divided into a major (*akbar*) and minor (*asghar*) unbelief. A major unbelief is based on a conscious decision to do wrong, whereupon the person becomes an apostate. A minor unbelief is caused by minor sins that do not lead to excommunication.
LF	Lebanese Forces, mainly Christians, whose leadership came from the Phalange Party.
LNM	Lebanese National Movement. Organized and led by Kamal Jumblat, the LNM included leftist and pan-Arabist parties and groups.
LNP	Liberal National Party.
madhab	School of jurisprudence; Islamic canonical/legal school.
manhaj	Methodology; method; way of life; practical implementation of Salafist beliefs and *da'wa* in relation to politics.
Marja' al-Taqlid	The supreme Islamic legal authority to be emulated.
masjid	Mosque.
maslaha	Interest.
MNF	Multinational Peacekeeping Force.
MOA	Memorandum of agreement.
mudahana	Concession.
muhadana	Truce.
mujahideen	Those who carry out jihad.
mukhabarat	Secret service.
murtad	Apostate; major sin or denying sources of Islam.

musaliyat	Prayer and discussion places.
mustad'afin	Oppressed.
mustakbirin	Oppressors.
nafsi	Spiritual; mental.
naha	Ban; prohibit.
nakd	Torment.
nakr	Denial; disavow; renounce.
nasiha	Advice.
NATO	North Atlantic Treaty Organization.
nidal	Struggle.
PFLP	Popular Front for the Liberation of Palestine.
PFLP-GC	Popular Front for the Liberation of Palestine–General Command.
PLO	Palestine Liberation Organization.
PSP	Progressive Socialist Party, mainly a Druze party founded by Kamal Jumblat and now led by his son Walid Jumblat.
qadar	Divine destiny.
qawanin wad'iyah	Positive laws; man-made laws.
qital	Fighting.
qiyas	Analogical reasoning.
raq	Bondage; slavery.
rawafid	Rejectionists; deserters. A derogatory term ascribed by many Salafists to Shi'ites.
ra'y	Personal opinion. Although they support *ijtihad* as a derivative reasoning/ruling from the Qur'an and *hadith*, Salafists reject the use of *ra'y* by religious scholars.
Salaf	Prophet Muhammad's virtuous/pious companions.
Salafism	A school of Islam whose adherents advocate the emulation of the first three generations of Muslims (*al-Salaf al-Salih*), the pious ancestors.
Salafists	Adherents of Salafism.
salat	Prayer.
SALSRA	Syria Accountability and Lebanese Sovereignty Restoration Act.
SAM	Surface-to-air missile.
SANA	Syrian Arabic News Agency.
sawm	Fasting.
shabha	Obscurity; vagueness; doubt; uncertainty.

shahada	Testimony of faith.
shahid	Martyr.
shari'a	Islamic law.
sheikh	Honorific title for a religious scholar or a respected man.
shirk	Idolatry; polytheism.
shura	Consultation.
SLA	South Lebanon Army. Created in 1978 and dismantled in 2000, the SLA was supported, equipped, and funded by Israel.
SSNP	Syrian Social Nationalist Movement. A Pan-Syrian party founded by Antun Saade.
sumud	Steadfastness.
sunna	The customs and practices of Prophet Muhammad.
taghut	Idol. Also applied to tyrannical rulers.
taghyir	Transform; change.
Taifa	Sect; religious community.
tajdid	Renewal.
takfir	Leveling the charge of unbelief on a person; excommunicate.
ta'lih	Deification; apotheosis.
ta'lim	Apprenticeship; instruction; training.
taqiyyah	Dissimulation.
taqlid	Emulation.
taqwa	Devoutness.
tarbawi	Pedagogical; learning; knowledge.
tarbiyah	Education; teaching; instruction; upbringing.
tasfiyah	Purification of everything that is alien and corruptive to Islam.
tashri'	Legislation.
ta'til	Obstruction; interruption; theological concept denying God all attributes.
tawhid	The oneness/unity of God.
thawabit	Immutable fundamentals/principles.
ulema	Muslim religious scholars.
ummah	The worldwide Muslim community of believers.
UNIFIL	United Nations Interim Force in Lebanon. UNIFIL is deployed in southern Lebanon.
wahi	Revelation (theology); inspiration.

wajib	Religious duty.
wasatiyah	Centrism.
za'im	Feudal leader; leader.
zakat	Almsgiving.

Selected Bibliography

Al-Bouti, Muhammad Said Ramadan. *Al-Salafiyah Marhalah Zamaniyah Mubarakah La Madhab Islami* (Al-Salafiyah Is a Blessed Period Not an Islamic Canonical Law School). Beirut: Dar al-Fikr al-Mu'asir, 2004.

Al-Fahad, Abdulaziz H. "From Exclusivism to Accommodation: Doctrinal and Legal Evolution of Wahhabism," *New York University Law Review* 79 (2004).

Algar, Hamid. *Wahhabism: A Critical Essay.* Oneonta, NY: Islamic Publications International, 2002.

Al-Hilali, Abou Usama Salim bin 'Eid. *Ta'rif 'Am bi-Manhaj al-Salaf al-Kiram* (A General Introduction of the Methodology [Way] of Honorable Salaf). Amman: Al-Dar al-Athariyah, 2004.

Al-Jisr, Basim. *Mithaq 1943, Limadha Kan? Wa Hal Saqat?* (National Pact 1943, Why It Was Founded? Did It Collapse?). Beirut: Dar al-Nahar lil-Nashr, 1978.

Al-Khaliq, Abd al-Rahman Abd. *Al-Usul al-'ilmiyah lil-Da'wa al-Salafiyah* (The Scientific Fundamentals of the Salafi Propagation). Kuwait: Sharikat Bayt al-Muqadas lil-Nashr wal-Tawzi', 2006.

Al-Kibbi, Sa'd al-Din ibn Muhammad. *Dhawabit al-Takfir for Ahl-Sunna wal-Jama'a* (The Regulations [General Rules] of Excommunication for the Partisans of the Sunna and the Group). Beirut: Al-Maktab al-Islami, 1997.

———. *Fiqh al-Taghyir bayna Ahl al-Sunna wa Ahl al-Ahwa'* (The Jurisprudence of Change between the Partisans of the Sunna and the Dissenters/Heretics). Tripoli, Lebanon: Markaz al-Bahth al'Ilmi al-Islami, 2010.

———. *Ta'rif al-Bari'ah bi-Manhaj al-Madrasa al-Salafiyah: (Ahl al-Hadith wal-Sunna)* (Introduction of Devoutness [Godliness] through the Methodology of the Salafist School: [Partisans of Hadiths and Sunna]). Tripoli, Lebanon: Center of Islamic Science Research, 2009.

————. *Ulama' al-Islam bayn Ahl al-Sunna wa Jama'at al-Takfir* (Muslim Religious Scholars [Ulema] between the Partisans of the Sunna and the Groups of Takfir). Tripoli, Lebanon: Markaz al-Bahth al'Ilmi al-Islami, 2010.

Al-Maqdisi, Abu Muhammad. "Al-Bara' min Kul Shar' Ghayr Shar' Llah min Aham Ma'ani 'La Ilah ila Llah'" (Disavowal of Every Revelation [Law] other than the Revelation [Law] of God Is the Most Important Meaning of "There Is No God but God"). In *Kashf al-Niqab 'An Shari'at al-Ghab* (Removing the Veil from the Law of the Jungle). Available at www.tawhed.ws/pr?i=5367.

————. "Al-Fasl al-Awal; fi Bayan Millat Ibrahim" (First Section; In the Statement of the Religion of Ibrahim). In *Millat Ibrahim wa-Da'wat al-Anbiya'wal-Mursalin* (The Religion of Ibrahim and the Propagation of the Prophets and Messengers). Available at www.tawhed.ws/pr?i=1394.

————. "Al-Jihad wal-Khuruj" (Jihad and Egression/Severance). In *Hathihi 'Aqidatuna* (This Is Our Creed). Available at www.tawhed.ws/pr?i=4784.

Al-Masri, Zakariya 'Abd al-Razaq. *Al-Islam wa Huriyat al-Insan* (Islam and the Freedom of the Human Being). Beirut: Mu'assassat al-Risala, 2001.

————. *Al-Qiwa al-Dawliyah fi Muwajahat al-Sahwa al-Islamiyah: Dawabit Shar'iya fi al-'Amaliyat al-Jihadiyah* (International Powers Confronting the Islamic Awakening: General Rules (Regulations) for Jihadi Operations). Tripoli, Lebanon: Maktabat al-Iman, 2004.

————. *Al-Usul wal-Thawabit wa Atharaha fi Wihdat al-Umma al-Islamiyah* (The Fundamentals and Immutables and Their Influence on the Unity of the Islamic Umma). Tripoli, Lebanon: Markaz Hamza li-Wala' wal-Bahth al-'Ilmi wal-'Amal al-Islami, 2006.

————. *Istratijiyah al-Sahwa al-Islamiyah fi Kayfiyat al-Ta'amul ma'a al-'Ilmaniyah al-Sharqiyah wal-'Ilmaniyah al-Gharbiyah* (The Strategy of the Islamic Awakening Regarding How to Deal with Oriental and Western Secularisms). Tripoli, Lebanon: Markaz Hamza li-Wala' wal-Bahth al-'Ilmi wal-'Amal al-Islami, 2009.

————. *Usul al-'Aqida al-Islamiya: Durus wa Tamarin* (The Fundamentals of Islamic Creed: Studies and Exercises). Beirut: Mu'assassat al-Risala, 2003.

Al-Qassem, Abd al-Malak. "Al-wala' wal-bara'." Available at www.said.net/arabic/ar45.htm.

Al-Sawda, Yusuf. *Fi Sabil Lubnan* (For Lebanon). Alexandria: Madrasat al-Farir al-Sina'iyah, 1919.

Al-Sayydi, Radwan. *Al-Jama'a wal-Mujtama' wal-Dawla: Sultat al-Ideologiyah fi al-Majal al-Siyasi al-Islami* (The Association [Congregation of Believers], the Society and the State: The Ideological Authority in the Islamic Arabic Political Field). Beirut: Dar al-Kitab al-'Arabi, 1997.

————. *Siyasiyat al-Islam al-Mu'aser: Muraja'at wa-Mutaba'at* (Politics of Contemporary Islam: Revisions and Follow Ups). Beirut: Dar al-Kitab al-Arabi, 1997.

Al-'Utaybi, Juhayman ibn Sayf. "Bab; fi Fadl al-Hub fi Llah wal-Bughd fi Llah." In *Awthaq 'Ura al-Iman; al-Hub fi Llah wal-Bughd fi Llah* ("Door; in the Graciousness of Love for the Sake of God and Hatred [Enmity] for the Sake of God," Faith the Firmest of Ties; Love for the Sake of God and Hatred for the Sake of God). Available at www.tawhed.ws/pr?i=2351.

———. "Fasl; fi Bayan Millat Ibrahim" (Section; in the Statement of the Religious Community of Ibrahim). In *Raf' al-Iltibas 'an Millat man Ja'alahu Allah Imaman lil-Nas* (Removing the Ambiguity from the Religious Community that God Made an Imam for the People). Available at www.tawhed.ws/pr?i=1349.

Al-'Utaybi, Juhayman. "Risalat al-Imara wal-Bay'a wal-Ta'a wa-Hukm Talbis al-Hukam 'ala Talabat al-'Ilm wal-'Amma," (The Message of Governance, Pledge of Allegiance and Obedience, and the Reign of Rulers' Deception of Students of Knowledge and Commoners). In *Manbar al-Tawhid wal-Jihad* (The Pulpit of Tawhid and Jihad). Available at www.tawhed.ws/r1?i=6513&x=fcchouzr.

Amarah, Muhammad. *Al-Salaf wa al-Salafiyah*. Cairo: Dar al-Hilal, 2010.

Amin, Kamaruddin. "Nasiruddin al-Albani on Muslim's Sahih: A Critical Study of His Method." *Islamic Law and Society* 11, no. 2 (2004).

Amnesty International. *Lebanon: Arbitrary Arrests, "Disappearances" and Extrajudicial Killings by Syrian Troops and Syrian-backed Forces in Tripoli*. AI Index: MDE 24/02/87, February 1987.

———. *Lebanon: Torture and Unfair Trial of the Dhinniyyah Detainees*. AI Index: MDE 18/005/2003.

Anjun, Ovamir. *Politics, Law and Community in Islamic Thought: Taymiyyan Moment*. Cambridge: Cambridge University Press, 2012.

Azzam, Abdallah. *Jihad Sha'b Muslim* (The Jihad of a Muslim People). Beirut: Dar Ibn Hamza, 1992.

Banasi, Shawqi. *Al-Tasfiyah wal-Tarbiyah 'Inda al-Sheikh al-'Alamah Muhammad Nasir al-Din al-Albani* (Purification and Education of Distinguished Sheikh Muhammad Nasir al-Din al-Albani). Beirut: Dar Ibn Hazm li-Tiba'a wal-Nashr wal-Tawzi', 2007.

Barress, Maurice. *La Colline Inspirée*. Paris: Plon-Nourrit, 1922.

———. *Le Culte du Moi*. Paris: Plon-Norrit, 1922.

Batatu, Hanna. *Syria's Peasantry, the Descendants of its Lesser Rural Notables, and Their Politics*. Princeton, NJ: Princeton University Press, 1999.

Bayyumi, Zakariya Sulayman. *Al-Ikwan al-Muslimun wa al-Jama'at al-Islamiyah fi al-Hayat al-Siyasiyah al-Misriyah, 1928–1948* (The Muslim Brothers and the Islamic Association in the Egyptian Political Life, 1928–1948). Cairo: Maktabat Wahbah, 1979.

Baz, Sheikh Abd al-Aziz bin Abdallah bin. *Al-'Aqida al-Sahiha wa Nawaqed al-Islam* [The Correct Creed and Islamic Contestations (Violations)]. Beirut: Mu'assassat al-Risala, 1413 H.

Bonney, Richard. *Jihad: From Qur'an to bin Laden*. New York: Palgrave Macmillan, 2004.

Bori, Caterina. "A New Source for the Biography of Ibn Taymiyya." *Bulletin of the School of Oriental and African Studies* 67, no. 3 (2004).

Brown, L. Carl. *Religion and State: The Muslim Approach to Politics*. New York: Columbia University Press, 2000.

Commins, David. *The Wahhabi Mission and Saudi Arabia*. London: I. B. Tauris, 2006.

Cook, Michael. *Commanding Right and Forbidding Wrong in Islamic Thought*. Cambridge: Cambridge University Press, 2000.

Corm, Charles. *La Montagne Inspirée: Chasons de Geste*. 2nd ed. Beirut: Éditions de la Revue Phenicienne, 1964.

Court of Justice. Assassination of Sheikh Nizar Al-Halabi, decision no. 1/1997, January 17, 1997. Available at Special Tribunal for Lebanon's website: www.stl-tsl.org/en/docu ments/relevant-law-and-case-law/relevant-case-law/terrorism-cases/court-of-justice -assassination-of-sheikh-nizar-al-halabi-decision-no-1-1997-17-january-1997.

Dekmejian, R. Hrair. "The Rise of Political Islamism in Saudi Arabia." *Middle East Journal* 48, no. 4 (Autumn 1994).

Dick, Marlin. "Hizballah's Domestic Growing Pains." *Middle East Report Online*, September 13, 2010. Available at www.merip.org/mero/mero091310.html.

Enayat, Hamid. *Modern Islamic Political Thought: The Response of the Shi'i and Sunni Muslims to the Twentieth Century*. London: I. B. Tauris, 2005.

Fadlallah, Hassan. *Harb al-Iradat: Sira' al-Muqawamah wa al-Ihtilal al-Israili fi Lubnan* (The Battle of Wills: The Struggle of the Resistance and Israel's Occupation in Lebanon). Beirut: Dar al-Hadi: 2009.

Fadlallah, Shaykh Muhammad Hussayn, and Mahmoud Soueid. "Islamic Unity and Political Change: Interview with Shaykh Muhammad Hussayn Fadlallah." *Journal of Palestine Studies* 25, no. 1 (Autumn 1995).

Gambill, Gary C. "Ain al-Hilweh: Lebanon's 'Zone of Unlaw.'" *Middle East Intelligence Bulletin* 5, no. 6 (June 2003).

———. "Syria and the Shebaa Farms Dispute." *Middle East Intelligence Bulletin*, May 2001.

Gerges, Fawaz A. *Journey of the Jihadist, Inside Muslim Militancy*. Orlando, FL: Harcourt, 2006.

Gleis, Joshua L. "National Security Implications of Al-Takfir Wal-Hijra." *Al-Nakhlah* (the Fletcher School's online journal for issues related to Southwest Asia and Islamic civilization), Spring 2005.

Haim, Sylvia. *Arab Nationalism: An Anthology*. Berkeley and Los Angeles: Cambridge University Press, 1962.

Hamzeh, A. Nizar. "Islamism in Lebanon: A Guide to the Groups." *Middle East Quarterly* 4, no. 3 (September 1997).

————. "Lebanon's Hizbullah: From Islamic Revolution to Parliamentary Accommodation." *Third World Quarterly* 14, no. 2 (1993).

Hamzeh, A. Nizar, and Hrair Dekmejian. "A Sufi Response to Political Islamism: Al-Ahbash of Lebanon." *International Journal of Middle East Studies* 28, no. 2 (May 1996).

Harik, Judith Palmer. *Hezbollah: The Changing Face of Terrorism*. London: I. B. Tauris, 2004.

Haykel, Bernard. "On the Nature of Salafi Thought and Action." In *Global Salafism: Islam's New Religious Movement*, edited by Roel Meijer. London: C. Hurst, 2009.

Hegghammer, Thomas. "Islamist Violence and Regime Stability in Saudi Arabia." *International Affairs* 84, no. 4 (2008).

Hegghammer, Thomas, and Stéphane Lacroix. "Rejectionist Islamism in Saudi Arabia: The Story of Juhayman al-'Utaybi Revisited." *The International Journal of Middle East Studies* 39, no. 1 (2007).

Hilmi, Mustapha. *Qawa'id al-Manhaj al-Salafi fi al-Fikr al-Islami* (The Fundamentals of Salafi Methodology in Islamic Thought). Beirut: Dar al-Kutb al-'ilmiyah, 2005.

Hourani, Albert. *A History of the Arab Peoples*. Cambridge, MA: Harvard University Press, 1991.

Hoyek, E. P. "Les Revendications du Liban, Memoire de la Delegation Libanaise à la Conference de la Paix." In *La Revue Phenicienne*, edited by David Corm and Son. Beirut: Éditions Maison d'Art, 1919.

Ibrahim, Fouad. *Al-Salafiyah al-Jihadiyah fi al-Sa'udiyah* (Jihadist Salafism in Saudi Arabia). Beirut: Dar al-Saqi, 2009.

'Imad, Abd al-Ghani. *Al-Harakat al-Islamiyah fi Lubnan: Ishkaliyat al-Din wal-Siyasah fi Mujtama' Mutanawe'* (Islamic Movements in Lebanon: *The Ambiguity of Religion and Politics in a Diverse Society*). Beirut: Dar al-Tali'a lil-Tiba'a wal-Nashr, 2006.

————. *Hakimiyat Allah wa Sultan al-Faqih: Qira'a fi Khitab al-Harakat al-Islamiyah al-Nu'asara* (Sovereignty of God and Jurisprudent Sultan: Reading in the Discourse of Contemporary Islamic Movements). Beirut: Dar al-Tali'a, 2005.

'Itani, Fida'. *Al-Jihadiyun fi Lubnan: Min "Quwat al-Fajr" ila "Fath al-Islam"* (Jihadis in Lebanon: From "al-Fajr Forces" to "Fath al-Islam"). Beirut: Dar al-Saqi, 2008.

Jaber, Hala. *Hezbollah: Born with a Vengeance*. New York: Columbia University Press, 1997.

Jansen, Johannes J. G. *The Neglected Duty: The Creed of Sadat's Assassins and Islamic Resurgence in the Middle East*. New York: Macmillan, 1986.

Kaufman, Asher. "Phoenicianism: The Formation of an Identity in Lebanon in 1920." *Middle East Studies* 37, no. 1 (January 2001).

Kepel, Gilles. *Jihad: The Trail of Political Islam*. Translated by Anthony F. Roberts. Cambridge, MA: Belknap Press of Harvard University Press, 2002.

Khashan, Hilal. "Lebanon's Islamist Stronghold." *Middle East Quarterly* 18, no. 2 (Spring 2011).

Khoury, Philip. *Syria and the French Mandate: The Politics of Arab Nationalism, 1920–1945*. Princeton, NJ: Princeton University Press, 1987.

Lacroix, Stéphane. *Awakening Islam: The Politics of Religious Dissent in Contemporary Saudi Arabia*. Translated by George Holoch. Cambridge, MA: Harvard University Press, 2011.

———. "Between Revolution and Apoliticism: Nasir al-Din al-Albani and His Impact on the Shaping of Contemporary Salafism." In *Global Salafism: Islam's New Religious Movement*, edited by Roel Meijer. London: C. Hurst, 2009.

Lagha, Ali. *Fathi Yakan: Ra'ed al-Harakah al-Islamiyah al-Mu'asirah fi Lubnan* (Fathi Yakan: The Pioneer of the Contemporary Islamic Movement in Lebanon). Beirut: Mu'assassat al-Risalah, 1994.

Lammens, Henri. *La Syrie: Précis Historique*. Beirut: Imprimerie Catholique, 1921.

Maila, Joseph. *The Document of National Understanding: A Commentary*. Oxford: Centre for Lebanese Studies, 1992.

Maktabi, Rania. "The Lebanese Census of 1932 Revisited: Who Are the Lebanese?" *British Journal of Middle Eastern Studies* 26, no. 2 (1999).

Marah, Ra'fat Fahd. *Al-Harakat wal-Qiwa al-Islamiyah fi al-Mujtama' al-Filistini fi Lubnan: al-Nasha', al-Ahdaf, al-Injazat* (The Islamic Movements and Forces in the Palestinian Society in Lebanon: Emergence, Objectives, and Accomplishments). Beirut: Markaz al-Zaytuni Lil-Dirasat wal-Istisharat, 2010.

Moosa, Matti. *Extremist Shiites: The Ghulat Sects*. Syracuse, NY: Syracuse University Press, 1987.

Moussalli, Ahmad. "The Views of Islamic Movements on Democracy and Political Pluralism." In *Islamic Movements Impact on Political Stability in the Arab World*, edited by the Emirates Center for Strategic Studies and Research (Abu Dhabi: The Emirates Center for Strategic Studies and Research, 2003).

Muhammad, Ali Ibrahim. *Muhammad Nasir al-Din al-Albani*. Damascus: Dar al-Qalam, 2001.

Naccache, Georges. *L'Orient*, March 10, 1949. Reproduced in *Un Rêve Libanais: 1943–1972*. Beirut: Éditions du Monde Arabe, 1983.

Nasrallah, Fida. *Prospects for Lebanon: The Question of South Lebanon*. Oxford: Centre for Lebanese Studies, 1992.

Norton, Augustus Richard. "Hizbullah: From Radicalization to Pragmatism?" *Middle East Policy* 4, no. 4 (January 1998).

———. "Lebanon after Ta'if: Is the Civil War Over?" *Middle East Journal* 45, no. 3 (Summer 1991).

Office of Foreign Assets Control, U.S. Department of the Treasury. "Terrorism: What You Need to Know about U.S. Sanctions." Available at www.treasury.gov/resource-center/sanctions/programs/documents/terror.pdf (accessed on July 8, 2013).

Pakradouni, Karim. *La'nat Watan: Min Harb Lubnan Ila Harb al-Khalij* (Curse of a Fatherland: From the Lebanese War to the Gulf War). Beirut: Trans-Orient Press, 1992.

———. *Sadmah wa Sumud: 'Ahd Emile Lahoud (1998–2007)* (Shock and Steadfastness: The Era of Emile Lahoud [1998–2007]). 2nd ed. Beirut: All Prints Distributors and Publishers, 2009.

Pall, Zoltan. *Lebanese Salafis between the Gulf and Europe: Development, Fractionalization and Transnational Networks of Salafism in Lebanon.* Amsterdam: Amsterdam University Press, 2013.

Phares, Walid. *Lebanese Christian Nationalism: The Rise and Fall of an Ethnic Resistance.* Boulder, CO: Lynne Rienner, 1995.

Qassem, Naim. *Hizbullah: Al-Manhaj, al-Tajribah, al-Mustaqbal* (Hizbullah: The Curriculum [program], the Experience, the Future). 6th ed. Beirut: Dar al-Hadi, 2009.

Qutb, Muhammad. *Jahiliyat al-Qarn al-'Ishrin* (The *Jahiliyah* of the Twentieth Century). Cairo: Dar al-Shuruq, 1995.

Qutb, Sayyid. *Milestones.* Cedar Rapids, IA: The Mother Mosque Foundation, n.d.

Rabbath, Edmond. *La Formation Historique du Liban Politique et Constitutionnel.* Beirut: Librairie Orientale, 1973.

Rabil, Robert G. *Embattled Neighbors: Syria, Israel, and Lebanon.* Boulder, CO: Lynne Rienner, 2003.

———. *Religion, National Identity, and Confessional Politics in Lebanon: The Challenge of Islamism.* New York: Palgrave Macmillan, 2011.

———. *Syria, the United States, and the War on Terror in the Middle East.* Westport, CT: Praeger Security International, 2006.

———. "The Syrian Muslim Brotherhood." *The Muslim Brotherhood: The Organization and Policies of a Global Movement.* Edited by Barry Rubin. New York: Palgrave Macmillan, 2010.

Ranstorp, Magnus. "The Strategy and Tactics of Hizballa's Current Lebanonization Process." *Mediterranean Politics* 3, no. 1 (1998).

Rougier, Bernard. *Everyday Jihad: The Rise of Militant Islam among Palestinians in Lebanon.* Translated by Pascale Ghazaleh. Cambridge, MA: Harvard University Press, 2007.

Saab, Bilal Y., and Magnus Ranstorp. "Securing Lebanon from the Threat of Salafist Jihadism." *Studies in Conflict and Terrorism* 30, no. 10 (2007).

Sa'd, Adel ibn. *Fatawa al-'Alama Nasir al-Din al-Albani* (Religious Edicts of Distinguished Scholar Nasir al-Din al-Albani). Beirut: Dar al-Kutub al-'ilmiyah, 2011.

Sakr, Etienne Sakr (Abu Arz). "Syria and the Islamist Movements in Lebanon." *The Guardians of the Cedars National Lebanese Movement*, February 23, 2003.

Salibi, Kamal. "Islam and Syria in the Writings of Henri Lammens." In *Historians of the Middle East*. Edited by Bernard Lewis and P. M. Holt. London: Oxford University Press, 1962.

Samra, Muhammad. *Trablus: Sahat Allah wa Mina' al-Hadatha* (Tripoli, Lebanon: Square of God and Port of Modernity). Beirut: Dar al-Saqi: 2011.

Secretary-General of Hezbollah Nasrallah's speeches on the party's Al-Ahed News website, www.alahednews.com.lb/.

Shahadah, Mirwan. *Tahawulat al-Khutab al-Salafi: Al-Harakat al-Jihadiyah-Halat Dirasa (1990–2007)* (The Transformations of the Salafi Discourse: Jihadist Movements; A Case Study [1990–2007]). Ras Beirut: Al-Shabaka al-Arabiyah lil-Abhath wal-Nashr, 2010.

Sharara, Waddah. *Dawlat Hizb Allah: Lubnan Mujtama'an Islamiyan* (The State of Hezbollah: Lebanon a Muslim Society). 3rd ed. Beirut: Dar al-Nahar, 1998.

Solh, Raghid. "The Attitude of the Arab Nationalists towards Greater Lebanon during the 1930s." In *Lebanon: A History of Conflict and Consensus*, edited by Nadim Shehadi and Dana Haffar Mills. London: I. B. Tauris, 1988.

Taymiyah, Taqi al-Din Ibn. *Al-Fatawa al-Kubra* (Great Religious Edicts). Vol. 5. Cairo: Dar al-Kutub al-Haditha, 1966.

Tibi, Bassam. *Arab Nationalism: A Critical Enquiry*. 2nd ed. New York: St. Martin's, 1990.

Wagemakers, Joas. *A Quietist Jihadi: The Ideology and Influence of Abu Muhammad al-Maqdisi*. New York: Cambridge University Press, 2012.

Walzer, Richard. *Greek into Arabic: Essays on Islamic Philosophy*. Cambridge, MA: Harvard University Press, 1962).

Wiktorowicz, Quintan. "Anatomy of the Salafi Movement." *Studies in Conflict and Terrorism* 29 (2006).

———. *The Management of Islamic Activism: Salafis, the Muslim Brotherhood, and State Power in Jordan*. New York: State University of New York Press, 2001.

Yakan, Fathi. *Abjadiyat al-Tasawor al-Haraki lil-'Amal al-Islami* (The Elementary Facts of the Conceptual Movement of Islamic Activism). Beirut: Mu'assassat al-Risalah, 1981.

———. *Adwa' 'ala al-Tajribah al-Niyabiyah al-Islamiyah fi Lubnan: Al-ida' al-Niyabi bayn al-Mabda' wa al-Tatbiq* (Lights on the Islamic Parliamentary Experience in Lebanon: The Parliamentary Performance between Principle and Practice). Beirut: Mu'assassat al-Risalah, 1996.

———. *Adwa' 'ala al-Tajribah al-Niyabiyah al-Islamiyah fi Lubnan: Al-'Ida' al-Niyabi 'Ubr al-I'lam* (Lights on the Islamic Parliamentarian Experience: The Parliamentarian Performance through the Media). Book no. 2. Beirut: Mu'assassat al-Risalah, 1996.

————. *Al-Masa'la al-Lubnaniyah min Manthur Islami* (The Lebanese Question from an Islamic Perspective). Beirut: Mu'assassat al-Risalah, 1979.

————. *Al-Mawsu'ah al-Harakiyah* (The Encyclopedia of Activism). Amman: Dar al-Bashr, 1983.

————. *Madha Ya'ni Intima'i lil-Islam* (What Does It Mean Being a Muslim?). Beirut: Mu'assassat al-Risalah, 1977.

Yamak, Labib Zuwiyya. *The Syrian Social Nationalist Party: An Ideological Analysis*. Cambridge, MA: Harvard University Press, 1966.

Yasushi, Kosugi. "Al-Manar Revisited." In *Intellectuals in the Modern Islamic World: Transmission, Transformation, Communication*, edited by Stephane A. Dudoignon, Komatsu Hisao, and Kosugi Yasushi. New York: Routledge, 2006.

Newspapers

Al-Akhbar (Beirut)
Al-Diyar (Beirut)
Al-Hayat (London)
Al-Mustaqbal (Beirut)
An-Nahar (Beirut)
As-Safir (Beirut)
Ash-Sharq al-Awsat (London)
Le Monde (Paris)
L'Orient–Le Jour (Beirut)

Websites

www.al-ahbash.org (al-Ahbash)
www.al-jamaa.org (Islamic Association)
www.almoslim.net (Islamist)
www.alqassem.arabblogs.com (Usbat al-Ansar)
www.attawhed.org (Islamic Unity Movement–Command Council)
www.boukhary.net (al-Bukhari Institute)
www.ikhwansyria.com (Syrian Muslim Brotherhood)
www.islahonline.org (Islamic Reform Association)
www.jinan.edu.lb (al-Jinan University)
www.moqawama.org (Hezbollah)
www.tawhed.ws (Salafi)

Index